Looking Inward

THE MIDDLE AGES SERIES

Ruth Mazo Karras, Series Editor
Edward Peters, Founding Editor

A complete list of books in the series is available from the publisher.

Looking Inward

Devotional Reading and the Private Self in
Late Medieval England

Jennifer Bryan

PENN

University of Pennsylvania Press
Philadelphia

Published by
University of Pennsylvania Press
Philadelphia, Pennsylvania 19104–4112

Printed in the United States of America on acid-free paper
10 9 8 7 6 5 4 3 2 1

Library of Congress Cataloging-in-Publication Data

Bryan, Jennifer.
   Looking inward : devotional reading and the private self in late medieval England /
Jennifer Bryan.
      p. cm. (Middle ages series)
   Includes bibliographical references (p. 241) and index.
   ISBN-13: 978-0-8122-4048-1 (hardcover : alk. paper)
   ISBN-10: 0-8122-4048-0 (hardcover : alk. paper)
   1. Devotional literature. 2. Self (Philosophy). 3. Identity (Philosophical concept). 4.
England—Religious life and customs. I. Title.
BV4818.B79 2007
242.0942'0902

                                                                2007023275

For Nick

Contents

A Note on Spelling and Punctuation

Throughout this book I have used modern spelling conventions, replacing thorn and eth with *th* and yogh with *y*, *g*, *w*, or *gh* according to my best judgment. In Chapter 3, I have also modernized the punctuation in quotations from *A Talkynge of the Love of God* and *The Prickynge of Love*.

Introduction

. . . ther are bokes ynowe
To telle men what Dowel is, Dobet and Dobest bothe
—*Ymaginatif to Will the Dreamer*
   (Piers Plowman xii.17–18)

There are books enough. The objection—familiar to writers everywhere—comes from Will's own mind, from the personified faculty of his imagination. Responding to Will's announcement that he plans to turn his dream-visions into a book, Ymaginatif questions the usefulness of the project. "There are enough books like that already," he says—enough visions transformed into instruction manuals, enough works on doing well, better, and best, enough spiritual ladders for the whole field full of folk. How many such books does the world need? Will is growing old; he should forget about writing and concentrate on amending his own life.

We might not normally think of *Piers Plowman* as a book of devotional instruction. Yet Ymaginatif assumes that this is what Langland's poetic persona intends to write—not a complex allegorical dream vision, not a fierce quest for Truth or a scathing social critique, but a three-step program of vernacular spiritual guidance such as already existed in burgeoning numbers in late fourteenth-century England. Thus imagined, Will's book would merely duplicate the effects of treatises such as *A Ladder of Four Rungs*, *The Scale of Perfection*, *The Form of Living*, *Book to a Mother*, *The Charter of Christ*, *The Abbey of the Holy Ghost*, *The Pricke of Conscience*, *The Prickynge of Love*, or *The Mirror of Holy Church*.

Will was not the only late medieval English devotional "writer" to suffer the anxiety of redundancy. The author of the fifteenth-century *Speculum*

Devotorum relates his great disappointment on hearing that Bonaventure had "made a boke of the same matere," and that another Carthusian had already "turnyd the same boke into englyishe."[1] (He underestimates his belatedness; Love's *Mirror of the Blessed Lyf of Jesu Crist* was but one of half a dozen English translations of the pseudo-Bonaventuran *Meditationes* already in circulation.) Similarly, the author of the *Seven Poyntes of Trewe Love and Everlastynge Wisdame* dreads that his work will be "sumwhat as in waste" given the number of devotional treatises already available. There are so many books "of vyces and vertues and of dyverse doctrynes," he writes, "that this short lyfe schalle rather have an ende" than allow time to read them all.[2] His lament seems to affirm the grounds of Ymaginatif's rebuke: yes, there are books enough about these things.

It also points us to a striking fact about late medieval English textual culture, one highlighted by numerous modern studies of book ownership and circulation: the fact that English men and women owned and presumably read more devotional treatises than any other kind of English book.[3] Beginning in the mid-fourteenth century and gaining momentum through the fifteenth, an immense and various body of devotional texts was written, translated, adapted, compiled, and copied in the English language. Works ranging from simple instructional tracts to graphic Passion meditations to advanced treatises on contemplation made their way into the hands of an increasingly diverse group of readers, from nuns and anchoresses to pious gentry widows; from lay clergy to merchants and urban tradesmen. Some of these readers were inside the cloister and some were outside, but their devotional reading blurred traditional boundaries between the active and contemplative lives. Texts that might previously have been addressed to a "dear brother" or a "ghostly sister in God" were translated for "all god's lovers," or for the many "wiche have ful gret liking to speke of the love of God, and al day askin how thei schul love God, and in what maner thei schul live."[4] The twelfth-century *Scala Claustralium*, a contemplative work for monks, became a fourteenth-century *Ladder of Four Rungs* peopled with wine merchants and poor old women, its lessons illustrated at one point with a homey hound-and-cheese analogy.[5] Lorens d'Orléans's thirteenth-century French *Somme le Roi* became an English *Ayenbite of Inwyt*, and then an English *Speculum Vitae*, and then a *Book of Vices and Virtues*—all between about 1340 and 1380. By 1486 there were nine versions, and one in print.[6] Indeed, much of the early printers' output was in this vein, testifying to its market appeal; Michael Alexander estimates that from Caxton's first editions through the 1540s, somewhere between 40 and 50 percent of printed books were religious and devotional.[7] There were certainly "bokes ynowe" to tell English readers about all aspects of doing well, better, and best, and yet the flood of devotional texts and translations continued unabated right up to the eve of the Reformation—and beyond.

This, then, is a study of what was arguably the most popular kind of literature in late medieval England. More particularly, it is a study of how this literature taught generations of English readers in the period between 1350 and 1550 to "see themselves" and to reflect on what they saw, initially as a habit of reading and then as a habit of mind. I seek to understand the intimate languages and techniques of subjectivity that medieval readers found in their devotional books, and to illuminate the role these played in a long, winding cultural conversation about the nature, status, and potential of the private, literate self in England. For the vernacular works of spiritual guidance evince an abiding concern with the processes of self-envisioning, self-knowledge, and affective and rational self-transformation. In teaching literate men and women the basic disciplines of contemplation, they encourage them to watch, search, and improve their "inner" selves. They map the boundaries of the heart and script the affective life of the soul, amplifying and reorienting desire through the passionate rhetoric of devotional meditation. They provide mirrors for self-reflection, identification, and imitation. They advise readers to "labor in themselves," using reading to "profit" themselves inwardly. And they attempt to balance detachment from and accommodation to "the world" against which readers are to define their quests for self-understanding and self-betterment. In this book I chart some of the most common and powerful means by which English devotional texts sought to shape the hidden selves of their readers, and by which they allowed readers to engage in the project of seeing and shaping their own reflections. "You must see yourself," they instructed their readers—and then showed them how to do it.

Hence I want to suggest that these texts were popular not because late medieval English readers were dull and pious, as has often been assumed, but because they were eager to know about and to improve what they took to be their deepest, truest, and most important selves. They were looking for ways of thinking and feeling that would help them to live better lives—as Langland put it, to do well, better, and best. (We are not unfamiliar with the idea that understanding ourselves, and developing certain ways of thinking and feeling, are the first steps to better living. Likewise, our own self-help books often rely on popularizations of specialized psychological and spiritual discourses.) The broad program of transforming individual spiritual experience into cultural practice was not a simple one, and the preoccupations of devotional discourse often highlight the difficulties and anxieties involved in re-envisioning the relationship between a solitary self and the social world it inhabits. But the languages of subjectivity that developed out of this matrix of problems and opportunities would have enduring expressive and explanatory power.

The relationship between reader and book has long shaped Western culture's imagination of what it means to be a self.[8] In a literate society, how we read—*why* we read—and what we think we are doing to ourselves in the process informs our notions of an "I" that is itself a kind of text, itself both object and subject of our reading and reflection. Do we read for pleasure, for knowledge, for improvement, for transformation? Does reading make us more or less self-aware, more or less autonomous? When we pick up a book, do we learn to assume a kind of authorial or critical control over our own experience, or do we submit to being inscribed by someone else's authority? In late medieval England, it was vernacular devotional literature that most directly and systematically foregrounded such questions. Few other genres engaged their readers' textual, reflective, and self-disciplinary practices more insistently or compellingly.

Of course, devotional writing by nature tends to highlight questions of use and practice—of the reader's response to and potential alteration by the text. More explicitly than in many other genres, the reader becomes the text's direct subject and the object of its operations. But the texts under consideration here were produced in response to a specific and unprecedented context that made such operations particularly urgent. They arose, that is, at a crucial juncture between rising vernacular literacy and the trend toward private, affective forms of piety—between new groups of readers just shaping their relationship to texts, and broad new expectations for religious experience that were influencing the sensibilities of people across the social spectrum. The new piety required subjective response; it also required a subject constituted in acceptable form, capable of responding in appropriate ways. As personal experience and private conscience mounted repeated challenges to public authority and clerical mediation, as the heart became an increasingly privileged and contested location, as competing modes of "vision" sparked intense debates about images and texts, popular devotional works both encouraged and regulated English habits of reading and self-reflection. They came into being because there was a suitable audience for them, a growing number of readers who "all day asked." At the same time, they helped to develop and define that audience through the very reading habits and preferences that had called them into being.

These changes by themselves might have been significant enough to reshape ideologies of the subject and the ways in which they were produced. But late medieval England was also a world where traditional categories of public identity were under growing strain. Following the upheavals of the plague years, new social realities and new possibilities confronted English men and women. As readers of Chaucer know, for example, men and women might now aspire to be "gentil" without benefit of noble blood. So too, as traditional distinctions between the active and contemplative lives eroded, they might be "God's lovers" without being strictly enclosed. Increasingly, such relatively fluid forms of identity depended on the shaping and training of the self through some kind of reading, whether that involved conduct manuals, romances promoting gentle behavior (as Caxton advertised), or devotional treatises. And increasingly, these forms of identity were anchored by an appeal to inner experience— indeed, were understood as the product of inner experience—whether erotic or spiritual (or both). As literate practice reached new audiences, so too did forms of self-fashioning that had previously been restricted to specific groups leading particular kinds of lives, often under explicit codes of external conduct.

Not just devotional texts, then, but late medieval English literary culture more broadly reflects this growing interest in the complexities of personal identity. Scenes of self-scrutiny, explorations of first-person utterance, fascination with the boundaries between inside and out—all these devotional preoccupations can be found throughout later Middle English poetry and prose. As Lee Patterson has argued, the struggle to reconcile an inner self with external social codes lies at the heart of many of the period's most powerful literary creations.[9] From Dreamer Will's peripatetic efforts to find "kynde knowynge" of Christ and himself to Margery Kempe's innovative autobiographical testimony, from the Wife of Bath's confessional prologue to the *Pearl*-poet's sly exploration of when Gawain is and is not "Gawain," late medieval English literature exposes repeatedly the problems involved not only in being or having a self, but in expressing and enacting the truth about it. We have become familiar with this period as one in which experience rises to challenge "auctoritee," in which dreamers explore the landscapes of their own muddled understandings, in which writers become *personae*, both earnest and ironic reflections of their makers. At the climax of the *Confessio Amantis*, John Gower/*Amans* finds his own aged countenance reflected back at him from the mirror of Venus. Dreamer Will/Langland claims never to have seen Christ "but as myself in a mirror." Thomas Hoccleve's autobiographical persona rushes to his chamber to assess his own reflection in a looking glass. Yet he is bitterly conscious of how little the countenance he sees there has to do with his "inly pensif" self, the self he presents himself as driven to expose in his poetry. As we shall see, the mirror scene is a fixture of devotional discourse too, and devotional texts often center on the reader's confrontation with his or her own complex, only partially available image.

Indeed, if we have been slow to attend to the psychological complexity of late medieval devotional discourses, it is partly because of the narratives provided by secular writers themselves—especially influential humanist writers like Petrarch, who is so often characterized as the source of poetic subjectivity in the English Renaissance and a turning point in the history of the Western self. In the *Canzoniere*, Petrarch sets up an opposition between the public, universal, eternal subjectivity of Christianity and his own deeply individual, historical, complicated, erotic subjectivity. The third sonnet, which relates how the poet fell in love with Laura on Good Friday, makes the point:

It was the day the sun himself grew pale
with grieving for his Maker—I was seized
and made no effort to defend myself;
your lovely eyes had held and bound me, Lady.

It didn't seem a time to be on guard
against Love's blows, so I went confident
and fearless on my way. My troubles started
amid the universal sense of woe.[10]

My troubles: the Petrarchan "I" comes into being against the universal grieving of Good Friday and the vision of the crucifixion. We tend to take the poet at his word when he suggests that his personal sorrow—interesting, rhetorical, self-conscious—exists in tension with, over and against, the threatened submersion in a timeless, faceless, ritualized emotion. Following Petrarch's lead, scholars have been quick to associate the secular and the erotic with the self-aware, the complex, the modern—indeed, even with subjectivity itself.

But English devotional texts pose a powerful challenge to this simplistic narrative. The Passion meditations discussed in Chapter 3, for example, articulate not a "universal sense of woe" but a set of shifting, freshly painful emotional trajectories that are as self-obsessed as any Petrarchan lament. And if the devotional "I" fashions itself in relation to a divine rather than a human lover, to the ever-more-human Christ rather than the ever-less-human Laura, it does so in similarly personal, confessional terms. Devotional texts are neither "high literature nor high theology," as Andrew Taylor remarks; but for precisely that reason, they are a crucial place to look for the discursive traces of readerly subjectivity that late medieval English culture left behind.[11] Precisely as non-"literary" texts, they help to address an important gap in our understanding: "the general absence from medieval evidence," as Nancy Partner puts it, "of the sorts of writing that document the interior life—diaries, personal letters, intimate memories and revelations of private life." This absence, Partner writes, together with the "prevalence of didactic genres . . . which stress conformity with religious and social norms encourage the notion that in some way the pre-modern era of history was populated with pre-individuals."[12] But vernacular devotional texts are exactly the sorts of writing that document the interior life—or, if they don't document it, at least represent and construct it in ways that suggest a serious and sustained cultural concern. (It remains true that large numbers of average English people did not begin to *write* about their private feelings and experiences until the Renaissance.) They bring crucial questions of will, desire, agency, and self-understanding into the sphere of daily life and literacy.

*   *   *

In the early sixteenth century, Syon monk Richard Whytford described contemplative life as "a diligent inward beholding with desire of heart."[13] His definition encompasses four categories that had, over the previous two hundred years, become central to the discourses of private devotional reading and self-construction in England: diligence, or "business"; inwardness, often associated with solitude and/or spiritual isolation; beholding; and desire. These categories were also controversial, however, and open to a considerable degree of interpretation, as we shall see in the chapters that follow. By weaving them together, devotional writers could stabilize their meaning to some extent, creating practical, self-regulating models of contemplative psychology and spiritual independence. But it will be useful in the beginning of the book to consider somewhat fuller ranges of possibility.

Thus Chapter 1 explores how the nebulous, highly prestigious, highly controversial concept of interiority could be variously defined and constructed for English readers, as it was interwoven with varying notions of flesh and spirit, reason and affect, orthodoxy and heterodoxy, and public and private. Several critics have remarked on the importance of "inwardness" to late medieval English devotion, though recent fascination with the status of the body in religious practice has perhaps prevented the term from garnering as much attention as it deserves. What critical discussion there has been has tended to assume that late medieval interiority is all the same kind of thing, so that although critics might disagree about what to make of late medieval devotion's inward turn—Was it bourgeois? Anti-Catholic? Reformist? Deeply conservative?—there is little sense that vernacular interiority was as interpretively fluid and problematic for medieval readers as it is for modern critics. I will argue that it was. Not everyone thought that vernacular readers should be—or were capable of—looking inward. Yet it was the idea of interiority, in all its vagueness and flexibility, that made it possible for new readers to appropriate older religious discourses, and that concerned both sacred and secular authorities anxious not to be excluded from the powerful space where the mother tongue met the secrets of the heart.

If broad ranges of significance had developed around the category of "inwardness," "beholding" was equally problematic. Scholars like Jeffrey Hamburger and Barbara Newman have emphasized that vision was at once a crucial category for medieval worship, and a contradictory and unstable epistemological and theological category with serious implications for controversies about, among other things, the nature of divine inspiration and the role of images in Christian worship.[14] Chapter 2 shows how English devotional writers sought to reshape their audience's subjective and "visionary" expectations through the increasingly ubiquitous trope of the mirror. One of the signature tendencies of English devotional writers and translators is to emphasize vision, and to downplay other modes of knowing and sensing. But they also tend to represent devotional vision as ideally private and self-reflexive, looking back to Augustine for models of specularity—and inwardness—that would render the practice more self-referential and self-contained. Whereas the mirror trope could still signify everything from comprehensiveness to illusion, in this literature it came to be more frequently linked to notions of introspection and spiritual progress, as self-reflexivity became the measure of spiritual authority and insight.

Yet Augustinian interiority, which was essentially imageless and rational, posed problems for a devotional culture that was fundamentally imaginative and affective. The version of Augustine's "radical reflexivity" that came to be disseminated in the vernacular was a much less radical, more practical kind of self-examination, closer to the *Confessions* than to *De Trinitate* in its emphasis on personal experience and memory. To illuminate the ways in which such "self-envisioning" could valorize personal narrative, Chapter 2 focuses on works where private history presents a problem: *The Myroure of Oure Ladye*, where the literate, self-conscious tendencies of English devotion run up against monastic ideals of self-effacement, and the mystical *Cloud of Unknowing*, where they conflict with the contemplative ideal of self-annihilation.

Building on this discussion but narrowing it to a particular genre, Chapter 3 follows the effort to construct certain kinds of readerly desire and inward beholding in the popular genre of Passion meditation—for "desire of heart" was needed to stimulate the inward turn and to make self-envisioning into productive self-transformation. English readers expected emotional intensity, and English writers needed to find ways to cultivate it in the context of private reading, where they could not rely on light pouring through glass, the smell of incense, or the heightening powers of public worship (though these could still be expected to form part of the reader's broader religious life). Instead, they created expansive, lyrical soliloquies to heighten and shape readers' affective experience. Here readers learned to explore the contours of an "I" not just visually but rhetorically. With their careful scripting of first-person response and their agitated, graphic, erotically expressive showings of Christ's crucified body, English Passion meditations sought to "imprint" their readers with particular visions of violence and yearning, circumscribed by the framework of private self-examination. They established clear expectations for what it meant to "see" Christ on the cross, and their tormented and gender-bending formulations of desire and identification may have helped to strengthen the boundaries between readers' inner and outer lives. The practices of the translator/adaptors of the late fourteenth-century *A Talkynge of the Love of God* and *The Prickynge of Love* render the expectations of English devotion particularly clear, as both writers weave the bloody vision of the cross together with painfully abject and reflexive visions of the reading self.

My focus tightens still further in the final two chapters, where I consider innovative works produced by single writers—a religious recluse and a lonely clerk—working within and against devotional tradition. Chapter 4 examines the *Showings* of the anchoress Julian of Norwich, whose longing to know herself, and to know how God sees her, makes enclosed self-reflection a theologically creative act. In Julian's response to the vision of Christ, though she frames her vision as inspired rather than readerly, we can trace all the assumptions and mechanisms of vernacular Passion meditation, as it puts the reader in visual and rhetorical dialogue with the bleeding, double-gendered body of Christ. Julian pushes this dialogue to its epistemological and theological limits—how far *can* we know God by reflecting on our own rational and affective responses?—even as she challenges the abjection and privacy typically associated with the inwardly beholding devotional subject.

For a different but equally creative revision, I turn to Thomas Hoccleve—not just a devotional translator (though he was that too), but a court poet and bureaucrat. Hoccleve turns familiar devotional paradigms into political and commercial forms of self-fashioning—profitably occupying, rather than dissolving, the boundaries between public and private. His remarkable autobiographical persona struggles with the disjunctions between inner and outer, religious and lay, in the context of urban alienation and intense political concern about the private hearts of English subjects. It thus demonstrates with particular clarity the deep connections between devotional, political, and poetic concerns in this period.

For its part, the remainder of this introduction provides a broad overview of the contexts for late medieval English devotional reading, highlighting some of the emerging patterns and problems of the cultural moment. For it was a changed environment, a changing readership, that gave fresh significance to many of the ideas in these works. Much of what was "new" or newly translated in late medieval English devotion was inherited from earlier traditions—from Augustinian Neoplatonism, from twelfth-century monasticism, from English anchoritic writings. New expectations about devotional reading and contemplative readers affected the reshaping and repackaging of these older ideas, as well as the formation of new ones. It will thus be useful to review some of the general trends in English devotion in this period, and some of the social and spiritual challenges confronting English readers and writers as they faced each other across the manuscript—and early printed—page.

Private Literacies

It is a critical commonplace that the period between the mid-fourteenth and mid-sixteenth centuries saw significant changes in the relationship between English readers and books. A "quiet revolution" in education led to significant increases in literacy; alterations in book production and distribution—even before the arrival of the printing press in the 1470s—improved access to texts.[15] As the ability to read in English became more common, as production moved out of the monasteries and into the hands of a diverse array of scribes, and as books became cheaper thanks to the introduction of paper and eventually print, more and more of the devout expressed their piety through the ownership of books. It is no surprise to find literacy and book ownership among the social elite, but by the mid-fifteenth century we begin to encounter readers like Robert Thornton of Yorkshire, a "modest and unexceptional" landowner who had two volumes compiled for his household: one a book of romances, the other a collection of devotional materials addressing contemplative piety, the mixed life, the Passion of Christ, and various penitential and visionary themes.[16] Thornton's interests are echoed in the wills of fellow northerners Elizabeth Sywardby (d. 1468), who left a substantial collection of Passion literature and other devotional works, and Agnes Stapleton (d. 1448), widow of Brian Stapleton of Carleton, who mentions among her bequests a French book, a work by Bonaventure, the *Prick of Conscience*, the *Chastising of God's Children*, and the *Book of Vices and Virtues*.[17] Further south, the will of Margaret Purdans of Norwich mentions two psalters (at least one in English), works by Hilton and St. Bridget, and a *Doctrine of the Herte*.[18] Evidence of steady increases in book ownership during the fourteenth century and exponential increases in the fifteenth led W. A. Pantin to assert that it would be "impossible to exaggerate the importance of the educated layman" in this period.[19] New patterns of circulation—lending libraries among the gentry, aristocratic women's reading circles, the informal networks of book exchange established by Lollard groups—made it easier for texts to move through communities of readers. Michael Sargent has discussed the phenomenon of "common profit books" as they circulated through a group of London tradesmen: in the last half of the fifteenth century, one volume of Hilton's works passed from a London grocer to a stationer to an organ-maker.[20] The early printers were able to build on this audience, which by the 1480s constituted a ready-made market for pious printings such as Caxton's *Book of Diverse Ghostly Matters* (1490) and Hilton's *Scale of Perfection* (1494).[21]

At the same time, the scene of reading itself was changing. Paul Saenger has argued that the spread of silent reading from clerics to the laity in the later Middle Ages encouraged more intimate relationships between readers and texts, and facilitated both private devotion and private erotica (or private devotional erotica, as the case sometimes seems to be).[22] Architectural developments further enabled and encouraged the practice of private reading. Many religious houses partitioned communal dormitories into separate cubicles, the "pryve closets" to which nuns and monks were urged to retire in order to collect and examine themselves. Aristocratic households acquired private chapels, and fashionable urban houses now had private rooms or closets for reading and meditation. A growing number of churches provided side-chapels and pews for individual prayer.[23] In the Middle English poem *Sir Gawain and the Green Knight*, Gawain and his host attend mass together in the castle chapel, but the lady of the house—rather ominously—secludes herself in "a cumly closet" or private pew.[24]

This is not to say that all late medieval devotional reading was either silent or solitary. The routines of Margaret Beaufort and Cicely of York, those Lancastrian and Yorkist icons of lay female devotion, included both private reading and group edification at mealtimes. Likewise, private reading at the famously literate Bridgettine Abbey of Syon was partly a preparation for later oral prelection and group study.[25] A short work of instruction for one layman admonishes him to "let the book be brought to the table as readily as the bread." Aristocrats might have chaplains or clerks to read to them at dinner, but this layman's family was in charge of its own mealtime edification, hearing reading "now by one, now by another, and by your children as soon as they can read."[26] Margery Kempe, who claims to be illiterate, relates how she spent seven or eight years listening to a priest read her the Bible with commentary, plus "Seynt Brydys Boke, Hyltons boke, Boneventure, Stimulus Amoris, Incendium Amoris, & swech other."[27] Joyce Coleman has offered an important corrective to the idea that public reading was generally in decline in late medieval England.[28] She points out, moreover, that literary depictions of private, solitary reading often present the practice as unnatural and unhealthy. We need to be careful not to assert too transparent a connection, then, between the material practices of silent, solitary reading and the expectations of privacy, inwardness, and self-reflection that Middle English devotional texts tend to construct. As numerous scholars have observed, late medieval devotional practice was often predicated on the assumption that public images or rituals could serve as the basis for very private, subjective devotional experiences—and even the most public-minded of texts, like a mirror for princes, could of course be read silently and alone.[29] In his study of medieval discourses of idealized love, Stephen Jaeger writes that "the private aspects of love come to saturate the public without overwhelming them."[30] This seems to me a perfect description of what is happening with vernacular English devotional culture.

For however they were read in practice, in theory most vernacular de-votional texts—unlike their literary counterparts—privileged the experi-ence of solitary, private reading. "Who evere purpose to come to inwarde & to spiritual thinges, it behoveth him to decline fro the cumpany of peple," writes Thomas à Kempis (or, more accurately, his English translator).[31] Nicholas Love similarly observes that "fort have gostly solitude the bodily helpeth ful miche."[32] *The Seven Poyntes of Trewe Love and Everlastynge Wis-dame* advises readers to seek "a place of rest, and there take the prive silences of contemplacyone and flee the periles of turblance of this noyous worlde."[33] *The Tree and Twelve Frutes* asks readers to "sitte solitarily and alone with in him self. seclusid from al outeward lettynges," and to "entre in to the pryvy chaumbre of thin hert."[34] In a similar vein, *The Book of Vices and Virtues* notes that the world is a prison for the contemplative reader, "and to be alone is his paradise. . . . For than he is with his tweye beste fren-des, that is with God and hymself."[35] One meditative work puts its proper context in the title: "A ful good meditacion for oon to seie by him-self al-oone."[36] These and many other works imagined the ideal devotional reader as a hermit, a recluse, a solitary self collected and drawn into itself, com-muning only with God in its devotions. Yet much as spiritual writers might have idealized physical solitude, many also assumed that with practice, read-ers could achieve isolation even in very public settings—on the model, for example, of Love's Saint Cecilia, who is so absorbed by the inner recounting of Christ's life that even amid "the grete pompe of weddyngis," she remains untouched by worldly vanity.[37] It was the *idea* of solitude and bodily con-tainment that was important to the reader's experience of the text, though a private pew or closet might have helped "ful miche." The relationship be-tween external and internal structures of privacy, as we shall see in Chapter one, was a crucial one for Middle English devotional texts, impinging on the very notion of what it meant to be a private self, or an "inward man."

It is worth recalling too that many of the emerging modes of devotional reading emphasized a subjective encounter with the text—an emphasis that made private experience primary, even if it did not preclude public reading. The practices associated with Franciscan visual meditation, for example, encouraged readers to use the text as a starting point for independent, interactive meditation and prayer, so that even public readings would produce private experience. As Brian Stock has argued, vernacular reading practices across Europe after the fourteenth century were mainly derived from the tradition of *lectio spiritualis*, a subset of the traditional monastic practice of *lectio divina* centered not on the biblical text but on the reader's emotional response and spiritual progress.[38] Whereas *lectio divina*—conceived of as one kind of ascetic experience among many—depended on "the recreation of the biblical text through oral reading and recitations," to be followed by prayer and meditation, *lectio spiritualis* could take place entirely in silence.[39] While *lectio divina* helped the reader to slowly internalize the biblical text, creating a more exact correspondence between reading and prayer, *lectio spiritualis* emphasized the subjective words and images that might arise in the reader's mind both during and after the textual encounter.

As reading habits became more subjective, the form of books changed, making it easier for readers to find specific material appropriate to their spiritual status and emotional state. The ubiquitous *kalendars* and tables of contents that preface much devotional literature emphasize readerly control, demonstrating their authors' desire to respond as directly as possible to their audiences' shifting and subjective needs. At Syon Abbey, elaborate systems of page tabs made even large books easily navigable.[40] "Walke aboute where ye wolen with youre mynde & resoun, in what aleye you lyke," writes the translator of *The Orcherd of Syon*, comparing his work to a private garden; "taste of sich fruyt and herbis resonably aftir youre affeccioun, & what you liketh best, afteirward chewe it wel & ete thereof."[41] Here the notion of reading as eating, where the fruit of doctrine is to be chewed and internalized—as in *lectio divina*—meets the metaphor of the book-as-pleasure-garden, where fruit is nibbled and chosen according to the individual palate. In Chaucerian terms, the reader can "turne over the leef and chese another tale."[42] The Vernon manuscript's extensive index allows readers to do just that, providing not only a list of works, but also a thematic guide to individual sections of particular works—so that readers seeking, for instance, the

Holy Name of Jesus, or remedies against temptation, might find them wherever they appear in the collection.[43] "The maner of preyere may diversely eche or encrece devocion aftir sondry disposicions of man," notes the author of the *Myrour of Recluses*, "In orisons that bien take of a mannes owen wil, lat every man holde & use for a tyme that manere, that forme, & that mesure that he felyth that his devocion is moost aplyed or vowyd to."[44] It was an exhortation to be found in a growing number of treatises, as medieval readers were encouraged to be more aware of their own dispositions, moods, and preferences. In the collective routines of the liturgical day and year, medieval men and women still submitted themselves to the communal moods of joy or grief, comfort or chastisement, appropriate to the passing hour or season. But in their encounters with vernacular devotional texts they attended to more localized vicissitudes of taste and feeling, so as to produce more effective personal responses.

Religion *sans* Rule: Solitary Readers and English Solitaries

As these habits of literacy spread to new groups of readers, the figure of the religious recluse—the hermit, anchoress, or anchorite—assumed ever-greater importance in the English devotional imagination. The recluse had been a distinctive part of the English religious landscape since the age of Cuthbert, but in late medieval England, solitaries were increasing in number and becoming icons of popular devotion and models for both lay and monastic reading. (This is in contrast to the situation on the Continent, where new spiritual energies tended to result in the formation of small communities like the Beguines, and where recluses were not particularly important to or associated with the broader forms of lay piety.)[45] How did these extreme, ascetic, marginal figures come to be associated with lay devotional practices?

In part the growing popularity of solitaries seems to stem from their association with the early desert saints and hermits. A culture preoccupied with corruption and reform might be expected to look back to its early heroes, whose piety stands apart from the institutions to which it has given rise. But as Anne Warren has shown, the solitary life was also undergoing basic shifts in the public imagination in this period; it may have evoked the stability and purity of the past, but it also responded remarkably quickly to current devotional trends.[46] Warren notes that descriptions of anchoritic enclosure were beginning to focus less on asceticism—on the anchorhold as a penitential, tomb-like space—and more on contemplation, where the small room is no longer seen as punishment but as liberation, a means of getting closer to God by being alone with him. Everywhere in Europe, of course, Christianity was being reoriented toward the affective and personal. But in England, those trends not only *influenced* the public perception of the solitary life; they seem to have become associated particularly *with* it.

The strong association of English eremiticism with affective, personal spirituality can be traced in part to Richard Rolle, whom Hope Emily Allen calls "one of the great formative influences in England during the later Middle Ages."[47] This northern hermit fired the imaginations of his contemporaries and influenced the devotional habits and expectations of English men and women for over a century.[48] Hundreds of copies of his works survive—most of them from after 1390—and still more works bear his name or image. Indeed, Rolle was almost more important as an icon than as a writer. If the Franciscans can be credited with introducing and spreading the doctrines of affective and lyrical piety in England, Rolle nonetheless took credit in the popular imagination—and particularly in the fifteenth century, as the friars' image became increasingly tarnished. Certain kinds of literature, as Margaret Connolly observes, "assumed his name indiscriminately," especially the works of sensual and emotional devotion to Jesus.[49] This new Desert Father became the distinctively English *joculator Dei*, the minstrel of God. In the popular mind, lyrical longing for Christ belonged not to the wandering Franciscan, but to the fiercely solitary voice of a hermit singing (and sometimes wandering) in the northern wilderness.

But if Rolle made spiritual solitude glamorous and romantic, the literature of eremiticism had already rendered it imitable—at least textually—by the unenclosed. English solitaries, and anchoresses in particular, comprised one of the earliest audiences for vernacular devotional texts, and their spiritual needs often overlapped with those of lay readers. Like laypeople, anchoritic readers needed templates for spiritual improvement that did not depend on the fortifications of external community, routine, or discipline. The hermit, Langland grumbled, was essentially "an ordre by hymselve— / Religion saunz rule and resonable obedience" (B xiii.284–85). Thus while monastic works tended to emphasize obedience and humility, anchoritic ones tended to focus on the problems of daily motivation, spiritual sluggishness, and the temptations of the world beckoning seductively outside the window. These were problems to which laypeople could relate.[50] St.

Anselm instructs a twelfth-century English recluse: "be unwilling to consider so much what you may do, but what you should desire; not so much what should be your tasks, but rather what is your inclination."[51] The *Ancrene Wisse* is divided explicitly into an "Outer Rule," which briefly addresses the anchoress's material existence, and an "Inner" one, which more extensively treats the daily struggles and fortifications of her spiritual life. Such an emphasis leaves the door open for lay audiences to eliminate formal requirements altogether, or to construct their own. As we will see in Chapter 4, the anchoress Julian of Norwich assumes that her experiences will be directly relevant to all her "even-Cristen."

These anchoritic works, along with numerous other vernacular texts, reached a broad spectrum of English readers in part through the efforts of the Carthusians, who were responsible for much of the writing, copying, preservation, and dissemination of English devotional literature—including Rolle's—and who provided a unique model of eremiticism in community. It is another mark of the tremendous prestige of solitaries in late medieval England that almost all new foundations in the period were Carthusian. (The other expanding order was that of the Bridgettines, which also had eremitic associations.) Dead to the world and sworn to silence, Carthusian monks lived in adjoining cells that were essentially private houses, with such features as fireplaces, studies, latrines, and gardens with small, private cloisters. Here they ate, slept, meditated, worshiped, and labored in solitude, coming together only infrequently in the central church. Yet their lonely labors of writing and copying—their silent "preaching"—definitively marked England's textual culture and connected them to a wider literate community. Developed for a world of silence and solitude, their contemplative practices shaped those of a broad spectrum of devout men and women who were eremitic only in their reading.[52] As the Carthusian prior Nicholas Love saw it, Christ's nine-month enclosure in his mother's womb showed that everyone should be in some sense enclosed. Love's *Mirror of the Blessed Lyf of Jesu Crist*, a translation of the pseudo-Bonaventuran *Meditationes* and one of the most widely read texts of the fifteenth century, demonstrates the power of popular Franciscanism harnessed to eremitic literacy—a peculiarly English yoking of affectivity, textuality, and the idea of solitude, to which we will return in the next chapter.

The increasing presence of solitaries in populated areas reinforced their potential to serve as models for lay reading. Anchoresses in particular became familiar fixtures in English urban spaces—"close and visible sign[s] of holiness."[53] Many hermitages were located at bridges; many anchorholds' windows looked out on streets leading to busy market squares—which explains frequent anxieties about anchoresses becoming hubs for town gossip. Anchoresses and anchorites were generously supported by every social class, and they were ideally positioned to offer spiritual counsel and comfort in return. Margery Kempe famously sought the advice of the anchoress Julian in the bustling town of Norwich, and was herself identified as an "ancress" in Pepwell's 1521 edition of extracts. And Hughes chronicles the importance of solitaries to the educated and powerful, especially at Cambridge and Westminster. Thus enmeshed in yet divorced from the social world, English recluses represented a category-defying spiritual detachment that even a layman might hope to imitate.[54]

Not everyone thought such imitation was a good idea. In Chaucer's *House of Fame*, the Eagle voices his disapproval of Geoffrey's hermit-like practices. Accusing the poet's persona of being a little too bookish, a little too antisocial, the Eagle describes a comically eremitic existence:

Thou goost hom to thy hous anoon,
And, also domb as any stoon,
Thou sittest at another book
Tyl fully daswed ys thy look;
And lyvest thus as an heremyte,
Although thyn abstynence ys lyte. (652–60)

Plump Geoffrey is no ascetic; lacking an outer rule, his "abstinence" is light indeed. His eremitic living consists merely in his habit of reading alone, silently, in his house. Like Langland's hermit he is an order by himself, reading without rule or reasonable obedience.

Langland's own "field full of folk" positively swarms with hermits and anchorites, both proper solitaries who keep to their cells and "grete lobies and longe" that wander the countryside (B i.55). But even Langland's own persona, "longe" Will, commences his spiritual journey "in habite as an heremite, unholy of werkes" (B i.3). The suspiciously garbed wanderer—who perhaps inevitably decides to write a book of vernacular spiritual guidance—evokes the romantic, half-liminal status of the Rollean solitary, but also his paradoxical ordinariness. In some sense, anyone could assume the habit of a hermit. For the literature of anchoritic formation made intentions more important than works, the inner more important than the outer rule. The representation and dissemination of vernacular spirituality in England was decisively shaped by this largely self-contained, text-centered, individualistic model of ideal devotional reading and subjectivity.

Women's Reading, Lay Reading

In the spread of monastic and eremitic ideals to a broader readership, women played a particularly important role. Because of their declining familiarity with Latin, female religious—anchoresses, but also nuns—were the original audiences for most vernacular devotional writing. Rolle's and Hilton's English works were written for women, as were the *Ancrene Wisse* and "Wooing Group" texts, *The Chastising of God's Children*, *The Myroure of Oure Ladye*, *The Orcherd of Syon*, *Speculum Devotorum*, and many others. But not only enclosed women were interested in devotional reading. As numerous important studies have shown, the reading habits and preferences of women outside the cloister were remarkably similar to those on the inside. The evidence of patronage and wills, as Carol Meale points out, suggests that "religion was by far the dominant reading interest of medieval women," regardless of religious status.[55] Secular women with money and leisure sought to imitate the routines of the abbey, marking time with the help of beautifully illuminated books of hours, and scheduling daily seclusion for reading and prayer. Those who sought shelter in religious houses during their later years were especially likely to leave devotional books to those houses in their wills. Mary Erler speculates that "their greater freedom and greater wealth may suggest that in some cases laywomen acquired books and nuns preserved them."[56] And not only nobly born women were involved. Women of the gentry and urban trading classes were also eager to acquire devotional books and to be instructed in devotional matters. Margery Kempe's yearning for someone to read to her is perhaps the best-known example, and it points to the ways in which even those women without solid literacy might become part of the "textual communities" of vernacular devotion. Given women's pervasive marginalization from much official and public religious culture, it is not difficult to understand why they might have been attracted to more autonomous and private forms of spiritual practice, to venues where they could effectively "turn the leaf" and choose material that suited them.

Yet in late medieval England, female textual culture cannot easily be divorced from lay culture in general—a point worth emphasizing, I think, not only because of its implications for the gendering of the inner life, but because devotional literature has so often been discussed as the special province of women readers. Margery Kempe, for one, seems to think that a wider spectrum of people profited from her devotional reading. When her reader-priest gained his own benefice, she relates, he had "gret cur of sowle," and was very glad "that he had redde so meche be-forn."[57] Presumably the texts that Margery had been so eager to hear were useful in ministering to parishioners of both genders. This movement of devotional discourse from religious women to the laity, often with the special interest and promotion of laywomen, is typical throughout the period. A chorus of scholarly opinion affirms that the pastoral care of religious women "set a standard for the *cura laicorum*, regardless of gender"; that as literacy spread, "the laity . . . came increasingly to occupy a position in the educational hierarchy similar to that which had long been occupied by female religious"; that "it was the nuns . . . who stood at the fore-front of English spirituality."[58] Given the close ties between convents and their communities, this is not surprising. Women in religious orders tended to maintain close ties with their benefactors, relatives, and surrounding communities. They lodged short- and long-term guests, educated both male and female boarders, and shared their churches with lay congregations.[59] It was perhaps inevitable that as vernacular literacy increased and demand for devotional instruction grew, the texts created for their needs should reach a broader audience.

The Bridgettine abbey at Syon (considered further in Chapter 2) stands at the peak of this phenomenon. Populated largely with former anchoresses at the time of its founding, the abbey's reputation for extraordinary piety and learning made it a great center for the dissemination of lay spirituality throughout the fifteenth and early sixteenth centuries, and it became an important source of devotional material for the early English printers. The textual interactions between these Bridgettine nuns, the Bridgettine brothers charged with their pastoral care, and the prolific Carthusian monks at nearby Sheen—not to mention several generations of Lancastrian, Yorkist, and Tudor patrons—modeled an idealized set of relations between devout readers, writers, and translators; between crown and church; and even between devotion and scholarship, as the Syon brothers accumulated a vast humanist library.

But even in the fourteenth century it had become common for writers to assert their works' relevance to lay as well as religious readers. The author of a treatise "agence fleshly affeccions" urges "every man havyng discrecioun" to learn from his work just as if it had been written "specially" for them, rather than for the particular needs of women.[60] Inscriptions in manuscripts of *The Contemplations of the Dread and Love of God*—a popular imitation of Rolle's works—indicate that it was read by Cistercian and Benedictine nuns, a countess, and one Agnette Dawn; but also by a sixteenth-century friar, a London pewterer named Alin Kyes, "master governor" Robert Cuttyng, and the unknown Peter Pungyarnar.[61] *The Seven Poyntes of Trewe Love and Everlastynge Wisdame* was first translated for a "worshipful lady," but quickly achieved wide circulation. It was popular with nuns, but it also turns up in the possession of aristocratic ladies, far-flung recluses, Yorkshire clergy, and Carthusian monks. It appears in the will of a Bristol merchant in 1393; it was owned by a Nottinghamshire knight and a royal judge in the fifteenth century. As the major part of William Caxton's *Book of Diverse Ghostly Matters* (ca. 1490), it must have reached an even wider audience.[62] We might take as emblematic Wynkyn de Worde's 1494 edition of Hilton's *Scale of Perfection*: originally written for a "ghostly sister," perhaps an anchoress, the *Scale* became popular with laypeople and was circulated in common-profit manuscripts in London. It was promoted by the Carthusians and became a standard at Syon; Lady Margaret Beaufort, Henry VII's mother, who had close ties to Syon, insisted that it be printed; and it came into print addressed to the spiritual good of every sort of person.[63] Thus did monastic and eremitic ideals, particularly those considered suitable for women, work their way to the heart of lay culture. Whether we look to urban women like Margery Kempe, religious houses like Syon, or aristocrats like the Lady Margaret—who herself translated the fourth book of Thomas à Kempis's *De Imitatione Christi*—the connections between women's reading and the broader forms of devotional literacy are everywhere apparent.

Mixed Lives and Bourgeois Dilemmas

By the time it appeared in print, the *Scale of Perfection* had acquired an unofficial third book: Hilton's *Epistle on the Mixed Life*. This too is emblematic, for as laypeople increasingly appropriated the forms and texts of the professional religious, the concept of the mixed or "medled" life helped to facilitate the shift.

The mixed life was not a new idea, but it had earlier been applied mostly to the secular clergy. Such men could imitate both Martha and Mary, the favorite symbols of active and contemplative life. They could attend to Christ's domestic needs with Martha, but also choose "the better part" of sitting at his feet in contemplation with Mary. They could take Leah to wife, but Rachel for love. They could be like Christ himself, who ministered actively but also retired to the wilderness to pray. But in his *Epistle on the Mixed Life*, Hilton cautiously extended this ideal to "sum temporal men": men, that is, with "sovereynte . . . of wordli goodis and . . . lordschipe overe othere men for to goveren and sustene hem."[64] The extension depends on a careful analogy between spiritual and temporal lordship; Hilton's work was written for a male landowner. The text quickly became the standard pronouncement on the subject for all kinds of readers, however, not just the propertied men Hilton had in mind. Nicholas Love recommends it to his own readers, declining to translate Bonaventura's discussion of active and contemplative lives in the largest single suppression of material from the *Meditationes*.[65]

Hilton advises his reader to temper the pursuit of his spiritual gifts and yearnings with an awareness of his worldly responsibilities. The reader should not spend too much time in meditations, "as it were a frere, or a monk" (112). He should not stay up all night or put off meals by excessive praying, nor neglect his obligations to dependents. He should not struggle to feel more devotion than comes naturally. Most important, he should maintain a strict segregation of his active and contemplative occupations. "*Omnia tempus habent*," Hilton writes; "Alle thinge hath tyme" (129). There is a time for outward deeds, for service and obligation, and there is a time for inward deeds, for sweet longings and emotional meditations. The resulting "continuel desire to God" may influence the reader's active life; but there is a "diversite," Hilton admonishes, "bitwene goostlie and bodili dedis" (121, 124). Therefore the reader must "departe wiisli thi lyvyng in two: o tyme to oon, another tyme to that othere" (116). Within these limits he may aspire to a higher form of living, pursuing the private stirrings of a spiritual desire that is not his assigned vocation.

Hilton insists on a compartmentalization of time, not of the self. But other devotional texts, in exhorting their mixed-life readers to internalize the ideals of the cloister, created the potential for substantial fissures between the inner life and the outer. The popular *Abbey of the Holy Ghost* insists that all those who "may noghte be bodyly in religyone . . . may be gostely," for they may build their abbeys "in a place called Conscience."[66] Here elements of the human psyche are allegorized as a community of busy religious women. A familiar physical space is re-imagined as the region within; a religious rule becomes a habit of mind. The text's admonition to "hold thee within the cloister, closed and locked" applies to a reader isolated from the affairs of the world in spirit only. Among the text's owners was ambitious Sir John Paston, of the famous letter-writing family. One wonders to what extent he considered himself spiritually isolated from the political and personal turmoil around him—including the terrible and drawn-out conflicts with his father, who wrote Margaret in 1465 that her newly knighted son was neither "politic nor diligent in helping himself" at court, and needed "to know the better himself, and put him in remembrance what time he has lost and how he has lived in idleness."[67] What kinds of self-knowing might John have engaged in—and with what help, one wonders again, from books?

Monastic and eremitic literature had long urged its readers to internalize the enclosures in which they spent their lives, imagining themselves as microcosms of their environment. Such internalization, however, must have had an entirely different effect where those inner structures no longer corresponded to material facts. A nun imagining her heart as a convent brought harmony and unity to her inner and outer realities. A layperson doing the same created a distinct divide, as this admonition in the *Contemplations of the Dread and Love of God* suggests: "Y sey not thou schalt fle bodili from the world or from thi wordeli goodis for thes ben principal ocasiones, but I counsele the in herte an in wil that thou fle al suche vanites, for thay thou be a lord or a laidi, housbond-man or wif, thou maist have as stable an herte and wil as some religious that sitteth in cloistre."[68] Here the reader's social identity becomes distinct from the inner reality of his or her heart and will. The outer self remains free to pursue worldly goods in the spaces of secular life, but the heart remains ideally disengaged, a world unto itself rather than a reflection of the self others see. Whereas in the cloister and anchorhold the heart's architecture had served to validate an external order, here it undermined it—or simply made it irrelevant.[69] Instead of giving away all his worldly goods, the rich layman could labor to be "poor in spirit" as works like *The Prickynge of Love* and *Dives and Pauper* advised. (This problem is discussed further in Chapter 1.)

Still, many laypeople continued to mix their active and contemplative lives in external, temporally segmented ways, as Hilton recommended. Tiny, elaborate books of hours helped them to imitate the prayer routines of the abbey. Some retired to convents or took vows of chastity at appropriate

times in their lives, while others became members of lay fraternities associated with contemplative orders or built private chapels. The distinctions between actives and contemplatives continued to blur both internally and
externally, and the physical and psychic boundaries of the "mixed life" continued to expand.

The idea of the mixed life helped to address what critics have characterized as one of the major bourgeois dilemmas of the later Middle Ages: as
Kathleen Ashley puts it, "how to achieve spiritual validation while remaining an active member of mercantile society."[70] Ashley and others describe a
world where new wealth creates bourgeois guilt, where the purchase of devotional books and devotional artifacts is meant partly to assuage the sense
that a life devoted to the pursuit of money and status is not the ideally
Christian life. Popular fifteenth-century plays such as the Digby *Mary Magdalene* and the Macro *Wisdom*, as Theresa Coletti has argued, dramatized
the desire to reconcile powerful economic interests with spiritual ideals.[71]
Like the audiences for those plays, readers of private contemplative literature must have been comforted by the thought that they could pursue
worldly success through all its vicissitudes and yet "have as stable an herte
and wil as some religious that sitteth in cloistre." It has been called an age of
ambition, an era of swiftly rising and falling fortunes, epitomized by the rise
of people like John Paston and his family. Such an age could create anxiety
and guilt, to be sure—but also "a sense that more was possible," as Rosemary
Horrox puts it. Devotional texts could not only compensate for their readers' material wealth, but help them actively to negotiate and articulate different kinds of possibilities for themselves.

Horrox argues for "a surge of interest in self-improvement" in the fifteenth century, indicated by the demand for education, school books, and
"handbooks of practical self-instruction."[72] As behavior became more important as an indicator of gentility, courtesy manuals found a wide audience. Women studied minute points of proper bearing, gesture, and address,
and urban guilds assembled strict codes for regulating the appearance and
behavior of their members.[73] Thomas Hoccleve's urban, clerkly persona
practices public faces in his mirror at home, obsessing over his ruined reputation, his alienating bureaucratic work, his failure to prosper. Urban readers are not my only concern in this study, but their social mobility and
habits of disciplinary self-instruction contributed to a broader environment
in which self-improvement was a familiar concept and books could be seen
as a means to that end. By the 1480s, William Caxton was promoting his

chivalric romances as conduct books of virtue and citizenship: "by whyche we may come and atteyne to good fame and renomme in thys lyf, and after thys shorte and transytorye lyf to come unto everlastyng blysse in heven."[74] It is not far from Spenser's purported aim of "fashion[ing] a gentleman or noble person in vertuous and gentle discipline" by means of *The Faerie Queene*.[75] If the abundance of educational and behavioral manuals in late medieval England suggests a growing interest in the tools and habits of self-betterment, the purchase of devotional literature indicates a similar eagerness to climb the ladders of doing well, better, and best—to participate vigorously in the sometimes anxious project of self-assessment and improvement, not least through the buying and reading of books.

The overlapping of material and spiritual values in this period has not gone unnoticed by religious historians, many of whom have derided fifteenth-century English spirituality as conservative and mercantile, especially compared to the fervid, presumably less materialistic and individualistic devotional activity on the Continent. Chaucer gives us the self-promoting guildsmen and the Wife of Bath to confirm the picture; theirs is a piety of precedence, a Christianity "out of alle charitee."[76] It is easy enough to point to figures like Margery Kempe, whose admissions of social pride and material ambition are so clearly mirrored in an often nakedly competitive spiritual life. Her rise in spiritual status seems to compensate for her failure to improve her social standing through marriage and business ventures. Yet Margery's religious life is not merely economics crudely translated, though it sometimes speaks in that register. Even Chaucer's Wife of Bath, as her hag's "pillow sermon" so amply demonstrates, has a remarkable grasp of the spiritual principles so entirely belied by her social behavior. This ostensibly shallow and materialistic layperson turns out to understand her faith better than she lets on—and far better than the churchmen who periodically interrupt and critique her performance. To ascribe to English spirituality a "fatal lukewarmness" is to miss the eagerness with which the same classes who admittedly spent more on their houses than anything else—a typically public and private gesture—also embraced the project of "knowing themselves" beyond the limits of material comforts and social identity, business and marriage negotiations.[77] In assuring readers that their inner selves, like their social personae, required constant examining, conforming, and disciplining, devotional literature may have echoed an already familiar habit of mind. But the focus on the inner life may also have provided a welcome relief—a small, liberating private space—from the relentless behaviorism required of people struggling, like Chaucer's Franklin, to establish and maintain their "gentilesse." (The Franklin, of course, ties himself in knots trying to reconcile private relation with the need to keep up public appearances.) Or perhaps that inner focus served as a source of friction with bourgeois values, as in Kempe's case. In any case, devotional literature was a crucial genre for a society trying to envision the proper relationships between self and community in an irrevocably "mixed" world. It seems only proper that the readers who poured so much energy into shaping their outer selves should approach their inner ones with equal enthusiasm and determination.

Writers, Translators, Copyists, Compilers

> *I think of myself as being essentially a reader. As you are aware, I have ventured into writing; but I think that what I have read is far more important than what I have written. For one reads what one likes—yet one writes not what one would like to write, but what one is able to write.*
>
> —*Jorge Luis Borges,* This Craft of Verse[78]

This study crosses a divide between what scholars sometimes think of as writerly England—England between about 1350 and 1410—and readerly England, from 1410 to about 1530. Marked by Archbishop Arundel's restrictive Constitutions of 1409, the divide has been seen as marking a dramatic change in the direction of English spirituality. In the long century after the Constitutions banned biblical translation and Parliamentary statute approved the burning of heretics—a century too of ruinous foreign and civil wars—English writers asserted their reliance on tradition and authority. Canonizing the past and apologizing for their own meager abilities, they claimed to think of themselves more as readers than as writers. They wrote what they were able, they insisted, not what they liked.[79] The devotional output of the fifteenth and early sixteenth centuries seems at best borrowed and unadventurous, and at worst reactionary, when compared to the native classics of what Nicholas Watson has called the "brilliant years" before 1410—years that produced not only John Wyclif, but Richard Rolle, Walter Hilton, Julian of Norwich, *The Cloud of Unknowing, Piers Plowman,* and *Pearl,* not to mention such important adaptations as *The Chastising of God's Children, A Talkynge of the Love of God,* and *The Prickynge of Love.*[80] Watson has argued that this outpouring of English vernacular theology was paralyzed by Arundel's Constitutions: a "vibrant tradition," he writes, was censored "almost out of existence"; the "life [went] out of English theology."[81]

Yet the existing tradition continued to lumber along, growing ever more expansive, ubiquitous, and popular. For it was during the fifteenth and early sixteenth centuries, as literacy grew by leaps and bounds and books became easier and cheaper to acquire, that those brilliant fourteenth-century theologies achieved their broadest readership and worked themselves into the fabric of English devotional culture. Since the censorship was not retroactive, even the most daring works were "grandfathered" into orthodoxy—even canonized after a fashion, as Watson argues.[82] The dramatic expansion of interest in English devotional literature, combined with this simultaneous narrowing in original vernacular writing, meant a broader market for previously sanctioned but hitherto inaccessible or unavailable writings—not just earlier works in English, but especially translations from Latin and the Continental vernaculars. It was a great age of translation, in which the works of writers like Guillaume Deguilleville, Bridget of Sweden, Catherine of Siena, Mechtild of Hackeborn, Henry Suso, and Thomas à Kempis became part of English devotional culture. Writers such as Thomas Hoccleve, John Lydgate, and Nicholas Love (and the rest of his Carthusian brethren) could hardly translate fast enough. The introduction of print in the 1470s only intensified these trends. The printers' sudden need for publishable material and the subsequent growth of the English book market meant that fresh translations, new compilations, and old standards reached a much wider audience than before.

It seems unlikely that fifteenth- and sixteenth-century readers considered these works conservative, lifeless, or outdated. Where devotional fashion did render a text out of date, it was often altered to suit contemporary tastes—as was the case, for example, with the Passion narratives in the *Cursor Mundi*.[83] The nuns at Syon must have been delighted to have their Latin rule in a fresh, accessible English translation. Margaret Beaufort was excited enough about the century-old works of Walter Hilton and Thomas à Kempis that she wanted to share them with other readers. Indeed, if we view the period from the perspective of English reading rather than English writing, the continuities across this apparent chasm in vernacular devotion are striking. The fifteenth century begins to look less like a near-extinction, and more like a dramatic expansion of possibilities only tentatively considered by earlier English writers.

Thus, since my focus is on constructions of the reader rather than on the originality or theological daring of any given writer, this study takes the period from about 1350 to 1530 as an untidy but coherent arc, loosely defined by the growth of devotional reading in English before the Reformation. Many of the texts discussed here were written in the late fourteenth century but read through the early sixteenth, and I consider them as "belonging" to the entire period. The age of Rolle's greatest popularity and impact, for example, is not the fourteenth century but the fifteenth. The *Stimulus Amoris* became the English *Prickynge of Love* in the late fourteenth century, but most of the ownership records are likewise from the fifteenth century. The *De Imitatione Christi* of Thomas à Kempis was translated into English in the mid-fifteenth century, was noticed by key readers in and around the Syon community, and became a runaway best-seller and perennial classic of Christian spirituality only after the Reformation. The great power of such texts to shape devotional subjectivities and to explore the possibilities for readerly self-envisioning comes precisely from their location in this culture of new audiences, evolving reading practices, and shifting religious ideals.

From this perspective, translations, compilations, and adaptations take on new interest. We have seen that in addressing the growing audience for devotional literature in English, spiritual writers often turned to discourses originally designed for specific religious audiences: hermits, nuns, anchoresses, Franciscans. Works that had enjoyed only limited circulation in their own day suddenly answered a general need: Edmund Rich's *Speculum Ecclesiae*, for example, with its systematic exercises on the Passion of Christ, was rarely read before the mid-fourteenth century, when it became extremely popular and inspired several translations into English.[84] Writers frequently borrowed from more than one source, creating more and less coherent works out of old standards and favorite quotations. The author/compiler of the *Chastising of God's Children* (ca. 1382–1410) augmented substantial borrowings from Alphonse of Pecha's *Epistola Solitarii* and Jan Ruusbroek's *Spiritual Espousals* with additional snippets from Augustine, Anselm, Bridget of Sweden, and others. Composed for nuns and owned by at least five female houses, the *Chastising* also circulated widely among the literate laity and male religious, particularly Carthusians. It survives in fourteen manuscript copies, is mentioned by name in two fifteenth-century wills, and was printed twice by Wynkyn de Worde in the early sixteenth century.[85] Yet it has received almost no critical attention. Michael Sargent describes the *Chastising* as an "eviscerated" version of Ruusbroec, a watered-down version of Continental mysticism for an unsophisticated English audience.[86] His description exemplifies the critical reception of English devotional literature, long influenced by the values and hierarchies of mystical and theological scholarship. The *Chastising* may not be particularly original or theologically compelling. But it does represent a considered and consistent attempt to shape an appropriate form of religious subjectivity for its readers: readers who are already represented in the text itself as questioning old habits of belief and religious practice, desiring new forms of devotion, and requesting new texts. For this restless audience the *Chastising's* author attempts to negotiate the competing claims of Latin and vernacular, inside and outside, "prevy" and public. He seems determined, that is, to shape and modify the trends of which his text is itself a sign. His carefully structured spiritual program—which, for example, eliminates almost all erotic metaphors in favor of maternal ones, emphasizes the busy labor of the inward life, and casts suspicion on both "visionary" and imageless devotion—seeks to control what vernacular reading and private devotions can mean by constructing what the inward selves of readers will ideally look like.

We should remember that the processes of translation, compilation, and extraction so typical of late medieval devotional writing were not limited to that genre, but were the most significant and characteristic features of the broader literary culture of the age. James Simpson speaks of a "dynamic interaction" between fifteenth-century English and Continental literatures, forming a textual culture where "writers . . . often represent themselves as readers, whose rereading of old texts produces a rewriting."[87] The most popular romances in fifteenth-century England were those composed a century or two before; new translations from the French continued to bring older materials to new audiences.[88] Malory's *Morte d'Arthur* is of course the great capstone of the phenomenon. Romances and devotional materials often appeared side by side in manuscript anthologies such as the famous collections of Robert Thornton, or the Harley manuscript. Both genres benefited tremendously from the expanding audience for English writing, and both were especially popular with urban and gentry readers. But while we no longer see English romances merely as watered-down or eviscerated versions of Continental traditions, we still treat their devotional brethren as uninteresting spiritual pablum. As Luce Guillerm observes, "In the fissures between original and adaptation we may choose to read not the insufficiency of a derivative discourse, but rather the traces of the aesthetic, social, and geopolitical preoccupations shared by translators and their im-

plied audiences."[89] Reverence for the Continental and English spiritual classics should not blind us to the ways in which their appropriation for and by
English readers participates in a lively process of cultural appropriation and
assertion.

Such a process does not necessarily show clear lines of development
and influence, or of efflorescence and decline. It is not a tidy narrative, beginning with Rolle and ending with Caxton and the dissolution of the
monasteries. How can we think about a literary culture of translation and
recirculation? As Fradenburg remarks, "Raymond Williams's distinctions
between 'emergent,' 'dominant,' and 'residual' cultural strains point out how
many epochs people might, at the 'same' time, be living in. But how do we
know what is dominant and what is residual, especially if the signifier can
always return?"[90] In late fourteenth- to early sixteenth-century England, we
might say, the signifier returned again and again in a vast eddy of emergent,
dominant, and residual cultural strains—making it notoriously difficult for
scholars to tell what epoch or epochs late medieval English men and women
might really have been living in. We continue to debate whether English culture was tending toward the "modern" or doubling back on itself to produce
ever-more "traditional" versions of its medievalness. (Were the Lollards
proto-Protestants or weren't they? Was chivalry a moribund fiction or a
lived ideal?) In the case of devotional literature, where so much that was old
was new again, where discourses crossed boundaries and took on different
meanings, and where all reforms tended to be couched as returns—both answers seem at least partly right.

Literacy and Orthodoxy

Such questions about tradition and innovation, repression and reform, lead
inevitably to two further, closely related questions of power and politics.
First, what is the relationship between ostensibly orthodox devotional texts
and the Lollard heresy, the most obvious target of Arundel's Constitutions?
And second—again a question of epochs—what is the relationship between
late medieval devotional reading and the Protestant Reformation? With regard to the first question, the production of orthodox devotional literature
might well be seen as an institutional response to the challenges of Lollardy.
Various scholars have suggested that the Vernon and Simeon manuscripts,
two of the most comprehensive medieval collections of devotional writing,

were the products of "a resurgent orthodoxy under siege," an orthodoxy challenged by Lollard activity in the district of Worcester where the manuscripts were produced.[91] Love's *Mirror* was approved if not actually commissioned by Arundel for "*hereticorum sive Lollardorum confutationem.*" Many other devotional texts show the strain of clerical authors trying to keep pace with and maintain some degree of control over the diverse devotional fashions affecting their literate but varyingly sophisticated audiences. Arundel and his clergy, especially, seem to have considered the dissemination of devotional literature a pastoral necessity, indispensable in the effort to extend church influence as far as possible into the intimate lives of parishioners.[92]

Nevertheless, there are good reasons not to see the devotional literature of the period in terms of a clear dichotomy between subversive heterodoxy and repressive, "here, read this instead" orthodoxy. First, considering non-Lollard devotional texts as monolithically "orthodox" obscures the fact that such texts contain various and often conflicting responses to issues of silent prayer, confession, interiority, visions, and mystical espousal. Most writers seem less worried about "heterodox" John Wyclif than about "orthodox" Richard Rolle, whose works were often criticized for creating expectations of sensory and emotional rapture among the susceptible and untrained, thus rendering them vulnerable to hubris, or disappointment, or, in a worst-case scenario, demonic fraud. Moreover, heterodox and ostensibly orthodox texts offered their readers quite *similar* positions on many issues, so much so that Lollard interpolators often had little work to do—adding an extra sentence here, a word there—to make approved texts into "Lollard versions."[93] Even where there has been no interpolation, many manuscripts include both orthodox and heterodox texts without comment. Finally, the possession of almost *any* vernacular text—including those we might consider safely or even defensively orthodox—could help to confirm if not initiate a charge of Lollardy. The boundaries between heterodoxy and orthodoxy often had as much to do with context (especially social class) as with theological content. Wycliffite Bibles, which seem to have been among the most popular texts of the period, were approved for the use of the wealthy and powerful, while even the most innocuous vernacular text in the hands of a laborer was cause for concern. The enthusiastically orthodox Margery Kempe, a voracious consumer and imitator of devotional literature, claims to have suffered repeated accusations of Lollardy—apparently based on the noisiness, rather than the nature, of her devotions. Such accusations usually came from her fellow laypeople, moreover, not from the church. As Kempe tells it, the responses of the numerous priests, friars, anchoresses, and bishops she encountered varied as dramatically as Kempe's own behavior. Ecclesiastical opinion was similarly divided on the orthodoxy of texts like *Dives and Pauper*; as Anne Hudson observes, a copy was commissioned by the conservative abbot of St. Albans in the same decade (1430s) that Bishop Alnwick confiscated one from a chaplain of Bury St. Edmunds, who had been loaning it out a little too indiscriminately.[94] (Indiscriminately or not, the text was printed in 1493, 1496, and 1536.)[95] This study assumes that devotional literature is the complex product of relationships between monastic, clerical, and lay cultures that were sometimes cooperative, sometimes resistant, earnest, cautious, flexible, conscientious, pragmatic, or condescending—but rarely reducible to binary models of cultural power and subversion.

The looming presence of the Protestant Reformation at the end of the period presents similar problems of interpretation, with some scholars asserting that private devotions, especially Christ-centered ones like the Passion meditations in Chapter 3, are essentially "anti-Catholic"; that the emphasis on intimate, vernacular, readerly relationships with Jesus, unmediated by clergymen, paves the way for sixteenth-century reforms.[96] If everyone's heart is an abbey, what need is there for brick-and-mortar foundations? Others, meanwhile, argue that late medieval devotional literacy is essentially conservative, so that the Reformation represents not an outgrowth from, but a violent break with the devotional tradition. After all, no religious order resisted the Act of Supremacy more adamantly or at greater cost than the Carthusians. Syon's famously readerly nuns were among the first to get an English translation of the Divine Service, but among the last to bow to Henry VIII's will. The most sustained popular uprising against the Reformation, the Pilgrimage of Grace, came from the North, where native son Richard Rolle was revered and ownership of devotional books was especially high. Could such readers have been essentially anti-Catholic without realizing it?

I do not consider late medieval devotional literature a prelude leading inevitably to Protestant forms of reading and self-examination. At the same time, it seems irresponsible to shrink from noticing continuities between pre- and post-Reformation devotion in order to preserve a hermetically sealed Middle Ages. Many of the themes of late medieval English devotional texts do resonate across the medieval/early modern divide, and many of the texts themselves survived the Reformation with only a few lines crossed out or pages excised. That they were amenable or adaptable to Protestant spirituality does not mean that they *caused* Protestant spirituality. But I think we need to be able to consider continuities, resurfacings, influences, and adaptations, despite the perils of teleology and our desire as medievalists not to see the period simply as background to the Renaissance. Part of my own abiding fascination with medieval devotional texts is about the moments where something seems familiar to me, another version of something I know from elsewhere, whether or not there is a straight line between the two. Part of it is about the moments that are dramatically *un*like anything I might have expected. What I try to do here is less to track a developing mentality than to describe an array of particular forms offered by the late medieval literature of contemplation, and to try to understand how they work. These forms are often richly diverse, as will be apparent in the next chapter. So I would like to turn now to the subject of interiority: one of those themes that echoes powerfully across the boundary between medieval and modern, as we shall see.

Chapter 1

A Very Inward Man

Though our outward man is corrupted, yet the inward man is renewed day by day.
—*Paul, 2 Corinthians 4:16*

What does it mean to have an "inward man"? If one wishes to live an inner life, search oneself within, or see with an inner eye, how exactly does one go about it? Where and how do we cross the boundaries from the outside to the inside? According to the author of the *Cloud of Unknowing*, most fourteenth-century Englishmen had not the slightest idea. Warning his readers against common pitfalls of contemplative practice, the *Cloud*-author complained that hapless cultivators of the inner life, responding eagerly to popular devotional rhetoric, were reversing the course of nature and driving themselves mad:

Thei reden & heren wel sey that thei schuld leve utward worching with theire wittes, & worche inwardes; & forthe that thei knowe not whiche is inward worchyng, therfore thei worche wronge. For thei turne theire bodily wittes inwardes to theire body agens the cours of kynde [nature]; & streynyn hem, as thei wolde see inwardes with theire bodily ighen, & heren inwardes with theire eren, & so forthe of all theire wittes, smellen taasten, & felen inwardes. & thus thei reverse hem agens the course of kynde, & with this coriouste thei travayle theire ymaginacioun so undiscreetly, that at the laste thei turne here brayne in here hedes.[1]

The *Cloud*-author was not the only English writer to suggest a connection between madness and the misguided or unqualified pursuit of interiority. (Indeed, the link between inwardness and insanity recurs from Hoccleve to Hamlet.) The author of the early sixteenth-century *Pomander of Prayer* advises laypeople to pray vocally rather than mentally—not because they are in danger of mistaking spiritual for bodily coordinates, but because mental prayer "is so laborous and so vyolente that within shorte space it wyll brynge a man unto such debilitacion and wykenes of brayne that it wyll cast hym in great danger of seckness or some other inconveyence."[2] Only the safely cloistered contemplative elite, he cautions, should practice this higher and more inward, if more intense and dangerous, form of address to God.

These two authors' warnings bracket more than a century of serious concern over the meaning, possession, and pursuit of interiority in England. The difference between inner and outer, as many of the spiritual writers of the day agreed, was the difference not only between corruption and renewal (as Paul had written), but between the active and contemplative lives, or sometimes between the lower and higher stages of contemplation. Richard Rolle—whose followers were probably the target of the *Cloud*-author's satire—assures readers of his popular *Form of Living* that while "Actife lyfe es mykel owteward. . . . Contemplatyfe lyfe is mykel inwarde."[3] Similarly, Walter Hilton begins his *Scale of Perfection* by explaining that active life consists "in love and charité schewyd outward in good bodili werkes," while contemplative life "is in perfight love and charité feelid inwardli bi goostli virtues."[4] And though Richard Whytford claims to be unable to describe the active and contemplative lives so clearly, after much hemming and hawing he still defines contemplation "in playne englyshe" as a "diligent beholdyng or inward lokyng with a desyre of hert."[5]

Indeed, as the boundaries between the active and contemplative lives blurred and became more difficult to define, the Middle English texts that were such a crucial factor in that blurring spoke habitually and insistently of inward affections and inward understanding, inward lovers and inward labor, inward devotion and especially inward beholding. Bridgettine nuns at Syon were advised to "laboure in your selfe inwardly. to sturre up your affeccyons" when reading in the library.[6] The English *Imitatio Christi* explained that "the inwarde man . . . nevere pourith himself holy to outwarde thinges."[7] In a particularly hyperbolic passage from Mechtild of Hackborne's *Booke of Gostlye Grace*, Christ tells the nun that she contains him "in the moste inwarde parties of thy sawle so that y be more inwarde to the[e] be my beynge with the[e] than alle thyne inwardness."[8] One of the most striking features of English devotional translations is their translators' tendency to insert the word "inward" at every opportunity (as in Nicholas

Love's *Mirror of the Blessed Lyf of Jesu Crist*, the English *Stimulus Amoris*, and Mechtild's *Booke*, for example). Surely the fifteenth-century translator of *The Doctrine of the Heart* was disingenuous to lament that so many devotional texts "speken to the bodi outward but fewe to the hert inward of simple soules"—a deficit his own work would of course remedy.[9] Few advertisements could have recommended his work more effectively to late medieval English readers. Just as surely, the Lollard writer who complained in a treatise against miracle plays that "the weeping that falleth to men and women by the sight of such miracles-playing . . . is not principally for their own sins, ne of their good faith withinforth, but more of their sight without forth" was making an accusation that would resonate not only with confirmed Lollards, but with a broad spectrum of readers.[10]

Yet for all their valorization of the interior—Rolle assured readers it was "lastandar and sykerar, restfuller, delitabiler, luflyer, and mare medeful"—it is not always clear what English writers actually mean by the term. We might assume that "inward" comprises thoughts and feelings as opposed to actions, the mind as opposed to the body: thus Hilton's assertion that active life is about performing charity through works, while contemplative life is about feeling it through virtues. And there are many other texts in which "inward" does seem to conjur a relatively straightforward mind-body split. Lollard attitudes toward penitence, for example, emphasize inner contrition—contrition in the heart, before God alone—over formal confession and bodily penance. What, though, are we to make of writers who speak of "inward affections" or "inward understandings"? Is "inward" in such cases merely an emphatic, a habit of usage?

In some cases the term does seem to mean simply devout, or spiritual, or inclined toward God. In others it indicates sincerity or intensity— "depth" of emotion, we might say. But inwardness could evoke a flesh-spirit dichotomy without relying on a mind-body one, since for many medieval thinkers the flesh was not precisely the same as the body. Rather, the flesh extended into the heart and mind through sensory perception and sensual imagination—the internalized forms of outward things. For Augustine as for the Neoplatonists, thoughts became more inward as they became less dependent on these sensory images and bodily forms. (It is worth noting that Augustine's works were enjoying something of a renaissance in fourteenth-century England, a point to which we will return.) According to Augustinian hermeneutics, the abstract, spiritual meaning is the "inner" kernel of truth, while figurative language is the outer, fleshly husk that conceals it. The outer is sensual, while the inner is rational. The human soul works the same way: its outer levels correspond to—and respond to—the outer level of the text, while its inner reason penetrates to the hidden, spiritual meaning of things. Fifteenth-century bishop Reginald Pecock follows the Augustinian paradigm in asserting that Reason is "the seid inward preciose book . . . buried in mannis soule."[11] The author of *The Chastising of God's Children* relies on it as well, declaring that more inward visions have fewer sensory components and are thus more trustworthy than their more outward counterparts. Imagistic, sensual visions may be misleading; abstract, rational visions are the likelier results of divine inspiration. Yet this text's version of inwardness encompasses another dichotomy, that between private and public. More inward visions pertain more exclusively to the self and to the reader's personal pursuit of virtues and are less likely to be shared. Between private spiritual progress and public teaching, between what is proper to oneself and what might pertain to others, "inwardness" traces a multivalent and powerful boundary.

To further complicate matters, if inner affections and understandings could be understood to be *less* dependent on fleshly, sensory imaginings, they could also be understood to be *more* so. Intensity of affection was thought to be most effectively stimulated by intense sensory experience. As Thomas Usk writes, "rude wordes & boystous percen the herte . . . to the inrest poynte."[12] Thus in many devotional texts, "inward beholding" requires a concentrated and colorful imagination—as in Nicholas Love's vivid, see-it-as-if-you-were-there pictures of the life of Christ, which owe so much to the Franciscan tradition of visual meditation.[13] "Inward" here is more concrete and lifelike, piercing the reader's heart and drawing him or her further into a universe of imaginative experience. But like the author of the *Chastising of God's Children*, Love implies a private/public dimension to interiority as well. Inward beholding creates personal and intimate knowledge, knowledge that pertains to the reader's soul alone.

The hapless targets of the *Cloud*-author's satire, then, might be forgiven for some confusion about "worching inward." Although the Christian thematics of inner and outer stretch back to Paul and Augustine, receive extensive development in Gregory's works, and figure importantly in major intellectual currents of the eleventh and twelfth centuries,[14] in the vernacular culture of late medieval England they seem to spin out of control, taking on a puzzling range of significance and becoming the focus of varied attempts at restructuring, redefining, re-imagining. As the sine qua non of superior devotion and spiritual truth, the inner life might be more rational or more affective, more imaginative or more introspective, less bodily or less literal, more intense, more devout, or just more private. It might be less orthodox or more so. In the early sixteenth century, James Grenehalgh drew Joanna Sewell's attention to a passage in her copy of *The Scale of Perfection*, writing triumphantly in the margins, "Quid sit interior oculus / diffinitive" ("what the interior eye is—definitively").[15] Whether Sewell's interest or his own motivated this Carthusian's marginal *nota bene*, he was not the only reader in England looking for authoritative definitions of inwardness, or formulating them. The *Oxford English Dictionary* registers a proliferation of semantics during this period, listing "coming from the inmost heart" as a new usage circa 1402, "devout" circa 1450, and "intimate" circa 1475. (It does not list the first instance of "secret or private" until circa 1548, though the *Middle English Dictionary* illustrates that meaning with Lydgate's 1420 *Troy Book*.)[16]

But the meaning of inwardness is not only a question of semantics. Depending on how inwardness was understood and pursued, it could have important implications for many of the most hotly contested issues of the age: issues of understanding and faith, public ritual and private conscience, the nature of images, the right way to pray, the role of reading, even the proper attitude toward the sacraments. It mattered to the way men and women thought about the borders and makeup of their proper selves, and how they aspired to certain privileged ways of perceiving and being. The Middle English devotional texts of the period bear witness to a serious contest over the practical applications of this vague but crucial concept.

Such vagueness is not entirely surprising. Forms of human consciousness, while often central to claims of prestige and value, are notoriously difficult to define. Take, for example, the more recent scholarly controversy over the origins of the "modern self." As Eric Jager writes, "The whole controversy depends, of course, on what exactly is meant by the 'self' and what precisely are the criteria of 'modernity.' In many cases, 'modernity' and 'selfhood' turn out to be largely honorary titles conferred on whatever a certain critic happens to admire or approve of."[17] Medieval writers were not immune to such enthusiastic imprecision. In many cases, "inwardness" turns out to be largely a fashionable term conferred on whatever a certain devotional writer happens to admire or approve of, whether that be understanding or obedience, spiritual autonomy or silence in church. In its purported inwardness or its purported modernity, the self is an easier thing to gesture toward than to pin down. But just as the term "modern" has real power as a label—even its careless use participates in a serious argument about our place in the world and in time—so too the term "inward" acts as a kind of touchstone for late medieval devotional culture, whether it means the same thing, or indeed anything, across disparate contexts. Even its careless use can alert us to the power of the idea, its centrality to narratives of medieval self-hood in relation to God, the church, and the world.

Of course, "modern" and "inward" and even "selves" are often assumed to be coterminous, particularly in early modernist scholarship. The English Renaissance, it is said, witnesses the rise of an interiorized religion (Protestantism), an interiorized lyric tradition (Petrarchan), and a widening gap between inner and outer selves influenced by a popular, secular dramatic tradition (Shakespearean)—among other cultural trends by which the English self becomes at once more inward, more exquisitely self-conscious, and of course more modern.[18]

Recently, however, some early modernists have begun to complicate this powerful narrative. Ramie Targoff, for example, has revisited the relationship between interior and exterior that "lies at the heart of early modern debates about devotional performance."[19] Revising accounts that insist on the radical separation of inner and outer selves fostered by Reformation theology and the Elizabethan settlement, Targoff demonstrates that prominent Tudor churchmen sought to *strengthen* the link between exterior behavior and interior devotion—partly, of course, in response to nonconformists who denied the outward readability of inner emotion and belief. Looking past Bacon's famous assertion that Elizabeth did not "make windows into men's hearts and secret thoughts,"[20] Targoff finds not "a triumphant embrace of the individual's private and invisible self," but a Protestant mainstream committed to the reliable correspondence between spiritual states and behavioral signs, and an ecclesiastical establishment eager "to shape personal faith through public and standardized forms."[21]

Targoff's provocative analysis suggests that the "inwardness" that was the focus of so much negotiation and concern in late medieval England continued to be a source of conflict after the Reformation. Like medieval churchmen a hundred or more years before them, Protestant authorities in Elizabethan England sought to reassert the transparency of the self and the efficacy of public prayer. But like earlier Lollard dissenters, Elizabethan recusants and nonconformists had a tremendous stake in asserting the hidden autonomy of the devotional subject. Meanwhile, ordinary churchgoers in both periods seem to have had a range of habits and beliefs. It would seem that we are looking at a long, winding, complex, and very productive cultural obsession indeed, one that cannot be reduced to simple contrasts between one externalized and another internalized culture, one public and the other private. Even less can it be forced into a clear trajectory of development—or loss. In Brian Stock's words, "within the problematics of reading, writing, and selfhood we have a phenomenon of *la longue durée* in Western intellectual history."[22]

Stock's observation returns us to the role of textuality, of "literate" modes of thought and interpretation, in cultural imaginings of selfhood. In *The Implications of Literacy*, Stock suggests that as literate paradigms permeated Western culture, textual hermeneutics began to structure other kinds of experience as well. The self became a kind of metaphor, composed of a bodily outer shell and a spiritual inner kernel that cried out for evaluation, interpretation, and commentary. Stock sets the allegorical, intellectualized search for hidden meaning in opposition to the spoken, the concrete, and the performative—an opposition increasingly apparent in the tensions between silent and spoken prayer, private piety and communal worship, that will concern us throughout this study. For now, I want to observe simply that in late medieval England, as vernacular literacy grows and private reading assumes greater importance in the lives of ever-larger numbers of English men and women, it makes sense that textual negotiations of selfhood should be so obsessively concerned with inner and outer, with literal surface and spiritual depths. Stock argues that literate modes are a function of broad cultural consciousness rather than individual literacy; such modes would have been solidly in place in England long before the late fourteenth century and not limited to the technically literate. Yet the increasing centrality of reading to English devotion and the steady movement of textual hermeneutics from Latin to vernacular culture, where established conceptual structures could suddenly break loose from their traditional semantic and contextual moorings, must have contributed to the urgency of these particular paradigms.

What, then, were the options for late medieval men and women seeking to turn inward without turning their brains in their heads? In the remainder of this chapter I offer a series of brief sketches drawn from this messy and recursive conversation, a number of different English models for the inner life. In doing so, I hope to suggest both the sustained concern and imagination inspired by this rather nebulous concept, and some of its particular implications for categories such as gender, social status, ritual, interpretation, politics, protest and heterodoxy, and the scene of reading. These different models were not as discrete nor as simplistic as my schematic overview must make them out to be. But I think it will be useful to separate out some of the contributing and competing strands in these negotiations, in order to appreciate the diversity of ways in which English men and women might attempt to look inward, to renew "the inner man" from day to day, by reading in the vernacular.

Seven Ways of Looking at an Inward Man

1. Richard Rolle: Inwardness Is "Luflyer and Mare Medeful"

As the *Cloud*-author's complaints might suggest, the charismatic hermit Richard Rolle was one of the most popular promoters of inwardness in late medieval England.[23] Surviving manuscripts of his English works number around a hundred, representing every Middle English dialect; there are thirty complete manuscripts of the *Form of Living* alone. For more than a hundred years, Rolle's name was a watchword of popular English devotion.

Rolle's mystical experience was revealed through sensory impressions, his (in)famous *fervor*, *canor*, and *dulcor*, or heat, song, and sweetness. But his English works focused most heavily on the emotions—joy, desire, and above all love—as the defining features of a spiritual life so fully personal and inward that no one but God could judge it.[24] For Rolle the inner life, far from transcending or turning away from sensory and affective experience, was a heightening and personalizing of such experience, a private world of sweetness in love-longing. The outer world against which the inner man would define himself was the public world of action, with its hypocrisies, distractions, and persecutions. Again and again Rolle rails against those who think they know "a mans hert, that nane knawes bot God."[25] He complains about actions divorced from emotion: "What gude, hopes thou, may come tharof, if thou lat thi tonge blaber on the boke and thi hert ren abowte in sere stedes in the worlde?"[26] But Rolle goes well beyond calls for concentration and sincerity, coming perilously close to rejecting *all* actions, all works, as potentially tainted with hypocrisy: "Lufe es in the hert and in the will of man," he writes, "noght in hys hand, ne in his mouth . . . noght in hys wark, bot in his sawle." And further: "Na thyng that I do withowten proves that I lufe God; for a wicked man myght do als mykel penance in body, als mykel wake and faste, als I do."[27] Rolle even fled the music of the choir, complaining that it interfered with his own inner harmonies.[28] Liturgical experience was hardly allowed to complement, let alone compete with, his singular devotion to God. Part of the external world, the church was inevitably shot through with that world's failings and conflicts, its lack of understanding and true perfection.

Inwardness on the Rollean model, then, threatens to sever the reader entirely from the authority of the community, making the heart its own authority. As Nicholas Watson writes, Rolle's teachings "bring out the radical potential latent in pastoral theology's pedagogical programme, which cannot but risk emancipating people from dependence on ecclesiastical structures by letting them take responsibility for their own souls."[29] This is strictly true only for the perfect, of course, for the contemplative elect and especially for Rolle himself. But as Watson has also argued, Rolle's rejection of outward religious disciplines made his doctrines "instantly adaptable to the general reader."[30] His insistence on love as the only criterion of holiness and God as the only judge of love made it impossible to impose any real boundaries on the community of the spiritual elite, and the wide circulation and influence of his works suggests that many men and women aspired to some version, however partial or temporary, of his experience.

And no wonder—for the inner life Rolle describes is relentlessly, radically upbeat. Separating himself from the conflicts and ugliness of the world, the Rollean contemplative enters a new world of gladness and joy, sweet song and "lyghtsumnes"—with a bare, perfunctory minimum of humility and sorrow, very little call to self-examination, and no discernible discipline other than the constant repetition of the name of Jesus. "If thou be in prayers and meditacions al the day," Rolle promises cheerfully, "I wate wele that thou mon wax gretely in the lufe of Jhesu Cryste, and mikel fele of delyte, and within schort tyme."[31] "Luf es a lyght byrthen," he sings elsewhere; "Lufe es withowten pyne."[32] Another song admonishes, "Loke thow lede thi lyf in lyghtsumnes; and hevynes, helde it away. Sarynes, let it noght sytt wyth the; bot in gladnes of God evermare make thow thi gle."[33] To be inward on Rolle's model is to be ravished by ecstatic love, to exist wholly in desire, to sing like a nightingale.

The fact that Rolle's desire for Jesus often sounds like a happier and more democratic version of courtly love was undoubtedly part of its appeal. Secular elites had long predicated at least part of their cultural superiority on the emotional complications of *fin amour*, the discourse of a "gentil" heart. As Hope Emily Allen puts it, "Chivalry and courtly love had been re-fining the emotions of secular men and women during hundreds of years, and those who, like Rolle, offered the lover as the ideal religious type, thus added to religion a pattern rich in the glamour of the most highly civilized traditions of secular medieval life."[34] Rolle's inward lover is glamorous in-deed, with his sensuous fire and languishing melodies, his sweet sorrow for the beloved body of Christ. His passionate interiority bursts forth in song as if he were some Troilus, singing of his endless delight in loving Criseyde. (And like Chaucer's Troilus, Rolle believes that you *can* run away with your lover—because the world is nothing, and love is all you need, and it doesn't matter what people think, though they will inevitably think the worst.) If the courtly lover frequently seems more interested in the complication and expression of his sensual, emotional life than in the actual presence of the beloved, Rollean inwardness shares that peculiar self-absorption. His own feelings and outpourings, because they signify his spiritual status, dominate his concern.

Part of the mystique of *fin amour*, however, is that not everyone can practice it. Such love is an "exceptional feeling," a way of justifying the social superiority of those who experience it.[35] Not everyone's heart will be capa-ble of such exquisite subtleties and sufferings. Neither can everyone live in Rolle's rarified love-longing—but anyone can try. For in Rolle's world, love no longer attends exclusively on noble blood and birth. Rolle's own father was a small householder, and surely there were others of approximately that station, women as well as men, who were eager to cultivate emotions asso-ciated with the "most highly civilized traditions" of medieval life, to believe their own hearts capable of such fine feeling. Adam the Carthusian makes similar claims for residents of the hermit's cell: "no other human being can be compared to you. Some exceed you in the temporal sphere, but their ca-pacity for joy and delight is less than yours."[36] Here too emotional capacity grounds the claim of personal value. But Rollean joy and delight is not strictly confined to the cell, any more than it is strictly confined to aristo-cratic readers. (Rolle himself was notoriously itinerant and indifferent to bodily discipline.) Rolle offers the prestige of an inner life to anyone with access to his works.

Perhaps this is one subtext for the *Cloud*-author's mocking, "and at last they turn their brains in their heads." If would-be Rolleans attempting to turn "inward" were mocked as too literal-minded, too bodily—they try to see inward with their bodily eye!—similar charges could be leveled at commoners fancying themselves "in love" when they were overcome by mere sexual attraction. (Think of Chaucer's *Miller's Tale*, with its hilariously literal, bawdy versions of both the delicate rituals of *fin amour* and the erotic language of the Canticles.) Surely natural creatures were incapable of experiencing such artful feelings, of understanding such advanced concepts. Similar charges were leveled at their language—at English itself.[37] Contemporary concerns that English might capture the letter but not the spirit of biblical utterance hinged on the notion that it might be too literal and bodily a medium to convey spiritual truth. Like its one-dimensional readers, English was all outer husk, no inner kernel. But Rolle's English readers were promised full access to and ownership of the interior, the world "lastandar and sykerar, restfuller, delitabiler, luflyer, and mare medeful." In this sensual, emotional, highly prestigious yet glamorously antisocial realm, the self could be made both autonomous and eloquent by desire. Rolle's inward lover of Christ rises above the wretched world and, like Troilus in the eighth sphere, laughs.

2. "Inaccessible to Others": Inwardness as (Female) Enclosure

> *I've known her—from an ample nation—*
> *Choose One—*
> *Then—close the Valves of her attention—*
> *Like Stone—*
> *—Emily Dickinson[38]*

Women were some of Rolle's earliest disciples and an important initial audience for his vernacular works. But if some fourteenth-century women flocked to Rolle's teachings and aspired to his glamorous, self-possessed spirituality, many others were busy cultivating an interiority imagined not as the exquisite emotionalism of the lover but as the erotic privacy of the bride, possessed body and soul by her husband. This was primarily an interiority of the cloister and anchorhold, and it was a matter not of refined spiritual sensibilities, but of enclosure and inviolability. Troped as a small, tightly contained space, this inner self was created and maintained through an obsessive attention to its borders, where as little as possible was allowed in or out, and where the purity of inner communion was perpetually endangered by incursion from the outside.

The ideal of the monastic soul as God's sexual possession was an ancient and familiar one. In the 1130s, Peter Abelard sought to console and instruct his enclosed wife Heloise by explaining that she had become the Ethiopian bride of the Canticles, she who is black but beautiful:

indeed, the disfigurement of her blackness makes her love what is hidden rather than open, what is secret rather than public. Such a wife desires private, not public delights with her husband, and would rather be experienced in bed than seen at table. Moreover it often happens that the flesh of black women is all the softer to touch though it is less attractive to look at, and for this reason the pleasure they give is greater and more suitable for private than for public gratification.[39]

Abelard's consolation takes the form of a lesson in biblical exegesis: he asks Heloise to consider the relationships between the literal and the allegorical meanings of the text, between the appearance of her black habit and its symbolic significance, and between her suffering in this life and her exaltation in the next. "She is black outside but lovely within," he writes, and that distinction becomes the basis for an entire range of interpretive associations, part of an intellectual and theological argument he is still having with his formidable ex-student.

Yet for later writers, particularly those addressing religious women in the vernacular, the inner/outer distinction would come to refer not to the process of interpretation but to the "more suitable" hidden space of erotic privacy itself, where interiority enabled the secret delights proper to that disfigured-but-desirable bride. As Roberta Gilchrist has shown, the bridal metaphors of female monasticism made the nun "a private space inaccessible to others."[40] Texts for nuns and anchoresses "seized on the complex apparatus of confinement," Jeffrey Hamburger observes, imagining inwardness in terms of the well-fortified spaces that constituted both the enclosed woman's physical environment and her body.[41] Hamburger describes the nun's subjectivity as a convent in miniature, a "womblike enclosure at the heart of [her] body."[42] She—or her heart—becomes a locked space, a privy chamber or a *hortus conclusus*, surrounded by thick stone walls and heavy, barred gates. Here, sealed off from the temptations and distractions of the outside world, she can await her spouse, the exclusive focus of her attention. By keeping the inner chamber as clean and inviolate as possible, she hopes to create an inviting space for him to enter, a private bower for secret ravishing. (As the fourteenth-century "Goodman of Paris" wrote to his young bride, "you ought to be very loving and privy toward your husband . . . moderately loving and privy towards your good and near kinsfolk . . . and very distant with all other men.")[43] Like the black bride, her soft flesh is meant to give pleasure, not to experience it. She focuses on the bridegroom's desire for her smooth and docile heart as intently as Rolle attends to his own passionate emotions and sensations.

And in a cloistered world where texts for women often focus obsessively on the sins of the tongue, to be properly inward is above all to be *silent*. The heart cannot be secured—and the lover may be frightened off—if the mouth is allowed to run free. *The Doctrine of the Heart* is typical in exhorting its readers to receive Christ into the houses of their hearts, where rest and quietness are "lokked up with a kay" through the careful regulation of speech.[44]

Privy chambers and enclosed love gardens, locks and keys, sturdy gates and dangerous windows appear as images of the self throughout Middle English texts associated with female religious, texts such as *A Ladder of Four Rungs, The Seven Poyntes of Trewe Love and Everlastynge Wisdame, The Tree and Twelve Frutes,* and *The Amesbury Letter.* Many show the influence of the still-popular *Ancrene Wisse,* with its famously inventive, elaborate, and privileged "Inner Rule" for the keeping of the heart.[45] Struggling to keep her heart sealed, the *Ancrene's* implied reader does incessant battle with her own outward-leaning flesh. That flesh threatens perpetually to betray her besieged heart to the world, leaving the windows ajar, stealing glances and a bit of gossip through the cracks. For she herself contains the boundary between inside and out, in the relentless stirrings of her own senses, the unruly movements of her own fleshly will. She looks—and the window swings open. She listens, and Death steals across the threshold. She speaks, and the wild heart leaps out. The internalization of external threat marks an important difference from Rolle: whereas Rolle can rely on his elevated feelings and judgment with utmost confidence, reserving his distrust for a world imagined as fully other, this model teaches the reader to distrust her own senses and keep constant watch over her own impulses. Rolle doesn't *have* an inner man—he is one, and this makes him as self-consistent, stubborn, and independent as the *Ancrene's* ideal reader is divided, self-conscious, and unsure.

It must be emphasized that in shutting out the blandishments of the sensual world and her own fleshly, sensory nature, the enclosed-inward reader is not abandoning sensual *imaginings*, not making the Neoplatonic distinction between pure reason and sensory affect. Nor is she learning to distinguish between the literal and the spiritual meaning of the biblical text. This model of interiority seeks rather to replace the "outer" world of the senses with an "inner" world of images and feelings that are "inner" largely because they are kept secret and directed exclusively toward God, not because they do not have a colorful fleshly and imaginative life of their own.

3. Enclosure Unenclosed

This distinction has important implications for the lay readers whose devotion would eventually bring them into contact with the discourses of female enclosure—for unlike the anchoress herself, the discourses did not stay obediently cloistered. Though Adam the Carthusian insisted that "the life of the cell is as essential to the interior life as water is to fish and the sheepfold to sheep,"[46] the notion of inwardness seems to have rendered anchoritic devotional works quite portable. The *Ancrene Wisse* may not go as far as Richard Rolle in disparaging all external religious forms, but its minimal "Outer Rule" claims so little attention that it is easily discarded, if not actively disdained. Consequently, the *Ancrene* seems to have been popular with various kinds of readers all the way through the sixteenth century.[47] Several of the surviving manuscripts went to lay audiences: the Pepys text to a Lollard group, a French copy to Eleanor Cobham (second wife of Humphrey, Duke of Gloucester), and a Latin version to Henry VIII's library. An English copy went to a Franciscan friary in Hereford, from whence its ideas and tropes were doubtless disseminated to the laity. Another good example is the *Seven Poyntes of Trewe Love and Everlastynge Wisdame*, adapted from a text written originally for nuns; it became quite popular with devout lay readers.[48] Laypeople of both genders pored over its instructions for arraying the "priviest" chambers of their hearts with roses and lilies for the bridegroom's arrival, and for receiving the spouse with most "inward lust of heart."

But if these readers were not enclosed, not silent, not betrothed to Christ in any formal sense, how did they apply such instructions to their own devotional activity? Perhaps they imagined an outer shell of social identity—the Nottinghamshire knight who owned the *Seven Points*, or the royal judge—concealing the inner truth of the soul's spiritual espousal behind stoutly locked and heavily guarded walls. According to the *Abbey of the Holy Ghost*, the abbey in the heart could be just as impermeable as that of the literally cloistered religious: "It is called 'cloyster' because it closes and sticks, and warely shall be locked."[49] In order to achieve the inwardness of bridal enclosure, lay readers had to enclose *some* part of themselves—if not their chastity, then some other version of their most important part—for

God. They had to imagine some inner core of true selfhood as being inaccessible to the rest of the world, kept pure and clean for their spiritual spouse. If the anchoress's heart-as-house looked like an anchorhold, the layperson's might have looked more like one of the private chambers or closets in aristocratic and bourgeois homes where devout readers could retire—temporarily—to read and pray before rejoining the world outside.

The inwardness-as-(modified)-enclosure model reached perhaps its broadest lay audience in Nicholas Love's *Mirror of the Blessed Lyf of Jesu Crist*, translated from another text for religious women, the *Meditationes Vitae Christi*.[50] As prior of the Carthusian house at Mount Grace in Yorkshire, Love would have known something about isolation, enclosure, and silence, and he shares the *Ancrene Wisse*'s distrust of sensory distractions. Recommending solitude to his readers, he explains: "he that seeth & hereth many thinges, shal ful harde ascape unclannes of herte & offence of conscience, for oft sithes deth entreth be oure windowe in to the soule" (72). Those who seek Christ, he advises, should flee the company of men, striving to be as "blynde, defe & doumbe" as the desert fathers (72). It would have been relatively easy to be so at Mount Grace. Love's primary audience was composed not of Carthusians but of lay readers, however, who could hardly have expected such luxuriously fortified solitude. Such readers, Love acknowledges, would need to create for themselves a different kind of enclosure:

This solitarye beynge & this fleyng as seynt Bernard seith is more vertuesly in soule than in body, that is to say, that a man in his entention in devoucion & in spirite be departed fro the world & men. & ioynede so in spirite to god, that is a spirite, & asketh not solitarye beinge of body bot in manere & in tyme, as specialy in tyme of speciale preyer. . . . And therfore seith the same seynt, thou that art among many bodily.' thou maiht [be] solitary & alone gostly if thou wille not & love not these wordly thinges, that the comunate loveth. And also if thou despise & forsake tho thinges that al men comunely desiren & taken. (72)

The lay reader's enclosure is largely one of intention and devotion. Living among many, he or she creates spiritual solitude by refusing to love or will or desire what "the comunate" does. Still, Love finds plenty of room to praise a fugitive and cloistered virtue, and advises the lay devotee to be alone whenever possible. For "the bodily [solitude] helpeth ful miche," he writes, in avoiding those external "occasion[s] . . . that miht drawe the soule withinforth fro the onyng & knittyng to hir spouse Jesu criste" (73). Like the inwardness of the anchoress, this program requires a certain bodily containment—blind, deaf, and dumb—to protect the purity of will to which it aspires. Seeing, hearing, and especially talking—these things let death in, and call the soul out from her private "oneing and knitting."

Thus the insistent rhetoric of interiority in Love's text—which would have its reader see inwardly, take heed inwardly, have compassion inwardly, speak in heart with fervent inward affection, set scenes most inwardly in mind, have grace inwardly—serves partly to enforce the boundaries between private devotional experience and social practice. Proper (inward) meditative practice produces correct (inward) feeling, which in turn brings divine reward. But that ravishing reward cannot be described or expressed: "thei kunne not tell, & . . . noman may knowe, bot onely he that by experience feleth it."[51] Love tells two stories of eucharistic visions, Edward the Confessor's and Hugh of Lincoln's, to confirm the principle. Both saints prove their worth by keeping their visions absolutely secret. After Edward and his noble friend are overwhelmed by ghostly drunkenness, tears, and inward sighings, Edward lays this charge on his companion: "that never while we lyven this thinge be brouht forthe in to the comune knowynge, leste we therebye fall in to veyn glorie & pride, thorh the opinion of the comune peple to oure gostly deth, or leste the envye of misbylevyng men lette & destruye trewe byleve to the wordes hereof" (231). Bringing forth the vision would create an opening for vainglory and perhaps even heresy. The vision going outward (to envy and mis-belief) would make a way for the sins coming inward. Silence thus protects not only the inner purity of anchoresses and Carthusians, but of kings, earls, and bishops. The lay reader's silence helps to create proper boundaries between his inner and outer lives.

As I mentioned earlier, the private closet might well have served as a useful space for helping to contain and protect the layperson's interiority. But an even more useful space in this respect is the world of the text itself, which creates its own inner room in the heart of the reader. The *Mirror*'s most powerful model for lay devotion is Saint Cecilia, whose spiritual enclosure is so complete that even amid the "grete pompe of weddyngis, where so many vanytees bene usede, whene the organes blewene & songene, she set hir herte stably in god, seying & praying, *Lord be my herte & my body clene, & not defilede*" (12). The valves of Cecilia's attention, as Emily Dickinson might say, have closed like stone, shutting out the bombastic music of the wedding. Now in the standard versions of Cecilia's legend, it is her own wedding that the virgin martyr resists, wearing a hairshirt underneath her bridal garments and refusing her husband's advances on their wedding night. Remarkably, however, Love fails to mention any of this. His Cecilia could be any bride or even wedding guest. Her extraordinary impenetrability is a strategy for a world of many "weddyngis," and it is accomplished by meditating on the life of Christ in precisely the way Love's readers are advised to do: "in the whiche she set her meditatcion & her thouht night & day with a clene & hole herte. And when she hade so fully alle the manere of his life over gon, she began agayne. And so with a likyng & swete taste gostly chewyng in that manere the gospell of crist. she set & bare it ever in the privyte of her breste. In the same manere I conseil that thou do" (11). While Cecilia traditionally has an angel with a flaming sword to keep her undefiled on her wedding night, this any-reader version of Cecilia has filled her heart so fully with the life of Christ that the world "might not entre in to her" (12). Repeated meditative reading has bricked up the doors and windows of her heart, keeping it private and clean for her true spouse. (*Book to a Mother*, by contrast, emphasizes the out-going of Cecilia's inner gospel, noting that she "[bore] ever the gospel of Crist in her herte *and secede not nyght ne day fro holy speche.*" A Lollard manuscript of the *Pore Caitif* adds, "withouten leeve of ony prelatis.")[52]

Yet we never hear of Cecilia's rapturous meeting with that spouse. For the *Mirror*'s inner compensations are not those of the divine lover but of the holy family romance. They are the compensations of narrative—of the *Mirror*—itself. It is an undeniably seductive read: vivid, well paced, uncluttered with theological argument but full of lively incident and affecting human detail. It is not difficult to see why fifteenth- and sixteenth-century readers enjoyed it—or how they might be tempted, like Cecilia, to begin it again. In doing so, they could replace the outer "comunate" with an inner one, and direct their willing and loving toward that compelling "inner" world of people, emotions, and events. Here the inwardness-as-enclosure model swerves away from private eroticism toward the vivacity of what Love himself calls "ymaginacions." This swerving aligns the pleasure of reading with inner space, moving away from an expectation of shared textual experience toward one of private, silent response. It reframes devotional reading as a kind of escapist fiction—another way in which the act of vernacular reading could produce "interiority" for late medieval readers.

4. Inaccessible to Whom? Enclosure Against Orthodoxy

Recent critical appraisals of Love's *Mirror* have not been kind to the narrative that received Archbishop Arundel's damning seal of approval for the
"confutation of heretics or Lollards."[53] It has been called condescending and
anti-intellectual, guilty of promoting a shallow, disengaged, silent spirituality easily managed by ecclesiastical authority. It is tempting to dismiss the
lay version of spiritual enclosure as one more strategy for controlling the
faithful, for keeping a spiritually restive group of readers closed off from
the perceived dangers of religious enthusiasm, intellectual inquiry, or a
more active engagement with the "outside."[54] So I would like to pause here
to point out that even this version of inwardness, once divorced from the
physical cloister, could be the source of considerable contemporary anxiety—
anxiety stemming in part from the flexibility of the concept, its ability to
signify differently depending on where that extremely well-fortified line between inside and out was drawn. Once the inner realm becomes both so
heavily privileged and so completely opposed and inaccessible to the
wretched "outside world," once the devotional life is assumed to be such an
intimate and private part of the individual believer, it requires only a small
interpretive shift for quietly pious orthodoxy to slide into a determined and
unreachable religious individualism. Here my different varieties of interiority come crashing back together.

Orthodox and Lollard opinion are perilously close on this point, as
Nicholas Love among others was well aware. Consider the Lollard assertion
that "schrift of mouthe is not needful to helthe of soule, but only sorowe of
hert."[55] Lollards objected to auricular confession partly because absolution
depended on the penitent's state of mind, which no one but God could
know.[56] (Recounting sinful and private matters, moreover, might spark lust
between priest and penitent—an anxiety that directly echoes the anchoritic
text's strict regulation of dangerous speech.)[57] For his part, Love rather per-
functorily denies that it is enough for a believer to "shryve him onely in his
herte, to godde" (135). Yet this brief disclaimer occupies much less space
than, for example, his explanations of how the reader can flee the world
more virtuously in soul than in body.[58] In the inner abbey, why may not
Contrition be general confessor? We can see how easily the heart-as-cloister
trope is turned to critique in *Book to a Mother*, which proclaims that where
Christ alone is abbot, there is no entrance fee, no simony, no hypocrisy, and
no worldly vanity. Hamburger observes that the heart-as-house so familiar

in medieval German convents would later become Martin Luther's personal emblem.[59]

Consider the Lollard rejection of the real presence of Christ in the sacrament. Elizabeth Stamford, a Chiltern Lollard, asserted that "Christ's own body . . . is not received by chewing of teeth but by hearing with ears and understanding with your soul."[60] Similarly, Love's Saint Cecilia internalizes Christ by "eating" the gospels, "with a likyng & swete taste gostly chewing . . . the gospell of crist." And while Love takes care to add several passages of effusive praise of the Eucharist later in the text, these do little to dilute the general emphasis on Christ as a narrative and moral exemplar, as opposed to a mediated sacramental body. In the *Seven Poyntes*, the Disciple asks Wisdom whether it is really better to eat God bodily than ghostly, since the Bible says, "believe and thou hast eaten."[61] Like Nicholas Love, Wisdom replies that it is best to have both together. But the idea of spiritual communion was gaining ground in fifteenth-century devotional culture. At impeccably orthodox Syon, nuns could "receive our lorde spiritually at every masse," and by the early sixteenth century, laypeople too could expect to be "all enflamed and fyered with desire and devotion" through such internally imagined, rather than physically realized, acts of reception.[62]

But perhaps the most dangerous potential slippage was the one in which the reader's interpretation of the "world" from which she needed to isolate herself might shift so as to include the worldly church itself. Cecilia's imperviousness to the pomp and vanity of great organs is not so far removed from the Lollard rejection of the "externals" of church ceremony. (Rolle too, remember, complained of the distractions of church music.) If the Lollards inhabited "a physical world detached from the spiritual realities beyond . . . driving a wedge between the material and the spiritual,"[63] the enclosure model risked driving a similar wedge—particularly when spiritual enclosure was divorced from an outer rule. Cecilia lives contentedly in a heart completely disengaged from her sensible surroundings, occupied wholly by her relentlessly internal narrative. Likewise, at his heresy trial in 1499, Thomas Boughton confessed that when receiving the Eucharist, "I feyned with myn hondys to honour it as cristen men use to doo, but my mynd and entent was nothyng therto, but to God almyghty above in heven."[64] One might say that amidst the great pomp and ceremony, "where so many vanytees bene usede, whene the organes blewene & songene," he set his heart stably in god, praying *"Lord be my herte [. . .] clene, & not defilede."* Love's Cecilia asks for a clean *body*, too—but again, the lay-friendly emphasis on the heart makes it a small leap from purity of body to purity of intent. The body "helps," Love says, but it is not the main thing.

Still worse was the potential for the church to find itself in the disparaged role of the worldly persecutor. As Mary Teresa Brady has observed, Lollard interpellators tended to reinforce passages on the value of suffering in orthodox texts.[65] Such passages are often seen by modern critics as instruments of orthodox power and oppression; they are said to create docile subjects whose misery is theologically justified, and thus passively accepted.[66] But the Lollard strategy of emphasizing just these passages suggests once again just how labile the category of "the world"—whose persecutions were to be suffered in patience—could be. Describing three late medieval and early modern heresy trials, Thomas Betteridge writes, "All three [heretics] construct themselves as lone, almost asocial or acultural, individuals holding out against the massed ranks of their worldly persecutors." Betteridge describes this "peculiarly 'modern' subjectivity" as a construction of "persecutive machinery"—but the deployment of a lone heart stubbornly holding out against a threatening world is hardly peculiar to dissenting traditions.[67]

English writers, then, had some reason to be wary of interiority taken too far, or in just slightly the wrong direction. Even if their readers did not develop heterodox opinions, there was the danger that in investing so much energy in their interior worlds, they might withdraw some of it from liturgical and communal engagement. In neither the abbey nor the urban parish nor even the private gentry chapel would this have been desirable. Thus even some of the most inwardly focused English devotional texts display a certain ambivalence on the subject, expressed in repeated but inconclusive confrontations between inward pleasure and outward duty, inner spiritual sufficiency and formal outward dependency. Walter Hilton advises a lay reader not to spend too much time meditating like a friar or monk, "or another man that were not bounden to the world."[68] Yet Hilton was one of the most important promoters of monastic spirituality for lay readers. Thomas à Kempis's translator, while extolling the "wonderful famyliarite" to be achieved in secret solitude, nonetheless cautions his readers to "be not slowe to common thinges, and more redy to private & singuler exercises."[69] William Caxton printed Hilton's works, but complained about women who studied "overmoche" in books of contemplation. He proposed that they would be better occupied with romances, which teach virtuous behavior and promote proper civic engagement.[70] He would have found little to fault in Robert Thornton, the northerner who collected so much devotional literature—for Thornton collected romances as well. Hughes writes, "Many of the secular and religious works that he copied into [his] volume warned the reader of the dangers of insularity and introversion and reminded him of his duties in a society beyond the family and its library."[71]

Works like *The Seven Poyntes* and *The Chastising of God's Children* attempt a careful balance, frequently cautioning their readers that inner devotion, no matter how rewarding, needs to be coupled with outward observance and good works. The *Chastising* presents the Virgin Mary—often used to represent silent, enclosed, readerly inwardness, particularly in scenes of the Annunciation[72]—as an exemplar of "outward and inward" virtues, the full offering of the self in charity "inwardly and outwardly," and the acceptance of "wilful travaile, inward and outward." The *Chastising's* author cautions readers that no matter how much more spiritual feeling they *think* they achieve in their private devotions, they must under no circumstances neglect the performance of the common liturgy (a subject taken up in the next chapter). The *Seven Poyntes*, in turn, identifies contemplative life with a radically inward eroticism and emotionalism, idealizing the wounded heart and its private ravishing, and spurning the "noyous worlde" and the "fleschly wittes" that serve it.[73] Yet it also cautions readers that their inner espousals should have some outward signs: the writing of the beloved's name in a secret place, for example, or three prostrations with a Pater Noster and Ave, or the daily praying of hours (380). Tears are fine, Wisdom instructs the Disciple, but he should conform himself to the Passion through deeds (339). And when his "inwarde confort" is withdrawn, he should cast his inward beholding to the Father in heaven; and the "more that is the forsakynge & desolacione of (thi) innere manne, with thi wille onede to godde, so myche the more thou schalt be like to the crucifixe" (343). Here the Disciple imitates the Passion by suffering the desolation of his inner world, a desolation that drives him relentlessly outward. The feminine world of inner weeping and ravishing is balanced by the masculine one of spiritual knighthood: a world of self-denial and emotional emptiness, but above all a world of outward deeds and things. This may explain Caxton's willingness to print the text as early as 1490.

Not every text struck the right balance at the right time. In 1525, Wynkyn de Worde had to retrieve all sixty copies of a book called the *Ymage of Love* that he had sold to Syon Abbey. The work's message is that the true image of love cannot be found in the world, but is the reflection of God in one's own soul—a message echoed in many other books available to Syon readers.[74] But in the wake of Luther's attacks on images, that message was too politically charged for the bishop to let it pass.

A little treatise published by Wynkyn de Worde in 1501 and reprinted by Henry Pepwell in 1521 further demonstrates the interpretive problems interiority might pose, for both medieval and modern critics. Made up of extracts from the *Book* of Margery Kempe, this treatise gives the rather astonishing impression that Kempe's teaching is all about the interiorization of the spiritual life.[75] She tells her readers that there is more merit in thinking with the mind than in praying with the mouth; that silence is better than wearing hairshirts; that desire for martyrdom is as good as martyrdom; that patience is *better* than martyrdom; that thinking about Jerusalem is as good as being there; and so on. Scholars have criticized the edition as an example of the orthodox, misogynistic recuperation of Kempe's spirituality, wherein the itinerant, married, boisterous Kempe becomes self-enclosed—and literally enclosed in Pepwell's 1521 edition, which names her an "Ancress." Sue Ellen Holbrook, for example, argues that the extractor has eliminated everything "radical, enthusiastic, feminist, particular, potentially heretical and historical" from the text.[76] Karma Lochrie writes that Kempe's voice and experience are "erased."[77] Kempe's words have certainly been appropriated by a different genre; a devotional pamphlet is not a Life, in either the hagiographic or the autobiographical sense. But how passive and contained have those words become? What does it *mean* to be inward? If inward means "silent, private, and self-regulating," then the text looks considerably different than if inwardness "lies behind and support the entire reformist enterprise," as Patterson argues.[78] The printed editions end with Christ telling Margery that she receives his grace as religious men and priests cannot—for they dread of "the shames of this worlde." If this represents a conservative appropriation of Kempe's work, it also authorizes exactly the sort of behavior that it supposedly seeks to erase from Kempe's own biography. Might the reader not infer that *wanting* to be a virgin is better than actually being one? Or that Margery is better qualified to hear confession than a world-fearing priest? Or, for that matter, that the image of God in the heart is better than the one in the church? So much depends on the context of reception. The Pepwell edition of 1521—which, as Jennifer Summit points out, was published after months of controversy surrounding Luther's attacks on images—reframes Margery's interiority as the spiritual enclosure and espousal proper to an anchoress. Its relevance to lay readers is ostensibly explained by the indulgenced "Image of Pity" at the front of the text; their reading becomes an externalized action designed to secure pardon. But the text itself does not change. And if Pepwell's nervous edition makes Kempe into a literal anchoress, it does not do the same for her readers, who might still apply the text's adaptable wisdom to their own lives—as another version of Margery had done with other texts before them.[79]

5. Transparency, Community, and the Vernacular

> *And seynt Austen seith, 'What is it worth to move and to patere with the lippes, whan the herte is al y-hid?' Suche difference or straungenesse as is bitwexe the stree and the corne, or bitwexe the bran and the flour of wheete, or bitwexe the skyn and the best, right suche difference is ther bitwexe the sowne of the bedes and the devocion of the herte. . . . Who-so biddeth God with-oute devocion of herte, he speketh to God a langage that men clepen patrolard, as who-so speketh half Englische and half Latyn. For he speketh to God with his mouth on, and with his herte a-nother.*
>
> —The Book of Vices and Virtues[80]

If inwardness threatened to create a breach between the reader and her world—or between her heart and her mouth, or between imagination and everyday identity, or between individual judgment and public authority, or between ritual and belief—some English writers tried to reframe the idea in an attempt to bridge those gaps, to intensify the reader's sense of meaning and participation in ritual and community. Particularly in liturgically oriented texts like *The Lay Folks Mass Book*, the *Meditations for Ghostly Exercise In the Time of the Mass*, and *The Myroure of Oure Ladye*, to be "inward" is to be fully integrated into the experience of the mass and the body of the Church, often through the mediation of vernacular translation. It is to access the kernel of spiritual meaning veiled by the material shell of ritual: as the Host is veiled by the rood screen, as a relic is enclosed by its reliquary, as the flesh of Christ is hidden in the form of bread. In this formulation of inwardness, inner and outer are not diametrically opposed, not implacable enemies like the heart and the world. They work together, two parts of a whole.

In some ways, this is another version of the anchoress's striving for perfect correspondence between her inner and outer enclosures, her physical and spiritual chastity. But unlike the anchoritic reader who becomes inaccessible in her interiority, this inward self has nothing we might call a *private* inner core, nothing he or she needs to keep safe or enclose. We might rather speak of a public inwardness that the self can access and participate in—thus shattering, rather than reinforcing, his or her isolation. Inward vision, rather than marking the special grace of the contemplative, comes to characterize the general grace of the community of understanding believers. In an illumination showing the elevation of the host in one layfolk's mass book from circa 1320, the congregation kneels together behind the priest, their hands raised in supplication and their eyes directed toward the elevation.[81] We see the wafer in the priest's hands; but behind it, in a square colored blue to indicate a different plane, we see what the worshippers are really looking at: the bleeding, crucified Christ. They see it not separately, as a solitary, inward vision—as in woodcuts showing, for example, the visions of a lone St. Bridget or an enclosed St. Catherine—but as a group, in a body. And that vision welds them together in sorrow, compassion, and communion. To help English readers "see" the inner reality of their common ritual, to help them penetrate its Latin-shrouded mysteries and be penetrated by them in turn, vernacular guides walked them through the mass step by step, explaining not only what they should do but also what they should understand, feel, and pray—not so as to remove themselves from the service and their fellows, but so as to connect with them at the deepest level, in an inwardness transparent to all.[82]

One such guide is John Lydgate's "Interpretation and Virtues of the Mass."[83] In this long poem, commissioned by Alice Chaucer (Geoffrey's "bookish" granddaughter),[84] Lydgate exhorts readers to busy themselves "[w]ith all your inward contemplacion" to understand the meaning of the priest's garments and actions, "As in a myrrour presentyng in fygure" (3, 4). The mirror shows truth but darkly, as a figure needing explication and understanding. Lydgate's vernacular text provides the key. With their "verray contemplatyfe" eyes, his readers are called to see inwardly—to remember, that is, the true meaning of the mass, the events it commemorates, and its function in their lives (9). They should hasten early to church with the "inward intent" of the women running to Christ's tomb to seek "theyr spouse dere," making their daily church attendance into a devotional and amorous *imitatio*.[85] Lydgate's thorough explication of the service includes an emotional prayer of nine stanzas to "say," presumably aloud, at the crucial moment of the elevation. Thus is affective vernacular reading linked surely and transparently to ritual performance. The subjective interiority offered by the mother tongue—the language of emotion and intention—meets the hermeneutic interiority of the liturgy, with its penetrable shells of sign and symbol, gesture and raiment. In a neat twist, the supposedly fleshly, one-dimensional vernacular becomes the tool of penetration, simply by virtue of being closest to the believer's heart. Rather than separating heart from mouth, this model brings them into perfect alignment.

Lydgate's promotion of a communitarian, liturgically oriented model of inwardness is very much in line with what historians such as Jeremy Catto have described as Henry V's strategies for reuniting England and re-establishing the power of the monarchy, in part through well-publicized and transparent "private" piety and the defense of orthodoxy.[86] Literary scholars have noted Henry's rhetorical crusade against "doubleness"—a term covering a host of ills, including French duplicity, Lollard secrecy, and just plain femininity, but applying as well to the psychic divisions fostered by some popular devotional paradigms.[87] Catto describes Lancastrian England as a country where the variety of independent religious initiative and private conscience contributed to a fractured and unstable polity. Instead of trying to fight the tide of popular devotion, Henry and his circle of powerful churchmen sought to regularize it, giving liturgical expression to popular lay initiatives and making "inward" devotion the hallmark of orthodoxy and the vital wellspring of public worship. Henry's own theatrical private devotion gave legitimacy to his leadership of church and state (though the most famous dramatization of such a strategy belongs to Shakespeare's Richard III). In Chapter 5 we will see how Thomas Hoccleve's intensely inward-looking political poetry makes brilliant use of this paradox.

And just as the English vernacular played an important part in the promotion of liturgical inwardness—as the medium of intellectual and affective penetration—so too it was crucial to Henry's attempts to create transparent harmony in the national community, realigning outward authority with the inward hearts and wills of his subjects. The records of the Brewer's Guild famously point out that Henry has chosen "to declare the secrets of his will" in "our mother-tongue, to wit the English tongue . . . for the better understanding of his people." Henceforth, they declare, their guild records will also be kept in English. Patterson points to the guild's decision as evidence that English was becoming the natural language of selfhood.[88] We might say rather that English was already the natural language of selfhood—"yhour kynde langage," in the words of the *Speculum Vitae*[89]—and that what is significant here is the increasing use of the mother's "kynde" language for public discourse, and the emergence of an official language that was also a personal one and that had unprecedented power to express and to intervene in the private realm. For the monarch as for the mass, the mother tongue renders the secrets of the interior ("the will") visible, so that they can be understood, internalized, and imitated by the faithful. Where the vernacular had been associated with privacy and Lollardy, Henry would reorient it toward nationalism and orthodoxy.[90] He would lay claim to the inner world of private desire and personal relation and recuperate it for civic participation and public sacrifice. Henry's "secrets" penetrate and harmonize popular consciousness, just as the English translation of the Divine Service for the nuns at the Abbey of Syon allows what "goyth daylly throughe your mouthes" to "synke & savoure contynually in youre hartes."[91] The nuns at Syon—Henry's powerhouse, along with Sheen, for the spread of vernacular devotions to the laity—were expected to internalize every aspect of the service in order to perform their devotions more accurately. Continually beholding the Virgin inwardly with the help of vernacular translation, they could better "show" her outwardly in the language of officially scripted ritual. I will have more to say about the *Myroure of Oure Ladye* in the next chapter; here I wish only to note its articulation of a typically Lancastrian (and Lydgatian) ideal: the perfect conformity of heart and mouth, inner devotion and outward performance, each inextricably bound to the other, as sovereign tongue to subject heart and subject heart to sovereign will.

It is by focusing almost exclusively on such liturgical devotions that Eamon Duffy can argue, in *The Stripping of the Altars*, that the religious interiority of late medieval England should not be seen as opposing public ritual, that it presents no challenge to orthodox faith. Duffy asserts that any distinction between inward and outward in late medieval English religion "would be artificial."[92] Indeed, when elevation prayers ask for a honey taste in "myn inward mowthe . . . of thin helthful presence," or when a meditative guide encourages readers to "Imprinte Inwardly In your hart" the Passion as performed by an officiating priest, inner devotion is clearly being harnessed to liturgical participation.[93] Describing a Suffolk recusant recalling the religious culture of his youth, Duffy observes, "what is striking about Martin's account is the convergence between inner and outer, private and public, the timeless and meditative on one hand, the seasonal and external on the other."[94] I do not think Duffy is wrong about the material he cites.[95] But as I have suggested, this particular construction of inwardness was not the only one available to English readers. It seems, in fact, to have been a considered response to other formulations, and not simply the universal and natural form of medieval Catholic devotion. No doubt the distinction between inward and outward *is* artificial—but that was true in the later Middle Ages, too, when writers sought to artifice and thereby naturalize that distinction over and over again.

Duffy's argument is partly a response to scholars who have seen late medieval interiority as incipient Protestantism, a Reformation already underway in the hearts and minds of English readers as an inherently, immovably externalized Catholicism decayed and crumbled. But the inwardness of fifteenth-century English devotion has also been criticized by scholars as the tool of a repressive, backward-looking Catholic orthodoxy—as we have already seen in responses to the inward Margery Kempe. Again the questions arise: is it radical theology or devotional paternalism? Peculiarly modern or resolutely conservative? Individualistic or communitarian? Does it produce social passivity or enable resistance?[96] This is one of the problems with seeing late medieval "interiority" as a monolithic and stable category. I would suggest that modern disagreement over what English inwardness *means* might be productively mapped onto late medieval arguments about the same thing. From this perspective, the interiority of late medieval English Catholicism is all of these: incipient Protestantism, invigorated and meaningful tradition, paternalistic and repressive social control, and self-absorbed bourgeois individualism—among other things.

Arguments about the relation between inner and outer worlds continued unabated through the Reformation, and the Lancastrian model of a self penetrated by the communal and public, responding inwardly in harmony with exterior practice, remained an ideal for many of the period's most influential and eloquent churchmen. In his "Necessary Doctrine and Erudition for any Christian Man" of 1543, Henry VIII insists that "besides the inward and secret calling which God hath always used, and yet still doth use, he hath also ordained an outward calling of the people unto him, by preaching of his most holy word." Henry calls for preaching of the scriptures so that people "may observe and keep them inwardly in their heart."[97] Like Lydgate's mass-book, Henry's preachers create inner conformity through vernacular instruction, bringing the outward performances of *ecclesia* into line with the secret callings of God's grace. But much later, in a sermon of 1622, John Donne would question even the possibility of inward and secret calling, apart from the common rituals of the church: "Where shall I find the Holy Ghost? I lock my door to myself, and I throw my self down in the presence of my God, I divest myself of all worldly thoughts, and I bend all my powers, and faculties upon God, as I think, and suddenly I find my self scattered, melted, fallen into vain thoughts, into no thoughts." Thus isolated and locked, divested of all worldly thoughts and inclinations, the medieval contemplative might have expected to feel the inward and secret calling of God, to melt in momentary rapture. For Donne, however, it is devotion that melts; it is God who is lost in this private room. His enclosed self is not whole but scattered, not full but devastatingly empty.[98] "*I believe in the Holy Ghost,*" he continues, "but do not find him, if I seek him only in private prayer; but in *Ecclesia,* when I go to meet him in the *Church,* when I seek him where he hath promised to be found . . . instantly the savor of this *Myrrh* is exalted, and multiplied to me; not a dew, but a shower is poured out upon me."[99] Only in the company of others, in the common performance of human salvation, is Donne showered with the sweet savor that had long been the promise of inward devotion. Like Lydgate, Donne refuses to surrender the affective experience of God to the realm of the private, the silent, and the self-enclosed.

6. What's Inside—Literally

Let us return to the pre-Reformation period, however, to take up two final models for the inward-looking man, which would become especially important to English devotional discourse. In contrast to the communally shared inwardness we have been considering, both these models take as their mantra the ancient theme, "know thyself," and ask their practitioners to set before their inner eyes not a divine lover nor a bustling narrative nor a liturgical ritual, but *themselves.* As we have seen, the inwardly turned Rollean subject is acutely aware of his own passionate emotions and sensations. The self-contained anchoress, in turn, scrutinizes every movement of her fleshly impulses and sinful tendencies, making herself a watchdog at her own gates. But in these last two models—which are really just the extreme poles on a continuum of ideas about self-examination—the inner self becomes a different kind of object-problem, a different source of awareness and insight.

At the one pole we find the almost perversely literalist outlook of works like the *Pricke of Conscience,* perhaps the most popular English poem of the Middle Ages. Surviving in more manuscripts than any Middle English text except the Wycliffite Bible, the *Pricke of Conscience* speaks out of a grimly, exuberantly materialist epistemology.[100] Cataloguing the endless miseries and sins of man and their eventual punishments, it presents its readers with a universe of slime, worms, lice, stinking carrion, and excrement—and with that familiar imperative, "know thyself." Like the Augustinian texts reviewed in the next section, the *Pricke of Conscience* links self-knowledge to the knowledge of God, and insists that both begin with an inward turn. Anyone seeking virtue or learning must begin by "knaw[ing] him-self with-inne," for "if he hym-self knew kyndely/ He suld haf knawyng of God almyghty."[101] Yet in the materialist universe of the *Pricke of Conscience*, self-knowledge is almost entirely constituted by the recognition that man is made of dirt, that he takes his beginning in the loathsome blood and slime of the womb, is home to nits and vermin, produces foul odors and excretions, dies an ugly death, and ends as a rotten, polluting corpse. In this nightmarish world, the proposition that the inner man is the true self gains a whole new meaning:

Bot som men and women fayre semes
To the syght with-outen, als men demes,
And that shewes noght elles bot a skyn;
Bot wha-swa moght se tham with-in,
Fouler carion moght never be
Than he suld than of tham se. (569)

We also like to say that "beauty is only skin deep," but in so doing, we assert a different kind of truth about the inner self: that it is character, not appearance—the mind, not the body—that really matters. Here, the self-knowledge offered by inward vision stops at blood and guts (with an emphatic glee that reminds one vaguely of Jonathan Swift: "Celia, Celia, Celia shits!"). Anyone looking "with-in" can see that even the most attractive woman is nothing but "ful wlatsom [loathsome]" slime: "Thus foul with-in ilk man es / Als the buk says and bers witnes" (586–87). The body is the truth.

The lesson can be found in a wide variety of other texts. The short "Mirror of Sinners," for example, exhorts its readers to use that titular mirror to set themselves busily and carefully before their own eyes: "Be-hold in this myrour and see what thow hast been, what thou art, and what thow schalt bee. Thenk of how vile a mater thow woxe up in thy modris wombe, how vyl al thyng is whan it passeth fro thee, be it never so deynteuous whan thow receyvest it; and last of alle, bihold how vile wormes mete thow schalt be lyggyng in thy grave."[102] Like the *Pricke of Conscience*, the "Mirror of Sinners" seems particularly interested in things that are inside the body and then outside of it (fetuses, excrement). This was of course a familiar rhetoric of humility and world renunciation in the Middle Ages, elaborated especially gruesomely in popular lyrics and in the visual arts. Simple folk were thought to understand bodily matters best—and here again we may recall the *Cloud*-author's concern for people trying to "see inwardly" with their bodily eyes.

Such texts do not just play to the lowest common denominator. They also assert a theological proposition: that spiritual value resides *outside* the self, not within it. Properly understood, the self is the space of the profane, the abject, the fallen; it has no inner kernel of transcendence. As in the world of Chaucer's despairing, fragmented, relic-peddling Pardoner, bodies are just bodies, and bones are just bones. Things are what they seem (only perhaps a bit worse than you think). As the Pardoner himself apostrophizes to the sinner's inner god:

O wombe! O bely! O stynkyng cod,
Fulfilled of dong and corrupcioun!
At either ende of thee foul is the soun.
How greet labour and cost is thee to fynde!
Thise cookes, how they stampe, and streyne, and grynde,
And turnen substaunce into accident
To fulfille al thy likerous talent! (VI.534–40)

The inner self is filled full, all right—literally. Across its borders come grotesque, gaseous parodies of speech. In a horrific abjectification of eucharistic language, substance, or inner reality, turns into accident, or outward appearance. More to the point, substance and accident become one and the same, and this is as true for language as it is for the body. For Pardoner hermeneutics, signs are husks through and through, devoid of spiritual significance.[103] Ironically, Chaucer creates one of his greatest illusions of psychological depth—and mordant self-awareness—in a character who appears to reject interiority as a theological and interpretive principle.

7. Specially Behold Thyself: Inwardness as Introspection

> *Thou shalt never be inwarde & devoute man, but yf thou kepe silence of othir men, & specialy beholde thiself.*
> —*Thomas à Kempis*, De Imitatione Christi[104]

But the rhetoric of self-knowledge that is put to such grotesquely material ends in texts like the *Pricke of Conscience* also circulated widely as a more complex psychological imperative—and looking in the mirror was not always a *memento mori*, a vision of poor Yorick's grinning skull. Rather than insisting on the earthenness of the body, the other extreme of this kind of interiority makes a muddy field of the heart. Rather than asking the reader to "remember" his future burial in the grave, it urges him to take a shovel and dig for what is already buried in a memory that has become its own problematic object. The inwardness-as-entrails model assumes that readers can and should know what they are. But this last formulation suggests that it is not so simple—that the self is almost impossible to really understand. "Who can plumb its depths?" Augustine asks of the "profound and incalculable complexity" of his own mind. "What, then, am I, my God? What is my nature?"[105] Rooted in an essentially Augustinian program of self-knowledge and self-reform, this version of interiority is actually the one with the deepest roots in medieval theology and monastic tradition. I have saved it for last in part because it will seem in many ways the most familiar—but also because it will be the most important for the rest of this study, and because it connects inwardness to the thematics of vision and reading that I want to investigate in the following chapter.

This Augustinian model of interiority, as it made its way into Middle English devotional texts, imagines the inner life as a scene of much greater unpleasantness and uncertainty than some of the others we have surveyed. Here the heart is not an enclosed bower but a field, or an orchard, where readers learn to toil mightily and busily at cultivating virtues out of stony soil, and where they are required to be endlessly conscious of their likeness and unlikeness to the divine image. As Augustine himself writes in the *Confessions*, "O Lord, I am working hard in this field, and the field of my labors is my own self. I have become a problem to myself, like land which a farmer works only with difficulty and at the cost of much sweat" (10.16). As we have seen, the discourse of feminine enclosure cajoled its readers to welcome the amorous Christ graciously into their hearts: to sweep clean the bridal chamber, invite the bridegroom in, and shut the doors behind him. But devotional writers like Walter Hilton asserted that Christ was always already there in the depths of the heart, and that the task was not so much to invite him in as to discover him in the hidden landscape of the self—a landscape, as Augustine described it, that was "ever varying, full of change," a country of "wide plains . . . innumerable caverns and hollows . . . full beyond compute of countless things of all kinds."[106] For the Augustinian devotional culture of late medieval England, inwardness was increasingly about self-examination and self-consciousness—the reflexive operations of the inner eye, operating in concert with the busy labors of self-reform.

Interest in Augustine's writings was strong in fourteenth-century England. The Augustinian orders flourished—the Bridgettine rule, for instance, was adapted from the Augustinian one—and Augustinian canons like Walter Hilton were often in the forefront of an introspective, psychologically oriented spirituality.[107] The Austin friars were also influential; William Flete's *De Remediis contra Temptaciones*, composed at Cambridge in the 1350s, survives in twenty-two Latin copies and sixteen English, with Hilton serving as translator. As Hughes observes, "Augustinian realist philosophy . . . had dominated the Oxford theology schools under Bradwardine and FitzRalph," where it influenced both Wyclif (who was especially impressed by the *Confessions*) and orthodox theologians.[108] *De Trinitate*, in which Augustine works out most fully his theories of the resemblance and reformation of the soul in God, was particularly popular, and its influence can be felt throughout the corpus of English religious writing, from sophisticated theology to basic devotional tracts (it was another of Wyclif's favorites, too). English writers were looking for ways to conceptualize the inwardness of their readers and to control the direction of its reformation; in Augustine's writings, and particularly in his elaboration of the Neoplatonic connections between vision, identity, and reading, they found practical technologies for doing just that. The busy beholding of self and Christ that would come to characterize so much late medieval English writing is largely an Augustinian inheritance.

Augustine himself was heir to a biblical dynamic of likeness and unlikeness, a dialectic that received its fullest articulation in the writings of Saint Paul, whose characterization of temporal existence as a state of seeing only *per speculum in aenigmate* would resonate through the period as one of its favored images of the human condition.[109] Now we see through a mirror, in an enigma; then, face to face. Originally created in the image of God—*ad imaginem et similitudinem nostram* (Gen. 1:26)—man could once again become a perfect reflection of his maker only in the immediacy of that final vision. The image distorted and defaced by sin would once again be clarified by the presence of its divine source. We see as though in a mirror because we *are* that mirror: an analogy that would become fundamental to Augustine and to those who came after him as a way of conceptualizing the relationship between man and God.

In *De Trinitate*, Augustine tries to explain how we can go about knowing God "through this image which is ourselves."[110] The enigmatic image through which we may glimpse the workings of the divine, he argues, is the human mind, particularly in its triune nature as memory, reason (or understanding), and will. In the threefold activity of remembering, understanding, and loving itself, the mind experiences its likeness to the Trinity, and its ability to remember, understand, and love God as well. Proceeding from "outer" to "inner" knowledge, it progressively abandons external, sensory information for the more abstract experience of its own self-conscious mental activity. Rational self-consciousness—Augustine's "radical reflexivity"[111]—becomes the means of both knowing and reflecting God.

But no one can fully know or reflect God in this life, both because the soul has added so many layers to itself through love of external things, and because it can only function in language and in time. Setting itself "as it were in its own view," the soul experiences a two-fold vision, a perception both of likeness and unlikeness: "for even in its very ungodliness, the more severe our condemnation of its fault, the more unhesitating must be our appreciation of its natural dignity" (104, 142). This double vision becomes the means of a slow and painful reformation, as the soul rationally analyzes and assesses the distance between image and original and renews itself as a clearer and brighter reflection, "in the spirit of the mind, in the knowledge of God, not outwardly but inwardly from day to day" (123). For Augustine, bodily and sensory experience is the outer husk, while rational self-consciousness is the kernel of the inner life, where the truth about the self in its relation to God may be sought. (As we will see in the next chapter, one of the primary ways of achieving this rational self-consciousness is through reading.)

It is important to remember the doubleness of Augustinian self-envisioning. It is not just that one can never get rid of the husk of personal experience; rather, the husk itself becomes crucial to the project. As Brian Stock explains, "Our understanding of our lives is inseparable from the stories by which we represent our thoughts in words. Every understanding, therefore, is a reading of ourselves, every genuine insight, a rereading, until, progressing upwards by revisions, we have inwardly in view the essential source of knowledge, which is God."[112] So Augustine is driven to contemplate his own memory, his emotions, his motivations (why did he steal pears?), the whole complex territory of caverns and hollows that is his understanding of himself in memory and in time. In doing so, he is able to experience the *process* of remembering, and thus to learn something crucial about his own nature, and the likeness to God that is buried in the workings of that nature. If *De Trinitate* insists on rational self-consciousness, the *Confessions* (written at about the same time) makes it clear that one needs something to be self-conscious *about*, and that thing is the text of one's own life. When the soul sets itself in its own view, it has to see both ways.

Augustine's emphasis on returning to "the inner man" never really ceased to affect medieval theology. His ideas were taken up with particular enthusiasm by twelfth-century spiritual writers, particularly Cistercians such as Bernard of Clairvaux and Aelred of Rievaulx.[113] The notion of self-concentration and self-examination as prerequisites to mystical experience, to self-knowledge and knowledge of God, was one of the defining themes of that period's intellectual life. The *Confessions* appear in a large number of twelfth- and thirteenth-century English manuscripts, and as we have seen, English interest in Augustine's works expanded through the period.[114] By the late fourteenth century, his ideas were spreading beyond monastic and university elites to reach a broader audience, in a language they understood.[115] Filtered in part through Bonaventure, the Augustinian inner trinity appears in *The Myrour of Recluses*, *The Orchard of Syon*, the treatise "How Mans Soul is Made to the Image and Likeness of the Holy Trinity," the morality play *Wisdom*, and many other late medieval English texts and sermons. The mirror-soul is still more prevalent.[116] "Austyn" is everywhere in works like *The Book of Vices and Virtues*. Insisting that self-knowledge is fundamental and memory is key, the *Book* observes that "the brighter that a creature is, the more [he] coveiteth to see himself, but he seeth wel that he is not worthy ne fyn to see hym. & than a good herte wexeth hot and is wroth with hireself; than taketh he a pycoise and a scholve and bigynneth to delve and to myne, and entreth forth with-ynne the hert & fyndeth there so many synnes and wikkednesses and defautes" (107). Such self-envisioning leads inevitably to inward labor—here, in the form of even greater self-scrutiny. The fourteenth-century English aristocrat Henry of Lancaster records a similar process. Desiring to know himself better, and so to reform himself in the image of God, he declares his intention to write his own devotional book, the *Livre de Seyntz Medicines*.[117] In so doing, he exercises his self-reflexive faculties in the "underground cesspool" of his heart, re-creating through his own labors of self-understanding the rational image of his Creator.

Book one of Hilton's *Scale of Perfection* serves as a particularly good example of how an Augustinian model of interiority made its way into the consciousness of Middle English readers.[118] The work was popular with the laity all the way through the early print era, often circulating in the company of Love's *Mirror* or Hilton's own *Epistle on the Mixed Life*.[119] What English readers found in Hilton's treatise was a program of contemplation centered almost entirely on self-knowledge and the reformation of the soul in the image of God. For Hilton, as for Augustine, the image in the soul was discernable, if miserably defaced by the dark image of sin, and the key to its reformation was an intense engagement with the deepest recesses of memory and consciousness. Thus Hilton describes spiritual progress, not in terms of higher or sweeter, but of deeper and more inward. He imagines the heart as a muddy depth of earth traversed by the concealed roots of sin and the poisonous springs of guilt, but hiding also the treasure of Christ. "He is in thee, though He be lost fro thee," he admonishes; "It nedeth not to run to Rome ne to Jerusalem for to seke Hym ther, but turne thi thought into thyn owen soule, where He is hid" (87).[120] But that is not all. The image of sin, too, lies hidden in the heart, "that thou felist not" (108). This image, this heavy "black schadewe," is born about "whereevere thou goost" (90), and the reader must delve for that as well. The *Scale* gives its readers, religious and lay, a vision of the contemplative life not as obedience to a rule, rumination on the scriptures, mystical contemplation of the godhead, or even marriage to a divine spouse, but as a search and a struggle in a dark heart, a dark mind: an intensely and often uncomfortably self-conscious life.

But if Hilton's treatise is one of the most sustained articulations of *De Trinitate* in late medieval England, it is not an entirely coherent one—even without the addition of the very different Book Two. Indeed, Book Two opens with an account of Hilton's first reader asking him to explain again about the image of God in her soul, and it is easy to see how she might have gotten confused. Like Augustine, Hilton begins with the Pauline mirror passages and the proposition that self-knowledge is essential to the knowledge of God. He assumes that the soul is an inner trinity, and that rational analysis can illuminate this interior likeness. He encourages his readers to become "more inward" by stripping their mental processes of bodily, imaginative images. But Hilton cannot seem to settle on how such rational and imageless reflexivity will mesh with typically affective and Christ-centered English piety, or where the exercise should fit into his progressive ladder of the spiritual life, or whether it is even a fruitful exercise, given the frailty of human reason and will.

He offers it at first almost incidentally, as a way of preventing idleness between periods of active temptation. "Thou shalt, yif thou wolt," he says, "bigynne a newe travaile, and that is for to entre into thyn owen soule bi meditacion, for to know what it is" (74). He pauses for a chapter to explain that each man must know and work according to his own unique gifts. Then he starts in again with greater urgency: "Nevertheless, there is oon werke whiche is nedful and spedful to to traveile inne," he writes, "And that is a man for to entre into himsilf, for to knowe his owen soule and the myghtes therof, the fairenesse and the foulenesse thereof" (76). Such inward beholding is necessary and profitable for his reader, he argues, for no one can come to the burning love of Jesus without it. "As longe as he fyndeth not His ymage reformed in thee," he warns, "He is straunge and fer fro thee" (88).

Yet this orientation toward *Jesus* changes the nature of the project in important ways. Although Hilton initially invokes the Augustinian trinity of memory, will, and understanding as the inner image of God, he quickly abandons that trinity in favor of the image of Jesus hidden in the soul. "Seke thanne that thou hast lost, that thou myght fynde it," he writes; "desire, morne, prai, and seke" for "al that thou hast loste . . . Jhesu" (83). Jesus becomes the drachma, the penny, the heritage, the treasure, hidden deep in the muddy field of the soul: "Thee behoveth for to delve deepe in thyn herte, for thereinne He is hid" (85). More than the mind in its three-fold rational activity, Jesus becomes the perfected image and inmost truth of the self.

The text remains full of Augustinian gestures. To aid the inner search, Hilton advises illuminating one's inner spaces with the lantern of Reason (86), recalling Augustine's discussion of memory in the *Confessions*: "The woman who had lost a coin searched for it by the light of a lantern, but she would never have found it unless she had remembered it" (10.18). (Augustine frequently refers to his memory as a treasure house full of lost things.) And in some chapters Hilton does insist that all bodily imaginings be removed from the inner eye. Elsewhere, however, he advises simply that "bi what maner of praier or meditacioun or occupacion that thou mai have grettest desire to Hym, and have most felynge of Hym, bi that occupacion thou sekest Hym best and best fyndest Hym" (84). It seems doubtful that many late medieval English readers would have found greatest "desire" and "feeling" in abstract contemplation, which ill accords with most contemporary affective practice—not to mention the extremely vivid and concrete language of Hilton's own text.[121]

Besides, even if a soul in properly Augustinian meditation successfully manages to "draw inner thi thought from al ymaginynge," what she finds is not the rational image of God but the unbearably painful and heavy and squalid image of sin (90). The most imageless inner vision described in Hilton's text finds not Trinitarian likeness, but a dark nothingness in which the reader must "swynke and swete," a poisonous spring from which rivers of sin well up and flow through the garden (92–93). Augustine's radical reflexivity here becomes something more like radical abjectivity, a vision of the human will infected to its deepest core. Incessantly beholding herself, saying "what am I?" every day, the soul becomes so conscious of her vile wretchedness that she can barely endure herself (48). She can hardly do even a good deed without defilement, through vainglory if nothing else, and her desires for material objects seem to make desire for God impossible (78).

Thus Hilton's call to "know thyself inwardly" ends up surprisingly close to that of the *Pricke of Conscience*, though it approaches through the putrid psyche rather than the decaying flesh. If the rational image of God is within, it is almost un-findable there, except in distant flashes and glimmerings. Called to ransack and labor in her soul, the reader is constantly thrown back by her own inadequacy upon faith and longing for Christ—the same Christ whose perfected image will remain strange and distant, a memory forgotten, until her soul is reformed. Hilton makes the inner life a scene of loss and unknowing, a place where the self can "desire, mourn, pray, and seek," where it can dig and delve, swink and sweat, but where it is inaccessible not only to others, but even to its own most rational, inward understanding. In this text, Christ is both the key to and a decided retreat from the problems of Augustinian self-knowledge and identity. The collision between Augustine's radical reflexivity and Christ's affective particularity results in a strangely compelling failure—or rather, a series of compelling failures, as Hilton returns repeatedly to the idea of inner reformation, re-imagining and restructuring the process each time.

This collision would play out repeatedly in late medieval English culture, as various Augustinian, semi-Augustinian and pseudo-Augustinian ideas about interiority, reflexivity, and reformation intersected with contemporary modes of piety and devotion, gender and vocation. In the next chapter, we will see how the idea of self-reflexive inward beholding came to be reshaped for a specific English community: the influential Bridgettine community at Syon, where Hilton's works were studied seriously for nearly a century. That investigation will shed more light on the broader transformations afoot in literate devotional culture. Before closing this preliminary survey of vernacular interiority, however, I would like to glance briefly toward the *Showings* of Julian of Norwich—the period's other great Augustinian writer. Julian is fascinated by the problem of self-knowledge and, like Hilton, she is deeply concerned to reconcile Augustine's Trinitarian hermeneutics to the affective, Christocentric piety of her own day.[122] Chapter four will examine Julian's text in more detail. Here, I want only to underline her careful and deliberate use of the word "inward" in the Long Text.

For Julian, as interested as she is in images of both enclosure and introspection, only rarely uses the word that so characterized what we assume to be most of her textual environment. It comes into play only at a few crucial moments in her visionary experience. The first of these is the moment when, as she tells it, she receives an offer from heaven: a friendly "profyr" in her reason, inviting her to raise her eyes from the crucifix to look directly to God the father in heaven. In the Short Text, she refuses in the following way: "I answerde and sayde: Naye, I may noght, for thowe erte myne heuen."[123] Rejecting the opportunity to ascend from a material representation of Christ's humanity to an unmediated experience of the godhead, Julian anchors her devotion in the affective contemplation of the Passion so often associated with beginning contemplatives, women, and the laity.

In the Long Text, written some twenty years later, Julian formulates her response to the proffer somewhat differently: "I answeryd *inwardly with alle the myght of my soule,* and sayd: Nay, I may nott, for thou art my hevyn" (19.10–11, emphasis mine).[124] It is easy to overlook the adverbial "inwardly" here, assuming Julian means only that she did not speak aloud. But nowhere else in the text does Julian use the word in this way—again, she rarely uses it at all—even though she is very careful to indicate which parts of her vision were bodily, which were ghostly, which were ghostly in bodily likeness, which were words formed in her understanding, and so forth. Unlike so many of her contemporaries, Julian does not throw inwardness around. In the case of the proffer, she goes on to explain:

Repentyng and wylfulle choyse be two contrarytes, whych I felt both at that tyme; and tho be two partes, that oon outward, that other inwarde. The outwarde party is our dedely flessh, whych is now in payne and now / in woo, and shalle be in this lyfe, where of I felte moch in thys tyme; and that party was that I repentyd. The inward party is a hygh and a blessydfulle lyfe, whych is alle in peece and in loue, and this is more pryvely felte; *and this party is in whych myghtly, wysely and wyllfully, I chose Jhesu to my hevyn.*

And in this I saw truly that the inward party is master and souereyne to the outward. (19.24–34, emphasis mine)

It is important to Julian that she chooses Jesus willfully and *inwardly*. Like Hilton, she is eager to reconcile her sense of the centrality of the Incarnation with her understanding of Augustinian introspection. In order to do so, she revises the inner/outer split, creating an Augustinian double vision in which the inner self, because it never consented to sin *and* willfully chose Jesus, is essentially unfallen. In this model, inwardness—though set in opposition to the outward "dedely flessh"—cannot be stripped of fleshly imaginings because it is itself the hidden image of the fleshly part of God, the "lower" part from which Julian refuses to raise her gaze. For Julian, none of the three faculties is more "inward" than any other; as she observes in the fourteenth revelation, "only by oure reson we may nott profyte, but yf we have *evynly therwith* minde and love" (56.51–53, emphasis mine).

Julian's discussion of this crucial choice in vision eight looks forward to her discussion of the Lord and Servant in vision fourteen—the other place in the text where inwardness becomes a critical concern, and the only place in the text where Julian reports receiving "inward teaching," "inward learning," "inward ghostly showing," and "inward sight" (51.54–185). Suddenly and strikingly, inwardness is everywhere, suggesting that the nature of this experience is fundamentally different than any other in the *Showings*. The experience—which is not recorded in the Short Text—begins with another mighty inner outburst: "I cryde *inwardly* with all my myght, sekyng in to god for helpe" (50.35, emphasis mine). With its careful echo of Julian's earlier rejection of the proffer, this mighty cry prompts God's answering example: the "wonderfull example of a lorde that hath a servannt" (51.2). The inward showing of its meaning, she writes, "descended into my soul," but it took another twenty years of inward teaching for her to fully understand (51.55, 51.87).

And what is the teaching Julian receives in this most enigmatic and hermeneutically inward of her visions, but a vision of inwardness itself—a vision rendered in the most carefully sensory, imagistic terms of any of the showings? Julian sees a servant with two selves, one inner and one outer. The outer, clad simply as a laborer, is Adam, and all mankind, whom God—himself double—beholds with an outer countenance, or "cheer," of pity. The inner is Jesus, the ground of love, whom God beholds with an inner countenance of endless joy and love. Each human being is composed of inner substance and outer sensuality; the outer falls into the slough, but the inner is endlessly enjoying in the godhead. ("Though our outward man is corrupted, yet the inward man is renewed day by day.") The two parts cannot be separated from one another, any more than God's two countenances mean that God himself is separable. The servant is Adam and Christ and humankind, all at once. The husk and kernel are the same.

This, then, is Julian's version of the two-fold vision of likeness and unlikeness, and of that lost or hidden self that is to be dug for in the muddy fields of its own mind. Even the metaphor of digging, though, has a slightly different cast here. As Julian reports, the servant sets out because in his inward understanding, he sees that there is a treasure in the earth that the lord loves: "the wysdom of the seruannt sawe inwardly that ther was one thyng to do" (51.175–76). For though the treasure is grounded in the lord, he cannot enjoy it until the servant has dug it up and presented it in his own person. Thus the servant "shuld do the grettest labour and the hardest traveyle that is. He shuld be a gardener, deluyng and dykyng and swetyng and turnyng the erth vp and down" (51.193–94). His laboring in the earth is to the worship of the father, and his fall comes from the mighty inward understanding that it is the only thing to do.

At the end of the section Julian again mentions the earlier proffer: "with this was a suttell felyng and a prevy inwarde syghte of the hye partys, and that was shewed in the same tyme, where I myghte nott for the mene profer loke up in to hevyn" (55.54–57). Thus does she link her inward asking and choosing tightly to the inward understanding of the Lord and Servant. The servant falls because he sees inwardly that there is one thing to do; Julian chooses Christ to be her heaven because she also understands that the treasure of Christ is his humanity, and that the hard labor undertaken by the Incarnation is the right choice for the inner life.

Julian's inner self is not the emotionally exceptional lover of Christ nor his silent and impenetrable bride. It does not require special discipline for its creation or maintenance, nor does it depend on firm distinctions between the sensory and the rational. It does not create the space for a private nor a transparently public self. It is not a vernacular penetration of the mass nor an intensified awareness of mortality. It is not purely Augustinian. But it is part of the same conversation as all of these, and made possible in part by the creative strains arising from a world where there are so many ways of looking and thinking about the intersections and gaps between inside and out. Across more than two centuries, the question of the inner life would resonate through English religious and devotional culture.

Chapter 2

Seeing a Difference: Mirrors and Texts

"I have lyved in londe," quod I, "my name is Longe Wille—"
(*B xv.152*)

Clerkes kenne me that Crist is in all places;
Ac I seigh hym nevere soothly but as myself in a mirour:
Hic in enigmate, tunc facie ad faciem.
(*B xv.161–63*)

In *Piers Plowman*, as in the *Scale of Perfection*, the image of Christ in the soul becomes central to apparently unsolvable problems of self-understanding. Where Hilton struggles with *De Trinitate*, however, Langland's text stands closer to the *Confessions* in its monumental attempts to find the meaning of a life in language, memory, space, and time. At the beginning of passus fifteen, Will seems to have gone mad in his efforts to understand Do-Well. Raving in his folly, he falls asleep again, rocked by Reason, only to find himself confronted by the strange creature *Anima*, who tells him, "wherof I cam and of what kynde" (xv.14). Will's subsequent attempts to rationally examine this creature *Anima*, his own soul, lead to the two declarations quoted above: the first, Langland's most complete and definitive occulted signature, followed closely by the second, Long Will's puzzled invocation of the Pauline mirror and the image of Christ. The transcendent self follows the historical one—and both of them are riddles.

With some effort, we can figure out that "londe" + "Long" + "Will" = William Langland, who is at once the author of the poem and the persona in the poem, though those identities do not wholly overlap. But when Will cannot see Christ except as "myself in a mirror," does that mean that the true image of Christ is unavailable to him, hidden behind the distancing enigma of Will's own historical face? (I *never saw him*, truly; all I could see was myself in the mirror—where "myself" refers to a tallish rural person named Will, whose surname encodes both physical stature and background.) Or does it mean that he can only "soothly" see Christ in his own humanity? (I never saw him *truly*, except as myself in a mirror—where "myself" refers to the universal human nature assumed by Christ in his incarnation.) What does the mirror show? Will is and is not the image of Christ, just as Piers Plowman is and is not a figure of Christ or an ideal laborer, just as Will is and is not Langland, who thus is and is not himself the image of either Piers or Christ. The self remains somewhere in the enigmatic distance between ideal and real, allegory and autobiography, psychology and ethics, where these overlapping images reflect, illuminate, and complicate one another.

In the previous chapter, I described some of the ways in which English men and women might have tried to become more "inward." But if readers were not definitively sure what it meant to have an inner man, they were confronted with equally complex and multiple ideas about what it meant to behold, to "see."[1] This chapter and the next focus on how English writers took advantage of long-standing associations between vision and identity formation—between what we see and what we are—to create ideal models of the reading self. Vision comes to stand for and regulate interiority in complex and interesting ways. In its multiple associations, it provides English religious writers with an effective means of imagining and constructing the devotional reader—often by means of the same interplay between ideal and real selves, between images and exemplars, that we find in Will's search for Christ and himself in the dream-vision world of *Piers Plowman*.

In its broadest sense, vision carries a complex network of meanings far beyond the scope and purpose of this chapter. My goal here is not to survey the various and complicated uses of visual perception and visual understanding in medieval thought, for that has been done often and well. Instead, I focus more narrowly on those discourses of sight that made English readers visible *to themselves* in some fashion, whether through visual identification or specular self-examination (or both). For while visual language could have a multitude of connotations and implications, in late medieval England we find many different kinds of vision being re-directed in the same way, in accordance with the notion of "interiority" as ceaseless self-reflection (a model considered in Chapter 1). The mystic's vision, the lover's gaze, the "sight" of the understanding intellect—all become more and more specular and introspective, as English writers work to define "contemplation" as self-consciousness and self-reform, and the literate devotional subject as continually aware of her own image. (I will take up the re-formation of the reading subject through soul-imprinting vision in the next chapter.) *Self*-envisioning made vision appropriate for a wide range of readers who knew that contemplation was a kind of *seeing*.

The argument of this chapter is built on a series of jumps from one thing to another, so let me lay out its general direction. I begin here with a short discussion of mirror-tropes and ideas about them, since these would become so important to English notions of contemplative vision. First I revisit Augustine, whose notions of books and selves as reflective surfaces helped to link devotional vision to textual practice. Then I look briefly at the growing prevalence of mirror-tropes in late medieval England, where Augustinian mirror-books and mirror-minds came into contact with numerous other traditional, figurative uses—exemplary mirrors, compendious mirrors, mirrors of vanity—and with rising interest in material mirrors as domestic objects. These overlapping associations would make devotional uses of the mirror-trope richly suggestive and widely appealing.

I return to my main argument, about how English writers were reshaping the meaning of devotional vision, through a more extensive consideration of one exemplary text, *The Myroure of Oure Ladye*. Much of the chapter is devoted to this text, which uses its titular mirror to refocus intellectual and affective "beholding," and thus to negotiate the relationships between Latin and English, private reading and public prayer, group identity and devotional interiority. Written for the nuns at Syon and promoted by its printer in 1530 as being "very necessary" to all devout Christians, the *Myroure* offers important evidence of the devotional preoccupations affecting monastic and lay spirituality alike. Here late medieval English impulses toward the inward and the specular intersect tellingly with controversial questions of vernacular translation, Continental influence, and feminine piety.

Finally, and more speculatively, I consider the implications of the imperative to "see yourself" echoing through vernacular devotional literature. How does it matter? If English readers were told repeatedly to look in the mirror, what did they see? As a way of thinking about this question—though I can't answer it—I bring together two diametrically opposed texts, the mystical *Cloud of Unknowing* and the popular *Chastising of God's Children*. The otherworldly *Cloud* makes the case for "blindness and forgetting"; in doing so, it helps to illuminate what is at stake in the *Myroure*'s insistence on busy beholding and remembering. For the *Cloud*-author is afraid that such beholding is inevitably identity-making, that it anchors a worldly, particularized version of selfhood that prevents the reader's full absorption in God. The more typical *Chastising*, on the other hand, mounts a scathing attack on the "blind, naked unbusiers" who neglect the self in the pursuit of mystical rapture. The emphasis on practical, active modes of devotion and self-improvement in texts like the *Myroure* and the *Chastising* helps to account for their popularity outside the cloister, with men and women who were more interested in creating new identities for themselves than in melting into God.

The Augustinian Mirror-text

In the last chapter we reviewed part of Augustine's answer to the question, In what way is the human soul made in the image of God? How does it see (itself) now *per speculum in enigmate*, and how will it come to see face to face? Part of Augustine's answer involves the reflexive study of one's own mental capacities, the created trinity of memory, will, and understanding. It also involves a reflexive study of one's own imperfections in relation to the perfection of God. This double vision is not achieved through Platonic self-reflection alone, however; it is made possible by reading, especially the reading of scripture.[2] The human soul may be a mirror, but it needs another mirror in order to see its own reflection, to study its own reflective powers. That secondary mirror is the text.

Augustine would agree with Walter Ong that reading "makes possible increasingly articulate introspectivity, opening the psyche as never before not only to the external objective world quite distinct from itself, but also to the interior self against whom the objective world is set."[3] For Augustine, reading initiates the project of self-knowledge, serving as the indispensable means of turning inward into the mind.[4] As the text turns the reader toward the inner self, it also displays a vision of the standard that that self has not met. "The mirror has set its writing before you," Augustine asserts, "it is read to you: blessed are the pure in heart, for they shall see God. The mirror is set forth in this reading; see whether you are what it has said. If you are not yet so, then groan, that you may become so. The mirror will disclose your face to you. As you will not see a flatterer in the mirror, so you will not wheedle yourself. Its brightness will show you what you are: see what you are."[5] It became a favorite theme of medieval theologians. Gregory the Great was among the many who echoed the idea that reading "presents a kind of mirror to the eye of the mind, that our inner face may be seen in it. There indeed we learn our own ugliness, our own beauty"—and there, consequently, we "transform what we read into our very selves."[6]

In the *Confessions*, Augustine represents his spiritual transformation as a sequence of textual encounters that turns him repeatedly back upon himself. The books of the Platonists initiate the process, opening Augustine's psyche to his own increasing introspectivity. The culmination of his awakening, however, is a series of nested Christian stories. Bishop Simplicianus tells him the story of Victorinus, a rhetoric teacher (like Augustine) converted by his attentive reading of Scripture. The story makes Augustine "glow with fervor to imitate" the converted man.[7] Yet he is still divided; part of him wants to convert, while the other part resists. Then a visitor named Ponticianus happens to pick up a book of Paul's epistles that Augustine has left lying on a game table. The book inspires Ponticianus to tell the story of the Egyptian monk Antony—converted by reading Scriptures—and how one of Ponticianus's friends, coming upon a book of Antony's life, was converted by it in turn. "He read on," Augustine confides to God, re-narrating the story of the friend, "and in his heart, where you alone could see, a change was taking place."[8] Meanwhile, a change is taking place in Augustine's heart too:

while he was speaking, O Lord, you were turning me around to look at myself. For I had placed myself behind my own back, refusing to see myself. You were setting me before my own eyes so that I could see how sordid I was, how deformed and squalid, how tainted with ulcers and sores. I saw it all and stood aghast, but there was no place where I could escape from myself. If I tried to turn my eyes away they fell on Ponticianus, still telling his tale, and in this way you brought me face to face with myself once more, forcing me upon my own sight.[9]

Augustine continues to struggle in himself, one will pitted violently against the other, but in the midst of his weeping, he hears the mysterious voice of a child chanting *tolle, lege*—take it, and read. He remembers Antony's conversion; he remembers how in that story, the gospel had addressed itself directly to a listener; he seizes Paul's epistles, reads the first passage he sees, and is converted.

What the book says is hardly the point; both Augustine and then his friend Alypius find themselves reflected on that page. (Everyone remembers the chiming "tolle, lege," but who remembers the anticlimactic verse itself?)[10] In this long series of reflective readings and examples, the text is simply a means for Augustine to get outside himself so that he can get back *inside* himself, so that he can get some purchase on what he already intimately knew but had forgotten. Reading stimulates his desire and shows him his own struggle in the lives of others. It goads him to look in his memory for what was always there, but has been lost or hidden.

Reading, moreover, allows Augustine to negotiate the problems of self-understanding in language and time. The process of reading and understanding one's life becomes analogous to the process by which one reads and understands scripture, so that learning to read the one is learning to read the other.[11] Both require holding the past and future in one's mind, comparing them with what one is reading now, and seeking to understand the relationships between them. And both require an understanding of the differences between the literal (outer) and spiritual (inner) meanings of things, between the imperfect things that are necessary to increase one's desire (language) and the perfect things toward which one's desire should be directed (God).

Mirrors in English

In his monumental study of mirror-texts and titles, Herbert Grabes records two striking observations about late medieval English culture: first, that from about 1200 England was "very much associated" with the rise of mirror-titled texts, and that English monastic libraries managed to acquire most of the Continental mirror-titles.[12] And second, that although mirrors rarely appeared in English poetry before the mid-fourteenth century, they were represented with increasing frequency thereafter.[13] How are we to understand this interest? In what sense are or aren't these textual mirrors Augustinian, and how do they reflect contemporary beliefs about the meaning of reading, the acquisition of knowledge, and the process of self-understanding?

In England as on the Continent, the rising interest in mirrors may be partly attributable to material conditions. In the thirteenth century, glass mirrors had gradually replaced polished metal ones, and scholars have noted the subsequent growth of interest in mirrors as domestic objects.[14] Yet most of the earlier mirror-titled texts do not refer to functions we normally associate with a material mirror—if only because our own mirrors are usually flat. Most medieval mirrors were convex, containing little worlds that they both reflected and reduced. Thus one kind of book-as-mirror was compendious, encyclopedic: it gave one, like Tennyson's Lady of Shalott, a panoramic view of the world outside, all without ever leaving the house. Mirrors and mirror-texts were also, however, associated with a visual function neither miniaturizing nor literally reflective, but exemplary: they showed one an image that was one's "own" only insofar as it was meant as a warning (so *The Mirror of Sinners* shows a *memento mori* version of "what you are"), or as an imitable example, as in a "mirror of virtues," or "mirror for princes." Such mirrors, like Augustine's nested conversion stories, allowed readers to see what they would or should or might become. There were many other ideas associated with mirrors: there were soul-capturing mirrors of witchcraft, flickering mirrors of worldly transience—like Langland's mirror of Middle Earth[15]—and the very common mirrors of vanity and flattery. These last came closest to reflecting the actual usage of material mirrors, in medieval as in modern culture: to examine one's own exterior, either to make sure it is properly composed, or to assist in making it that way.

In the mid-fourteenth century—around the time that images of material mirrors begin to appear in English poetry—we start to find mirror-titles that are more explicit about reflecting readers back at themselves, not as they will be or should be, but as they already *are*. Such reflection is still conceived as a preliminary step toward improving the image. But the "real" image begins to compete with the "ideal" as a locus of the reader's attention; self-knowledge becomes more prominently associated with both mirrors and texts. In *The Myrour of Recluses*, for example (originally written in Latin for an English solitary), the reader learns how to "behold and seeth your calling" (a version of 1 Cor. 1:26), but also how to "Seeth and beholdeth your owne self, list ye lese that ye haan doon and wroght" (2 John 1:8).[16] The text presents an Augustinian conception of both the solitary self—the created trinity of memory, will, and understanding—and of self-reflexive reading, where the book helps the reader to see his vocation both as an ideal and as he is currently practicing it. Encouraging readers to assess their progress every day, to examine the movements of their will and affections, to choose appropriate devotions, and to see their failings reflected in the Passion of

Christ (a third kind of mirror, inwardly beheld), the text represents the mirror-book as crucial to each of these self-reflective tasks. Here we are not far from the mirror in which Gower's *Amans*, soon to be named as "John Gower," remembers his own age. Seeing himself not as the lover he had imagined, but as the old man he really is, Gower calls home his Reason, makes full confession to Venus, and achieves grace and reform at the end of the book. In secular as in sacred writing, the mirror allowed its beholders to write and rewrite, to recognize as well as misrecognize themselves.

As the idea of the book as a self-reflective mirror became more popular, so too did the idea of Christ as a mirror that Long Will so intriguingly invokes in the epigraph to this chapter. Christ had fulfilled the promise of reciprocity inherent in the creation: man having been formed in the image of God, God now took on the image of man. As Nicholas Love writes, "the first man Adam . . . deformede in him that ymage of god. . . . Bot this day the seconde Adam crist god & man reformed this ymage in his Incarnation."[17] The image of man looking *per speculum in enigmate* came to be understood as a visual dialogue between the viewer and Christ, the perfect, spotless human image at once obscured by the individual's imperfect shadow and casting it into sharp relief. As *Book to a Mother* puts it, "yif thou wolt knowe sikerliche [truly] thi soule and thi lif . . . thenke ofte and loke inwardlich in Crist. . . . For that is the boke and the mirour withouten wem [blemish]."[18] The second Passion meditation attributed to Richard Rolle also asks readers to look into that mirror-face and restore its likeness in their own souls. The "Fifteen Oes" tropes Christ as the mirror of everlasting clearness and the mirror of truth; in *The Prickynge of Love* he is the mirror without spot.[19] The figure of Christ-as-mirror also appears regularly in both popular drama and late medieval sermons. In *The Orcherd of Syon*, a translation of Catherine of Siena's *Dialogues*, the reflection enables Catherine to refute the notion that woman might *not* be created in God's image. Christ, she asserts, is a "mirrour that needis I moste biholde, in the which myrrour is representid to me that I am thin ymage & creature."[20] As a "myself in a mirror," Christ could be both exemplary and reflective, combining the functions of image-mirror and reality-mirror, the impetus for recognition and reform as well as prime ground for arguments about the nature of human likeness to God.

There are intriguing examples of the Christ-mirror connection in material culture. The crucifixion was a prominent subject on medieval ivory mirror-cases, where the image of one's own particular features could be juxtaposed with the image of suffering perfection.[21] A large tondo owned by the duke of Burgundy around 1400 seems to have created a similar juxtaposition. As Hans Belting describes it, "The reverse has the duke's coat of arms, and the fact that the roundel is painted on both sides reveals its use as a portable image in the court's travels. At such times it was protected by a leather case, from which the duke drew it to use as a devotional image. The owner would look into the expensively painted mirror to see, not himself, but the image of the suffering Christ."[22] The duke's "mirror" combines a symbol of his temporal identity—his coat of arms, painted on one side of the roundel—with an image of his transcendent one. Yet they are *not* combined; the worldly and the spiritual can never be seen at the same time, so that the duke has to choose which side to look at. One wonders whether he thought of the roundel as having an "inside" and an "outside." We find a similar object in *Sir Gawain and the Green Knight*: Gawain's shield, which displays the Pentangle on the outside—the knightly image of masculine perfection and wholeness that Gawain shows to the world—and the image of the Virgin Mary on the inside, where only Gawain can see it.[23]

It is a Marian mirror to which we now turn. (The subject of Christ-as-mirror surfaces again in the next chapter.) Like Christ, the Virgin Mary was often represented or symbolized by a mirror. After all, she had received light and reflected it perfectly.[24] If Christ was the incarnate image of God, Mary was the glass that had received that image, making it visible to human eyes by clothing it in human flesh. Mary's purity made her a good exemplary image too, a mirror without spots in which all might see their own blemishes. The Marian mirror could show Christ, Mary herself, and/or the viewer's own face. In one fifteenth-century text, *The Myroure of Oure Ladye*, it also shows the correct understanding and performance of the Divine Service at the Abbey of Syon. The mirror trope grounds that text's attempts to harmonize the affective devotions of the heart, the reformation of the individual soul through study and reflection, and the external performance of public ritual. A closer examination of the *Myroure* will begin to suggest the richness and importance of the mirror for fifteenth-century English devotional culture, and show how writers could use it as a kind of visual master-trope for reshaping other modes of beholding in an environment where vision, inwardness, and vernacular devotional reading were subjects of intense concern.

Our Lady's Mirror

The Monastery of St. Saviour and St. Bridget of Syon of the Order of St. Augustine was a double monastery of sixty women and twenty-five men living on the north side of the Thames, upstream from London and across the river from the Carthusian foundation at Sheen.[25] Though there is much we do not know about the abbey, Syon does give us a landscape, a Rule, a history, and a list of specific names in particular manuscripts, many—like the *Myroure*—made especially for this community. We can picture the Bridgettines filing into their chapel, the sisters crossing over a bridge to a gallery suspended above the nave, while the brothers come in on the ground floor.[26] Their chanting echoes back and forth through the day, first the higher voices in the loft, then the lower voices on the ground (in constant expiation of Lancastrian sins). We can hear too the work of construction—no doubt loudest when anyone was trying to concentrate—that continued through most of the fifteenth century. The chapel was finally finished in 1488.[27] We can imagine the sisters assembling for daily devotions around an open grave, singing *De Profundis* and pinching up a bit of earth, and later participating in the evening ceremony of *Indulgete*, or mutual forgiveness of the day's transgressions, those in the right stalls inclining to the left, and then the left to the right.[28]

Syon gives our quest for late medieval interiority and self-reflection a satisfyingly local habitation. But this unique community was also an important symbol of national piety and a center for the dissemination of vernacular spirituality throughout the fifteenth and early sixteenth centuries. For more than a century it reflected and channeled lay devotional interests.[29] Thus its specific attempts to regulate the readerly life of private and public prayer open out onto the concerns of late medieval English devotional culture more generally. From its founding in 1415 to the eve of the dissolution, when Henry VIII sought repeatedly to gain its approval for his reforms, Syon was constantly cited as one of England's most spiritually vibrant communities. Its monks fostered a close relationship with London's various elites by serving as spiritual directors for influential laymen, hearing confessions, preaching in the vernacular, and handling the many visitors to the abbey.[30] (Generous indulgences attached to those sermons helped draw crowds, as did other indulgences available at the abbey.) Donations suggest the social range of their influence: Duchess Margaret of Clarence, Henry V's sister-in-law, gave £200 in books and gifts, while Johanna Buklonde, a fishmonger's widow, gave a book costing four marks, two shillings.[31] Margery Kempe took care to pay a visit. Syon's rapid rise to the forefront of England's wealthiest foundations indicates broad national support, as does the careful patronage of Lancastrian, Yorkist, and Tudor families in turn.[32] The abbey had strong northern associations and close ties to the East Anglian aristocracy and merchant classes, men and women who remembered Syon generously in their wills, and who often became lay brothers and sisters.[33] The hybrid spirituality suggested by this practice is evident even within the convent, where many sisters owned books of hours: a genre typically associated with lay *imitation* of monastic ritual, not with monastic ritual itself. Rebecca Krug finds "remarkable similarities" between Bridgettine and aristocratic lay devotion, similarities she attributes in large part to the practice of having prospective nuns spend a year reading Bridgettine texts before entering the abbey.[34]

Indeed, books were at the heart of the nuns' relationship to England at large. While the brothers amassed a stunning academic and humanist library,[35] the sisters received a good deal of the vernacular spiritual literature of the day, and their partnership with Sheen assured that many books written or well received there would be copied and disseminated to a broader audience. When the printing presses went into production, the abbey provided them with a steady supply of texts.

As an English translation and rationale of the Divine Service, the *Myroure* confronts head on the role of the vernacular in orthodox worship. It does so in what would seem to be a context of growing discontent with the almost wholly externalized experience of the Latin liturgy. Remember that vernacular guides to the mass were a popular genre in late medieval England. Texts written for nuns suggest that even in the convent, the lack of widespread familiarity with Latin, alongside the expanding discourses of affectivity and inwardness, were causing murmurs of dissatisfaction.[36] Women wondered how they could pray devoutly when their thoughts did not match the words on their lips. How could they summon the proper emotion in their hearts without using the mother tongue?[37] The *Tree and Twelve Frutes* tries to finesse the problem, observing that vocal and mental prayer "ben so nygh of kynned. that almost the ton is never fownde with oute the tother."[38] The *Chastising of God's Children* offers this caution:

[S]um now in these daies usen to sei on ynglisshe her sautir and matyns of oure ladi, and the sevene psalmes and the letanye. . . . I wil nat repreve such translacion . . . but uttirli to usen hem in englisshe and leve the laten, I holde it nat commendable. . . . If yee wil aske hou ye shuln preie devoutli in preier whiche ye undirstond nat, i answere you therto and seie that for the vertu of the wordis and your lowness and obeisaunce to holi chirche, with a fervent desire upward to god aftir youre entent, though ye understonde no word that ye seie, it may be to you more medeful, and more acceptable to god thanne grete devocioun that ye wene ye have in other prevy devocions.[39]

While acknowledging his readers' desire for deeper involvement in their prayer lives, the author of the *Chastising* insists that intent is ultimately more important than understanding, and that humble obedience and the inherent power of the words will bring greater reward than private, vernacular devotions—even if the praying subject feels otherwise. Mental involvement, he asserts, is not crucial to fervent desire or devout prayer.

The Myroure of Oure Ladye owes its production to quite the opposite conviction (though in other respects, as I will argue later, it has much in common with the *Chastising*.) Like the many lay guides to the mass but on a larger scale, it provides its readers with the means of understanding just what they are saying and doing and meaning as they progress through their weekly Office. The author tries not to undermine the use of Latin: "This lokeynge on the englyshe whyle the latyn ys redde," he writes, "ys to be understonde of them that have sayde theyre mattyns or reed thyr legende before. For else I wolde not counsell them to leve the herynge of the latyn."[40] Yet he does reject the *Chastising*'s emphasis on obedience over understanding, asserting that inward involvement *is* crucial to proper worship. Explaining why the *Ave Maria* and *Pater Noster* are said in silence when entering the church, for example, he insists that "god ys more pleased wyth the prevy devocyon of the harte . . . then with the outwarde noyse wyth the voyce" (73). In another place he instructs, "at the begynnynge of eche howre saye thus to our lorde. bothe with harte. and with tongue. *or at the leste with the harte*" (276, emphasis mine). For if the heart is well kept, "all the lyfe ys well" (64). Neither abstinence nor virtues nor any outward deeds make a man truly religious, he insists, and so "thys gostly study to kepe the harte, ys youre chyefe laboure" (64). "Inward" love, devotion, and understanding are the keys to worship. Such attitudes reflect the abbey's deep involvement with anchoritic spirituality, and echo the sentiments of many late medieval theologians who felt that although oral prayer was necessary for the liturgy, and more profitable for the simple and unlettered, internal prayer was otherwise the higher form, capable of more intense and intimate expression.[41] The author's rhetoric on this point speaks to his respect for the inner capacities of his readers.[42]

At the same time, the *Myroure* is careful to honor the external signs of obedience and community that are so important to conventual life. Inner devotions are desirable precisely because they deepen one's engagement with liturgical performance; "outwarde observaunces," in turn, assist in the extraordinary effort required to gather the mind for its inner devotions (62–63). In the *Scale of Perfection*, Hilton had advised readers to keep whatever exercises engaged their desire, whether "praiynge or thenkynge, stillenes or spekynge, reedynge or heerynge, oonlynes or comonynge, goynge or sittynge."[43] "Sitting" seems to have been a touchy subject, since Rolle had insisted that he sometimes felt the most love of Jesus when he was just sitting. The *Myroure*'s author cautions, however, that books "that say how som have moste devocyon syttynge, or else . . . syttynge or knelynge or goynge or standynge" pertain only to *private* devotions that the nuns have chosen to say on their own (63). The service is a different story. The legislated forms must be kept, and it *matters* whether one sits, stands, or kneels. But there is room for both Rollean sitting and formal worship. In fact, private devotion is specifically legislated by the Bridgettine Rule.[44] It is not an optional supplement but the dialogic complement to and foundation for public acts of praise.

Syon's commitment to the vernacular may have been influenced by its founder Bridget, who received her revelations in Swedish and had the Bible translated into that language. It may also have been influenced, as I suggested earlier, by the Lancastrian promotion of English as a national language. Whatever else it was, it was a practical corollary to the Bridgettine embrace of devotional reading. The *Myroure* calls such reading "one of the partes of contemplacyon," and no convent in England had a higher reputation for literacy or for intellectual rigor (66).[45] The rule allows sisters an unlimited supply of books for study, lists them among the items to be provided for novices, and stipulates that "silence after some convenience, is to be kepte in the lybrary, whyls any suster is there alone in recordyng of her redynge."[46] An order for twenty-three pairs of spectacles placed by Dame Bridget Belgrave, Chambress for 1536–37, suggests that the sisters took their studies seriously, as does Syon's practice of putting user-friendly indexing tabs on manuscripts and printed books.[47] The abbey owned Rolle's English Psalter and probably English Bibles as well.[48] The Augustinian *Rule* with Hugh of St. Victor's commentary was translated for their use, as was David of Augsburg's *De Exterioris et Interioris Hominis Compositione*.[49] Catherine of Siena's *Dialogue* became their *Orcherd of Syon*; both *Disce Mori* and the

Speculum Devotorum were probably written for them. Extant manuscripts from Syon also include works by Hilton, Love, and Thomas à Kempis, as well as the *Cursor Mundi, The Tree and Twelve Frutes, The Chastising of God's Children, The Treatise of Love, A Ladder of Four Rungs, Benjamin Minor,* and the *Ancrene Wisse.*[50] Wynkyn de Worde had to recall sixty copies of the potentially heretical *Ymage of Love*—enough for all sixty nuns to have had their own copies. Works arguably less conducive to devotion include a mid-fifteenth-century collection of English works including Vegetius, Lydgate's *Siege of Thebes,* and Chaucer's *Parliament of Fowles.*[51] Henry Parker, a priest of Syon, gave Margaret Windsor, a nun, an early printed copy of Boccaccio's *De la ruine des nobles hommes et femmes.*[52]

Syon's reputation for spiritual and intellectual rigor, then, was to be founded on a serious program of vernacular reading, and a careful rapprochement between communal worship and private exercise. Eager for the more advanced and fulfilling experience of inner prayer and for the private devotions increasingly adopted by lay elites, Bridgettines needed modes of worship that would encourage the pursuit of an inner life without seriously damaging collective experience and identity. This was a convent, after all, even if its nuns read like laywomen. As Syon's own Richard Whytford wrote, "al the covent shule be of one hert, one mynde, one affection and one felynge & assent of our lorde. So were the disciples."[53] In giving the sisters an English "key" to the daily services, feasts, and masses of the Virgin, the *Myroure* attempts to bridge the threatening gulf between the oral performance that links the sisters in community and obedience, and the internal devotion that links them privately to God. Rather than setting vernacular devotions in opposition to the Latin service, it makes an English text the means by which the sisters may internalize that service, thus weaving corporate experience, vernacular reading, and private devotions inextricably together.

The *Myroure* stages this agenda through a series of oppositions: not only between Latin and vernacular, mouth and heart, external and internal, but also and most insistently between oral and visual, between saying and *seeing.* The language of seeing and beholding pervades the introductory sections of the text, where the translator explains his text's rationale and use.[54] From the oft-repeated introductory phrase, "*Viderunt eam Filie syon, et beatissimam predicaverunt. . . .* The doghtres of Syon have sene hyr; and thye have shewed hyr moste blessed," to the frequent exhortations to "lyfte up the eyen of your soulles towarde youre soverayne lady, and often & bysely loke and study in this her myroure," vision serves as the central metaphor for talking about translation, interiority, reading, and performance. Before they begin to praise, they see, explains the translator; when they perform their praise, they show (note that *praedicare* is rendered in visual rather than oral terms). "Ye ought to be doughtres of byholdynge by contemplacione," he writes; "ye ought to se her"; "beholde and se wyth youre gostly eyen" (2, 5).

The visual theme is many layered, but the first prominent sense at work here has to do with the traditional association of vision and understanding, of sight and *in*sight ("Oh, I see," we say). A long intellectual tradition— partly Augustininan—associated vision with meditative reading and with biblical hermeneutics in particular.[55] To "see" properly in this mode was to go beyond the literal level of the text, to understand its hidden meanings through careful, meditative *lectio*. Part of the *Myroure*'s visual language derives from this traditional way of talking about textual knowing: "Many of you," writes the translator, "though ye can synge and rede, yet ye can not se what the meanynge therof ys: therefore . . . I have drawen your legende and all youre servyce in to Englyshe, that ye shulde se by the understondynge therof" (2–3). The book makes visible to the nuns' understanding whatever knowledge they need to improve their performance. (The book makes words literally visible as well; recall that the nuns are not to leave the *hearing* of the Latin in order to *look on* the English.) How can they show properly by outward praising, "but yf ye have fyrste syght therof by inwarde understandinge?" Looking busily in this mirror, they must study "not lyghtely but contynually . . . labouryng to knowe what you rede that ye may se and understonde" (4). By studying what they see on the page, they acquire inward vision of the meaning of the service. Finally they become mirrors themselves, reflecting understanding back outward through liturgical praise.

But if "sight" was linked to textual understanding, it was also central to the traditions of affective piety and visionary mysticism that were transforming Christian devotional expectations. For late medieval religious women, as Hamburger and others have argued, "the meaning of vision . . . had undergone a subtle transformation."[56] Vision was becoming divorced from reading as it became more closely associated with both empirical knowledge and spiritual authority, and as the Franciscan discipline of imaginative visual meditation on the life of Christ became increasingly popular.[57] While such practiced visualization was not granted the same status as received visionary experience, the line between the two was often confused, as Barbara Newman points out.[58] The number of confirmed female "visionaries" across Europe was rising rapidly, even as Franciscan texts such as the *Meditationes Vitae Christi* were being translated and retranslated for laypeople. Even books of hours contained more images of eyes, more references to vision, as the fifteenth century progressed.[59] From the elite spirituality of the authorized mystics to the relatively pedestrian devotions of the lay primers, an obsessive interest in visuality was increasingly associated with subjective experience of God, with individual sanctity—and with women. Newman suggests that in many female religious communities, some kind of visionary experience "was considered normal, even normative."[60] We might expect it in an order founded by Bridget of Sweden, whose revelations had such a powerful influence on fifteenth-century devotion, iconography, and politics.

To a certain extent, the *Myroure* plays to these expectations, exhorting readers to create deeper and sweeter contemplation by "beholding" the Virgin and visualizing imaginatively the actions narrated in the service. It invokes several times, in fact, the visions of "St. Maud," or Mechtild of Hackborne, a German nun and mystic. The catalog of the men's library lists six copies of Mechtild's *Booke of Gostlye Grace*, and this well-known work would seem to be an ideal model for the kind of paraliturgical visionary experience that the nuns at Syon might be trained to practice, since Mechtild's visions were inspired almost exclusively by the liturgical cycle in her own convent at Helfta.[61] Mechtild's revelations read like a nun's life in technicolor: full of devotional fervor, majestic and affective images, symbolic ceremonies and ritual "oneings" with God. Mechtild *sees* the invisible community inhabiting her convent and surrounding her sisters as they go about their daily devotions. She sees the Virgin Mary walking through the choir with the infant Christ during the service; she sees ten-year-old Christ running down the corridors; she sees St. John standing by the bedside of a nun who is particularly devoted to him. The mysteries of the service reveal themselves in sensual form: she sees the words of the gospel streaming like sunbeams, Christ raising the golden chalice, the angelic host worshipping the Virgin. Mechtild really does "see" the service, not in a textual but in an imaginative and inspired—even a dramatic—way. One thinks of Margery Kempe making soup for the Virgin Mary, or watching as Jesus ascends very slowly into heaven.

So too the *Myroure of Oure Ladye* gives the Syon nuns access to the service's dramatic and imaginative associations, to the ghostly presence of the Virgin in their conventual life. They are promised the same kind of rich and full interior world that Mechtild inhabits—an existence of "inward delyte and devocyon," of "holy and hevenly medytacyons," of "deper or swetter contemplacion"—if only they too will learn to "see" (3–4). The book recommends devotional use of Mechtild's revelations, and even recounts the story of a young nun who saw the choir lifted up to heaven with all the angels and martyrs during the singing of *Te Deum* (117).

Yet vision in *The Myroure of Oure Ladye* is not quite the same thing as vision in the convent at Helfta, though it promises similar rewards. One difference is the text's more traditional emphasis on the insight produced by reading and understanding. Rather than being unpredictably or eccentrically inspired, the Bridgettines experience appropriate liturgical emotions based on the text's interpretation of their service, which harmonizes their experiences of "love and ioye . . . dreade . . . hope . . . sorow & . . . compassyon" by linking them to a common understanding, internalized through serious textual study (70).

But the crucial difference between Mechtildian and Bridgettine vision is the trope of the mirror itself, which grounds and refocuses all of the text's other visual associations, making both textual and imaginative vision ideally self-referential—while still anchoring it to the performance of group identity. Explaining his book's title, the translator writes: "For as muche as ye may se in this boke as in a myroure, the praysynges and worthines of oure moste excellente lady therfor I name it. Oure ladyes myroure. Not that oure lady shulde se herselfe therin, but that ye shulde se her therin as in a myroure, and so be styred the more devoutly to prayse her, & to knowe where ye fayle in her praysinges, and to amende: tyll ye may come there ye may se her face to face wythouten eny myrroure" (4). Several associations are twisted together here. First the exemplary function: in the book-as-mirror, the nuns can see Mary's worthiness. Then the material function is invoked, albeit negatively: Mary does not use this mirror to see herself. Finally we come to the model of self-envisioning and self-reform, underpinned by Paul's imperfect vision: know where *you* fail, and amend, until you can see her face to face. The mirror-book shows the nun to herself in both ideal and real form: as the exemplar and symbol of her community and vocation, and as the imperfect individual imposed upon the exemplar. So many of Syon's other texts would have reinforced the paradigm; the *Orcherd of Syon*, for example, explains, "right as a spott or a filthe of a mannys visage may ligtly be parceyved in a myrrour, so a soul, which with a verray knowynge of hymsilf . . . [lokes] ynward with the ighe of intellecte to se hersilf in the holy myrrour of God, knowith and parceyveth myche the moore the foul spottis of his owne soule."[62] Looking in the mirror of our Lady, the Bridgettines assess the foul spots they have made on her image in their imperfect showings of praise. And then they labor—not just to improve their performance of the service, but "in clensyng of theyr conscyence" (68). As the translator emphasizes, "ye ought . . . to be doughtres of byholdynge by contemplacyon & specyally in byholdynge of youre owne wretchednes" (2, emphasis mine).

The dynamic here is not a simple comparison of sinful Bridgettine self to perfect externalized ideal, viewed like a picture in the book. The perfect image is also inside the self, in the rational soul; the external mirror gives the reader access to an internal one, in the complicated but familiar Augustinian dynamic. The translator explains, "Oure resonable soulle ys called owre lordes chere. for yt ys made to hys lykenesse. but yt was defoyled. and darkyd. and mysshape by synne. But by the lyghte of grace in our baptym. and by penaunce doynge. yt is now sealed ageyne. and reformed to the lykenesse of god. as waxe taketh lykenesse of the seale. and as a peny hathe impressed the image of the kynge" (98). Here is Hilton's lost penny, re-imprinted with the likeness of Christ. *Pace* Augustine, the soul needs the text to see itself, to initiate the inward turn that makes visible the improvable image of God in the soul. The ideal Bridgettine reader becomes ceaselessly conscious of herself. Even in public ritual, she performs as if watching and correcting herself in the mirror—often, continually, busily. The mirror, then, effectively focuses diverse expectations of the visionary inner life. All kinds of intellectual and affective vision ultimately refer back to its doubled images.

Mechtild of Hackborne, by way of contrast, participates in her visions but rarely describes *seeing* herself. When she does, it is only to illustrate her immediate union with Christ—emphasizing identity, not difference, the erasure rather than the foregrounding of self as a category of experience. Rather than preserving visual distinctions, she feels herself melting into Christ like wax. Her inwardness is a rapturous bridal chamber, not an inescapable mirror. There are no mirrors in her text. Never is there the kind of intense and critical self-scrutiny that emerges from the *Myroure* as the ideal of the visionary, inward life. Mechtild is not interested in seeing who she is and where she fails. In the *Booke of Gostlye Grace*, vision is not really about the self. In the *Myroure*, ultimately, vision is about almost nothing else.

And while Mechtild's interiority is fundamentally erotic, grounded in her status as the private vessel and special lover of Christ, the *Myroure* shies away from any suggestion that its visual dialogue is about erotic attraction or sexual union. This dialogue is between a self and a better self—a Mary figured as a teacher, an apostle, a counselor, a comforter, and a tender mother. The events of her life structure the calendar of feasts; she suffers most of the pains of the Passion. Christ receives much less attention. It is Mary who grounds the nuns' self-assessments and their attempts, not to melt into God or receive "hevenlie privetees" as a token of special favor, but simply to do better.

The *Myroure*'s reflexive imperative erects some key boundaries around the interpretive autonomy fostered by the abbey's rigorous program of vernacular reading. For if inspired visions could confer spiritual authority, so too could the textual penetration offered by English translation and private study. Whether textual, bodily, or imaginative, "seeing" could destabilize institutional control by creating an individual locus of interpretation. One fourteenth-century sermon revealingly insists that because of original sin, "all the knawyng that we hafe in this werlde of Hym, es of *heryng*, and of lerynge, and of techyng of other, of the law and the lare that langes till Haly Kyrke."[63] The *Myroure*-author, on the other hand, insists that the nuns study until they understand even difficult passages for themselves; "saynt Austyn sayeth" that one reading is never enough, he admonishes (67). Through busy labor and with the help of others if necessary, they may become masters of their own learning: "For as a clarke writeth. there be thre thynges that make a dyscyple passe his master. One is often to aske & to lerne that he can not. Another is bysely to kepe in mynde that he lerneth & herith. And the thyrde is redely & frely to teche fourth to other. tho thynges that he hath lerned & can" (67). But here our author quickly qualifies himself, admonishing that reading and study are "not only for to be connynge. or for to . . . speke yt fourthe to other; but pryncypally to enforme your selfe. & to set yt a warke in youre owne lyvynge."[64] Again "sight" becomes self-reflexive, a vision in the mirror. When reading books "made to enforme the understondynge," the sisters must strive primarily to understand themselves, polish their mirrors, and improve:

ye oughte to beholde in yourself sadly whether ye lyve & do as ye rede or no. & what wyl and desyre ye have therto. & what entendaunce & laboure ye do therabout. And yf ye fele that youre lyfe ys rewled in vertu accordynge to that ye rede; then ye ought hartely & mekely to thanke our lorde therof . . . and yf ye fele & se in youre selfe. that ye lacke suche verteows governaunce as ye rede of . . . ye ought to abyde therupon. & inwardly sorow for the defaulte & lacke that ye se in yourselfe. & besely to kepe in mynde that lesson that so sheweth you to youre self & ofte to rede yt ageyne. & to loke theron. & on your selfe. (68)

Here repeated reading becomes the means of more careful self-reflection and constant attention to one's own particular failings. If a difficult text requires multiple readings, how much more does the enigma of a reflected self: "rede yt ageyne." The same impulse is evident in the author's explication of the Rule's commandment to "contynuall studyes, " where "study" rapidly becomes "gostly study to kepe the harte" (64). At Syon, the library is the essential scene of self-examination, where the sisters "labour in [themselves] inwardly," both stirring up their affections and trying to evaluate their will and desire, their living and laboring, through the medium of the book (69). Take it, and read: the text places the Bridgettine reader before her own face, encouraging those introspective habits of thought and being that render the doubled image of the self perpetually and inescapably visible.

The self-reflective disciplinary program that helps to combine and refocus various kinds of vision and devotion in the *Myroure of Oure Ladye* figures prominently in many other works associated with Syon, including Catherine of Siena's deeply Augustinian *Orcherd of Syon*, David of Augsburg's *De Exterioris et Interioris*, and Hilton's *Scale of Perfection*, one of the first books donated to Syon (by new Bridgettine and former anchoress Margery Pensax).[65] Syon was also associated with the introduction and dissemination of the *Imitatio Christi* of Thomas à Kempis. Abbess Elizabeth Gibbs was one of the first recipients of the English translation, which instructed readers to "wake upon thiself, styre thiself, amonisshe thiself; and hou ever it be of othir, foryete not thiself."[66] Sister Clemence Tressham owned a 1523 print edition, and Syon brother Richard Whytford produced his own translation around 1530.[67] Taken together, these texts form a kind of core Augustinian canon, a syllabus of English works devoted to the disciplines of self-conscious reformation in the image of God. At the beginning of the sixteenth century, this would be the kind of spirituality that the humanist circle associated with Syon—including Margaret Beaufort, Bishop Fisher, and Sir Thomas More—would work to promote in England, using sermons, the power of the new presses, and the tremendous spiritual prestige of Syon and its libraries.

It was in the early sixteenth century that Carthusian James Grenehalgh—whose annotations in Joanna Sewell's copy of the *Scale of Perfection*

I have already had occasion to mention (what *is* the inner eye, anyway?)—made a trefoil in the same text next to the heading, "How a man shall see the grounde of synne wythin hymself." Grenehalgh added this notation: "se wele fro this to the end of the first boke & begyn at such a sygne."[68] Just as William Langland encodes his own proper name near the enigmatic mirror of Christ, so too Joanna Sewell's spiritual director and close friend encodes her name at the intersection of textual meditation—"se wele fro this to the end of the first boke"—and penitential self-reflection—"see the ground of synne wythin [your]self." Long Will has lived in land; Joanna Sewell sees well, and what she sees is herself, by means of a text. The book doubly reflects her: it has her name repeatedly, playfully, and artfully inscribed on its pages by someone she seems to have been close to, and it offers her a mirror in which she is asked to search for the image of sin within herself. It may even invite reflection on that very doubleness: the enigma of temporal and spiritual identity—a self who owns a book, a self who is in a book—that is Joanna Sewell.

Grenehalgh's wordplay evokes a conundrum of reception that we can hardly avoid nor really hope to answer. What might be the effect of the specular discipline promoted by *The Myroure of Oure Ladye* and other Syon texts as the best way to worship, read, live? Who *is* Joanna Sewell, and what does she see? Does all this focus on the self—beholding it, laboring in it, conforming it, remembering it—encourage a more intense interest in one's own temporally incarnated existence? Something, perhaps, like the scene depicted in a French manuscript of Boccaccio's *De claris mulieribus* (finished in 1420), in which the nun Marcia is shown painting her own portrait with the aid of a convex mirror?[69] As Gibson reminds us, the Virgin Mary was at the heart of fifteenth-century incarnational devotion; "mediating the dizzy distance from heaven to earth," her human life, joys, and sorrows were elaborated in English art, drama, and poetry in ever more specific and subtle detail.[70] The Marian mirror took in light and made it visible *as flesh*, fusing inner and outer, contemplative seeing and bodily showing. Is this, in part, how Joanna Sewell "saw" herself?

Or does the specular regime erase any sense of individual or bodily particularity by constructing the private self as an internalized image of the ideal, a communal ritual more perfectly assimilated? In the previous chapter I described *The Myroure of Oure Ladye* as one of those Lancastrian texts that sought to bring inner and outer into transparent harmony through targeted use of the vernacular, infusing liturgical participation with the cachet of private devotion and the power of shared emotional experience. Even as Henry V promoted English as the language of national community, this translation of the hours and masses of the Virgin as they were used at Syon presented its readers with an English template for monastic identity, allowing them to "see" Mary's presence in their Service so as to conform themselves more accurately to her image, and to "show" her in their oral performance. Krug has argued that the *Myroure* seeks to make the daughters of Syon "as similar as if they were mass-produced in God's factory,"[71] and indeed, the text's use of the mirror to link inner seeing with outer showing seems paradigmatic, not only of the monastic ideal of depersonalized identity, but also of a Lancastrian world where external obedience is not enough, where both secular and sacred authorities seek new ways of penetrating the privileged space of the interior in hopes of making it transparently visible to the outside.

Yet the work is more complicated than this, too, both because the textual and conventual world it speaks to is so complicated, and because the tropes it utilizes—vision, reflection, reformation, inwardness—are already so freighted, so complex. Ultimately, the adoption of the mirror trope as a controlling metaphor for corporate liturgical practice, affective visionary experience, and readerly intellectual insight makes a transparent link between private and public identity impossible, even undesirable; the two images are not, cannot be, the same. The rational soul may be a stamped penny, but readers of Hilton know that that penny is irretrievably hidden in the depths of the self; it is not available for clear outward projection. Krug herself observes that the *Myroure*'s ostensible attempt to mass-produce corporate selves at Syon does not seem to have worked very well—why, she asks, did sisters keep writing their names in books, when the Rule specifically forbids private property?—but she locates the disruption in secular conditions (like strong family identity): conditions originating outside the abbey and developing gradually over the course of the fifteenth century.[72] I think it a mistake to set the disruptive patterns of the secular world against the conformist machinery of the convent, the regulatory mechanisms of the text. This convent's intense vernacular devotional culture was surely disruptive enough. If the Bridgettines brought other kinds of identity with them to the convent, they learned there how to be more conscious of them, not less.

This still does not solve our conundrum of reception, which depends on a hopeless number of personal and social variables. For his part, the *My-*

roure's author observes that even one person is "contrary and diverse in himself," and that the diversity between people is much greater (151). Because a given text might apply to them or affect them differently depending on who they are and how they are feeling, he advises the Bridgettines to evaluate themselves before choosing reading material. Liturgical emotion may be tightly regulated and unified, but private reading is left open to individual inclination. If the *Myroure*-author cannot imagine a perfectly stable and coercive reading environment, we probably should not either. He might try to limit visionary authority in the convent, and he certainly does his best to connect the image of the literate and inward subject with that of the collective body. But he does not want his readers to cease meditating on their own particularity. It is worth noting that the only surviving manuscript copy of the *Myroure* bears the name of Sister Elizabeth Monton, who inscribed her particular ownership of this particular book at the end of the first volume.[73]

To consider this question from a different angle, however, I would like to return to *The Cloud of Unknowing*, whose author we met in Chapter 1, satirizing the ignorant in pursuit of inwardness. What does a contemporary writer say about the effects of all this labor in the self, all this looking in the mirror? What versions of identity does *he* think it might produce? The *Cloud*-author presents the case *against* self-envisioning—and he does so in part on the grounds that the introspective, self-reforming subject is a personal, even an autobiographical one, and thus irreparably separated from God. The *Cloud*-author's pursuit of blindness and forgetting helps to illuminate what is at stake in the more typical English devotional obsession with reading and seeing.

No Book, No Mirror: *The Cloud of Unknowing* and the Rejection of "Self in Special"

Medieval mystics seeking union with God through the oblivion of self often spoke of that oblivion as a termination of vision. Marguerite Porete, for example, writes that in the sixth stage of mystical ascent the soul no longer sees: God sees her, and he sees only himself in her. While obviously speaking to the Pauline perfection of vision, Porete also participates in a long tradition of equating the highest levels of contemplation with blindness. In Hugh of St. Victor's formulation, "The eye of the flesh is open, the eye of reason runs, the eye of contemplation is closed and blind."[74] The fourteenth-century English *Cloud of Unknowing* offers one of the most extensive meditations on mystical blindness in this period, turning the suppression of visual understanding, imagination, and memory into the dominant imperative of contemplative life. In doing so, it reflects contemporary fascination with the visual and its role in structuring human interiority.

The *Cloud* designates four stages of the spiritual life in theory, but only three in practice. In theory there are lower and higher actives, and lower and higher contemplatives. In practice, however, the higher actives and lower contemplatives occupy the same plane; we might be tempted to call that plane "the mixed life." Here are the literate nuns and anchoresses, the secular priests, lay brothers, devout gentry, widows, merchants—anyone, that is, who aspires to more than a rudimentary understanding of his or her faith (lower active), but is not mystically united to God (higher contemplative).

The *Cloud*-author then assigns a spatial position to each of these three stages. In the lower active life, a man is outside himself and beneath himself. In the higher contemplative life, a man is above himself and under God. But in the active-contemplative middle, a man "is with-inne him-self & even with himself."[75] It is to the middle people—the people within themselves—that the realm of subjectivity belongs, created and maintained by visuality, by "goodly goostly meditacions, & besy beholding" (31–32). These souls see their own sinfulness in Christ's Passion and God's word: "Goddes worde, outher wretyn or spokyn, is licnid to a mirour. Goostly, the ighe of thi soule is thi reson; thi concience is thi visage goostly. . . . With-outen redyng or heryng of Godes worde, it is inpossible to mans understondyng that a soule that is bleendid in custom of synne schuld see the foule spot in his concyence" (72–73). Like Augustine and the *Myroure*-author, the *Cloud*-author asserts that interiority comes from self-reflection, and that self-reflection is made possible by the mirroring function of the text, oral or written. A person is "within himself and even with himself" through visual, textual reflection.

But as the *Cloud*-author observes, "it is not so with hem that contynuely worchen in the werk of this book" (72). This text is not focused on the middle ground, and thus is not concerned with vision or reading or interiority or the self—except insofar as it strives to get rid of all of them together. The work of advanced contemplatives is in "*blynde* felynges of theire owne wrechidnes, or of the goodnes of God *with-outyn* any menes of redyng or heryng comyng before, & *with-outyn* any special beholdyng of any thyng under God" (72–73, emphasis mine). They seek to be not even with but *above* themselves, as language and vision fall utterly away. For the *Cloud*-author's goal is to dissolve the particular self, which is the greatest barrier to mystical "oneing" with God. Continental mystics described it as being ravished above the self, drunk with love, emptied out, or melted like wax. Marguerite Porete's *Mirror of Simple Souls* exhibits a typically Dionysian disdain for the mundane struggles of desire and will:

And again I say that even if they drive themselves each day with themselves to enlarge upon the perfection of the apostles by the effort of the will, they will not be unencumbered from themselves. . . . Truly not, says Love, since rudeness and the disputes about the interior life do not give deliverance, one cannot return there no matter what is done with oneself, it will still only be self-encumbrance. Those know this who undertake works with themselves without the whirling fiery ardor of the interior life.[76]

The *Cloud*-author also considers the self an encumbrance: a "foule stinkynge lumpe," a "hevy birthen" that prevents the soul's absorption into the Godhead (84). "Fle fro thi-self as from venym," he advises.[77]

And because it is *beholding* that creates and maintains interiority and memory, the erasure of vision becomes the soul's most important task. "Blind" is the *Cloud*'s mantra, repeated again and again. The reader must "put down all such beholdings, be they never so holy" and "let that meek derknes be thi mirour & thi mynde hole" (34, 136). For when the soul sees itself in "special beholding," it learns not only that "I am & I see & fele that I am . . . bot so I am & so & so & so & so" (141). It sees the "sotil condicions of the myghtes of thi soule & theire worchynges" (119), the "queinte qualities" and the "diverse corious meditacions of the qualities of thi beyng; the whiche . . . ben ful diverse and scateryng from the perfeccion of onheed" (140). Seeing is the condition of fragmentation, isolation, and particularity. It foregrounds loss; it inspires language.[78] Even seeing Christ's Passion is dangerous, for one beholding leads to another and quickly turns into looking back at the self: "he wil lat thee see thin olde wrechid living; & paraventure, in seing and thinkyng ther-of, he wil bryng to thi mynde som place that thou hast wonid in before this tyme. So that at the last, er ever wite thou, thou schalt be scaterid thou wost never where" (27). It may seem odd that a vision of Christ should evoke memories of particular *places*, but from the end of the twelfth century, confessional literature had been concerned to evoke the circumstances of sin: the *quis, quid, ubi, quando, cur, quomodo,* and *quibus adminiculis.* Its particular social dimensions were emphasized: what was the sinner's status? who else was involved?[79] So that if beholding Christ results in a beholding of the self in sin—the foul spots on one's inner countenance—it will very properly be a particular beholding, involving such distractions as the place where the sinner used to live (*I have lived in londe*), the things he used to do. In no time, the beholder is involved in his former sins all over again, caught up in the memory of his former self—like Augustine in the *Confessions,* remembering his youthful theft of pears and what that meant. His sins mark him out, defining the contours of a life en-meshed in history and allowing for the split between self-as-subject and self-as-object, which enables the confession of a life, an autobiographical stance. Sin, as the *Cloud*-author observes, is "onyd & congelid with the substaunce of thi beyng" (79). Sin is autobiography, and he wants none of it. Mary Mag-dalene was the worst of sinners, he asserts, but what did that matter? "Cam sche therfore doun fro the height of desire into the depnes of hir sinful liif, & serchid in the foule stynkyng fen & donghille of hir synnes, serching theim up be one & be one, *with alle the circumstaunces of hem,* & sorowed & weep so upon hem ich one bi hem-self? Nay, sekirly sche did not so" (46, emphasis mine). Instead of dwelling on the foul memory of her sins, trying to gain forgiveness but probably only inspiring herself with the will to sin again, "sche heng up hir love & hir longing desire in this cloude of unknow-ing, & lernid hir to love a thing the which she might not se cleerly in this liif bi light of understondyng in hir reson, ne yit verely fele in swetnes of love in hir affecion; in so mochel tht sche had ofte-tymes lityl specyal mynde whether that ever sche had ben a synner or none" (46). In Mary's languish-ing desire for God, she never sees herself at all. She has no "special mind" of herself or her sins; she has no "special beholding" of Christ, of either the beauty of his body or the horror of the crucifixion (47). Mary Magdalene shows readers how *not* to dig for the dark inner roots of sin, how *not* to search for Christ, how *not* to behold themselves. The contemplative cannot reconstitute the sins of the past in a former self, for to do so is to reify that self and make her part of the present. Thus the discursive, rational mind, which for Augustine reflects most clearly the image of the Trinity, is for the *Cloud*-author a hindrance. Feeling, not seeing; desire, not reason and mem-ory, leads to union with God. "Oneing" is impossible if the bounded self, in all its "special qualities"—its language, its will, its history, its vices and virtues—persists.

Unitive mysticism was not a popular phenomenon anywhere in Europe, but it seems to have been even less so in England.[80] Wolfgang Riehle, discussing the connections between Continental and English mysticism, has observed that "the spatial concept of emptying oneself (of all earthly images and ties) is rarely retained in translations into English."[81] We might simply assume that this stage of contemplation was felt to be irrelevant to the unadvanced readers of English prose, yet in popular treatises like the *Chastising of God's Children*, what we find is not mere omission, but active hostility.[82] The *Chastising* excoriates those who seek "a fals ydelnesse as for her perfeccion" (130). These "naked unbesiers" think they are the highest contemplatives, trying to forget themselves by living in blindness, idleness, and silence. They live without exercises, without working, and without the constant accusations of conscience. They have voided themselves, which goes against good love, fervent charity, "and the inward worchyng and touchyng of the grace of god" (131). Such practice, explains the writer, "brynggeth a man into suche *blyndenesse* that nought he shal knowe, and into a maner bowyng dounward to himsilf and into himsilf, without any dedis or werkis. This reste is nat ellis but a maner *ydelnesse* in himsilf, and a *voydance of hymsilf, forgetyng hymsilf,* god and al other thynge. This reste is contrarious to the reste of god, for the reste in god, which is above kynde, is a loueli *biholdyng* into an high cliernesse that may nat be comprehendid" (emphasis mine).[83] Unlike its principal Continental source, the *Chastising* contains no positive representations of unitive mysticism—only warnings against blind un-busiers who have no interiority, who have no selves, because they have chosen not to see. It is not so much that self-emptying is not a possibility for these particular readers, as that it is a false goal.

Though it eventually achieved wide circulation in both manuscript and print, the *Chastising* was originally written for nuns, and it was available at Syon. I began my discussion of the *Myroure* by quoting the *Chastising*'s conservative advice about the relative merits of Latin and English prayer; yet in many other ways, the two texts are strikingly similar. Both are concerned with the balance between inner and outer, though they do not come down in quite the same place. Both are engaged, cautiously, with Continental mystical traditions and the possibility of visionary activity. And both center their disciplinary programs around a scene of envisioning that is not quite "visionary."

Each of the *Chastising*'s twenty-eight chapters ends with the same admonition: "wake and pray, that ye fall not into temptation. *Vigilate et orate, etc.*" The verse is Matthew 26:41, and it invokes a favorite scene of prayer (and chastising). That scene is the Agony in the Garden, when Christ is praying at Gethsemane before his arrest. As Christ prays, the disciples repeatedly fall asleep. Each time, Christ rebukes them sorrowfully, telling them to "wake and pray." The scene defines prayer as a discipline of constant watchfulness, and its mantra is well suited to the *Chastising*, which also privileges the state of looking and seeing: "Chastising opens the eyes."[84] But like the *Myroure of Oure Ladye*, the *Chastising* directs the reader's watchful gaze constantly back toward the self, defining prayer as a vigilant inward vision that is also the key moment of self-discipline. "It is ful nedeful," the writer admonishes, ". . . that wiseli we deeme ouresilf first of ony thyng, and slighli serche oursilf that we see and knowe what we be withinne" (184). Struggle and temptation, constantly analyzed, constitute a state of grace: "A spirit troubled is a sacrifice to God" (216).[85]

And a troubled soul, importantly, is a *busy* soul, always laboring, working in itself like a bee storing honey for the winter. In language reminiscent of *Piers Plowman* or *Wynnere and Wastoure*, the text castigates the contemplative who "abidith stille as a deed stok or another instrument, that lieth stille ydel til the werker cometh and settith it awerke" (140). If it seems that busy exercises belong to the outer life, the writer is quick to point out the error of that assumption: it is the idle man who "forsakes himself inward." Like the Syon nuns who labor busily in the library and in themselves, the *Chastising*'s inward man is too troubled, too conscious of his fallen state, too involved with the "accusations of conscience," to allow himself any leisure, external or internal. The typical vocabulary of virtuous industry to be found in English devotional texts—busyness, labor, digging, working—harnesses terms more broadly associated with social idealism to a program of contemplation and spiritual progress. ("Thou shalt ever ioy at even," writes Thomas à Kempis, "if thou spende the day fruytfully.") No doubt this made such works more appealing to those in the "mixed" life: men and women who were certainly busy, and whose favorite images of the spiritual life thus reflected a belief that even the inner life ought to be as unceasingly vigilant and industrious as possible. The specular imperatives of texts like the *Chastising* and the *Myroure* created a kind of busy inward beholding that was easily transferable to the doubled, mixed selves outside the convent: selves intensely mindful of the ideal and the real, and the distance between them.

Gibson describes fifteenth-century English culture as having an "incarnational aesthetic," an "ever-growing tendency to transform the abstract and theological to the personal and concrete."[86] We see the tendency in Hilton's works, where Trinitarian and Christocentric devotions collide, where Hilton cannot seem to choose between Augustinian and affective meditation. We see it in *Piers Plowman*, where the abstract and the autobiographical jostle one another in social and theological speculation. The same quarter-century that produced *The Myroure of Oure Ladye* also produced Margery Kempe's magnificently detailed self-narrations and Thomas Hoccleve's moody auto-biographical poems. Especially given the *Cloud*-author's insistence that looking at oneself is inevitably about the particular "so and so and so and so" of personal experience, we might assume that the injunction to see one-self in the mirror would indeed have been subject to the personal and con-cretizing tendencies of an incarnational age.

I want to conclude, then, with a brief nod to the body, as it is tied up in notions of selfhood and identity. The *Cloud*-author is deeply concerned with the endless particularities of bodily behavior. He inveighs against those who

writhen here hedes onside queyntely, & up with the chin; thei gape with theire mouthes as thei schuld here with hem, not with here eres. Som, when thei schulen speke, poynted with here fyngres, or on theire fygres, or on theire owne brestes, or on theires that hei speke to. Som kan nouther sit still, stonde stylle, ne lige stille, bot yif thei be outher waggyng with theire fete, or elles sumwhat doyng with theire handes. . . . Som ben ever-more smyling & leighing at iche other worde that thei spike, as thei weren gigelotes & nice japyng jogelers. (99)

He condemns these gestures and expressions not because they are inherently sinful, but because "they be governers of that man that doth hem," habits that he cannot give up. They become tokens of personality, inextricable from the self. We still locate personality in gesture and expression, the way a particular person inhabits his or her skin. So does Chaucer, who uses such small details—the way the Pardoner stretches out his neck, the Prioress's prim lip-wiping—as an effective shorthand for character. In an incarna-tional and Chaucerian age, this must have been part of what it meant to be "within yourself and even with yourself," as readers found themselves re-flected in mirrors both spiritual and material, exemplary and reflexive, com-pendious and particular. If the *Myroure* can turn the vision of textual understanding and affective visionary experience back upon the self, then the proliferation of mirrors and other tropes of introspection in late medieval English texts, to say nothing of their proliferation in material culture, has the potential to shift the meaning of both vision *and* inwardness for a broad range of readers, reflecting a wide array of "queinte qualities," "sotil condicions," and "diverse corious meditacions," all meaning somehow that "I am & I see & fele that I am."

Chapter 3
Private Passions

The crosse therfore is ever redy . . . thou maiste not flee hit: whereever thou renne and wherever thou come, thou berest thiselfe with thee, and ever thou shalte fynde thiselfe. Turne thiselfe above, turne thiselfe bynethe, turne thi selfe outwarde, turne thi selfe inwarde; and in alle thes shalte thou fynde the crosse.

—*The first English translation of Thomas à Kempis's* De Imitatione Christi

We have been trying to understand inner gymnastics, invisible labours of concentration which are to us most strange.

—*Frances Yates,* The Art of Memory

While the Bridgettines at Syon were learning to see themselves in the mirror of the Virgin Mary, a Benedictine monk named John Lydgate was searching his own memory for the image of Christ. Like the Bridgettines, this prolific poet played an important role in the production of fifteenth-century English devotion. Like them, he enjoyed Lancastrian patronage and helped to foster that dynasty's reputation for nationalistic piety. And as we saw in Chapter 1, he shared their concern with enhancing and promoting particular models of interiority. He was as connected to the secular world by his writing as the Bridgettine sisters were by their reading.

Lydgate's *Testament*, moreover—the closest thing to a spiritual memoir the Benedictine ever wrote—both obeys the devotional exhortation to *see* oneself and affirms the grounds of the *Cloud*-author's critique: vision and memory enable Lydgate's relation to an ideal self, but they also confirm and even romanticize his particular separateness. Combining personal memory and confession with a beholding of the Passion, Lydgate's poem elaborates, however ambivalently and awkwardly, the essential connection between self and cross that will be the theme of this chapter. If Langland's Long Will never saw Christ truly but as himself in a mirror, Lydgate's *Testament* proceeds from the corollary assumption that he can never see *himself* truly except in the mirror of Christ. It will be worthwhile to consider Lydgate's recollections briefly here, as a link between the mirrors of Syon and the Passion meditations to follow.

The *Testament of Dan John Lydgate* (ca. 1459) is a meditation in five parts: two sections of memory and confession in rhyme royale (the "I, John Lydgate" sections), sandwiched between three sections of prayer to Christ in eight-line stanzas.[1] This formal dialectic between Lydgate and Christ is further complicated by the doubling of both figures. The Christ figure of the first section is a glittering imperial conqueror, liberally ornamented with classical allusions, who recalls the kings and heroes of Lydgate's secular poetry. This Christ inhabits the petitionary "now" of Lydgate's humble old age. The second Christ is a defeated, wounded body that Lydgate remembers seeing on a crucifix long ago, when he was just a boy.[2] This memorial image asks the wide-eyed child to behold his meekness "and leve thy pryde," to "gyf me thyn herte and be no more unkynde" (746, 869). His is the "pietous" but insistent exhortation to *see* that fills Lydgate's final meditation:

Beholde my woundes, behold my blody face,
Beholde the rebukes that do me so manace,
Beholde my enemyes that do me so despice. (756–58)

The two versions of John Lydgate, then, stand in inverse relation to the two Christs. The broken Christ on the crucifix, crowned with thorns, hangs before the eyes of a wild, jolly child, crowned with flowers, and asks piteously for his love.[3] The unwounded conqueror, on the other hand, receives petitions from a sick old monk whose mind is a great, gaping wound of remembrance and regret.

Memory connects these figures and allows for the transactions of life and energy, power and wounding between them. If Christ is to remember Lydgate, Lydgate must remember himself, and so the Boethian scene is set: as Lydgate lies sick and complaining in his bed, the Lady Memory appears,

Clad in a mentell, a woman sad of chere,
Blak was her abyte, sobre of countenaunce,
Straunge of hir porte, froward of dalyaunce,

Castyng here looke to meward in certeyne
Lich of me she hadde but disdeyne. (264–68)

Like Lady Philosophy, who directs an aged Boethius to "uncover his wound," Lady Memory prompts the aged Lydgate to reflect on the circumstances of his life. Unlike Boethius, however, Lydgate uncovers not a history of injustice and suffering, but one of pleasure and nostalgia. Memory carries him back to an exuberant Chaucerian springtime, "whiche sesoun prikkes fressh corages" (297). There, young John frolics like an unbridled colt—fighting, lying, breaking hedges, playing tricks and cherry-stones, avoiding bedtime, arriving unwashed at the dinner table. (Like Augustine, he is a stealer of fruit.) Memory ought to be stern reckoning for time wasted, "talent" misspent (220).[4] Instead, it becomes unvarnished yearning for a world where honeysuckle and primrose open against the sun, where birds salute the season with motets and carols and Aurora bedews the green world with silver liquor. In "this quykyng sesoun, nutrityf and good," children are "grene, fressh, and delyver of corage"—and inclined to cavort like wanton apes through anybody's grape arbor, heedless of walls and hedges or schoolmasters and sacring bells (311, 308). The portrait is of a familiar type, to be sure—but it is unmistakably infused with Lydgate's own pride in himself, not merely as an energetic child, but as a poetic maker: a master of difficult stanzas, of Chaucerian eloquence and ornament. Only thus obliquely does Lydgate acknowledge his particular history as a poet, a history that otherwise has no place in his narrative.

But after seventeen springtime stanzas, Lydgate stops to pray once more for a proper wound, asking for the name of Christ to be carved freshly into the midpoint of his mind. Carried away by the memories that accompany his reckoning, old Lydgate begs for a change of heart: "Brydel myn outrage under thy disciplyne; / Fetre sensualite, enlumyne my resoun" (448–49). He asks Christ as carpenter and "artificer" to "Repare my thought, broke with mysgovernaunce, / Visite my soule, my herte of stele to breste" (554, 556–57). Praying to be broken and repaired, re-engraved and re-imprinted, Lydgate imagines Christ as a fellow maker—one who seems to compete with Lydgate's own power to craft himself in memory, to enhance his recollections with lavish classical allusions and loving Chaucerian flourishes. As a young monk, Lydgate confesses, he preferred vain fables to holy histories (721, 729)—a preference, it would appear, that still colors his ability to remember himself.[5]

Young Lydgate not only gravitates toward the wrong kind of art, though; in an important sense, he *is* the wrong kind of art. Although he took up the habit of religion, he relates, his outward show merely counterfeited an inner "entent" (704):

Of religioun I wered a blak habite,
Only outward as be apparence,
To folowe that charge savoured but ful lyte,
Save be a maner connterfete pretence;
But in effecte ther was non existence,
Like the image of Pygmalyon,
Shewed lyfly, and was made but of ston. (691–97)

The Pygmalion image echoes and inverts a simile from twenty lines earlier, in which Lydgate had compared himself to Lot's wife, frozen in the act of looking back (676).[6] While Pygmalion's lover is a dead image that becomes a woman, Lot's wife is a woman who becomes a dead image. Lydgate himself, meanwhile, is still looking back. Presumably his looking has been transformed. Yet if his chief crime as a young monk was to make himself double and counterfeit, splitting body from heart and outward pretense from inner inclination, his current reflections seem to do much the same thing, separating his present from his past and masking an eager desire to re-live behind the somber intention to confess. The false young monk who wears the black habit and sober face of religion looks suspiciously like the lady Memory, with her sweeping black "habit" and sober countenance, casting a disdainful look while actually enabling a poetic infatuation with the past.

In the midst of his remembering and writing, however, Lydgate stops short—confronted by the image of the crucifix he saw as a child, an image glossed by the word "*vide*": behold. Only later, he relates, did he understand the meaning of that command, and when he did, he took pen in hand and wrote a "litel dite" to which he now turns, abandoning his past altogether except for the remembered verses of this song, written for the vivid memory of that terrible image (753). The word "*vide*" becomes an English Passion meditation of eighteen stanzas. The image is newly engraved and—to extend the Pygmalion metaphor—as it becomes a living, bleeding body, so too Lydgate's own mind is re-engraved, his stone heart broken. Christ becomes the poem's first-person voice, while Lydgate—an "I" no longer—never speaks again. The new "I" invites the poet to "turne home agyen," in a corrected version of the action of Lot's wife (866). "Tarye no lenger," Christ admonishes the aged poet; "[h]ast on thy weye and be of ryght good chere" (890–91). The heavenly court waits for him, and tarrying no longer, the poet finishes his *Testament*.

The poem speaks to the difficulties—even for a monk, even for Lydgate—of negotiating confessional history and personal memory through the ambivalent transactions between real and ideal selves.[7] The poet is haunted by memories of a false self that pretended and counterfeited, that was divided between outward show and inner intent. Confessing should help to heal the divide—he must see himself as he was—and yet doing so seems only to reconstitute the earlier self, reifying it as a dead image in stone or salt or verse. Is personal memory a first step or a false one? The broken Christ who can make Lydgate whole is an image recovered from his personal memories, inextricable from his penitential, if deeply nostalgic, reflections. That image must be rhetorically vivified through a painful process of recollected seeing, understanding, and writing, as Lydgate works himself up to breaking his own heart. The confessional poem can then become an exemplary narrative, suitable for other readers—and even for the cornice scrolls in the Clopton chapel at Long Melford, where it directed the literate visitor's penitential response to nearby images of pietà and Passion.[8] The *Testament* is a tool Lydgate uses to act on himself and others, and part of its lesson is about the way readers change themselves through the processes of meditation and desire, taking up various voices in turn—conventional ones, personal ones—to transform memory and inclination. It is significant that Lydgate's struggle to do so takes place in the context of a first-person confrontation with and meditation on the Passion of Christ.

For as the growth of vernacular literacy wrought its complex changes across the English religious and literary landscapes, it was Passion meditation above all other exercises that came to be considered the ideal focus of private devotion, particularly for mixed-life readers.[9] The devotional climate of late medieval England generated a massive demand for vernacular Passions that would continue unabated through the Reformation, and it was in this context that the visual and self-reflexive imperatives promoted across English devotional discourse were at their strongest. Nowhere were late medieval English readers enjoined to "behold" more frequently or more searchingly. The Passion became the preeminent place of self-reflection and self-reformation for English religious culture. At the heart of late medieval tendencies toward the affective and the personal, it had immense potential for defining the territory of the interior that English spiritual writers were so concerned to locate, enhance, and circumscribe for their readers.[10]

That potential was especially powerful in texts using the first-person voice to script readers' private responses to visions of Christ and themselves. The "I" of Lydgate's *Testament*, while exemplary, is still "John Lydgate," but the "I" of many Passion meditations is any reader's, and every reader's alone. If treatises like *The Myroure of Oure Ladye* or the *Scale of Perfection* exhorted readers to see themselves, meditations like *The Prickynge of Love* and *A Talkynge of the Love of God* actually talked them through it, using intimate, emotional soliloquies to construct the inward gaze and voice. Passion meditations were in effect the major psychological narratives of the later Middle Ages, elaborating readers' dramatic reactions not only to the torture and death of Christ, but also to the trauma of birth and separation, the yearning for absorption in the body of the other, the pain of erotic longing, and the anguish of self-recognition. This chapter considers how English meditations made "strange images of death," as Vincent Gillespie has memorably called them, into the wellsprings of the inner life, the psychic dramas of the everyday Christian self.[11]

Passion Meditation in English

Although this chapter explores only a few meditations, I want to emphasize that these were part of a broad and vibrant genre, with roots stretching back through the long and still vital tradition of Latin Passion writing in England. English recluses had been meditating on the Passion since at least the eleventh century, and Latin remained the language of most English meditations throughout the period.[12] By the fourteenth century, however, the Passion was coming to be considered an ideal subject for lay and female devotion—anchored as it was in the humanity, rather than the divinity, of Christ.[13] It was also central to the spirituality of the Franciscans, whose intense identification with the human Christ shaped their pastoral mission of creating compassion and contrition in the hearts of the laity. It was in the fourteenth century, then, as the vernacular audience developed and the Franciscan program really took hold, that English-language meditations began rapidly to multiply. The first translation of the crucifixion narrative from the pseudo-Bonaventuran *Meditationes Vitae Christi* was completed around 1320, and it would influence English treatments for the rest of the period. (It was followed by at least six other Middle English versions.)[14] Prose Passions such as the two attributed to Richard Rolle soon joined verse texts such as the anonymous *Meditations on the Life and Passion of Christ.* From the north came the *Northern Passion*; from the south the *Southern Passion* and *The Passion of Our Lord.* Older meditations were rediscovered, translated, updated: St. Edmund's thirteenth-century *Mirror of Holy Church*, for example, became suddenly popular.[15] Two meditations from the thirteenth-century "Wooing Group" were transformed into *The Talkynge of the Love of God.* The Franciscan *Stimulus Amoris* became *The Prickynge of Love.*

The multiplication of vernacular Passions did not end with the fourteenth century. Bridget of Sweden's *Revelations* enhanced fifteenth-century English meditations with new details. Her gory descriptions were excerpted and combined as "The meditacion of oure lordis passyon," and she was also credited with authoring the popular "Fifteen Oes."[16] These snippets of abstract, affective meditation appeared in four English versions—two prose and two verse—as well as in Latin, and retained their immense popularity through the Reformation.[17] From the pens of English women came the anonymous *Faits and the Passion of Our Lord Jesu Christ* and Dame Eleanor Hull's *Meditations Upon the Seven Days of the Week.*[18] From Scotland came the Passion poems of Henryson and Dunbar.[19] English translations of Ludolphus of Sweden's *Speculum Vitae Christi* and Jordanus of Quedlinburg's *Meditations* served as important sources for two of the latest and most comprehensive English treatments: Bridgettine John Fewterer's 1533 *Myrrour or Glasse of Christes Passioun* and Scottish poet Walter Kennedy's late fifteenth-century *Passioun of Christ.*[20] Most of the *ars moriendi* and books of comfort and consolation included Passion material, as did other popular devotional texts such as *The Seven Poyntes of Trewe Love and Everlastynge Wisdame.*[21] This is to say nothing of the immense body of lyrics and sermons, primers and prayers, that further elaborated English devotion to the Passion of Christ.

As this very partial overview suggests, excerpting and extracting as well as translation and adaptation fed the English hunger for Passion devotion, and such practices can tell us a great deal about devotional trends and audience expectations. As Sarah Horall has shown, for example, the Passion narrative of the thirteenth-century *Cursor Mundi* "seems to have been considered rather old-fashioned" by the end of the fourteenth century, and several scribes replaced it with more vividly emotional and affective versions.[22] In the fifteenth century, to take another example, scribes apparently felt free to choose between the two representations of Christ in Lydgate's *Testament*, generally preferring the crucified victim at the poem's end to the triumphant conqueror of its beginning. (Two manuscripts, however, preserve only the martial Christ.)[23] Or we might consider the "meditacion of oure lordis passyon," composed of several scenes from Bridget's *Revelations*. This graphic text, probably intended for laypeople, instructs its readers to apply the lessons of its bloody torture narratives to themselves just as Bridget does. *She* learns not to speak in anger or impatience—but when the angry stirrings are past, Christ tells her, she can speak as much as she likes. The cheerfully didactic ending feels strangely incongruous after the extremities of the text's imagined violence. Yet as we shall see, English lay readers were often expected to consider their own small failings in the hyperbolic terms of the Passion, and to transform narratives of frenzied emotion into the grounds of more routine self-awareness and practical imitation. English writers, compilers, and scribes made meaningful choices as they created the vast body of late medieval English Passion literature, and if we cannot always decipher their intent, we can at least attempt to describe the nature of those choices. Readers' actual experiences of the works may be likewise irrecoverable—but in the first-person voices of meditative texts, we can trace the responses of the text's ideal and expected readers, the "I's" that were in some sense readers' own. I should like to turn, then, to *A Talkynge of the Love of God*—a fourteenth-century compilation of earlier English texts for religious women, and a particularly revealing study in the expectations and objectives of English reading and Passion meditation.

"In Mind so Privily": *A Talkynge of the Love of God*

A Talkynge of the Love of God survives only in the two compendious devotional collections now known as the Vernon and Simeon manuscripts.[24] In Vernon it stands among the works of Rolle and Hilton and the *Ancrene Wisse*, and like those texts, it is rooted in the tradition of twelfth- and thirteenth-century English writing for religious women. Its two main sources are from the celebrated Wooing Group: its first section offers a mostly faithful rendition of *On Wel Swuthe God Ureison of God Almighty*, while its final section is a looser expansion of *The Wohunge of Ure Lauerd*. A shorter central section and a brief introduction are adapted from Anselm's eleventh-century *Liber Meditationum et Orationem*.

The *Talkynge* can thus be considered a "reading" of earlier meditations, in which existing devotional threads are brought together and transformed according the expectations of new readers. Our fourteenth-century writer uses the Wooing Group texts for his vision of the Passion, and for the rhythmic, ecstatic voice of erotic response. But between these texts he sandwiches Anselmian passages of abject self-consciousness, in which the rapt gaze of the viewer is forced back upon itself, and this self-reflexive vision reshapes the reader's subsequent approach to the vision of the cross. The work suggests, in ways typical of late medieval English devotion, that seeing Christ and seeing one's own image—desiring another and mourning the self—are inextricable parts of the same exercise.

It is worth pausing to consider the problems of authorship and audience. For if the Wooing Group texts were written for religious women, internal evidence suggests that the *Talkynge* was initially written for male readers, as Salvina Westra has argued. Unlike many vernacular texts, the *Talkynge* does not specify an audience, naming only "hem that hit reden" (2). But the meditative voice uses masculine terms and pronouns. The writer replaces the word "child" with "son." The reader's flesh is no longer a "whore"; neither has Christ made him "lady over all."[25] The meditative "I" describes being nailed to his order like Christ on the cross; he must be religious, perhaps a Franciscan. But what audience did the text in fact reach? The Vernon and Simeon manuscripts have often been linked to religious women—though Westra reads the continuing presence of masculine pronouns in Vernon as evidence of an audience at least not exclusively female. Other scholars have seen the two manuscripts as productions intended to reflect and shape lay devotion; Vernon has been linked to the aristocratic Bohun family.[26] Given the demand for vernacular Passion meditations, the *Talkynge*'s placement in Vernon among works popular with the laity is suggestive. But we might imagine an audience of Franciscans, other men in orders, religious women, lay readers, or all of the above.

I introduce this somewhat murky history not only because it points to the ways in which religious discourses were crossing boundaries of gender and vocation at the end of the Middle Ages, but also because the few critical discussions of *A Talkynge of the Love of God* have tended to assume that it is a straightforward work of bridal mysticism for religious women, and that its effusive meditations reflect masculine assumptions about the emotional and sexual needs of that audience.[27] These assumptions work better for the text's major sources, the *Wel Swuthe Gode Ureison* and the *Wohunge of Ure Lauerd*;

these texts offered their thirteenth-century female readers cadenced, alliterative rhapsodies on Jesus, their supremely worthy and desirable divine
spouse. The female "I" of those texts visualizes Christ's lovely face, beautiful
even on the cross. She gazes at his white body, marveling at his wealth, gen-
erosity, wisdom, strength, and bravery. "Iesu min heorte," she chants, "mine
soule hele. Swete iesu mi leof. mi lif. mi leome [light]. min healewi [balm].
min huniter [honey drop]."[28] He alone encompasses all things gentle and
love-worthy—why would a woman want anyone else? Such meditations
take the language of courtly romance, enrich it with the more actively desiring female voice of the *Song of Songs*, and use it to solidify the reader's commitment to her spiritual vocation. Within the confines of the cloister or
anchorhold, her desires can be reoriented and encouraged. Her anxieties can
be addressed: will her love be enough? Why has she not already wrapped
herself in his arms?[29] Only the purifying blood of the Passion, she concludes, can wash her clean, shut out the world, and bring her to bliss. The
courtly marriage plot helped to make the female reader a true bride of
Christ, not just symbolically or vocationally but also emotionally, imaginatively, mystically.

The *Talkynge of the Love of God*, however, is more than just a later
redaction of these bridal works. It is true that in adapting the *Ureison* for the
first part of his text, our reader/writer has changed very little. But we can no
longer imagine this as only a women's text, directed specifically at the (perceived) needs of female religious. Indeed it requires very little imagination
to see how the soliloquies might have appealed to a male religious reader, accustomed to imagining his own soul as the bride of Christ, and to styling his
religious longings as a certain kind of feminized yearning. (The interest in
Christ's masculine beauty is by no means exclusive to women's literature.)[30]
We need not even posit a homoerotic appeal for the meditation, at least not
for all of its readers. For as Caroline Walker Bynum has argued, medieval
men tended to pursue spirituality through structures of reversal: by becoming more like women, for example. This text's first-person meditations
would have allowed a male reader to step directly and intimately into a pre-
scripted "I" that reflected the inner truth of his feminine soul. In following
the *Ureison* so closely, the author of the *Talkynge* affirms the usefulness of
bridal longing and erotic praise to his own spiritual progress and pleasure.

But following his rendering of the *Ureison*, our writer makes a turn.
This narrative is not sufficient; he needs something else. And what he needs
he finds in one of the eleventh-century prayers of Anselm of Bec. (The

prayer is addressed to John the Baptist, as it happens, though no trace of the original addressee remains.) This is the moment of reorientation—the central hinge of the work—where the reader realizes that he cannot simply gaze with adoration at the beautiful body of Jesus. He needs to introduce that familiar dynamic of likeness and unlikeness, of self-envisioning and self-scrutiny. He needs to make it clear that the beloved is not only the object of vision and desire but also a mirror of the subject. Our reader must see *himself*, and what he will see is horrible. (I will continue to use the masculine pronoun for this first "reader," though subsequent readers may have been female.)

The Anselmian centerpiece begins with an address to the Virgin, for the speaker has become too wretched to address Christ directly. "Mi sunnes [sins] ben so gastliche, grisliche and grete," he mourns, they "maketh me so wlatsum [disgusting] and stinkinde foule that I ne dar him neighen [come near him] ne folwe my neode" (10). *I have embraced dirt*, he laments, and the stench of worldly filth. I am filled with horror of myself; I loathe myself; I cannot endure myself, the cause of all this sorrow and pain. And while he cannot approach Christ, his own repulsive countenance is unavoidable: "yif I seo myself, I ne may soffre my self. and yif I ne seo my self nought, thenne gyle I my self" (14). His original likeness in the image of God becomes the occasion for recognition of how far he has fallen: "thorw his grace he prented in my soule the ymage of him selve. And I enprented above the liknesse of helle. . . . hou have I chaunged that prente and dampned my selven" (12). Convinced that he has the devil's own face, he hardly knows where to look. If he beholds himself in the "develes Mirour," he sees himself with a pleasant countenance (16). But if he sees himself as he really is, he sees the changed print that he can hardly bear. "Allas my foule fulthe," he wails, "And my muchel unsleihthe [folly]. what schal I nou to rede [what plan shall I now follow]. whoder schal I now gon, wher schal I me beo tornen. Nou alle thing is thus risen ageyns me one, and wondreth thus on me" (18). Caught in the imagined gaze of "alle thing"—a gaze that magnifies the intensity of his own vision—he is utterly alone, lost and near despair. The horror instilled by this section's self-visualizing imperative is barely attenuated by the final, half-hearted reassurance that the mercy of the Virgin and her son will be enough to save him. (He does not echo Anselm in asking to be "Reconcile[d] . . . to myself.")[31]

We might consider further what our writer has and has not taken from Anselm. Anselm of Bec, archbishop of Canterbury from 1093 to 1109, is credited by R. W. Southern with having "created a new kind of poetry—the poetry of intimate, personal devotion," a genre of meditations "clearly unsuitable for public use."[32] So far this is promising territory for our fourteenth-century writer. Anselm's extravagantly emotional, deeply self-reflective prayers, with their profound interest in spiritual psychology and their professed relevance to laypeople, seem an ideal match for late medieval English devotional tastes. Anselm's prayers to the saints were meant to stir the meditative reader's heart, to create as vivid as possible an experience of horror and fear as a prelude to an outpouring of guilt, contrition, and petition. As Mary Carruthers writes, "[Anselm] scares himself, he grieves himself, he shames himself: this is literally *com-punc-tio cordis*, wounding oneself with the *puncti* of text and picture."[33] In the company of the righteous saints, the Anselmian sinner sees himself as "an intolerable horror": "I cannot fly from myself, / nor can I look at myself" (130). Powerless to save himself, all he can do is to entreat the saints for compassion and intervention.

Yet Anselm's prayers also serve as balanced arguments for mercy and reconciliation. They contend that the sinner will *not* be forgotten, largely because of the intercessory power of those benevolent saints. As Anselm confides to God, "I have a good hope that what you refuse me / on account of my sins, / you will grant me because of the merits of your friend [St. Nicholas]" (186). His meditations typically conclude with praise, hope, and gratitude. The *Talkynge*'s author has little use for this aspect of the prayers; he cares for neither the patronage of the saints nor the harmonious accord they are capable of bringing about. His genre is Passion meditation, and what he needs is a script for the wounding self-consciousness that such meditation must engender. His expectations are clear: the gruesome Passion—not the company of the glorious saints—is the proper context for abject self-reflection, a reflection bound up with the terrible longing and violence of desire. His romantic Wooing Group texts *need* Anselm's visceral abjection, and Anselm's self-wounding soliloquies need a beholding of the Passion.

Following his Anselmian interlude, the *Talkynge*'s author returns to the Wooing Group, beginning afresh with *The Wohunge of Ure Lauerd* and its alliterative love-longing for honey-sweet Jesus. But now he no longer follows his source text very carefully. The lover's emotional responses become increasingly intense. Along with the enumerations of Christ's courtly qualities, there are more interjections of "my dear one," "my sweet one," "my darling," "my lover." The lyrical opening apostrophe has more than doubled in length (I emphasize new material):

Ihesu *my derworthe lord. Ihesu myn oune Fader.* Swete Ihesu *hevene kyng.* Mi druri my derling. *Mi deoring. Mi lovynge. Myn hony brid. My sweting.* Myn hele & myn hony ter. *Min hony lyf.* Min halewy [balm]. Swettore art thou then hony *or Milk* in Mouthe, *Meode Meth or piyement madd with spices swete. Or eny lykinde licour that oughwher may be founden.* Ho ne may love, lord, thi leove *lofsum* leore. what herte is so over hard that ne may to melte in the monyg [remembering] of the, *loveliche lord.* And ho ne may love the swete Ihesu. (26)

The writing becomes more descriptive, more sensual. Where the *Wohunge*'s repeated refrain asks that the love of Jesus may be all the soul's "liking" (pleasure), the *Talkynge* adds, "Mi longyng. Mi mournynge," and sometimes, "My yeornyng." This is not mere amplification; the additions change the nature of the request, speaking not to the pleasure but to the pain of desire, the ache and absence of it. ("Longing, we say," Robert Hass writes, "because desire is full / of endless distances.")[34] The specular abjection of the central prayers seems to have conjured just such an endless distance. Bridging it will require increasingly intense desire on the lover's part—desire re-imagined as something that has to hurt. And the greater the reader's expressions of longing become, the more violently they seem to snap back toward the self.

The emotional trajectory becomes more complicated as the text approaches Christ's death for the second time. The *Wohunge*'s rendition of the crucifixion was already quite violent, part of an argument for the extreme merits of the beloved. But the *Talkynge*'s author has expanded those scenes to a gruesome and almost overwhelming extent, "with betyng & busting, and spittyng & spoutyng, with outen eny merci" (48). He adds more raving and ridicule, more descriptions of Christ's meekness and his livid, raw, stained flesh. The skin is all "to riven and to rent," and "ther stremes on uche syde a flood of water and of red blod" (48). The sinews stretch and the limbs leap out of joint; the eyes roll back as the sharp thorns are pressed into the brain. All the while, the "I" grieves heartbrokenly for his beloved and for his own sin. His heart breaks in pity; he cries to feel the pain of the wounds. Of the sixty lines leading up to the death of Christ, about two-thirds are new to the *Talkynge*, and two additional passages after it (totaling about fifty lines) repeat the trajectory, re-imagining it through the Virgin's swooning anguish as she beholds her son's body on the cross.

While characteristic of the gory excesses of many late medieval Passions, these amplifications also result from the ways in which desire and violence, reflection, identification, and self-recrimination are bound up together in this text. The "I" tortures and wounds himself by imagining the horrific wounding of his own mirror image, at once the beautiful and defiled object of his desire. He elaborates the truth of a self so violent and ugly that he can hardly bear to look at it—though look he must. Like the gruesome image on the cross, his own reflection is an intolerable but inescapable horror that he cannot flee. This is not the space of historical or exemplary narrative; despite the multiplication of tortures, there are no crowd scenes here, no frothing Jews or brutal Romans. One hardly notices the presence of anyone besides Mary, Jesus, and the "I." This is dream-space, psychic space.

And where *The Wohunge of Ure Lauerd* concludes with a final assertion of the crucified suitor's worthiness—"nis nan swa wurthi to beo luved as tu swete iesu"—the *Talkynge*'s writer breaks into yet another vision of the crucifixion, followed by still more desperate and violent expressions of love. When he sees Christ on the cross, the "I" confesses—citing the wrenched limbs, the twisted joints, the grisly face—he feels a marvelous taste of love. He sees the Virgin offering him the body to embrace as his own companion (60). His excitement intensifies: "the love teres of myn neb [face] rennen ful smerte. my song is likynge of love, al with oute note. I lepe on him raply [swiftly] as grehound on herte, al out of my self with loveliche leete [manner]. And cluppe in myn armes the cros bi the sterte [foot]. the blood I souke of his feet. that sok is ful swete. I cusse and I cluppe and stunte [stop] otherwhile, as mon that is love mad and seek of love sore."[35] This ferocious encounter, part ravishing and part devouring, is a long way from the decorous longing of the Wooing Group texts. The grayhound-like lover—the very emblem of desire—leaps on his prey, clasping and sucking. "Al out of my self," he is mad and sick and utterly out of control. (It brings to mind the *Pomander of Prayer*'s warning that inner prayer "is so laborous and so vyolente that . . . it wyll cast hym in great danger of seckness."[36]) Becoming suddenly hesitant, the lover looks to the Virgin for reassurance that such frenzy is authorized: "and heo [she] biginneth to smyle, as thaugh hire likede wel and wolde I dude more. I lepe eft [again] ther I was, and auntre [dare] me thore. I cluppe and I cusse as I wood wore. I walewe and I souke, I not whiche while [know not how long]. and whon I have al don, yit me luste more. thenne fele I that blood in thought of my Mynde, as hit weore bodilich warm on my lippe. and the flesch on his feet, bi fore and beo hynde, so softe and so swete to cusse and to cluppe." Christ's feet were a common focus of mystical desire in late medieval devotion. Margery Kempe adores the feet—probably in imitation of Mary Magdalene, who in the visual arts frequently appears under Christ's feet as he hangs on the cross. Many images of the pietà show her handling those feet while the Virgin Mary caresses the head. As Kempe recalls the scene, "And than the creatur thowt sche herd Mary Mawdelyn seyn to owr Lady, 'I pray yow, Lady, gyf me leve to handelyn & kyssyn hys feet, for at thes get I grace'" (93–94). But the *Talkynge*'s insatiable kissing and sucking goes well beyond the Magdalene's sorrowful caresses or Kempe's public foot-fondling. By the end of the text the voice of desire has been intensified and reoriented, so that a lyrical exercise in romantic yearning and wooing—designed to yield a self cleansed, comforted, and spiritually married—becomes a meditation on defilement, through an eroticism that is more about the ravenous needs of the beholder than the courtly worthiness of the beheld.

For what kinds of late medieval readers would the cultivation of such desire have been appropriate or desirable? What kind of readers would want to adopt this "I" as their own, and why would a writer want to construct their spiritual experience in this way? Our writer does not identify the future "speakers" of his passionate rhetoric. He does make it clear, however, that the experience pertains specially to the inner life, and that is meant to be strictly private. Adapting Anselm's preface for his own introduction, he explains that his treatise "is mad for to sturen hem that hit reden to loven him the more. And to fynde lykyng and tast in his love. Hit falleth for to reden hit esyliche and softe. So as men may mest *in Inward felynge and deplich thenkyng* savour fynden" (2, emphasis mine). Anselm's original language, by contrast, emphasizes the *pace* of reading: "They are not to be read in turmoil, but quietly, not skimmed or hurried through, but taken a little at a time, with deep and thoughtful meditation" (89). The *Talkynge*'s author is more concerned with *locating* the experience, a concern that surfaces repeatedly. Inward thinking and deep seeking during the reading process are followed by inward sight and feeling without any reading, "And swetnes wonderful, yif preyere folwe" (2). As we have seen, inwardness had multiple valences in English devotional writing, but the way this text constructs not only the content but the scene of its own performance makes interiority primarily a matter not of interpretive penetration nor of spiritual or rational insight, but of the inaccessibility of an individual psyche, constituted—perhaps transgressively—through the meditative encounter with the text.

In another revealing scene, the "I" is carried to the chamber of Christ, far from the false world, there to be united with him on the cross. This delicious bower is most obviously identifiable as the monastic or eremitic cell. Here is loving death, suffering and sweet reward, consummation through pain—a description that must have resonated as strongly for a fourteenth-century monk or friar as for thirteenth-century nun or anchoress. Indeed, our writer has expanded the passage considerably, meditating at length on the "love longyng" and "stille mournyng" of his vocation. There is no trace of community in the description. Christ has brought him out of the world (added material emphasized): "as thin owne derling to thin owne boure. *And as I weore thin owne brid, here in to thi cage,* to wone [live] with thi self in this holy place, *that no mon of al this world ne thar me with delen* [shares] *but thi self al one. Ihesu me deore lemmon, where that I may the sen* [see thee]. *In muynde so prively.* And wouwe the so lovely. And cluppe the swetely" (58; note that "delen" can have sexual connotations). The seeing and wooing occur, not just "in this holy place," but also "in muynde so prively," with no man in the world but Jesus. The reader is reclusive in imagination, if not in fact—a move that leaves the door open for unenclosed readers.

The climactic interaction between the soul and Christ also emphasizes private space. Perhaps disturbed by the violence of his passions, the love-maddened "I" finds himself suddenly wrapped in the comforting darkness of the Virgin's mantle: "heo openeth hir Mantel that ladi so kuynde, and happeth [wraps] us ther under in that muri fitte. yif eni mon us asketh, theer men may us fynde, as hem that lyketh ther thei ben & loth is for to flitte [leave]. Swete lemmon leove lyf. Mony wo have thei that are not holliche with the in thin holi cluppyng. But wel is me that I may ever more, niht and day, al this world forsaken. . . . I as on my Rode, sperred in myn ordre" (62). The visual imperative seems finally to relax; both the reader and the body of Christ disappear into the safe, enveloping darkness. The inner space of the order—the reader's cross but also his passionate refuge—becomes the acceptable location for and solution to his desires.

But the passage also constructs, through exclusion, the problems of those unenclosed readers whose desire for devotional contemplation and a deeper engagement with the Passion might have brought them to this text: an apparently well-respected example of a genre commonly prescribed for spiritual beginners, and conveniently available in English. *Mony wo have thei that are not holliche with the in thin holi cluppyng.* The mixed-life reader—lay or religious—might well have felt himself excluded, and lamented the many woes of his not wholly embraced self. For if the order (the birdcage, the

Virgin's mantle) is the only escape from his unbearable self-consciousness, then for the mixed-life reader there is no way out. Or rather, there is no way *in*. He (or she) remains in the space of anguished self-envisioning—where, as the *Cloud*-author might say, he is within himself and even with himself, endlessly talking out his own yearnings and frustration.

Of course, he might instead read "wholly within" as meaning wholly within the *self*, "in mind so privily." Interiority, as we have seen, was a language that made specialized religious discourses readily adaptable to broader audiences. By emphasizing the private space of reading and the inner space of the mind, this writer leaves open the possibility of something like an Abbey of the Holy Ghost, a darkly mantled birdcage in the heart. The lay-oriented *Book of Vices and Virtues* offers something along these lines, imagining the "meke herte" of the reader as a dove flying into a dovecote: "Whan the meke herte hath y-do so moche that he is entred in-to that roche as the colver in-to here colverhous, that is whan he recordeth wel the life of Ihesu Crist and his blessed passion, than forgeteth he al his woo.... The world is a prisone for hym, and to be alone is his paradise."[37] For lay readers already accustomed to thinking of their private meditations in such terms, the *Talkynge*'s final embrace might not seem so far out of reach.

The *Book of Vices and Virtues*, however, imagines that in the dovecote of Passion meditation a man is "with his tweye beste *frendes*, that is with God and hymself" (emphasis mine). If the discourse of erotic contemplation could pass relatively freely between male and female religious, its transition to lay audiences seems a greater stretch. For laywomen, the *Talkynge*'s presentation of violent longing must have seemed dramatically unlike other models of female desire and response circulating in late medieval English culture.[38] We might compare it to a work like *The Tretys of Love*, translated from a French text for an aristocratic female reader late in the fifteenth century, and printed soon after by Wynkyn de Worde.[39] In the *Tretys*, the female soul is the hard-hearted object, rather than the passionate subject, of desire. The knightly Christ covets her, sends her love letters from afar, performs feats of bravery, and finally suffers death for the love of her. He pines and complains, but the voice of the soul is never heard. She remains cold and silent, and in the end the reader is asked to pass judgment on her (on herself, that is) based on the rules of a courtly system in which she is called to serve as reward for the deserving suitor. Rather than desire, she is asked to feel pity—pity for Jesus the lover, wandering barefoot and weeping in the snow; pity for Jesus the little child, crying pathetically in his manger while she, the reader, lies in her large, warm bed; and pity for the Virgin Mary, lamenting the death of her son.

The Virgin's lament does offer a first-person female voice in the *Tretys of Love*. But her anguish is excessive, paralyzing. The reader is encouraged to pity but not to imitate her, not to assume that kind of selfish voice. The Virgin's complaint only worsens Christ's pain: "his blessid moder did him thenne more of sorow than of comforte" (63). Far better to have accepted passively her son's destiny, as the reader is cajoled to accept his love. The courtly *Tretys* translates secular ideologies of gender into the register of devotion. The domesticated response it inscribes for the aristocratic female reader throws into sharp relief the tormented voice of love from the religious tradition—radical not only in its presentation of feminine desire, but in its voicing of a feminine "I" at all. It is like comparing a silent romance heroine to Heloise.

The obstacles may have been greater still for laymen, faced with talking themselves through the dramatic rhetoric of feminine erotic desire. If for male religious, feminization created a structure of inversion across the boundaries between the world and the monastery, for laymen that structure of inversion needed to be relocated to the boundaries between private and public, or between inside and out—a move that must have strengthened those boundaries for many readers.[40] Indeed, Debora Shuger finds that well into the early modern period, "the specter of female desire is also the structure of religious (and male) subjectivity"—for males of all kinds.[41] The characteristic flexibility of gender images and pronouns in Passion texts may have helped readers to confront and somehow reconcile or interpret the differences between their social identities—with their attendant, appropriate desires—and their spiritual ones. (Shuger suggests, however, a divergence in the early modern period between the vengeful masculine allegories of the Calvinist Passion narratives—which seem to preserve the dynamics of punishment, objectification and anxiety from late medieval Passions—and an alternative model of erotic yearning.)

Part of the difficulty in pinning down late medieval English religious attitudes, then, is perhaps attributable not only to the multiplicity of religious identities during this period, but to the divisions within any single devout identity: contemplative and lay, masculine and feminine, abject and rapturous, inside and out. Gibson characterizes fifteenth-century East Anglians as people at once "indomitable and sentimental, intensely religious and rigorously practical."[42] These were the people of the Jesus masses and cults, the expensive windows and private prayerbooks. One wonders whether such people could have spoken and intensely *felt* the language of a meditation like *A Talkynge of the Love of God*, then gone to mass and headed off to daily business—satisfied that their inner selves had received a kind of deepening and enriching imprint, a taste of agonizing discomfort and "swetnes wonderful" that they could take as at least a partial, rhetorical basis for subjectivity. One wonders, too, whether they carried with them a lingering sense of alienation from their surroundings, an increased consciousness of their own emotions and impulses—a certain habit of disconcerting self-reflection. Did performing the Anselmian prayers change their own responses to the Passion, give them new lenses with which to see themselves?

Inward Vision with Desire of Heart

The transformative power of vision-with-desire was in fact one of the central tenets of late medieval devotion. Writers steeped in the traditions of visual contemplation and memory training would certainly have believed that seeing something with intense longing could imprint the beholder's heart and memory with the lingering image of the object beheld. (When Chaucer's Troilus looks on Criseyde: "of hire look in him ther gan to quyken / So gret desir and such affeccioun, / That in his hertes botme gan to stiken / Of hir his fixe and depe impressioun.")[43] This gives us another way of thinking about the amplifications of violence and desire in the late medieval practice of erotic Passion contemplation, and so I want to pause to review this tradition and its implications.

According to the ancient Neoplatonic understanding of the physics of bodily vision, the seeing eye produced a visual ray, or *species*: an emanation of the body's strongest life force that literally streamed out from the eye to touch its object and then returned to the viewer, imprinting his or her memory with the received image.[44] Subject and object touched only momentarily, but the cumulative effect of such moments was a lasting impression. By the fourteenth century, advances in the science of optics had changed people's understanding of the processes of physical vision. Yet as the visual ray was discredited in the bodily realm, it became even more ubiquitous and influential as a way of understanding the operation of the spiritual eye.[45] Augustine's writings on spiritual vision and transformation had been thoroughly informed by the Neoplatonic paradigm.[46] Positing a visual ray for the inner eye of the soul, he argued that the soul—already an image in a mirror, mutable and transient—could be transformed by what it reflected, and by what it reflected upon. The darkened image of God could be re-imprinted as a better likeness; the soul could reflect more accurately by see-ing more intensely. As Julian of Norwich writes, "the saule that thus behaldys, it makys it lyke to hym that is behaldene."[47] Or as the fifteenth-century English translator of Ruusbroec puts it, "that that we are we be-holde, and that we beholde we are."[48] Throughout the Middle Ages, vision was considered the strongest possible access to objects of devotion, an im-portant factor in later medieval theories of the image and affective piety.[49] It gave artists—and writers—a way of almost literally reaching into and *shaping* the inner selves of viewers and readers.

For Augustine, however, as for the Neoplatonists, merely seeing an ob-ject was not enough to create a strong imprint. The visual ray had to be con-centrated by strong emotion, such as fear or desire. Indeed the "visual ray" of the spiritual eye was desire itself, and that ray had to be trained and fo-cused before it could embrace its object and return a clear image or imprint to the soul. Augustine writes:

The will possesses such power . . . that it moves the sense to be formed to that thing which is seen, and keeps it fixed on it when it has been formed. And if it is so violent that it can be called love, or desire, or passion, it likewise exerts a powerful influence on the rest of the body of this living being. And where a duller or harder matter does not offer resistance, it changes into a similar form and color. Note how easily the lit-tle body of the chameleon turns very easily into the colors that it sees.[50]

The body may be hard and dull, but the chameleon soul will take the shape of any intensely viewed object. Passionate attention makes us what we are, and "the more vehement the fear or the desire, the more clearly is the eye in-formed."[51] Recalling the illicit sexual trysts of their youth, Heloise com-plains to Abelard that "Wherever I turn they are always there before my eyes, bringing with them awakened longings and fantasies which will not even let me sleep. . . . Everything we did and also the times and places where we did it are stamped on my heart along with your image, so that I live through them all again with you. Even in sleep I know no respite."[52] The abbess's heart and mind are not her own; instead, they are constituted by the lasting impact of her extraordinary desire for Abelard. Taking the veil has no im-pact on an inner self already marked by passionate vision.

The transformative operation of desire was central to the thought of spiritual writers like Bonaventure and Hugh of St. Victor, through whose influence it became widespread in both learned and popular forms.[53] We find it simplified, for example, in the fourteenth-century English treatise "How Mans Sawle is Made to the Ymage and the liknes of the holy Trinite," which observes:

> when a man is affecte or delited unordandly with a worldely desire, than on a manere he is transformed into the worlde, and is as it were in that manere even the self worlde. Here seynt Austyn saythe, that yf thou luffe the erthe or gold, thou art than erthe or gold. And yf thou luffe God, thou ert God; that is for to say, parcenere with hym by grace . . . than is a man unordandly affect or delyted in thees worldely thinges, when the forme, the shape or the lyknes of hem is undewly impressyd in hys affecyon.[54]

Catherine of Siena explains the same idea in *The Orcherd of Syon*: "Wordly men confoormen hem in al manere of wises by ynordynat love to erthely thinges, and thereby thei ben imaad al erthe. For thei han a maner of goostly inpressyoun of liknes with richesse."[55] And as we have seen, Richard Whytford defined contemplation itself as "inward lokyng with a desyre of hert," concisely summing up a vast body of vernacular devotional theory and practice.[56]

But how was such desire of heart to be generated? How could the soul's eye be focused in passionate attention? As Frances Yates and Mary Carruthers have taught us, a mnemotechnic tradition stretching back to antiquity held that the most effective way to focus the inner eye and engrave the memory was to make the images it concentrated on as vivid, graphic, and personal as possible. As the influential rhetorical treatise *Ad Herennium* puts it, "if we see or hear something exceptionally base, dishonorable, unusual, great, unbelievable, or ridiculous, that we are likely to remember for a long time.[57] Phillip Cary has suggested that Augustine's idea of the "inner self" was in fact influenced by this classical rhetorical theory and mnemotechnique—indeed, we might recall the centrality of memory to Augustine's sense of inner selfhood.[58] His model of inner vision and transformation depended on the viewer's emotional response to images—not just on the exceptionality of the images themselves—but it is a small leap from one to the other.[59] Certain kinds of exceptional images (violent rather than ridiculous, for example) would obviously work better than others. To focus the will and transform the soul, medieval devotional images would have to evoke desire, pain, pleasure, tenderness, nostalgia, or horror—the stronger the better.

Carruthers has described how, in the course of the Middle Ages, "*compunctio cordis* became elaborated in a variety of 'ways' to induce strong emotions of grief and/or fear, including an emotion-filled imagining as one recites or chants the psalms, the Passion, and other suitable texts."[60] For late medieval English audiences, the Passion was the imaginative "way" of choice. Here readers confronted the perfected image of God they needed to internalize, in a situation where violent scenarios and strong emotions could effectively imprint that image on their hearts. Innumerable English meditations and lyrics thus urged their readers to "behold" the events of the Passion and to be "imprinted" by them—works such as Lydgate's "Dolerous Pyte of Crystes Passioun," which exhorts its readers to look constantly on Christ's Passion and "Enprenteth it in your Inward sight."[61] To imprint the memory and transform the soul, Passion writers made their images as intimate, intense, shocking, and strange as possible. They urged their readers to *see* the Passion, as vividly and bodily as if they had been there themselves.

Thus the extraordinarily violent and surprising images and reactions recorded in a text like *A Talkynge of the Love of God* can be seen as mental machines for rhetorical self-transformation, for a performance of vision with desire that *changes* the reader-seer-speaker, imprinting him (or her) with longings and fantasies that stay before his eyes wherever he turns, even in sleep. The "I" of the *Talkynge* complains that he must always see himself, that he can never escape his own wretched image. But the text also ensures that the reader will never be able to escape from the image on the cross that shows him so intimately and painfully to himself. Talking himself through the vision, assuming the text's voice of desperate desire in response to it, he makes it a permanent part of his internal makeup.

Fantastic and gruesome images are also a hallmark of the *Prickynge of Love* or *Stimulus Amoris*, translated and adapted from the Latin contemplative work of the same name. Because this translation is apparently aimed at a mixed audience, it illustrates more clearly than does the *Talkynge of the Love of God* how these powerful narratives could be rendered appropriate for a broad spectrum of readers. It teaches us, that is, how to read the soulshaping techniques of Passion meditation from outside the cloister. In its difficult negotiations of erotics and ethics, mystical desire and social reality, the *Prickynge of Love* re-imagines the rhetoric of self-conscious longing as the preserve, not of the enclosed and ravished monastic interior, but of the restless, divided self outside—an "inward" self nonetheless.

The *Stimulus Amoris* in English

> *All the new thinking is about loss.*
> *In this it resembles all the old thinking.*
> —Robert Hass, "Meditations at Lagunitas"

The *Prickynge of Love* is perhaps most familiar to modern readers as an item on Margery Kempe's devotional syllabus. It was one of the many books of contemplation read to her by a willing priest, to her deep satisfaction and, as she emphasizes, *his* lasting profit—not to mention the benefit to his large congregation: "He red to hir many a good boke of hy contemplacyon & other bokys, as the Bybyl wyth doctowrys ther-up-on, Seynt Brydys boke, Hyltons boke, Bone-ventur, Stimulus Amoris, Incendium Amoris, & swech other. . . . The forseyd preste red hir bokys the most part of vii yer er viii yer to gret encres of hys cunnyng & of hys meryte. . . . Aftyrwardys he wex benefysyd & had gret cur of sowle, & than lykyd hym ful wel that he had redde so meche be-forn."[62] The work's appearance among such a formidable group of texts and writers—the Bible, Bridget, Hilton, Bonaventure, Rolle—suggests its considerable prestige in fifteenth-century England. So does its power, later in Kempe's *Book*, to convince a more skeptical priest of the legitimacy of her tears. Reading the *Stimulus Amoris* (the English version appeared under both titles), this priest learns how the soul longing for Christ cries out like a "wood man . . . in the stretys," irritating the people around him who do not perceive the desires of his heart; they do not know that he is drunk with love. "A, Lord," Kempe quotes from the *Stimulus*, "what shal I mor noysen er cryen? Thu lettyst [tarry] & thu comyst not, & I, wery & ovyrcome thorw desyr, begynne for to maddyn, for lofe governyth me & not reson."[63] The priest sees the likeness and is converted to Margery's cause. The passionate, allegorical rhetoric of Latin mysticism becomes justification for a laywoman's literal and rather obnoxious sobbing in the streets of town—a shift which is both remarkably appropriate and completely anomalous in terms of the text's translation and reception in late medieval England.[64]

The *Stimulus Amoris* was originally the work of a thirteenth-century Franciscan, James of Milan. It has been called "one of the most elegant of the formal handbooks of contemplation," and it presents its ascetic readers with rigorous instructions for their contemplative journey toward God.[65] It is a demanding work, given to extensive discussions of the horrors of sin and the necessity of obedience, and to long flights of abstract rhetoric, mystical speculation, and explorations of paradox. It is not overwhelmingly concerned with the Passion; there are meditations in two chapters, midway through the text, but although those meditations are quite famous and influential, they hardly characterize the work as a whole.

As the *Stimulus Amoris* circulated among the Franciscans, it was gradually expanded by the devotional outpourings of writers whose tastes reflected the age's growing preoccupation with Christ's humanity and Passion—and the realities of most Franciscans' active vocations. By the late fourteenth century at least thirteen chapters on the Passion had been added, along with some discussion of the mixed life and more prosaic materials appropriate for preaching and teaching. The chapters had been re-arranged, and the entire work had been attributed to Bonaventure, making it a good companion piece for the *Meditationes Vitae Christi*. At a time when English men and women were requesting Passion meditations and translators were looking for appropriate materials, it must have seemed a natural candidate. So it was that the bloated Latin compilation came to be pared down again into a much more concise and practical English treatise, emphasizing not ascetic discipline or religious obedience or mystical fusion with the godhead, but what English parishioners wanted and what those in charge of their pastoral care were concerned to provide: a Passion meditation for the mixed life. Indeed, it often circulated with Hilton's *Epistle on the Mixed Life*, and was even attributed to Hilton in four manuscripts.[66] Having crossed boundaries of time, space, language, gender, and profession, *The Prickynge of Love* came to take its place alongside Rolle, Hilton, and Bridget in the catalogue of works suitable for the instruction of laypeople like Margery Kempe.

By all accounts it was a popular and influential text. It survives in sixteen manuscripts of wide geographical distribution (eleven from the fifteenth century), alongside a broad range of other works.[67] It was owned by nuns, ladies, and prosperous commoners alike; the *Tree and Twelve Frutes* recommends it by name, assuring readers that it "shal enflawme thi soule fervently in his love. and teche thi forto despise this wrecchid world."[68] It appears in the Vernon and Simeon manuscripts, and Kempe's testimony suggests that it was available to the lay priests of East Anglia.

The translator's sensitivity to the needs of this diverse audience is evident throughout the work, as he carefully shapes, prunes, and reorients his material. He is everywhere direct, concrete, sensible, and moderate.[69] He eliminates long passages of repetitive hyperbole, tones down rhetoric, makes colorful examples out of clever metaphors and abstractions, and crafts touching, affective meditations out of allegory and paradox. *Bonitas immensa* and *summum bonum* become simply *iesu*, or *thou*.[70] Where the author of the *Stimulus* meditates hyperbolically on how any man could even *think* of giving Christ his wretchedly inadequate heart, the *Prickynge* has Christ say simply and directly, "Son gif to me thyn herte," and follows with the reader's doubtful but willing reply: "I wolde offere to the[e] my herte."[71] Satan is almost completely excised from the text, and Christ the stern judge and king has been replaced by Jesus the good shepherd, the kind healer, the friend. Demands for praise and honor have been transformed into pleas for love.[72] Derogatory remarks about women and laborers are out. So are exhortations to obedience and warnings against excessive pride in the contemplative life. Colorful descriptions of fishing nets, grain flails, and frying pans are in, as are frequent instructions to readers to act in whatever ways might be proper to their particular estate and degree.[73] Where the Latin text exhorts its readers to radical poverty, the English asks readers to be "poor in heart" and not to covet an excess of worldly goods—but not to give away their necessities either. In a typical addition, the English writer explains that "God asketh no more of us but yif we have mykel, gyve we mykel. yif we have litel, gyve we litil. yif we nought have, geve we thenne a goode wille or a good word with pite & compassioun, & that is i–nowgh" (65). Similarly, where the Latin text celebrates suffering for the souls of others, this translator adds a few sentences counseling readers who cannot preach, teach, or even perform deeds of mercy to pray, weep, "& do that thou may, & that suffiseth to the[e]" (52). If readers are unable to perform works of great holiness or self-sacrifice—"for parchaunce we are letted [hindered] for resonable causes"—it is enough that they have compassion for all in their hearts, and "specialli to hem that we knowe" (106). Radical holiness becomes domestic tenderness and social moderation, balanced carefully with the expectations of worldly obligation and identity. After strenuous meditations readers are allowed to say, "yif I mai not do this ay [always] in hoolnesse of deuocioun, ni in likynge of goostli ymaginacioun, at the laste that I mai do hit in stabilnesse of feith & in holi conversacioun."[74] Even the work's flexible pronouns, which often shift from the meditative "I" to "a man . . . he" or "the soul . . . she," position the work as accessible and encompassing.[75] (Modern research suggests that such gender-neutral practice does indeed make a difference to a reader's identification with and memory of a text.)[76]

We hear the voice of the translator—*now you should do this, here we should believe that*—trading places with the scripted voice of the reader: *now I see this, now I feel that, now I cry out in this way.*

Only once does the author say that contemplative life "hit-self is more plesaunt to god than actif life, & solitarie life more then in congregacioun" (153). But even here the statement merely qualifies a long discussion of how people come to God in sundry ways—and "whiche is better, no man wote" (149). While one chapter offers a severe critique of contemporary monastic practice, another ("How a man may in al doyngs be contemplatif") presents a stirring defense of the mixed life.[77] A person filled with Christ's love, we are told, does not differentiate "bitwixte gree & gree, woche were better than other, ne bitwene stat and staate, or lif & life, or persone & persone" (103). The mixed life is the best way to serve, and the key to that life is to imprint one's heart with a deep image of Christ that will remain fresh and painful no matter where one goes (104).[78] The visionary experiences created by Passion meditation—"when a man geder hym-self al to hym-self fro the clevynge-to of al owtwarde thynge and entre into his owne thought" (107)—transform the self inwardly, ravishing it from love of the world, so that it has no need of literal enclosure. Vision-with-desire becomes the mechanism through which an active person may achieve contemplation and inwardness while remaining in the world.

What kinds of visions, what kinds of desires, do we find in the meditations? The *Prickynge's* opening chapter takes its reader through the same kind of intense first-person exercise we found in the *Talkynge of the Love of God.* Its source is the fourteenth chapter of James of Milan's treatise, one of the two Passion meditations midway through the work. Those chapters were brought forward in the expanded Latin version and remained there in the translation, so that the text begins in something like *medias res*: not by articulating a spiritual scale, not by setting forth any preliminary discussions of contemplative life, but in the midst of rapturous meditation. The *Prickynge* begins where the *Talkynge* ends, with its reader's most fervid response to the crucifixion.

The text opens with a reminder that God's love is obtained only through the flesh of Jesus. "Prente ther-fore ihesu sadli [solemnly, fully] in thi thoughte," it advises, "for ofte mynd of his holy flesh & of his passioun shal waste in thee al fleshli & vicious love, and hit shall reise up thi desire to love of his godhead. Hit shall show hou thou shalt worche, & hou thou shalt fele, and hit shal enflaume the herte. . . . And in thought and in word and in werk hit shall reule thee" (6). So commences this new "rule" for thought, word, and work: "A thou precious Passion ful of desire. A thou deth full of love" (6–7). The reader imagines himself in the scene, first ruminating on its paradoxes (sweet bitterness, glorious shame, and so on), then reflecting on the paradoxes of his own soul (nobility and degradation), then finally beginning to participate, becoming more and more aroused as he follows the crucifixion. He wants to do everything Jesus does—to be crowned with thorns, to be cold and naked on the cross, "and he is kyndlid with a great brennynge of love." (And because we have already dealt with a similar scene in the *Talkynge of the Love of God*, there is no need to go into detail here.) At the climax of his imitation he is embraced by the dying Jesus, who raises up his head "with kissynge that is swete" (8). "A thow loveli deth," he rhapsodizes, wishing that he had been there in place of the cross. If he had been the cross he would have been buried with Jesus; nothing could have separated them, nailed fast together.

But this scripted "I" realizes that he cannot be the cross, and so he turns from Passion to nativity. (The two scenes often occurred together in the visual arts, so the meditative leap here is relatively easy.) Seeing Christ sucking at his mother's breast, he resolves to suck there too: "& thus shal I tempore to-gidere the swete mylke of marie the virgine with the blood of ihesu, and make to myself a drynke that is ful of hele." Birth and death mingle in the blood and milk, as Mary's lactating breast becomes Christ's bleeding one, and as the wounded heart is transformed in turn into an encompassing womb.[79] Recalling how Mary's soft womb nurtured Jesus, the "I" resolves to grope its way into Christ through what is now both bloody injury and birth canal, hoping to feast on a kind of placenta of charity:[80]

For on a time as I entrid in him with my eyen opened, me thoughte that myn yen were filled ful of his blod. & so I yeode in gropande, til I come to the innerest of his herte. and ther I wonne. and soche mete as he useth, I use, & drynke of the self drynke. Charite is bothe mete and drynke that hath he. & theroffe yeveth he me. there I habounde in swetnesse of his love and of his charite, so mikel that I mai not telle the[e]. & him that I eer fonde in his modres wombe, I fele now how he voucheth-saf to bere my soule as his child with-inne his blessid sides.[81]

It is a much more daring image than the maternal mantle that wrapped and hid the *Talkynge*-subject's "muri fitte" (again, at the *end* of that text). The meditator here reaches the extreme limit of his quest to be united with this multiply gendered body—to undo the trauma of identity and return to the plenitude of the mother-lover's womb. Yet almost as soon as he has reached his innermost goal, he is thrust back out again: "But I drede over-soone to be sperid out fro tho delites that I now fele. Certeynli yif he caste me ought, he shal neverthles as my modir yef me sowke of his pappis & bere me in his armes. or ellis yif he do not thus, I wot wat I shal do. I wote wel that his woundes are ai open & there-fore as ofte as I falle ought, as ofte shal I entre in ayen, un-tyl that I be unpartabelly to hym festend" (9–10). Resolving not to be thrust into a world where he cannot be certain even of a mother's comfort, he resolves to keep un-birthing himself until he is somehow re-fastened to the object of his desire.

One thinks here of the eerily despairing Old Man in Chaucer's *Pardoner's Tale*—knocking at his mother's gate, begging to be readmitted, longing for dissolution:

And on the ground, which is my moodres gate,
I knokke with my staf, bothe erly and late,
and seye "Leeve mooder, leet me in!
Lo how I vanysshe, flessh, and blood, and skyn!

. . . But yet to me she wol nat do that grace . . . (VI.729–32, 737)

Like the *Pardoner's Tale*, the *Prickynge of Love* uses the threat of the mother's rejection to highlight a terrible yearning for inclusion, respite, and comfort. It forces the meditative reader to inhabit the nightmare world of the excluded Pardoner and his deathless Old Man—if only for a moment. Then the reader, unlike the Old Man, forces his way back through the mother's gate, groping toward the place where he can escape the terrible isolation of the outside world.

It is a strange beginning. It might seem stranger still were we not familiar with the graphic maternal imagery of many late medieval female saints' lives, documented so vividly by Caroline Walker Bynum in her groundbreaking *Holy Feast and Holy Fast*. We have become accustomed to finding such language in the ecstatic visions of female mystics—and indeed, scholars have generally categorized the *Prickynge* itself as a "mystical" text, and left it at that. Vincent Gillespie, for example, finds no alternative to re-abstracting and re-intellectualizing the episode. "Through a kind of density of imagery," he writes, "the reader or meditator is provoked and challenged until a new pattern can be seen emerging from the ideas. . . . The extremity is such that the mind is almost forced to treat it mystically to defuse the aggressive physicality of the writing."[82] The fantastic, fragmented images of the Passion, he argues, facilitate "concentrated analysis," until the intellectual overload topples into enlightenment, or "the blind stirring of love."[83] Sarah Beckwith similarly emphasizes the mystical nature of the experience, remarking that the reader is "reborn and absorbed into Christ at the same time, so that the rebirth is *not* felt as a separation or bereavement" (emphasis mine).[84]

Indeed, if this episode were the climax of a Latin contemplative work, it would be easy enough to see it as a kind of interpretive conundrum designed to focus concentration, or as a daring allegory of mystical union, enacting the inexpressible violation of boundaries between the (embracing, penetrating, consuming) self and God. But as the opening salvo in a series of resolutely literal, personal, fleshly English meditations aimed at mixed-life readers, I think it does something quite different. Here, mystical discourse becomes almost its own obverse: a discourse developed to encourage the erasure of particular identity becomes instead a language of intense border anxieties. In translation, the fantasy of self-annihilation solidifies the boundaries of the self, effecting not a toppling over into the blind stirring of enlightened love, but a recognition instead of inevitable rejection, uncertainty, and longing. For though its eyes might be momentarily filled with blood, the English "I" never disappears from its own narrative view, never stops talking about itself and how it feels. Even in the womb, the infant-soul dreads violence and separation; once outside, his impossible hope is to become fastened, not melted or absorbed. And the new structure of the work—which will shift shortly into abject self-accusation—moves the reader not closer and closer to union, but farther and farther away. Instead of a mind-bending intellectual display or an expression of mystical *jouissance*, what we have in the *Prickynge of Love* is a psychological map for the re-formation of a subject. (As Catherine of Siena says in *The Orcherd of Syon*, "Thou wost wel that love causeth peyne whanne that thing is lost, to the whiche alle worldly men ben hoolly confoormyd.")[85] This powerful death-birth meditation is the text's dream of origins, of the traumatic creation of a self in the world: an outside self, or a "mixed" self, going in and out across the boundaries. Out of a deep desire to un-make the world, a world has been made.

And if this work is to "rule" a busy, distracted life, its images will have to cut deep. Its disciplines will have to be powerful and urgent. How appropriate, then, that its gateway meditation, its signature exercise, should stir up the affections and assault the memory with every active, grotesque, piercingly personal tool it can muster. It grabs hold of its reader's memory and desire and does not let go.

Following this delirious opening, the *Prickynge*'s initial trajectory proceeds to construct its readers as willing but not always able practitioners of devotional intensity. Chapter two descends to a more practical discussion of how the reader might go about stirring up, not rapture, but simple compassion. What if the heart refuses to open in longing? What if the reader sees the wounds but cannot feel them? The writer suggests different tactics, from imagining and amplifying particularly nasty tortures from saints' lives—like the flaying of Saint Bartholomew—to a little private scourging, though he is generally opposed to self-mortification (15–16). But what if the reader still cannot melt into tears? *Think what a sack of filth you are*, the writer advises, and cry for your sins, like this:

wat is wershe than I, wat is more thenne the malice of my herte. Alas wat shal I do that I am so over-don seeke. . . . The yen blynneth nought of wepynge until the moistour of teris may soften the hardness of my herte. wat may I do that I fynde nought the life of my sowle. That I mai nought taste of that swete doun-gettynge of cristes charite. I shal sitte wyth Iob in the myddynge of my synnes, and I shal pare a-wey with a shelle of sharpe sorowe the stynke of my conscience. I shal nought spare my soule fro siche turmentynge tyl I may fynde my ihesu in his passioun. (17)

The lament continues long in this vein, but the wounds of compassion she begs for will not come. At last she must content herself with waiting meekly for a new heart.

Yet this helpless waiting for grace turns into an even more passionate rhetoric of desire—the same rhetoric, in fact, that Kempe quotes to such good effect. Unable to melt in tears of pity, the "I" burns with desire to do so: "Never-the-lees I shal ubide . . . & longe in desire un-til my herte melte. A ryght now lord, my sowle bi-gyneth to longe for love, and al worldly likynge is even browt to nought in me. so I disire to be freshhid & counfortide with the hoote blode of thi swete woundes. A lord, delay me nought fer, . . . tarie not to wound me, lest that thourghe thi taryinge I be lost fro thee. . . . Renne sone lord & wounde me, lest that thou come to late" (19). Why does Christ not let her in? she asks. (Here I use the feminine pronoun to evoke the desiring soul and the frantic Margery.) Is she harder and rustier than the iron spear? The wounds are already made—may she not come in? Is her yearning too cruel? Is her appetite too intense? Though she eat the flesh for love, Christ will not be less. And yet he still will not wound or change her heart, will not let her in. He is the absent beloved; he tarries and comes not, and the lover, mad with yearning, runs like a drunkard or a "wodeman" through the streets, scorned by all who see her, her heart on fire with love (20). By making Christ himself responsible for the reader's lack of feeling—here the hard-hearted, absent lover changes places with the hard-hearted, unworthy beloved—the text turns that lack on its head, transforming the self-loathing rhetoric of emotional imperviousness and exclusion into a rhetoric of erotic longing. The more Christ keeps her out and stays away—the more she does not feel and cannot cry—the more feverishly she yearns and runs. (Readers familiar with Donne's Holy Sonnet 14 will recognize this strategy: begging God to ravish his captive heart, Donne makes passionate appeal out of the very absence of devotional fervor.) The repetitive, lyrical anguish of spiritual dryness and frustration is as powerfully moving as the language of ecstasy—if not more so. As the distinctions between yearning and ecstasy are eroded, so too are the distinctions between the wound of desire bestowed by grace, and the wound of desire brought into being by the reader's own scripted performance: a self-inflicted wound through which grace may penetrate.[86]

The dynamic is repeated over and over, with the reader appealing now to Christ, now to Mary. For even Mary, the epitome of fluid and overflowing grace, disdains to share her wounds with the frustrated reader, who resolves to fall at Mary's feet, to cry and beg and never leave unless she is driven away (25). If Mary strikes her, at least she will be wounded. And if she speaks fairly, that will wound her too. And if she will not answer, the "I" will wound her own heart with woe and sorrow (26). Again, the desire for connection and identity is forced to be content with the desire *for* desire, and sorrow for the Passion is replaced with sorrow for lack of sorrow, a self-wounded heart. The reader is powerless and yet imaginatively empowered by her own articulation of pain and longing. Her desolation can even, remarkably, become an imitation of Christ. Just as Jesus cried out, "My God, my God, why hast thou forsaken me," so too the reader can complain of her lack of grace: and "yif thou do thus, thenne folwest thou wel cristes passioun; in sum-wat art thou like hym" (28). Incredibly, the unsure, un-fervent reader becomes something like Christ in his most tormented outcry. An imitative rhetoric, not an identical depth of feeling, establishes the likeness.

Thus if the *Prickynge*'s opening meditation figures an originary fall from mystical ecstasy or the security of contemplative enclosure, subsequent episodes seek to negotiate the distances and ruptures resulting from that fall. The feared "spearing out" has become a terrible reality, and the reader's response alternates between anguished self-consciousness and desperate expressions of drunken desire, like the *Talkynge of the Love of God* on continuous fast-forward loop. The meditative voice careens from songs of ravishing love-longing and baroque excess—panting, groping, drinking, sighing—to abject reflections on the self, and the horrified, Anselmian wish to flee it: "[f]lee my-self may I not. ne I wrecche wole not flee. I may not flee. for I am fer & over-fer, thou I flee no ferther" (57). Unable to escape, the "I" turns on itself instead: "I shal dissese my-seelf with peynfulnesse & angwisshe" (58). He tortures and kills his own beloved, and wonders why all creatures do not rise up against him; he fights with his own conscience (21). Far from erasing the self or making it whole, seeing the Passion makes the "I" increasingly aware of its own conflicted impulses—about which there always seems more to say. I suggested earlier that the rhetoric of abjection might take on added meaning for unenclosed readers of the *Talkynge of the Love of God*. The *Prickynge* seems to bear that out, making such abjection a central practice of the mixed life.

The language of longing and pain allows the reader to manipulate his emotional responses, not merely for the pleasure of doing so, but in order to more effectively "imprint" his soul with the image of Christ.[87] For if the mixed self cannot be "inside" religion, the image of Christ can be inside the self. And if mystical union with God is no longer a possibility, there remains a more everyday model of "union": the soul's gradual inner transformation in the image of the human Christ. (To reinforce this point, the translator consistently adds or emphasizes references to the lost image of God in man's soul, and to the perfection of that image through Christ's incarnation.)[88] This transformation is made possible in part by the very *impossibility* of mystical union, and the consequent emotional labors of the soul. If she cannot melt rapturously into Christ, she can still find and improve in herself the image of what she loves, scraping herself with the shell of sharp sorrow until she finds the image of Christ underneath. The raptures and anguish are not ends in themselves; the fluctuations between them drive the soul's busy progress. Readers not securely nailed to an order need different crosses, different modes of imitation. But the desires that get them there will be very similar, even if those desires are for an object that seems further away and emanate from a subject that must stay closer to itself.

Inner transformation involves both desire and vision, of course, and this may be why the English translator seems so eager to impose a consistently visual paradigm on his text. He adds the language of seeing and beholding at every opportunity, frequently altering phrases of possession and union to convey vision instead. The act of "having God alone" becomes "a litel goostli syghte" of Jesus. Having compassion turns into "a depe and an inli be-holdynge of cristes passioun or ellis . . . gret fervour of disire longe kyndelid thourghe assiduell byholdynge."[89] While the Latin writer articulates various modes of experience—"to have this, to see you, to fly"—the English translator edits out everything but "to see you."[90] The English meditations are framed by the reader's gaze, evoked by the continual refrain of "I see thee . . . I behold thee," until the vision is so all-pervasive "that widerso I turne me, ai mote I se the crucified with myn inner yghe" (22). True contemplatives have Christ always in their sight, and the more inwardly and passionately they behold, the more they are conformed, "thourghe syche a depe prentynge of thoughte in hym that on siche side he turned hym he shulde not fele ne considere but ihesu criste" (107).[91] This omnipresent language of beholding doubtless reflects the powerful influence of the *Meditationes Vitae Christi* and its heirs, but it also reveals the English writer's interest in fashioning more effective mechanisms of internalization for his readers, whose distracting external lives require ever deeper memorial imprints, visions that will haunt them no matter which way they turn.

The constant vision of self is also relentlessly enforced. The reader must always behold, never forget himself—in part because God is always beholding *him*.[92] Comparison of the Latin and English texts is instructive. In chapter seven of the Latin *Stimulus*, for example, James of Milan describes how the contemplative should always think and act as if he were in God's presence—for contemplation, indeed, allows him to ascend to God in heaven. Is it not wonderful, he asks, that God could allow such a foul creature to stand in his presence?[93] He should be grateful for the honor, always thinking and behaving accordingly. If in his weakness he should fall from that honor, he should labor anxiously to return. In the *Stimulus*, contemplation is a privileged state, where the elite are free to concentrate all their attention on God and in so doing, to ascend to him.

In the *Prickynge of Love*, this chapter reflects a different reality. You must think that you are always in the presence of God, instructs the translator, adding "For-whi thou art ai [always] so thow thynke hit not" (86). This small addition establishes a situation in the indicative rather than the subjunctive mood, outside the reader's control rather than dependent upon his special vocation and focused concentration. Whereas the *Stimulus* assumes that the contemplative can fall out of God's presence through inattention or weakness, the reader of the *Prickynge* can only forget that he is there: "turne agen ther-to with a sorwe that thou hast been any tyme out *from biholdynge of his presence*" (87, addition emphasized). Christ is always there, seeing him, and he needs to see Christ so that he can see Christ seeing him—and construct himself accordingly. Where the Latin text advises that "the servant of God should never think, speak, or do anything otherwise than as if he saw God face to face," the English translator writes, "Goddis servaunt awghte *for to bi-holde himself so avisili that he shulde* ryght nought don speke ne thenke, but als he wolde yif he saw God face to face" (additions emphasized).[94] He adds that God "seth the lest thoughte of oure herte, and parceyvyth the leeste twynkelynge of oure yghe."[95] The reader must see himself just as minutely and carefully—for he is always being watched, whether he remembers it or not. And this has nothing to do with the elite silences of contemplation. "This settynge of thi herte," advises the translator, "may thou have yif thou wolt, whether thou shal preie or rede or thenke, or do any odir bodyli werke."[96]

Thus the reader carries a monitory mirror with him wherever he goes: "wat-so he do out-ward of wordeli bysyness. . . . god is ay present goostli before his yghen, & seeth al that he doth and thynketh" (77). Even the most aggressively fluid meditations are inscribed within the framework of mutual observation, where God's vision focuses the reader's own, forcing him to interrogate and bewail his own thoughts and desires. "I shal deeme my-self," he declares, "and arme me ageynys my-seelf" (58). For the question, "what am I?"—part of a traditional Franciscan question before the cross, "What are you, lord, and what am I?"—always leads back to the dung-heap and the stink of sin. The visual dialectic separates the abject body from the ideal one, emphasizing their discontinuity but also making possible the instruction of the one by the other.

As we might now expect, the meditations are also circumscribed by a spatial frame separating inside from out. The translator repeatedly qualifies his source with some version of the word *inward*, some reminder that the heart is the proper place for the reader's emotional exercises.[97] He emphasizes the *privacy* of contemplative experience, of "pryve speche & . . . daliaunce," even when its sweetness is felt burningly in the body (44). "Litel hede taketh he . . . of out-ward thynges," the translator observes, "that seketh for to fynde [Jesus] in preyvyte of his herte"—and here he has revealingly replaced *purity* of heart (*puro corde*) with privacy. *Cor altum* becomes "dep-nesse of herte . . . pryvyli."[98] He repeatedly underlines the hierarchy of inner and outer: tribulation, for example, is beneficial because it drives a man inward and opens the inner eye (96–97). More inward beholding is more intense, more ravishing (e.g., 33, 39). Criticism of others drives a man outward, while self-criticism keeps him inward. The outer flesh need not be mortified—only the fleshly will (4). And anyone who seeks Christ other than through his manhood will be deluded, for "whenn he weneth to be [believes himself to be] with-inne, he is ful fer with-outen" (124). (We have seen that the question of who is *really* inward and who only *thinks* they are is a contentious one in this period.) What began as a powerful desire to be wholly inside the womb of Christ is gradually channeled into a need to be wholly within one's own interior. For it is only when fully inside the self, all busily gathered within, that one can even contemplate being out of it—or *half* out of it, as the translator amends his source at one point.[99]

It often seems, then, as if the *Prickynge of Love* (or its translator) has two different voices, two different personalities. One (generally the instructional "you" voice) is sane, moderate, consistent, concise, and earthy. He makes sure that the reader is always keeping an eye on herself. The other (the meditative "I") is a drunken "wodeman" given to grotesque elaborations, masochistic yearnings. He (or she) wallows in extremes and revels in being out of control. These divisions more or less mirror the developing split between the two selves of the reader. There is the self of social moderation and propriety, and the self of passionate, eloquent desire for Jesus. One attends carefully and self-consciously to the expectations of the outside world, the other to the stylized violence of suffering and desire in the readerly interior. Thus "unenclosed" mystical discourse produces Christian identity not as more fluid and less self-conscious, but as ever more deeply divided, guilty, and self-aware.

It is on this point that Margery Kempe, in her unwillingness to separate any part of her identity from any other, gets the *Prickynge of Love* most insistently wrong. Margery takes the *Prickynge* at its word when it says that she should see Jesus in everyone and in everything she does, when it tells her to melt into sobs of compassion, roar and weep for her sins, fondle Christ's feet, collapse in sweetness of bodily sensation, or run through the streets, drunk with love. In making her seeing, sobbing, roaring, and running so public, so performative, so *loud*, she opens up her spiritual life—the private dialectic that should include only herself and God—to her fellow Christians.[100] If Margery is going to be inwardly chaste, she wants to signify it with her white clothing. If she is moved to weep over an infant that reminds her of Jesus, she is also moved to explain that motivation to an audience. Her determined externalism opens her up to repeated charges of hypocrisy, as we might expect; some of her fictional contemporaries, at least, expect there to be a gap. But there are no divisions for Margery. Like the nuns at Syon, she sees in order to *show*. If we compare her to Lydgate, we can see the difference between a monastic and a lay reading of the Passion, and of the inside/outside split. Lydgate's monastic identity should be seamless but isn't; Margery's lay-contemplative identity should not be seamless but is. Neither the doubled Lydgate nor the dramatically single-minded Margery are fully "within" in ways that accord with their social roles.

The frequent accusations that Margery manufactures her own tears point to a further problem: the *Prickynge of Love*, as we have seen, blurs the line between the uncontrollable actions of grace and self-produced feelings—between grace freely given and grace attracted, as it were, by rhetorical performance. It does so by encouraging its reader to take up a dramatic voice, to labor in herself until she achieves the proper emotional state. She thus creates real effects in her soul, reshaping her interior in the image of Christ. Begging for wounds, she wounds herself. But she also creates the potential for exactly the kind of anxious questions that surround Margery's more public devotional performances: what is inspiration and what is theater (a question that would haunt the Reformation)? When is self-fashioning spiritual progress, and when is it just self-absorption?

Yet Kempe gets the *Prickynge* right on two fundamental and related counts. First, by ignoring its call to inwardness, she gains the scorn of her community, or "the world." This is one of the primary lessons of the Passion. The *Prickynge*'s ideal reader longs to be reviled and despised, and hungers ceaselessly for the world's reproof; his own worship stinks in his nostrils (42). He is happiest when (in a passage new to the English version) "alle men scornen hym, holden hym but a fool, and summe callen hym ypocrite, and summe bacbiten hym, and summe openly mysseyn hym, but he goth forth & doth his werk myghtili."[101] Kempe's critics do call her a fool and a hypocrite, both "backbiting" and openly criticizing her. And although the *Prickynge* emphasizes inwardness and social responsibility, it is not without models for flamboyant and socially unacceptable behavior. In an address to the Virgin in chapter three, the reader asks why Mary ran out to Calvary instead of staying at home alone in her chamber, as would have been customary for "shamefastnesse of maydenhode" (24). She should have avoided such hideous noise and rabble; she foolishly put herself in danger, and it was "not custummable" (24). "But I hope thou may not here me," the reader adds. For by ignoring custom, propriety, and circumspection, the unruly Virgin has made herself a model for the ways in which everyone may be "turned in-to the woundes of crist." It is a brief but potentially instructive episode.

Margery also gets the text right by performing her passionate imitation of Christ through busy service to others, rather than by enclosing herself in a convent or anchorhold. For as much as the *Prickynge* insists that the reader's contemplative exercises are performed in the heart, it also insists that her ethical practice will be secretly but indelibly affected. We have seen that while the first chapter sets up a longing for enclosure and re-absorption, the remainder of the text moves inexorably toward a model of likeness through imitative practice, whereby meditation on the Passion not only stirs up desire, but teaches the reader how to behave. It becomes increasingly clear that imitating Christ means having pity and compassion for others: seeking him in the sick and suffering, performing the works of mercy, forgiving injury. It means having "a modir tendirnesse to all [one's] even-cristen"—having compassion for them as a mother would have compassion for her own children (75–76). Desire *for* the mother becomes desire to be *like* a mother, just as desire *for* Christ becomes desire to be *like* him. Perhaps the most powerful articulation of this ethic can be found in that crucial chapter on the mixed life: "thou that woldiste be a spouse of ihesu crist & wolte fynde hym that thi soule loveth, I shal telle the[e] where thi ihesu, thi spouse, lyghth, and where thou maight fynde him: not in the mydday cele, as holy writte seyth, but in thi seke brother that is croked & blynde or disesed in odir bodili sikenesse" (105). If you will ravish yourself by effort of your own desire, the writer advises, go to a leper or a sick man and kiss him—as indeed Margery does. For no one can love Christ who does not love his "even-cristen." (The maternal Christ, the nature of self-reflection and imitation, and the relationship between private devotion and public charity are themes important to Julian of Norwich as well, and so will engage us further in the next chapter.)

A Franciscan concern with the active works of charity thus becomes an ethical program for all Christians—and again, our translator makes sure that this program can be practiced by everyone, not just those called to radical holiness. If "resonable causes" prevent physical service, pity and forgiveness will be enough. And though he does not "reprove" the enclosed religious, he clearly prefers the life outside the cloister. "Make the gronde of thi herte in cristes passioun & sette hit in his blood," he advises, "but thenne shalt thou bigge on this grounde als many goode werkes as thou may & make thi hope stif and strong" (36–37). From the psychic ground of intensely solitary rapture and abjection—from what at first glance seemed to be one of the most self-absorbed and savage expressions of late medieval affective devotion to Christ's flesh—there emerges a way of charity in community. The confrontation with the Passion that constitutes the Christian interior is a vortex of erotic psychology, all gothic energy and excess, all blood and milk and wombs and wounds, where the inner self is transformed through violent stirrings and yearnings. But this interior belongs to a social self that performs whatever modest version of charity is proper and practical to its station. The bridge between them is a hermeneutic, whereby the reader is asked to interpret herself and her relations with others—both those who scorn her and those who suffer—through the dream-like inner narrative of her desire for Christ and transformation into his envisioned image.[102] The soul's passionate yearning becomes the engine driving its daily ethical imitation of Christ.

The text's final chapter brings us full circle—or almost full circle. This description of the state of the blessed in heaven follows two chapters of dramatic rhapsody on the tenderness of Mary and her ravishing womb. But at last we return to a vision of heavenly reunion that is *not* a womb, though God once again is a mother:

As the modir cherissheth the childe, so shal I counforte you, seith oure lorde. ye shulen be born in armes, & ye shul be cherisshed on knees. There shul we ioyen & have myrthe, uche man of otheris ioye as of his owne. and sovereynli we shul have ioye of the unmesurabel mykelnesse of goddis myghte and of his wisdam & of his godenesse, and we shul be led in-to the inner ioye. and what with-outen and what withinnen we shul been over-fillid with ioye, that we shul be als we were slokened therinne. (209–10)

In heavenly Jerusalem, inner and outer will at last overflow into one another. Desire will be slaked, but not through the lone child's ecstatic re-absorption into the mother. In this vision of heavenly rest, the mother holds her children—all her children—not in the womb, nor even at the breast, but in her arms and on her knees. Instead of a final rejection of visibility and the world outside, we are given a scene in which the outside is redeemed, is heaven. So too is human consciousness redeemed, for the eyes of the blessed are not closed nor filled with blood, but open in "stabel beholdynge with-outen blenke" of the Trinity (209). The hunger for seamless union has been redirected into a desire for community, for a "felaushepe beste" where each is "knyt to-gidere" with fervent charity and "clenneste shewynge of love uche of us to odir hertliest" (209). The reader's busy, active, self-conscious, communal life is no longer the horrific result of being "speared out" of the womb of rest, delight, and contemplation, no longer a terrible realm of unlikeness it is forced to inhabit in yearning and self-recrimination. It becomes instead an imperfect reflection of, and an entirely proper form of longing for, the ideal world.

*   *   *

This fervidly restless, Christ-beholding, self-envisioning strain of English devotion begins in the Middle Ages but does not end there. We can find versions of it, for example, in the extraordinarily popular works of the early sixteenth-century bishop and humanist John Fisher; or in the English translation of Thomas à Kempis's *Imitatione Christi*, cited in this chapter's epigraph; or in the anguished, strenuous devotional poetry of John Donne. Fisher imagined these exercises reaching all the way down the social scale: in one of the first works to be published in England (a work that went through seven editions), he wrote:

A man may easily say & thinke with him selfe (beholding in his hart the Image of the Crucifixe), who arte thou, and who am I. Thus everie person both ryche and poore, may thinke, not onely in the church here, but in every other place, and in hys business where about hee goeth. Thus the poore laborer maye thinke, when he is at plough earying hys grounde, and when hee goeth to hys pastures to see hys Cattayle, or when hee is sittyng at home by hys fire side, or els when he lyeth in hys bed waking and can not sleepe.[103]

The injunction to see oneself in the Passion of Christ could produce quite different forms of response—from the penitential, self-consciously literary monastic confessions of John Lydgate, to the increasing amplifications of desire and abjection in *The Talkynge of the Love of God*, to the inside-out negotiations of rapture, identification, and ethics in *The Prickynge of Love*. What remained relatively consistent was the visual imperative—*vide*—and the self-conscious turn it implied. The image of Christ on the cross was everywhere the image of the Christian interior.

And English Passion meditations were its voice. For one of the things that distinguishes this kind of Passion devotion and identification from that produced by other kinds of artifacts, in other contexts, is that it is always and fundamentally rhetorical. It produces an idea of interiority that is not in essence bodily or sensual or inexpressible, but brought into being and entered into precisely by taking up a voice, by assuming a position in a discourse. This is where we find an inner self not only gestured toward—and assumed to be unreachable and unknowable—but linguistically constructed and *expressed*: an "I" remembering, singing, mourning, praying, longing, and transforming itself in the process. And unlike the discourse of passionate secular love—the other great locus of rhetorical inwardness and self-transformation in late medieval culture—it was a discourse that aspired, at least, to a broad audience, in terms that moved far beyond narrowly prescribed and essentially static gender roles, seeking to imagine human life and longing in broader, more flexible, and (by design) more surprising terms.

Chapter 4

Profitable Sights: The Showings *of Julian of Norwich*

The remarkable *Showings* of Julian of Norwich constitute a vision of the Passion that is both strikingly like and subtly, profoundly unlike the meditations of the previous chapter. Deathly ill and failing fast, a "symple creature unlettyrde" who has long desired a bodily sight and more true mind of the Passion is reminded of that desire when her curate brings her a cross with the image of Christ on it and places it before her face to comfort her. "My eyen was sett upright into heaven," she explains, "but nevertheles I ascentyd to sett my eyen in the face of the crucyfixe, if I might, and so I dide, for me thought I might longar dure to looke even forth then right up."[1]

Having thus lowered her gaze to the eye-level human Christ, Julian experiences a series of visions of the Passion that recall *The Prickynge of Love* and other English meditations in their graphic, abstracted account of Christ's sufferings. Suddenly, she sees the red blood running down from under the crown of thorns, "hote and freyshely, plentuously and lively" (4.4). "The grett droppes of blode felle downe fro under the garlonde lyke pelottes," she notes, with a strangely aesthetic fascination, "semyng as it had comynn ouhte of the veynes. And in the comyng ouhte they were browne rede, for the blode was full thycke; and in the spredyng abrode they were bryght rede" (7.14–17). In the second showing she sees the beautiful face hideously disfigured by a spreading stain of dried blood. In the fourth she sees the body scourged, so that "The feyer skynne was broken full depe in to the tendyr flessch, with sharpe smytynges all a bout the sweete body. The hote blode ranne out so plentuously that ther was neyther seen skynne ne wounde, but as it were all blode" (12.2–7). At other times she sees the welcoming wound in Christ's side, his terrible thirst, the desiccation of his flesh, and the surpassing pain and suffering of his mother Mary. Julian's remarkable descriptions of, for example, drops of blood as round as the scales of a herring could never be mistaken for standard issue, but these visions of the Passion clearly share many of the basic conventions of their genre—just as Julian's earlier desires to be "with Magdaleyne and with other that were Christus lovers, that I might have seen bodilie the passion that our lord suffered for me" had reflected the piety of her day (2.9–11).

More than the fascination with blood and wounds, however, it is the self-reflexive, subjective quality of Julian's vision that marks her deep involvement with the paradigms of English Passion meditation. For it is clear that Julian conceives of the Passion as a scene of introspection and self-knowledge, where showings of God and self converge and reflect. In the second showing, when Julian sees Christ's face defiled and overspread with blood, she is not overwhelmed with emotion, with weeping, or with desire for physical imitation of the wounds. Instead, she examines the vision for its specular meaning, identifying Christ's defilement as "a fygur and a lyknes of our fowle blacke dede, which that our feyre bryght blessed lord bare for our synne" (10.36–38). The distorted face calls up a familiar paradigm of likeness and unlikeness, of difference and desire. Julian sees how the Trinity made mankind in his image, and how, in the wake of the Fall, Christ in turn assumed "the ymage and the lyknes of owr fowle blacke dede" (10.60). She remarks, too, that she can see this vision only darkly, though she desires a clearer sight; and from this she understands the familiar lesson that the soul's task in this life is "contynually sekyng" after the clearer image (10.68–69). As she writes in the fourteenth showing,

whan we know and see verely and clerely what oure selfe is, than shalle we verely and clerly see and know oure lorde god in fulhed of joye. . . . We may have knowynge of oure self in this lyfe by contynuant helpe and vertu of oure hygh kynd, in which knowyng we may encrese and wax by fortheryng and spedyng of mercy and grace. But we may nevyr fulle know oure selfe in to the last poynt, in which poynte thys passyng life and alle manner of woo and payne shalle have ane ende. And therefore it longyth properly to us both by kynde and by grace to long and desyer with alle oure myghtes to know oure selfe, in which full knowyng we shall verely and clerely know oure god in fulhede of endlesse joy. (14.2–15)

Taking up the Pauline and Augustinian resonances that echo through English devotional writing of the period, Julian approaches her vision of the Passion as a dark sign of much else besides suffering and sorrow. Her *Showings* offer us a unique opportunity to examine the way one English reader envisions herself, and God, as a result of the injunction to "beholde and se," to find oneself in the mirrors of vernacular devotional literature.

Julian's work is usually placed in the genre of mystical and visionary, rather than devotional, literature. She presents her vision of the Passion as inspired, not laboriously achieved; it is from experience, not from books. English devotional texts such as *The Prickynge of Love* and *The Contemplations of the Dread and Love of God* are said to be part of Julian's spiritual climate, her background, but they are not of a kind with her. Her claim of direct access to divine revelation places her instead in the category of female mystics such as Catherine of Siena, Mechtild of Hackeborn, and Bridget of Sweden—or, depending on organizational principles, with English mystics such as Richard Rolle and the *Cloud*-author. Julian's text never mentions reading of any kind. Indeed, she asserts that she is "unlettered," although that claim has been qualified or rejected, in varying degrees, by most modern scholars.

As I have already suggested, however, and as I will continue to argue in the rest of this chapter, Julian's work is seriously engaged with the conventions of English devotional writing and private reading, and with the ideals of seeing and selfhood that those conventions represent and construct. At the end of Chapter 1, I suggested that Julian was thinking hard about the multiple discourses of "inwardness" swirling through the devotional literature of her day. Taking advantage of contradictions already present in those discourses, Julian creates a vision of doubled humanity that takes advantage of Augustinian epistemology, but challenges its hierarchies of reason and sensuality, rethinking "inward" to make it answer to both Trinitarian and Christocentric paradigms. In this chapter, I want to explore further Julian's involvement with devotional narratives about what a human "I" *is*: how it comes to understand itself in relation to a "seeing" of the Passion, how it is disciplined and developed through pain and loss, how it understands its own separateness and individuality. By thinking of Julian-the-beholder as in some ways an exemplary devotional reader, presenting her own progress in learning to "see" what she is, we can better understand how the complexly interwoven text of Julian-the-writer depends on other vernacular devotional models, including Passion meditations, *planctus Mariae*, tracts on the "profits of tribulation," and other works aimed at literate English men and women. We can also gain a better appreciation of just how complicated and unpredictable the results of serious readings of such texts could be.

To suggest in general terms how much Julian's text is both of and about the busy self-beholding of the devotional "I," it helps to make some broad comparisons with contemporary visionary texts. It is telling, for example, that Julian never assumes the unified, unreflexive gaze of the mystic, the kind of total absorption in beholding and desiring God that ravishes the visionary out of or above herself. Julian is never drunk with love, never released from the strenuous engagement with the self that is a hallmark of English inwardness. She tells us in the sixteenth showing that she had wished to exult in beholding Christ without the simultaneous pain of self-reflection, but that she had not been permitted: "Whan he shewde me that I shuld synne, and for joy that I had in beholdyng hym, I entendyd nott redely to that shewyng, oure curteyse lorde restyd there, and wolde no ferther tech me. . . . And herof was I lerned, though that we be hyely lyftyd in to contemplacyon by the specialle gyfte of oure lorde, yett us behovyth nedys therwith to have knowyng and syght of oure synne and of oure febylnes" (78.31–37). Even in the midst of high visionary contemplation, Julian cannot stop seeing the ways in which, as she says, "I have made my selfe foule and unlyke to thee" (61.49–50)—a project of dizzying scope, for the complexity and "unsykerness" of the self creates endless variations, just as the vision of Christ's Passion shifts through numerous forms and moods. The soul is such a "mervelous medelur" of well and woe, Christ and Adam, rising one minute and falling the next, that we can hardly know anything about it (52.9–35). "I wot nott how I shalle falle," Julian admits, "ne I know not the measure ne the gretnesse of my synne" (79.12–13). She concludes that three kinds of knowing were the reason for everything she was shown: "The furst is that we know oure lorde God. The second is that we know ourselfe, what we ar by him in kinde and in grace. The thirde is that we know mekely what oureselfe is, anemptes oure sinne and anemptes oure febilnes. And for these thre was alle this shewing made" (72.54–58). Julian needs to know about a universal human nature, united to God "in kinde and in grace." But she also needs to know about the particular self constituted by sin and feebleness— a self that will be honored in heaven, as all faults are turned into matter of praise. The penitential knowledge of "what oureselfe *is*" (after "ourselfe, what we *ar*") is not a lesser step on the way to the higher, more difficult knowledges, and as she has seen, it cannot cease even during the special gift of high contemplation. As Julian muses elsewhere, in a radical reversal of Augustine, it may actually be easier to come to the knowledge of God than to the knowledge of the human self—though that does not excuse one from trying (56.1–9).

Compare this, then, to the more certain, authoritative opening of the work of Julian's Italian contemporary, Catherine of Siena (herself the most

Augustinian of the Continental mystics): "A soul rises up, restless with tremendous desire for God's honor and the salvation of souls. She has for some time exercised herself in virtue and has become accustomed to dwelling in the cell of self-knowledge in order to know better God's goodness toward her, since upon knowledge follows love. And loving, she seeks to pursue truth and clothe herself in it."[2] Catherine speaks of self-knowledge, but she has already gone beyond it; it is a stage, a prerequisite to her visionary experience, not the goal of the experience itself. There is no sense of an ordinary "I" here, nothing like the intricate, developing trajectories of emotional and intellectual response and inevitable human failing that come through so strongly in Julian's text, despite the lack of concrete information about her life, her surroundings, her external identity.

For Julian does nothing to present herself as a holy woman, a special mouthpiece of God. Her text is almost completely lacking—disappointingly lacking, many have felt—in those biographical details that might constitute the basis for a public hagiography. She is only a "simple creature," nameless and without status except through what is presumably a scribal introduction. And yet she manages to convey the presence of a real person: thirty winters old, devout, desirous of a deeper knowledge of the Passion, terribly ill, afraid. Few "visionary" texts have as immediate and subjective a feel as this one, or convey so powerfully the sense of a particular "I" speaking, thinking, looking back on her own feelings and responding to them.[3] As we have seen, meditations like *The Prickynge of Love* spend less time actually describing the Passion than elaborating the reader's relation and response to it. Likewise, Julian's responses to the images she is shown often receive more analysis and discussion than the images themselves—in part because those images are so fragmentary, indirect, and enigmatic that only by internalizing and "reading" them in relation to her own feeling can Julian recognize their meaning. ("I am suer by my awne felyng," she periodically asserts.) In important ways, the introspective assumptions of English devotional writing are what make Julian's uniquely first-person text possible. But those assumptions are also the subject of intensive revision and expansion in the course of that text, as Julian transfers the paradigms of English devotional vision from the context of private, meditative reading into that of revelation.

For Julian works hard to disrupt the purely private assumptions of the genre whose language, whose images, whose tensions between God and self, whose subjective vision she has taken up in order to reconstruct. She asserts frequently and urgently that her visions are *not* purely private, that

God does *not* mean them for "me alone." Perhaps only in *The Cloud of Unknowing* does the relationship between "special" and "general" selves assume as much critical importance as in Julian's text, and there only because the former is so dangerous to the *Cloud*-author's project. For Julian, though, special and general, personal and universal, coexist in a constant tension, like so many other contradictory pairs that she manages to hold in delicate, dangerous balance.[4] In examining her own sin, Julian is propelled into a consideration of the nature of sin itself. In assessing her own feelings, she finds a subjective standpoint that can coexist with the teachings of faith and Holy Church. Julian looks inward in order to reformulate what is assumed to be a private, often erotic relationship to Christ; for her, the heart is not the soul's bower but its city, large and fair. Her inwardness is not alienating but incorporating, so that in her showings, the self-regarding, self-fashioning, penitential models of private, vernacular reading and devotion become the way to a vision of God that is at once deeply subjective and confidently universal: like the wound in Christ's side, "large enough for all mankind." Julian's text posits a private, inward-looking self as both a legitimate and an immensely powerful place from which to speak, a place where it is possible to be "suer" of the whole by one's "awne felyng," in one's own language.

My approach to Julian as a writer who works within, and yet reimagines and rewrites, the dominant religious discourses of her day is now common among Julian scholars, including, notably, David Aers, Lynn Staley, and Nicholas Watson. Her ability to "activate an existing theological structure" (Watson), and yet "resist it, unravel it, estrange us from it, and, gradually but decisively, supercede it" (Aers),[5] has become a favorite explanatory paradigm for the way Julian's text can seem so orthodox, serene, and timeless, and yet so unfamiliar and even subversive at the same time. While earlier scholars sought to place Julian within the elevated circle of fourteenth-century mysticism, a spiritual outpouring unrelated to social and cultural turmoil, it is now common to emphasize Julian's position as— most likely—a member of the gentry class of East Anglia, a resident of the bustling and important city of Norwich (the center of so much religious and devotional activity in this period and boasting relatively high levels of literacy and book ownership), and a witness to times that provoked diverse, often radical responses from contemporaries such as Chaucer, Gower, Kempe, Arundel, and the Wycliffites.[6] Benedicta Ward suggests that Julian was probably a laywoman until at least the age of thirty, when her visions

occurred; but even as a nun or anchoress, she would hardly have been isolated from the issues and conflicts swirling through her urban environment.

Nicholas Watson, moreover, has argued for a closer connection between Julian's book and the explosion of vernacular devotional writing in
the early fifteenth century than has previously been accepted.[7] While most
scholars have located Julian's period of composition between 1373—the year
of her illness and visionary experience—and the 1390s, based on Julian's account of her twenty years of meditation and prayer, Watson argues that both
versions of the *Showings* are the product of a much longer, more hesitant
process of composition, one that would have benefited from the increasing
circulation of vernacular devotional literature, including translations of
continental visionary texts and works such as *The Chastising of God's Children*. Watson places the short text circa 1388 and the long text as late as 1410
or 1415, effectively rejecting the notion of Julian's short text as a spontaneous
record of visionary experience, and locating her long text in a much richer
vernacular environment than has previously been supposed (both the Vernon and Simeon manuscripts, for example, were produced just before 1400).
Lacking extratextual evidence, it seems unlikely that scholars will ever uni-
formly agree about the date of Julian's finished work.[8] Watson's re-datings
are not crucial to my argument, but they do provide a particularly suggestive context, emphasizing Julian's reading and her careful, prolonged thinking across a span of time when vernacular reading was becoming
increasingly widespread in English society.

Images of the Self Beholding: The First Showing

Let us begin with the problem of the beholding self. Julian locates her work
within this central devotional activity, within the system of vision and reflection that defined the parameters of literate devotional activity in late
medieval England. Seeing Christ, she is required to see her own deformed
image; knowing herself in sin, she desires passionately to know how God
sees her in that sin—so that she might know better how to regard herself. In
Julian's work, vision is at once bodily, imaginative, and intellectual, a way of
talking about knowledge, reflection, understanding, and experience all together.[9] But most of all, Julian uses the language of vision to define a complex relationship between humanity and divinity, simultaneously separated
and united by their beholding and reflection of one another. Julian's engage-

ment with this problem winds its way throughout the *Showings*, but it begins in the first revelation of the crown of thorns. In this showing, she explains, were "manie fayer schewynges and techynges of endelesse wisdom and love, in which all the shewynges that foloweth be groundid and ioyned" (1.5–7; see also 6.63–64). From this vision, which is both the genesis and the conclusion of all her searching, Julian works her way backward and forward, spinning out the implications of what she beholds.

The vision begins suddenly, in blood. Staring at the strangely illuminated crucifix, desiring to be filled with mind of Christ's Passion, Julian relates how "sodenly I saw the reed bloud rynning downe from under the garlande, hote and freyshely, plentuously and lively, right as it was in the tyme that the garland of thornes was pressed on his blessed head" (4.1–6). Julian continues to behold this image during the entire course of the showings. Whatever else she is given to understand, always before her bodily eyes she sees "the bodely syght lastynge of the plentuous bledyng of the hede," forming the context for everything else she sees (7.13–14). Now in the second vision, Julian will see the disfigurement of Christ's face as the reflection of her own sin. So too, in this first showing, we might expect the plenteous bleeding to cause Julian to reflect on her own response to, and responsibility for, the Passion. We might expect her, that is, to turn her gaze from Christ's face back to her own, to be forced inward by the pressure of self-consciousness. That will come later; what we are given here is something related, but quite different. Juxtaposed against the bleeding head, or reflected within it, Julian sees—not herself, exactly, but two enigmatic images, whose slow alteration develops a meditation on how the made soul envisions itself in relation to its maker.

The first image is that of the Virgin Mary. The Virgin often serves as a version of the reader's own image in Passion meditations, where she models both ideal response to and internalized imitation of Christ's suffering. For many readers, and especially religious women, seeing the Virgin was in an important sense seeing oneself. It is a little surprising, however, that Julian now sees the Virgin not in the context of the Passion or even of the nativity, but instead at the time of the Annunciation.[10] "I saw her ghostly in bodily lykenes," Julian explains, referring to something like an imaginative vision, "a simple mayden and a meeke, yong of age, a little waxen above a chylde, in the stature as she was when she conceivede" (4.28–31). This scene positions Mary as a beholder, but not as the agonized beholder of the crucifixion. Instead, she is the solitary, contemplative, inward beholder represented in so many visual and textual depictions of the Annunciation. In this tradition, Mary appears alone in her room: silent, enclosed, often engaged in private reading before Gabriel appears to her. It is thus that she appears in Love's *Mirror*, for example. A treatise on contemplation sometimes attributed to Rolle exhorts the reader to see Mary in her chamber: "Behalde howe devotely sche syttes, & hyre boke lyande on a deske before hyre, & sche aparty stowpande towarde hire boke & redinde pryvaly wyth-owtyn shewyng of voyce."[11] As the reader looks on, "bysely behalding" his exemplar, the Virgin turns her eyes from her book up to heaven—but only inwardly, since her outer eyes are closed. Julian's vision finds the young Mary likewise engaged in a reverent beholding (though again, Julian fails to mention the presence of a book in what is usually presented as a scene of reading): "she beheld her god, that is her maker, marvayling with great reverence that he would be borne of her that was a symple creature of his makyng. And this wisdome and truth, knowing the greatnes of her maker and the littlehead of her selfe that is made, made her to say full meekely to Gabriell: Loo me here, gods handmayden" (4.32–37). Gabriel's suddenly intimated presence barely intrudes on the intense, specular exchange between the contemplative Virgin and God, as she *sees herself* simple, little, and creaturely beside the greatness of her maker. Yet in this sight, Julian writes, "I did understand verily that she is more then all that god made beneth her in worthines and in fullhead" (4.37–39). Juxtaposed against the still-present bleeding head of the Passion, this vision offers a somewhat unconventional model of mutual beholding and self-envisioning—one suggesting the dignity and grace, rather than the misery and abjection, of the human beholder.

Julian continues to see the head bleed. But now she is shown a different secondary image: "a little thing, the quantitie of an haselnott, lying in the palme of my hand, as me semide, and it was as rounde as a balle" (5.9–11). The ball represents all that is made, including the made creature Julian. Julian's immediate reaction to the ball—another version of her own image— is to marvel at its insignificance, "for me thought it might sodenly have fallen to nawght for littlenes" (5.14). And indeed, she is given to understand that no soul can be in rest until it is "noughted of all things that is made" (5.31–32). On one hand, the image would seem to teach Julian how to disdain made things, including her own self, seeking instead the perfection of being "wilfully noughted for love" and "substantially unyted to [God]." And yet Julian is also told that the ball "lasteth and ever shall, for god loveth it; and so hath all thing being by the love of God" (5.15–16). Despite its insignificance, the ball will never be lost or absorbed. It will not be annihilated in a rapture of mystical union; it will not melt or empty into God—for God made it, and loves it, and keeps it.

Although the ball in Julian's vision is tiny, it is not—as we might expect, if it represents creaturely mankind as well as the natural Creation—either foul or deformed. Indeed, its perfect roundness (as round as any ball) suggests an inherent purity. It is a well-made thing. But Julian does not rest with this implication; she goes on to address more directly, and startlingly, what we might take to be one of the "foulest" aspects of fleshly, created humanity. Asserting that Christ's human flesh is the greatest mean between humanity and God, Julian turns suddenly to a discussion of human excretion:

A man goyth uppe ryght, and the soule [digested food][12] of his body is sparyde [closed] as a purse fulle feyer. And what it is tyme of his nescessery, it is openyde and sparyde ayen fulle honestly. And that it is he that doyth this, it is schewed ther wher he seythe he comyth downe to us to the lowest parte of oure nede. For he hath no dispite of that he made, ne he hath no disdeyne to serve us at the sympylest office that to oure body longyth in kynde, for love of the soul that he made to his awne lycknesse. (6.35–41)

English penitential laments speak vividly of the foul dung-heaps of sin, of the grotesque excretions and putrefactions of the human body and soul. Devotional self-consciousness, as we have seen, requires a certain abjection. Julian's discussion of excrement recalls a description of Mary's motherly tenderness in the *Prickynge of Love*: "sothli lady, I stynke foule in thy nose-thrilles. ye so foule that ne were that thi loue held the[e], thou woldest fleen the filthe of me as I wolde don the stynke of caryoun. but thou farist with vs as a modir with hir owne childe, that kisseth hym with her mowth & with hir handis makith clene his taylende" (190–91; cf. 201). In the *Prickynge of Love*, Mary's hands clean the "taylende" of her child in spite of its nauseating smell; her tender offices indeed "comyth downe to us to the lowest parte of oure nede." But Julian's description changes the terms of this merciful act. God does not stoop to cleanse the soul after it has fouled itself. Instead, God is in the act of excretion itself, opening and closing the digestive tract simply and "fulle honestly." Julian says nothing of filth, nothing of the stink of carrion, but only repeats that the soul is made in the likeness of God. If envisioning the Passion so often leads to meditation on the almost unbearable stench and degradation of the beholding "I," here in the presence of Christ's bleeding head Julian seems determined to face that stench head-on, confronting abjection and resolutely de-abjectifying it.[13] "Soule and body," Julian asserts, humanity is "cladde and enclosydde in the goodnes of god" (6.44).

Now Julian says more directly that the hazelnut (like Mary) represents the problem of the soul's self-reflexive beholding. Above all things, she writes, "the beholdyng and the lovyng of the maker makyth the soule to seme lest in his awne syght" (6.65). Not worst, not foulest, only *least*: small, but round. The soul's loving beholding (like Mary's earlier) "most fyllyth hit with reverent drede and trew meknesse, and with plente of charyte to his evyn crysten" (6.65–66). In the next chapter Julian returns to the Virgin Mary, but asserts that this showing was happening "in the same tyme" as the other: Mary turning her gaze from God back to herself, sizing up the differences between them. Mary sees God great, and high, and mighty, and good, "and with this she sawe hyr self so lytylle and so lowe, so symple and so poer in regard of hyr god that thys reverent drede fulfyllyd her of meknes" (7.7–9; notice the careful repetition of phrasing). In this moment, she is filled with grace. Her exemplary, self-reflexive vision of God becomes the very ground of the Incarnation.

Meanwhile, Julian continues to see the bleeding head. The visions of Mary and the little thing-like-a-ball cannot be divorced from the soul's contemplation of the Passion, for it is the problem of the Passion that Julian is trying to unravel here: the problem, that is, of the soul's core understanding of itself. Julian reminds us repeatedly that "in alle that tyme that he schewyd thys that I have now seyde in gostely syght, I saw the bodely syght lastyng of the plentuous bledyng" (7.12–13). She turns from Mary's reverent beholding to her own contemplation of the drops of blood, and how they reminded her of homely images from her own experience: raindrops coming off the eves of a house, the scales of a herring. She projects her own voice into the vision, asserting that "as longe as I saw thys syght of the plentuousnesse of bledyng of the heed, I myght never stynte of these wordes: Benedicite dominus" (8.1–2). Julian's Passional and Mary's Incarnational beholding overlay each other, linguistically and temporally, just as Julian's "Benedicite dominus" must resonate underneath Mary's "Lo, me here, God's handmaiden." The one determines the other; Julian's reaction to her vision of the Passion depends on the way she sees Mary beholding, and the way she sees the thing-like-a-ball in relation to God.

Thus in "the plentuousnesse of bledyng of the heed," Julian explains, she understood six things. The first was the Passion; the second was the maiden mother Mary; the third was the Trinity. The fourth was all created things—and here Julian adds another layer of interpretation. For although it may have seemed small as a hazelnut in her vision, Julian well knows "that hevyn and erth and alle that is made is great, large and feyer and good. But the cause why it shewyth so lytylle to my syght was *for I saw it in the presence of hym that is the maker*. For a soul that seth the maker of all thyng, all that is made semyth fulle lytylle" (8.9–13, emphasis mine). Having rejected the assumptions of foulness and abjection in Passional self-envisioning, Julian now shows that even the smallness and fragility of created things is merely a subjective illusion, a question of perspective rather than clarity. For there are different ways of "seeing" things, as Julian cannily understands, playing the subjective nature of vision, and the Pauline trope of partial sight, for all it is worth. The Virgin sees herself as small and simple, and yet she is more than all that is made. The thing-like-a-ball seems tiny and insignificant to its beholder, but it is great, large, fair, and good (and it will never be noughted). If the beholding of God "makyth the soul to seme lest in his awne syght," it is not because the soul is worthless, but because *from this perspective* it cannot seem otherwise. Julian will repeat this formulation in her fourteenth showing, where she again describes the creaturely soul in language that recalls the created hazelnut ball:

And evyr more it doyth that it was made for; it seeth god and it beholdyth god and it lovyth god. Wherfore god enjoyeth in the creature and the creature in god, endlesly mervelyng, in whych mervelyng he seeth his god, hys lorde, hys maker, so hye, so grett and so good in regarde of hym that is made that unethys the creature semyth ought to the selfe. But the bryghtnes and clernesse of truth and wysedome makyth hum to see and to know that he is made for love, in whych love god endlesly kepyth hym. (44.14–21)

The fifth thing Julian understands from her first showing of the Passion is that all things are made for love, and will be kept for love without end. The sixth thing is that God is all things that are good, and the goodness of all things is God.

Julian's account of her first vision confronts subtly but uncompromisingly the expectations fostered by so many other English accounts of the Passion, of a private self in visual dialogue with the image of the crucified Christ and the watching Virgin. Julian seems to have absorbed the process but rejected the suggested outcome, refusing to let the pre-scripted "I" of devotional meditation define her own beholding. Instead, she takes this immensely powerful paradigm on a long journey that is only begun in the first showing, playing with different images of the self beholding until she has built up, through linguistic repetition, sudden swervings, and simultaneous beholdings, a pattern of the soul's reflexive contemplation of Christ that can satisfy her sense of both its dignity and its humility. Julian ends her account of the showing, moreover, by stating quite plainly that her intimate vision of the Passion was not, in fact, meant to remain private—that as personal and subjective as her visions were, they can mean for humanity in general as much as they mean to her. In doing so, she ruptures the tight visual dialectic between Christ and the private, inward self so carefully constructed in English Passion meditation.

Of course, we might expect that since Julian is claiming a miraculous showing, rather than an imaginative or readerly one, the boundaries circumscribing devotional meditation would no longer apply. Surely direct inspiration is meant to be shared outwardly as well as imprinted internally? In part, this must be true; Julian's writing is in large extent authorized by the "visionary" nature of her experience. But in English texts, as we have seen, the line between imaginative and inspired vision is not always so clear. We might recall the visions given to King Edward and Hugh of Lincoln in Love's *Mirror of the Blessed Lyf of Jesu Crist* (discussed in Chapter 1). These inspired English visions too are kept secret, making the humble secrecy of Edward and Hugh's visionary lives as important a message as the real presence of Christ in the sacrament.

The Chastising of God's Children is also instructive on this point. It includes a cautious discussion of "the discernment of spirits," or how to distinguish between real and demonic visions. It observes, for example, that intellectual visions, which consist of inward understanding without any image (and which would therefore be difficult to frame as miraculously inspired), are the least dangerous, since wicked spirits are likely to appear bodily to the eyes. A lack of formal religious training is a bad sign; any kind of heterodoxy is obviously a mark of demonic deception. The most telling assertion for our purposes, however, is that even *true* visions are of little worth unless they inspire personal spiritual development and are accepted with proper humility. Some people have visions and devotions and tears, the author explains, and they counsel and convert others and write books in Latin and English (Richard Rolle, perhaps?), and yet they themselves are not holy or perfect, and so their names are not written in the book of life. Moses had great visions from God, and yet they did him no good: for one little sin, he was barred from the promised land. The emphasis here on private spiritual development, even in the context of the larger providential history of the Israelite people, is stunning. What good were Moses' visions? He should have been more self-aware. "It is ful nedeful," our author advises, "that wiseli we deeme ouresilf first of ony thyng, and slighli serche oursilf that we see and knowe what we be withinne" (184). And the first sign of selfish misuse of visionary experience is *telling others* about the experience. Such publication reveals a treacherous and self-defeating vainglory, a boastful self-satisfaction. Keeping one's visions secret, on the other hand, and using them for self-scrutiny and self-discipline, ultimately increases meekness, charity, and service to others. In private, one beholds and speaks; in public one only acts, without explanation.

All the more startling, then, is Julian's calm assertion at the end of her first vision of the Passion that "Alle that I say of me I mene in person of alle my evyn cristen," and that her vision is shown "generally in comfort of us alle" (8.33–39). She writes that she believed herself to be on the verge of death, about to be "demyde particulerly" in accordance with late medieval doctrine on immediate personal judgment. At this of all times, she should have been concerned to see her own image and to judge and repent of her own sin—lest she, like Moses, should be barred from entering the promised land.[14] But even here Julian's concern is that those about her and all her even-cristen might see as she saw, believing that this vision—far from being only about personal judgment—"was schewde for them that shuld lyve" (8.32).[15] Throughout her book, she continues to insist that what she sees in her own person applies to everyone, that "I" here is "we" as well, even when it refers to something as personal as sin ("Though oure lorde shewyd me that I shuld synne, by me aloone is understonde alle" [37.8–9]).[16] Julian refuses to keep the personal private, knowing that a small, enclosed space may contain the whole universe. Using the very means by which English authors circumscribed the sphere of visionary meditation, she fashions a daring public theology that, like Christ in his mother's womb, is much larger than that which contains it. Even Julian's own heart contains at its center not a bower or a ravishing couch, but the vast, public space of her soul, which she sees "so large as it were an endlesse warde, and also as it were a blessyd kyngdom . . . a wurschypfulle cytte" (68.2–4).

So it is that the question of personal sin telescopes out into the problem of sin in general, and the vision of self into a consideration of how God sees *us*. For in arguing for the inherent dignity of the meekly beholding soul, Julian does not simply gloss over human responsibility for the ugliness of sin; she does not rest with the perspectival reflections of the first vision. In her second vision, Julian returns to a more conventional visual exchange with Christ's tortured face. Her vision is frightening and dark; she wants to see more but cannot, and is greatly disturbed. She sees that the image of sin has transformed the once-lovely face, the image of God in man—and that as a result, the alienated soul must not only behold, but seek, mourn, weep, and long. Julian's subsequent explorations of the problem of vision are much more concerned with the soul's necessary beholding of its own sinfulness, and how that can be reconciled with the tiny yet lovely and expansive images of the first showing, where no foulness is seen.

Seeing the Fall

The horror of the soul's sinfulness, reflected in the defacement and defilement of Christ's image, continues to haunt Julian throughout the *Showings*. It is not until the last four showings, however (which constitute about three-quarters of the text), that she takes up the problem of sin again in earnest. Here, overtaken once more by the ache of separation, she sees that "nothing lettyd me but synne, and so I behelde generally in us alle, and me thought yf synne had nott be, we shulde alle have be clene and lyke to oure lorde as he made us" (27.2–6). She begins to mourn "withoughte reson and dyscrecion," sorrowing and wondering why God ever allowed sin to come between them in the first place. But before she can become entirely consumed by these terrible lamentations (here we might think of the Anselmian anguish central to *A Talkynge of the Love of God*), she is pointedly reproved by God's answer that "Synne is behovely, but alle shalle be wele" (27.13). In understanding how this can be so, Julian turns once again to the Passion—shown only briefly and generally this time, lest she be terrified by its ugliness—and to the visual dialectic that both creates her understanding of sin and may serve as its solution.

   The church teaches Julian that "me behovyth nedys to know my selfe a synner," and this is a tenet from which she never departs (45.19–20). "In alle this beholdynge," she writes, "me thought it behovyd nedys to se and to know that we be synners and do many evylles that we ought to leve, and leve many good dedys undone that we oughte to do" (46.26–28). Sin can be "behovely" only by virtue of being constantly in view: "it nedyth us to falle, and it nedyth us to se it," Julian insists, for "if we se it not, though we felle it shuld not profyte us. And comonly furst we falle and sethen we se it; and both is of the mercy of god" (61.18, 32–34). It was a medieval commonplace that the Fall was "fortunate," in that it allowed God to demonstrate his love through the Incarnation. Julian, though, is concerned to extend this blessing from Original Sin to particular sins, and from the general blessing of the Incarnation to the spiritual profit of the individual.

In part, this is a conventional concern of the "profits of tribulation" genre, a genre increasingly popular with the profit-minded residents of Julian's own prosperous region of East Anglia (and we'll come back to it later in the chapter). Julian's fellow East Anglian and contemporary Margery Kempe begins her book with a rather mercantile account of her tribulations and how they added to her spiritual profit. Thomas Hoccleve ends his "Complaint" comforted by a book on the profits of tribulation that he had borrowed from a friend. And the *Prickynge of Love*'s English translator digresses repeatedly from his source text's discussion of self-loathing to explain how beneficial it is for a man to suffer tribulations (since they drive him inward).[17] For a competitive and individually minded culture, assertions of general good and general punishment were losing some of their explanatory force. Visions should result in personal profit; so too should tribulations; and surely sin, if it is so needful, should result in some personal profit as well. So the first part of Julian's strategy is conventional enough: we need to behold ourselves in sin and unlikeness, she argues, in order to know what we are, to gain meekness, and to stimulate our desire for God. She writes, "when we se oure selfe so fowle, then *we wene* that god were wroth with us for oure synne. Than be we steryd of the holy gost by contriscion in to prayer, and desyr amendyng of oure selfe with all oure myght to slake the wrath of god" (40.5–8, emphasis mine). Here again, the soul sees itself as it imagines God sees it, and is overwhelmed—productively, profitably—with the self-consciousness thus generated, with the desire for self-improvement. Properly envisioned, sin is purgative; it is "the sharpest scorge that ony chosyn soule may be smytten with, whych scorge alle to betyth man or woman, and alle to brekyth hym, and purgyth hym *in his owne syght*" (39.1–4; emphasis mine). We need to see ourselves in wretchedness, Julian explains, in order that "we shulde be made ashamed of oure selfe, and brokyn downe as agaynst oure pryde and our presumpcion" (78.16–18).

But as my emphasis is meant to suggest, this self-envisioning is not, in fact, the way God sees things at all. If it is God's imagined, reflecting gaze that determines the way the soul can see itself—as in *The Prickynge of Love*—it is also the continual, inescapable presence of this gaze, in Julian's work, that rescues the soul from its own scrutiny. Julian takes the trope of surveillance, the eye that can never be escaped and that constitutes the soul's own visual imperative, and transforms it into something comforting and redeeming by her simple assertion that God, seeing us continually and always, sees things *differently.*

Thus the soul, in its confrontation with the human image of God, in the necessary beholding of its own sin and its own fall, *imagines* that it sees itself the way God sees it, *tries* to see as God sees, but in truth is thwarted both by its own inscrutability and by God's entirely other perspective. So Julian learns in her vision of the Lord and Servant, which she is given in response to her mighty desire to know "in what manner he beholdeth us in oure synne." In this vision she is made to understand that God sees one way, and man sees another way, but neither is complete without the other: "For other wyse is the beholdynge of god, and other wyse is the beholdyng of man. For it longyth to man mekely to accuse hym selfe, and it longyth to the propyr goodnesse of oure lorde god curtesly to excuse man. And theyse be two partyes that were shewde in the doubyll chere in whych the lorde behelde the fallyng of hys lovyd servant. . . . Thus wylle oure good lorde that we accuse oure selfe wylfully, and truly se and know our fallyng" (52.69–77). It belongs to man meekly to accuse his own fall, and yet "in the beholdyng of god we falle nott" (82.30). This is more than forgiveness, more than the "excusing" that is God's prerogative. Julian asserts here, extraordinarily enough, that there is nothing to forgive. In our own beholding we hardly stand; in God's beholding we never fall; "and boyth theyse be soth, as to my syght, but the beholdyng of oure lord god is the hygher sothnes" (82.31–32).

So even though humanity's failing is dreadful, and its falling shameful, and its dying sorrowful, as Julian writes, "in all this the swet eye of pytte and of love deperteth nevyr from us" (48.25–26). God beholds "so tendyrly that he seth alle oure lyvyng here to be penance," she argues (81.18–19). The constant pressure of the divine gaze is not the sorrowfully accusing one we think we see reflected back at us from the crucifixion—the "oygly syghte" that inspires fear and despair and is only briefly shown—but the comforting gaze of the mother who never ceases to behold her children with love and pity (28.35; 63.36–37).

The visual paradigms of English devotional writing thus provide a usefully subjective framework for Julian's theological explorations. The pervasive visual language of the *Showings* becomes a way of balancing two positions that seem antithetical only because they are viewed from different places. Julian habitually asserts that something seemed true "as to her sight," or that something else she might have expected to see was "not shown" to her, thus avoiding the problem of objective statement. We might recall again that sermon of John Gaytridge, asserting that "all knawing we have of hym in this life is of hering, and of lernyng and of teching of other." Julian does not frame her revelations as a hearing; God hardly *says* anything to her. Instead, she keeps to the mode that is subjective and private, enigmatic and partial—and yet has implicit claims to delimiting the deepest connection between humanity and divinity.

Yet if the visual standpoint allows for subjective judgments, it is also implicitly unstable and alienating; there is room for different perspectives because the subjects are standing so far from one another. Julian never really ceases to be concerned about the heavy burden of self-consciousness. The potential for solipsistic despair and self-loathing inherent in the soul's private dialogues with the Passion surfaces frequently and eloquently in these later showings. "Oft tymes when oure fallyng and oure wrechydnes is shewde us, we be so sore adred and so gretly ashamed of oure selfe that unnethis we witt wher that we may holde us," Julian observes (61.41–43), noting again later how horrible such beholding seems to the loving soul "that wolde be alle feyer and shynyng in the syght of god" (63.17–18; cf. 73.37–38). Despair is one of only two sins Julian sees in particular, and it is a real danger—one she illustrates in the retelling of her own sin, following the fifteenth showing. Here Julian, like Peter, forsakes Christ. The showings have ended; her pains have returned. But when a religious person asks her what has happened, she betrays the special comfort she has received, saying only that she has "raved." So ashamed and "astonyd" is she by this betrayal that she cannot even confess her sin, and that night she is visited by a horrible devil who clutches at her throat. "Here may yow se what I am of my selfe," Julian confesses, "but here in woulde oure curtesse lorde nott leeve me" (67.33–34).

Julian asserts, then, that although the soul must see its own wretchedness, it must not remain in that beholding, nor busy itself greatly about accusing itself, nor "be to wrechydfulle" on itself (79.35–36). It must see only as much as will work to its profit, and no more. In her final readjustment of the paradigms of surveillance and self-discipline, Julian argues that the soul beholding itself in the presence of God is not completely alienated from the divine perspective and will not be left to the horror of its own beholding. For sin is so foul and so horrible, she writes, that no one could endure the true sight of it; therefore God "mesuryth the syght to us," showing the soul only what will be useful to it (78.21). The soul beholds itself in God's presence, through God's image, *not* in order to point up the absolute horror of its own reflection, but so that it may reflect on itself partly through the merciful perspective of God: "Owre lorde of his mercy shewyth us oure synne and oure feblynesse by the swete gracious lyght of hym selfe, for oure synne is so foule and so horryble that he of his curtesy wylle not shewe it us but by the lyght of his mercy" (78.1–5). Viewing the self through the image and perspective of the other mitigates its foulness, shows it partly through the "swete eye of mercy." As Julian finally formulates it, meditating on how the Lord beheld his Servant in pity and not with blame, "this passyng lyfe askyth not to lyve alle without synne. He lovythe us endlessly, and we synne customeably, and he shewyth it us fulle myldely. And than we sorow and morne dyscretly, turnyng us in to the beholdyng of hys mercy clevyng to his love and to his goodnesse" (82.10–14). The profitable vision of sin culminates in a desire that, rather than turning the soul into itself and against itself, impels it toward God. Julian's sin of betrayal leads her to see what she is of herself, but God does not leave her there; instead, the horrors of her temptation drive her toward the embrace of the final showing. Only in heaven shall we see fully how grievously we sinned, Julian writes, but there too we shall see how we were never hurt in God's sight, and the vision of love will be complete.

Julian takes up the paradigms of reflection—of divine surveillance and human beholding, of self-scrutiny and discipline—in order to test their limits, running them through various permutations to see whether they cannot be transformed into redeeming and connective, rather than isolating and potentially despairing, configurations. We need to see our fall—but God sees it differently. God's surveillance is constant—and constantly redeeming. We must see ourselves—but not abide there. (Julian sometimes describes the soul's seeking as mournful, but at other times says that it should seek willfully, busily, gladly, and merrily, without "veyne sorow" [10.90].) Clearly, Julian feels that the interiorizing abjection fostered by private devotional models of the Passion is dangerous and excessive, threatening to cut the beholder off from the very mercy she seeks. Representations of such isolation appear in various texts of the period. Julian's refusal to confess her betrayal is echoed by Margery Kempe's refusal to confess her secret sin; Thomas Hoccleve's poems to the Virgin, discussed in the next chapter, speak of a shame so great that he cannot bring himself to cry for mercy. Lynn Staley aptly describes Chaucer's Pardoner as "the awful site where knowledge of sin and expectation of judgment intersect, as the comfortless landscape of despair."[18] There is nowhere he can hide from himself, no "leve moder" to let him in. Langland too, Staley observes, hints at "the tolls of self-awareness" through Hawkyn's "seemingly insurmountable problems with cleansing." But sin was no shame, Julian argues, for Mary Magdalene, or Peter, or Paul, or Thomas of India, or John of Beverly: a parade of individuals marked out and defined positively, in part, by their great sins.

Lovers, Mothers, and Others

We have seen that English Passion texts construct relationships of desire and development for their readers using both lover and mother figures, sometimes in quick succession or free alteration. As a writer, Julian excels at such imagistic shape-shifting and doubleness—yet she does not choose to work with the familiar mother-lover dynamic. Instead she abandons the trope of Jesus as lover or bridegroom almost entirely, devoting herself to the idea of Jesus-as-mother: an idea she develops more famously and perhaps more fully than any other writer of the Middle Ages.[19]

Given the strong association of the bridegroom trope with privacy, possession, and the keeping of secrets, it is not difficult to understand why Julian would want to avoid it.[20] The common insistence that Christ is a *jealous* lover suggests how much the lovers' attempts at union separate them from others, rendering them distant, inaccessible, a little world unto themselves. Yet they are separate from each other, too. The equally common theme of yearning and waiting for the absent beloved reminds us that moments of consummation—though rapturous—are few and fleeting, that full selfhood is always deferred. The narrative calls for an isolated, tragic, abject self: a model of subjectivity Julian assiduously avoids.

Yet it is not immediately obvious that the trope of Jesus-as-mother will offer her a suitable alternative. Indeed, the common overlaying of mother and lover in the Passion meditations suggests an easy identification between the two figures and their function in the psychic spaces of loss and desire. In the *Prickynge of Love*, the speaking "I" is forced from the mother's womb into a space of alienation and yearning. In one of the most frequently recounted passages from the *Ancrene Wisse*, a mother plays cruel games of abandonment and reunion with her young children:

> our Lord, when he allows us to be tempted, is playing with us as the mother with her young darling. She runs away from him and hides herself, and lets him sit alone and look eagerly about crying "Mother! Mother!" and crying for a while; and then with open arms she jumps out laughing, and hugs and kisses him and wipes his eyes. So our Lord sometimes lets us be alone and withdraws his grace, his comfort, and his support, so that we find no sweetness in anything that we do well, nor savor in our hearts.[21]

This mother seems to take a strange pleasure in tormenting her child. She hugs and kisses him, but as part of a manipulative strategy designed to increase his desire for her and take away his pleasure in everything else. (This strategy is assigned to Jesus the lover, not Jesus the mother, in the *Prickynge of Love*.) Notice too that this god-mother is invoked to answer almost the same problems that Julian is struggling with: Why does God allow us to be tempted? Why does God allow sin? The *Ancrene Wisse* might turn God into a rather selfish and manipulative mother, but its explanation is already far distant from the angry father-god whose thunderbolts had to be endured, not questioned, by earlier generations. And this points us again toward one of the major problems for later medieval devotion: once it had made the journey "from judgment to passion," as Rachel Fulton terms it, the problems of sin and suffering became increasingly troublesome.[22] True, fourteenth-century preachers could still invoke the wrath of an angry god to justify plagues and warfare; but an increasingly tender, loving, and self-sacrificing god who allowed sin and temptation to run rampant and innocent people to suffer was an increasingly inscrutable mystery. I have already mentioned the rise of the "profits of tribulation" genre and its emphasis on the individual benefits to be gained from trials both spiritual and material. From William Flete's *De Remediis contra Temptaciones* to Sir Thomas More's *A Dialogue of Comfort*, late medieval Englishmen asked with particular urgency *why* they were tempted, *why* they suffered. And while earlier generations had seen misfortune as a Boethian reminder of the world's instability, or as a sign of God's wrath, fifteenth-century English men and women were more likely to see it as a sign of his favor and tender care. Like their sixteenth-century descendants, they wanted to know how to interpret the signs of

God's involvement in their spiritual development, and how to generate the most personal benefit from those signs.

The Chastising of God's Children was one of the many English texts addressed to this persistent mystery—one of the manuscripts in which it appears seems to be an entire "profits of tribulation" collection—and it also presented its answer in the form of a mother.[23] Its translator/compiler, working sometime between 1382 and 1408, makes approximately the same choice Julian does: although he is writing for an audience of religious women, he eliminates almost entirely the Jesus-as-lover theme so prevalent in his main Continental sources—mostly Ruusbroek's *Spiritual Espousals*. In place of mystical espousal, he puts a carefully developed version of the *Ancrene Wisse*'s mother-who-leaves. And his choice of mother over lover is not the only thing his text shares with Julian's. Like Julian, he is uneasy with the notion of a wholly private devotional life, and uneasy with reading practices and spiritual tropes that might detract from the life of the community. His anxiety, however, comes from what we might characterize as a more "conservative" position, one more ambivalent about the consequences of even his own vernacular project. He worries repeatedly about the pitfalls of translation, the dangers of turning Latin concepts into English phrases. He tolerates translations of the Service, but insists that Latin prayers are "more medeful and more acceptable to God" (222). As we saw earlier in this chapter, he would like any *visions* his readers might have to be interpreted personally and kept private, though in other aspects of devotion he seeks a balance between inner and outer, personal and communal. This work gives us an opportunity to set Julian's Jesus-as-mother alongside that of a contemporary working on similar problems, in similar contexts.

For the author of *The Chastising of God's Children*, the idea of the absent mother proves a powerful explanatory and structuring device. He incorporates it into nearly every chapter of the work, creating a much fuller developmental narrative than was offered by the *Ancrene Wisse*. Initially he explains—following *Ancrene Wisse*—that God withdraws from his children in play. Here God is like a mother who hides herself from her child, allowing him to weep and mourn so she can see how much he loves her. Through this planned alteration of joy and sorrow, she increases the child's desire for her. But as her children grow, the mother withdraws for a different, almost opposite reason: in order to wean them, to allow them to stand on their own. She no longer offers them mild and soft foods, but harder meat (104). In the same way, God is soft and nurturing with spiritual novices, but gradually gives them tougher meat to chew in order to facilitate their development. Stronger temptations indicate a more advanced spiritual state. And just as the mother will sometimes speak harshly to the child and threaten him in order to educate him, so God will sometimes give harsh trials to his older children. Finally, if the child is bad, the mother will beat him. The stronger he gets, the bigger the stick she uses—but it is all done (as in Julian's scheme) for love. Suffering is the sign not of God's wrath, but of his love and care for the developing soul. When the child runs away, the mother disciplines him to keep him home. So too, "for love that oure lord hath to his chosen child, bittirli he betith him to purge hym for his trespas, and techith him with sharpnesse evermore to abide at hom in oure lordis service, and al this chastising is for love" (115). (William Flete's God-mother also beats her children for disciplinary purposes.)[24]

The mother-child narrative speaks to the reader's spiritual immaturity and to her continuing need for guidance. But the trope also suggests a conflict between the subject's competing desires for unity and separation in a way that the bridal trope does not. The *Chastising* posits a narrative not of increasing intimacy, but of increasing distance, as the mother grows further and further away, and that increasing distance necessitates greater and greater discipline, imposed both externally and internally. Bridal mysticism imagines inwardness as a space of private plenitude, where the soul seeks communion with her spouse: Ruuysbroec's text describes how the Bridegroom comes to his beloved in the privacy of her inner life, where the spirit may be naturally united both in itself and to God. The *Chastising*, by contrast, redefines interiority as a constant awareness of separation. The child is suspended between its growing independence—for which it is chastised—and its strong desire to return to the mother, which it knows to be impossible. Maternal absence replaces spiritual eroticism, producing contradictory desires within an interpretively unstable developmental framework.

An abbreviated version of the same theme appears in *The Seven Poyntes of Trewe Love and Everlastynge Wisdame*. Even in a text saturated with bridal mysticism, when the Disciple asks Wisdom why she allows her lovers to suffer so much, Wisdom turns the question into a narrative about mothering:

A yonge hynde-fowne that is newe-borne seketh refute of the modere & for to sowke here tetes; but whanne hit is growene & waxene eldere, sche leveth the moder milde & goth up to the hye hilles & there (is) fedde & felawechipede with the flokke. And so thou that art passede chiles condicione that hath nede to be fedde with milke, & art come nowe to saddenesse of mannus yeres, hit is tyme that thou, wenede fro milke and drawene fro tetes, be ioynede and felawechipede in the noumbre of stronge menne. Where-for bye ensomple of hem thou schalt lerne what thou schalt do & howe pacientlye thou schalt ber alle manere of adversitees, so that, whanne thou art provede with tribulaciones as thei were, thou maye be felawchepede to here noumbre with ioye with-owt ende. (348)

The results here are slightly different—this fawn/child joins the herd, whereas in the *Chastising* the child is beaten into staying home—but the similarity of the terms is striking. Adversity is about personal development. Tribulation is for profit. God is like a mother, leaving humans to suffer for their own good. (As Julian might observe, mother and child doubtless see things differently.)

In the *Chastising*, however, the various explanations within the mother-child narrative conflict and overlap, so that even if the mother's ultimate motivations are clear, her tactics foster radical uncertainty in the child with regard to his current status. Is his suffering about the play of presence and absence, a ploy to increase his desire? Is he being weaned on harder meats, indicating spiritual advancement? Or is he being punished? "I counceile everyman to rette it to his owne defaute that grace is withdrawe, bi sum maner necligence," advises the author, "and though his conscience deme nat this alweis in special, yit goode it is to drede" (111). The reader examines himself constantly, seeking those faults for which he is rightfully chastised, taking heed busily of the passions of his soul (cf. 199, 215). But if he must scrutinize his feelings, he must doubt them too—especially if he feels himself to be calm and untroubled, for this is the worst temptation of all: "then ought she sorriest to dread, for then she is most tempted when she feels herself not to be tempted" (97). And why would she *want* to be free of temptation and tribulation? For her own comfort? That too would be a sin; the inward man does not desire rest of heart, ease of conscience, or the peace of contemplation, for such things do not *profit* anyone. "Lord," Saint Bernard is quoted as saying, "give me always tribulation, that I may always be with thee" (201). The reader is reminded that "Hooli men and goode men bien more temptid than othir men," and that the Virgin Mary, in particular, "most was troubled" (96–97). (Recall this writer's attack on the self-emptying rest of "naked unbusiers," discussed in Chapter 2.) We might compare this to the *Ancrene Wisse*'s professed desire to make the heart "even and smooth, without the lumps and hollows of a crooked and accusing conscience which says, 'Here you sin,' or, 'This is not yet amended as well as it might be.'"[25] In the world of the *Chastising*, such lumps and hollows are devoutly to be wished. By centering his text on the mother-child relationship, the *Chastising*'s author constructs a model of subjectivity that is both independent and deeply constrained. As in the *Prickynge of Love*, it is the loss of the mother that drives the subject outward—into the ceaseless exercises of yearning and imitation—and inward, toward the confrontation with the self and the recognition of its inadequacy.

Like so many religious writers of the period, Julian is deeply concerned with the problematics of presence and absence. In the seventh showing, for example, she alternates rapidly between pain and joy, learning that "it is spedfulle to some soules . . . some tyme to be in comfort, and some tyme for to fayle and to be lefte to them selfe" (15.21–22). Like the *Chastising* and related works, she speaks the language of personal betterment. Like them, she believes in the power of abandonment and chastising. It would seem natural, then, for her to invoke God's motherhood in this context, following both her contemporaries and her own abiding interest in the theme of God as mother. But she does not.

For in Julian's work, Christ is not the mother who leaves, against whom the "I" emerges. She will not use the familiar trope even where it seems most appropriate, even called for. For Christ must be the mother from whom we are never fully separated, in whom a part of our soul always remains enclosed: "our savyoure is oure very moder, in whome we be endlesly borne and *nevyr shall come out of hym*" (57.49–50, emphasis mine). Nancy Coiner writes that for Julian (as for Freud), "the exploration of the 'homely' leads again and again to the image of the child enclosed and hidden within the mother's body. And for both, that doubleness-in-unity is a site on which oppositions meet and the distinctions between them blur."[26] The split between God and self is thus not nearly so violent and problematic here as in the *Chastising*, and the Passion no longer encodes increasingly aggressive attempts at reunion. (Julian does not beg to enter, eat, suck, be ravished or wounded, or melt into tears.) The subject is still split, but not traumatically. The doubleness of self becomes a way of keeping part of the soul hidden and unfallen in God, while another part falls with humanity.[27]

The theme of God's motherhood in the *Showings* has been well developed elsewhere; there is no need to explore it further here. I would like to end this chapter by returning to the other mother in the text: the Virgin Mary. For it is Mary—a mother, not a child, even if she is only "a little waxen above a child"—who figures the devout self-in-special, and therefore Julian herself. The figure of the Virgin Mary demonstrates that a universal model can be about "me alone," just as the particular experiences of an "I" can throughout the *Showings* stand for all.

Mary in Special

> And though it be so that thys dede [the unknown deed that God shall perform] be truly take for the generall man, yett it excludyth nott the specyalle; for what oure good lorde wylle do by his poure creatures, it is now unknowyn to me.
>
> —*Showings* (36.50–53)

I have argued that Julian works within the paradigms of vernacular devotional writing, but rejects the boundaries of the self they construct, using a typically private experience of the Passion to confront the universal problem of sin and the broader relationship not between Christ and one soul, but between God and humanity. Julian does not, however, reject the central importance of the individual self, constituted in time and in sin, any more than she rejects the value of personal feeling, in all its vicissitudes, or the importance of what we might call "private" experience. If she were unconvinced of the importance of the "special" self against the general good of the Church, after all, she would not be so concerned with the problem of universal salvation, with the good of each sinful person as well as the "generall man" who shall be saved. Julian thinks not simply in terms of Original Sin, but in terms of individual sins and individual sinners, and how each may profit by seeing his or her own fall. Julian's book is itself evidence of her faith in the power of human reason to find meaning in subjective experience—and in the very personal failure that she so scrupulously records and examines, convinced of its ability to reflect some aspect of the divine plan. For Julian, individual self-consciousness is always epistemological and theological ground zero.

As we have seen, Julian understands that ground through an Augustinian rationalism—fundamentally Trinitarian—filtered through the most familiar affective paradigm of her day, the personal and affective encounter with the crucified Christ. But Julian's text also deploys what we might call the autobiographical or confessional mode of self-knowledge and self-understanding: a mode that values the individual life, constituted through and understanding itself in terms of its encounters with time. Because the *Showings* are not constructed as a confession or a spiritual autobiography, it is easy to miss this operation of the text; we have to look differently, through the symbols and images of Julian's visionary experience, to find it. We might look productively to the representation of the Virgin Mary. In *The Myroure of Oure Ladye, The Chastising of God's Children*, and so many other texts, religious women were told to see her, and to see themselves reflected in this powerful self/other, this reflective and exemplary mirror. Julian clearly does. We are used to seeing William Langland cryptically written into his own work, glimmering through the enigmatic overlays of Will and Piers and Christ. Julian also inscribes herself into her visions, through the only figure in her text who is represented in a progression through time, in the fullness of a life.

For if Julian sees God in a single point, as she says, she represents the Virgin Mary as a line, stretched out from childhood to heavenly reward. "Oure lorde shewyd me nothyng in specialle but oure lady sent Mary," Julian writes, "and her he shewyd thre tymes. The furst was as she conceyvyd, the seconde as she was in her sorowes under the cross, and the thurde was as she is now in lykynge, worschyppe and joy" (25.37–41). Each of those three "specialle" showings occurs at a crucial moment in the text, and each is in some subtle way associated with Julian's own progression from the past to "as she is now."

The first showing of the Virgin Mary is at the Annunciation. I have already described how the young Mary, only "a little waxen above a child," serves in Julian's first revelation as a model for the contemplative vision that shows the made creature to itself through a vision of its maker. Mary's vision of herself as little and low next to God corresponds to the vision of the hazelnut-sized thing and the soul's vision of itself, all linguistically interwoven. More particularly, Mary's reverent beholding overlays Julian's own reverent beholding, and Mary's "Lo, god's handmaiden" resonates over and through Julian's "Benedicite dominus." The young Mary, in the moment of the Annunciation, serves as an enigmatic model for Julian's concurrent visionary experience, and for Passional vision in general. Her ability to contain so much more than herself is echoed in Julian's own enclosure of Christ, as he sits enthroned in the endless ward of her soul.

The second showing of the Virgin Mary is as she stands beside the cross in the eighth revelation—a mature woman now, suffering horribly in compassion for her dying son. The vision comes as Julian herself contemplates the final drying of Christ's body. "The shewyng of Cristes paynes fylled me fulle of peynes," she writes, repenting that she had ever asked for a vision of the Passion; "For me thought my paynes passyd ony bodely deth"—an assertion often made about the Virgin Mary, crucified "inwardly" with her son (17.50–56). Like the Virgin, Julian feels that she loves Christ so far above herself that there could be no worse suffering than to see him die. "Here I saw in parte the compassion of our blessed lady sainct Mary," she writes, whose "peyne passyd alle other" because of the greatness of her creaturely, "kynde" love for Christ (18.1–8). Mary traditionally models the compassionate response to, and inward imitation of, Christ's death for all Christians, so her appearance and function here are unremarkable. But Julian uses them to do something startling.

For Julian now experiences the friendly "profyr" in her reason: "Loke uppe to hevyn to hys father" (19.7). She refuses "inwardly with alle the myght of my soule," saying that Jesus is her heaven, and that she would rather be in pain until Doomsday than come to heaven any other way (see Chapter one for further discussion). "Myghtly, wysely and wyllfully, I chose Jhesus to my hevyn," she writes (19.31–32). Just as her empathetic suffering of the Passion is based on Mary's model, so too is her willful choice to stay with him in his human suffering. In numerous *planctus Mariae* and other devotional treatises (such as the *Tretys of Love* mentioned in Chapter 3, or Hoccleve's "Complaint of the Virgin," discussed in Chapter 5), the Virgin Mary refuses to "look up" toward the greater purpose of the Passion, positioning herself against Christ's heavenly father in her refusal to be consoled. Paralyzed by suffering, she too chooses unimaginable and lasting pain rather than betray her too-human love for her son.[28] In choosing not to look up to the father, Julian again positions herself alongside the Virgin Mary. *Planctus Mariae* often emphasized that Mary's refusal to be comforted increased her son's agony; Julian too observes that Christ suffered for his mother's sorrow (20.22). But Julian rewrites the moral of the Virgin's—and her own—stubbornness in the face of the hierarchies of salvation, insisting that her willful choice was also mighty and wise, and that it "hath evyr be a comfort to me, that I chose Jhesu to be my hevyn." She is taught "that I shulde evyr more do so," in well or in woe (19.19–20). Mary proves a "lernyng" to her, as she has before and will again. Whether standing willfully by the cross or seeing herself at the Annunciation, she becomes the ground of Julian's most striking assertions.[29] In both these scenes, Julian shifts the Virgin's association with vision and inwardness to make those associations limn much broader understandings of the connections between divine and human perceiving, feeling, and understanding.

The third and final showing of the Virgin takes her from the cross to her reward in heaven. The revelation begins: "And with thys chere of myrth and joy our good lord lokyd downe on the ryght syde, and brought to my mynde where our lady stode in the tyme of hys passion, and seyd: Wilt thou see her? And in this swete word, as yf he had seyd, I wott welle that thou wilt se my blessyd mother, for after my selfe she is the hyghest joy that I myght shewe the, and most lykyng and worschyppe to me, and most she is desyred to be seen of alle my blessyd creatures" (25.1–9). This is not merely a repetition of the previous vision. What is particularly intriguing here is the way Julian emphasizes the Virgin's singular and "special" status, even while quietly connecting her, visually and enigmatically, to the "I" of Julian's own text. Julian speaks of the "marvelous hygh and syngular love" that Christ has to this sweet maiden, and then understands Christ to be saying a second time, "wylte thou se how that I love her?" (25.12) And then again a third time, he speaks "to all mankynd that shall be savyd," but he speaks *as it were alle to one person*, as yf he sayde, wylt thou se in her how *thou* art lovyd?" (25.15–16, emphasis mine) Visual language saturates this section: the Virgin is most desired to be seen; she is the most blessed sight; Julian desires to see her; she is not shown her in bodily presence, but she does see her in ghostly showing.[30] A fourth time, Christ asks, "Wylte thou see her?" And in this ghostly vision, Julian writes, finally making it self-reflexive, "I am leernyd to know my self, and reverently drede my god" (25.21–22).

Now Julian beholds the Virgin no longer "lytylle and symple," but "hygh and noble and glorious and plesyng to [Christ] above all creatures," for he loves her "as yf a man love a creature syngulary a bove alle creatures" (25.32–33). Julian explains that "in thys worde that Jesu seyde: Wylte thou see her?"—and this is the *fifth time* the question has been repeated—"me thought it was the most lykyn worde that he myght geve me of her with the gostely shewyng that he gave me of her" (25.35–37). Why, we might ask, is this question so welcome to Julian, and why is it repeated so obsessively here? Jesus' question encourages Julian to recognize herself, and tells her how she is singularly loved. It is because, she continues, "our lorde shewyd me nothyng in specialle but oure lady sent Mary, and her he shewyd thre tymes": carefully summed up as a passage through age and experience and time, from "as she conceyvyd," to her "sorowes under the crosse," to "as she is now, in lykyng, worschyppe and joy" (25.37–41).

Julian has already seen herself lifted to heaven, in the sixth revelation, to be thanked and feasted with Christ and all his friends. In this revelation, she hears God saying: "I thangke the of thy servys and of thy travelle of thy yowyth" (14.3–4). We know nothing biographical about Julian's youth; only that she had desired three wounds, a sickness, and better feeling of the Passion. (Perhaps she had taken religious vows.) But immediately following these mysterious thanks, Julian's understanding is lifted into heaven, where she sees a lord in his own house, calling his friends to a solemn feast. She sees the bliss that each soul shall have, "And I saw that . . . the age of every man shal be knowen in hevyn, and be rewardyd for hys wyllfulle servys and for hys tyme, *and namly the age of them that wylfully and frely offer ther yowth to god*, passynly is rewarded and wonderfully thangkyd" (14.29–32, emphasis mine). Note here the focus on youth, age, and time. God values the life of service in history, the time that has been offered.

Watson writes, "The passing of time is not an incidental feature of the Long Text; on the contrary, dates, numbers of years, Julian's own age, are carefully brought before us at the work's most crucial moments, as though they are of thematic significance."[31] Julian's sickness and revelations occur when she is thirty years old and a half, on May 13, 1373. She had before, "in my jowth," desired three gifts by the grace of God, but two of them had passed from her mind. She is ill for three days and three nights, and on the fourth night she takes her last rites; then another two days and two nights pass, and on the third night she has her first series of visions, which last from about 4:00 A.M. to past noon (65.37–40). The sixteenth showing takes place the next night. More than fifteen years pass, during which time she desires constantly to know her Lord's meaning, and finally she is answered that love was his meaning. And of her showing of the Lord and Servant, she writes, "For twenty yere after the tyme of the shewyng save thre monthys I had techyng inwardly as I shall sey" (51.86–87). In the course of the book, we are told about Julian's desires—and service and travail—in youth; her pains and sorrows "beside the cross" during her illness; and her long, difficult process of coming to understand her experience and what it meant, as she now joyfully sees it. The passage of time and the passage of a life are vividly present. Julian is "learned" to know herself through the Virgin in many ways, but perhaps the most unexpected way is as a self "in special," as well as in general, represented in the progress of time as well as in the endless "now" of heavenly reward. Insisting on the general and universal, Julian still leaves the Virgin Mary as the place where the singular and special, the human, the temporal, the particular age of every man, can reside. Finding herself in the Virgin just at Langland finds his image in Piers and Christ—and defining herself, like him, through the movements of her restless and mighty "will"— Julian writes herself into the fabric of her work, a work carefully constructed to value the process of coming to a clearer vision as well as the perfected reflection that is its goal.

Chapter 5
Hoccleve's Glasses

Moving from Norwich to Westminster, this study ends with an author more famous for autobiographical poetry than for devotional reading: Thomas Hoccleve, clerk of the Privy Seal, self-promoting follower of Chaucer, and author of one of the fifteenth century's most popular texts, *The Regement of Princes*. What could be further from the serene self-effacement and theological optimism of Julian's *Showings* than the perpetual plights and gripes of this petty bureaucrat and sometime royal apologist, whom F. J. Furnivall would describe as a "weak, sensitive, look-on-the-worst-side kind of man"?[1] Julian addresses God in a mighty inward voice, seeking answers to the universal inequities of suffering and salvation. Hoccleve addresses Prince Henry in the squeakiest and most self-abasing of tones, complaining about his delicate stomach and seeking redress for the nonpayment of his small annuity.

In many ways, though, Hoccleve is a natural endpoint for our consideration of how English devotional discourses envisioned the private self, and how earlier religious models were transmitted and adapted for new audiences. A member of that literate "middle" group of people who have figured so prominently in this study, Hoccleve had meant to be a priest, but never received a benefice; instead he married and was absorbed into the bustling bureaucracy of Lancastrian administration. He wrote devotional poems for aristocrats as well as for the urban bourgeoisie: among them, a complaint of the Virgin for Joan Fitzalan, countess of Hereford; a poem to the Virgin for Thomas Marleburgh, a London stationer; and another for Robert Chichele, master of the Grocer's Company and mayor of London. A translation from Suso's *Horologium Sapientiae*, "Lerne to Die," was one of his last works; addressed to Humphrey, Duke of Gloucester, it stands near the end of his *Series*. So Hoccleve was in part a devotional writer, one of the many translators laboring to meet the laity's demand for vernacular works of piety and spiritual guidance.

Hoccleve's poetic reputation rests not on his mostly overlooked religious pieces, of course, but on his claim to being the earliest autobiographical poet in English, "our first chronicler of private worries."[2] This chapter explores some of the interplay between those two modes. For even Hoccleve's secular poetry bears witness to a deep engagement with devotional paradigms, with the voices of the meditative, confessional, and penitential "I." Like Julian, Hoccleve uses devotional discourse—and the discourses of vision and interiority in particular—to *think with*, and to ground his own experiments with poetic subjectivity. Where Julian makes public theology out of the paradigms of Passion meditation and Augustinian self-examination, Hoccleve turns private self-envisioning into secular and poetic self-fashioning. While Julian challenges the boundaries of private devotion, Hoccleve occupies and exploits them, crafting a witty, confessional persona that can move from private abjection to public speech and back again. No writer better illuminates the contested, paradoxical, politically loaded territory between inner and outer, private and public, spectacle and introspection in early fifteenth-century England than this plaintive, self-absorbed clerk.

In suggesting a connection between Hoccleve's devotional and autobiographical poetry, I am following a line laid out by Eva Thornley in her 1967 article, "The Middle English Penitential Lyric and Hoccleve's Autobiographical Poetry." In this thorough and convincing reading of Hoccleve's "La Male Regle," Thornley remarks that "the importance of the Middle English penitential lyric as distinct *literary* genre . . . has not been fully realized" (295). The form's literary potential, she remarks, "lies primarily in [its] autobiographical tendency," and this tendency can be seen clearly in Hoccleve's autobiographical parody of it. Arguing for the traditional and religious, rather than forward-looking and secular, nature of Hoccleve's self-examining aesthetic, she writes, "while his introspective tendency appears to anticipate the Renaissance, it would be truer to say that the actual and potential influence of the penitential lyric upon the poetry of personal revelation, both religious and secular, may be observed in his autobiographical verse" (296). Thornley's article has been much cited but little heeded, with critics generally preferring to find Hoccleve's influences in secular contexts: the French *dit* tradition, Chaucer's garrulous Wife of Bath and Pardoner, the form of the bureaucratic petition.[3] I don't discount the importance of any of these. As I noted in the introduction, interest in—and anxiety about—the private self was high in fifteenth-century England in a variety of contexts. This interest, I suggested, contributed to the popularity of devotional texts, which provided some of the most detailed and powerful discourses of identity available, and would have appealed to readers concerned to enhance and articulate their inner lives. Indeed, I think it would be strange if Hoccleve had not made use of these familiar paradigms. What I want to do in this chapter, then, is to show how Hoccleve explores the fissures of his social and political worlds in part by re-locating and rewriting devotional narratives and tropes. In various genres and contexts, he plays with the same kinds of questions we have seen in texts such as Julian's *Showings* and *The Myroure of Oure Ladye*. What kinds of authority—and danger—does the inward turn produce? What is the relationship between seeing inward and showing outward, between introspection and the poetics of personal display? What are the profits of tribulation? Hoccleve invests these questions with new significance by applying them to a particular historical and personal world, and by running them through different combinations and hybridizations of genres: not just devotional, but classical, political, petitionary, Boethian, Chaucerian. Swerving from one mode of speech to another, he highlights the dangers and difficulties of self-consciousness in the busy, precarious, shifting world of Lancastrian London. In doing so, he helps to remind us that however world-scorning and inward it was, devotional literature was not separate from, but deeply imbricated with, the social worlds of busy, interesting, historical people.

*   *   *

It will be useful to begin with a brief examination of Hoccleve's shorter devotional poems. We might think about these poems as experiments with the first-person voice, explorations of a mode that Hoccleve would transform in his secular verse—for the guilty, self-conscious, isolated speaker of these poems has strong affinities with Hoccleve's autobiographical persona.[4] This devotional "I," however, is not exactly the voice of "Thomas Hoccleve." Rather, it is intended to become the private voice of people like Thomas Marleburgh, Robert Chichele, or Joan Fitzalan. Shaping the devotional experiences, and the devotional selves, of his wealthy, London-area clientele was part of Hoccleve's business. These poems connect our introspective clerk to a pious, literate audience—not only through the mechanisms of patronage, but through a shared investment in certain forms of devotional rhetoric, certain models of subjectivity. In what respects, we might ask, might the professedly alienated, impoverished clerk at the Privy Seal share a self and a voice with the powerful and prosperous citizens of London?

Like the Passion meditations discussed in Chapter 3, Hoccleve's devotional verses articulate a subject whose meditative encounters almost invariably plunge him into painfully self-conscious lamentation. They are penitential rather than affective, confessional rather than celebratory. At the beginning of the "Ballad to the Virgin and Christ," for example, the meditator recalls how he was walking in a garden when he came across "A crois depeynted with a fair ymage" (10). The next line contains the turn: "I thoghte I nas but asshes and foul clay" (11). Rather than provoking his pity, the cross confronts him with his own foulness and mortality. The reflexive action is repeated forcefully in lines 68 and 69: "On the crois was thy skyn in-to blood died! / Allas! why have I me to synne applied?" Like his secular verses, Hoccleve's devotional poems return inevitably to his heart's "filthy privitee." Standing before the Virgin in "Ad beatam Virginem," he relates how the "beholdynge of [her] pured clennesse" makes him intensely aware of his own, humiliatingly exposed offenses:

My soule is stuffid so with stynk of synne,
that ay it dreedith beforn thee appeere,
Lest for the filthe which that it is ynne,
Thow torne away thy merciable cheere.

Addressing the infant Jesus in another poem, he sees himself in every aspect of the child's later suffering:

I am the wownde of al thy grevance;
I am the cause of thyn occisioun,
And of thy deeth, dessert, of thy vengeance
I am also verry flagicioun;
I causid thee thy grevous passioun. ("Ad filium," 8–12)

Placed forcefully at the beginning of each line, the "I" dominates the poem. "I am he," the meditator declares, "that wroght have synfully . . . I dide amis, I synned grevously" (36–38). Each of Christ's virtues shows him one of his own failures. He is proud while Christ is meek; his flesh is fat while Christ is thin; his own heart is "wrappid in unbuxumnesse; / And thow buxum our soules for to wynne" (45–46). The "greet dyversitee" between himself and Christ is like the divide between Eve and Mary: "Eve me gladith with a lawwhyng ye, / And weepynge up-on thee reewith Marie" (62–63). The subject of these poems talks endlessly about himself. He also talks *to* himself: to his soul (sometimes "she," sometimes "it"), to his spirit (gendered male, the abandoner of his sorrowful feminine soul), to his own sins. Talking to himself, or "raving" as he calls it, is also a hallmark of Hoccleve's self-absorbed secular poetry.

Again, these poems are translations, some doubtless undertaken by particular request. Yet as a body, Hoccleve's devotional pieces make sense; they speak with essentially the same voice, though that voice—solitary and self-conscious as it is—is partly a shared one, meant to be taken up by other readers. There are no celebratory hymns along the lines of, for example, Chaucer's "An ABC," a hymn to the Virgin translated from the French of Guillaume Deguilleville. Hoccleve also translated a Deguilleville piece—but an anguished complaint, not an exquisite ode. What interests Hoccleve (and his patrons) is not the rhetoric of praise but that of self-abasement, not the brilliance of poetic description but the articulation of emotional states. These poems fit comfortably into a devotional habit of mind that, as I have argued, was particularly popular with English writers and readers. At the same time, the translations are marked with the unmistakable signs of Hoccleve's own abiding poetic concerns.

"Ad filium," for example, ends with an odd and characteristically Hocclevean moment, which inverts the visual and affective paradigms of most Passion meditation. It closes with an injunction to "behold"—but not the familiar "behold Christ's wounds" or "behold thyself" (which this meditator is already doing to a painful extent in any case). It is instead a request for Christ to behold *himself*. "O Kyng of glorie," the speaker prays, "thow beholde & see / what peynes thow suffriddist for our sake!" (64–65) In other poems, he begs Christ to behold his mother, or implores God the Father to behold his suffering son: "The gracious yen of they magestee, / we the byseeche on thy sone thow caste!"[5] The sight of Christ's wounded sides will create memory and compassion—but in God, not the sinner. "Beholde his toren membres, fadir free," he implores, "And lat our substance in thyn herte impresse!"[6] The Virgin too is frequently asked to "impress" the Passion into her memory, or to behold and remember her own sufferings. The subject's self-recognition demands reciprocal action: the deity too must see, remember, and take pity. At the end of "Ad beatam virginem," Christ stands "Beforn his fadir, with his wowndes rede," and the Virgin stands before Christ, "mercy for to grede":

Thy sone his body shewith al bybled;
And to thy sone also, thy maydenhede
Shewith the pappes wher-with he was fed. (108–12)

The tableau makes divine showing the solution to the speaker's despair. From the bare-breasted Virgin (in the classic posture of maternal political intercession) to the wound-displaying Christ to God the beholder, the chain of exposure holds out the possibility of relief for a subject whose inward gaze threatens to lock him into a cycle of solipsistic isolation. These dynamics of power, petition, and visual exchange offer suggestive parallels to Hoccleve's secular verse, where powerful patrons are often asked to see, remember, and respond to the mirror images presented to them by the confessional and impoverished poet. Here we find Hoccleve thinking not just about the representation of fragmented, self-accusing consciousness, but about how that representation might generate recognition, connection, and response.

*   *   *

The depth of Hoccleve's engagement with devotional themes is apparent in his nondevotional verse as well, from the mock-penitential "La Male Regle" to the confessional episodes in the *Regement of Princes*. In his "Dialogue with a Friend," for example—the second part of the *Series*—Hoccleve explains that he wants to publish his "Complaint" as a confession of God's mercy: "In feythe, frinde, I thenke make an open shryfte, / and hyde not what I had of his gyfte," he says (83–84). His narrative may inspire some future reader, who "there-by shall / his consyence ful tenderly grope, / and withe hym self acompte, & reken of all / that he hathe in his lyfe wrowght, great and small" (219–22). But Hoccleve's confessional protestations are only awkwardly applicable to the self-serving narrative of the "Complaint." (What might his readers really learn from this?) As in so much of his secular poetry, Hoccleve's use of religious language and imagery seems to insert an ironic distance, underlining the fallenness of the urban, bureaucratic world, where Lady Money is "of the world goddesse, / That have al thynge under my buxumnesse" ("Three Roundels"). In the "Balade to Master John Carpenter," Hoccleve begs Carpenter to intercede for him with his creditors, after the fashion of a Marian plea for intercession. In a ballad to Henry Somer for the Court de Bone Conpaignie, he refers to that social club humorously as a "rule" of sorts, a foundation whose members are in need of a good "miroure" and whose observances are in need of reform. "First wern we fowndid to use largesse," he writes, reminding Somer that he has promised them a dinner, so "that th'entente of oure old fundacioun / Observed mighte been and to that plyt / Be broght as it was first."[7] And in "La Male Regle," the language of confession and penitence prefaces a supplication not for grace, but for money. In exchange for the exposure of his soul, Hoccleve expects his purse to be made well. This generic twist—a devotional subject in an economic context, a begging poem where the supplicant's troubles are his own fault—renders his personal revelations both intimate and ironic, both desperately sincere and entertainingly self-mocking. Much of the wry humor and wit of Hoccleve's social verse depends on this clever, slightly rueful displacement of religious language.

But Hoccleve's reliance on devotional convention is always at its deepest and most searching when he is representing the solitary self and negotiating the distances between inwardness and social identity. This is particularly evident in the famous and emblematic episode in "My Complaint," where the poet stands alone in his private chamber, looking at himself in a mirror.

He has come to examine himself, to try to see himself as others must see him—for his return to society following a period of madness has gone very badly. When he is out in public, people look strangely at him and then look away. ("The worlde me made a straunge countinaunce," he reports.)[8] They flee from him and gossip about him behind his back. Every external gesture is taken as a sign of mental illness or instability:

Men seyden, I loked as a wilde steer,
and so my loke abowt I gan to throwe;
myne heed to hie a-nother seide I beer,
full bukkyshe is his brayne well may I trowe. (120–23)

With these whispers ringing in his ears, the humiliated poet rushes home to his solitary chamber. (Tribulations, as so many texts observed, force a man to inhabit the house of his own heart.) Yet if anything, the public's gaze is even more pressing in his private chamber than it was on the streets of London, for Hoccleve reenacts it for himself through the technology of the mirror:

And in my chamber at home when I was
my self alone, I in this wyse wrowght:

I streite unto my myrrowr and my glas,
to loke how that me of my chere thowghte,
yf any other were it than it owghte;
for fayne wolde I yf it had not be right,
amendyd it, to my kunynge and myght. (155–61)

It is a virtual parody of the scene of devotional self-examination. Like the subject of *The Prickynge of Love*—or like Julian, anxious to know "how God sees us"—Hoccleve is driven to examine his own image by the sense that he is already the object of critical scrutiny. The mirror allows him to re-create for himself the gaze of "the folk" on the streets of Westminster, so that he might see—as *The Myroure of Oure Ladye* would put it—where he fails, and amend.

Even with the aid of his mirror, however, Hoccleve admits that he is not really sure he can see and know himself accurately. How can a madman tell whether he is really sane? (As Julian might ask, how can we really know ourselves when we have no perspective outside our own? We can't see ourselves properly until we know how God sees us, and God's vision may be completely unlike our own.) Hoccleve's struggle to erase the distance between ideal and real images highlights the epistemological problems inherent not only in the madman's, but in any solitary soul's attempts at self-reflection, self-knowledge, and self-improvement. "Men in her owne cas bene blind alday," he observes (170). Without external confirmation, how is the beholder to know how closely his envisioning aligns with God's? Especially since interiority is already so closely associated with insanity? Hoccleve believes that he is perfectly sane, but the picture of him leaping repeatedly in front of his mirror, trying to catch himself in the act of looking crazy, makes him seem "bukkyshe" indeed. If madness cast Hoccleve out of himself, separating him from his memory and wits, the mirror scene seems to do much the same thing, creating one person looking for another as if the other were not, somehow, himself.

Of course, the critical gaze Hoccleve is trying to re-create here is not God's, and the poet is not interested in amending his inner life. Instead, the mirror scene has been literalized and emptied of spiritual significance. Hoccleve wishes to amend only his appearance—not his substance, but his accident. (The "substaunce of [his] memorie" has ostensibly returned [50].) For although the folk are quick to judge his inward state by its outward manifestations, Hoccleve asserts that such judgments are wildly unreliable: "Upon a looke is harde, men them to grownde / what a man is;

there-by the sothe is hid" (211–12). Men cannot see into his inner life. And so he practices what he hopes will be convincingly sane faces for the crowd at Westminster. "Yf that I loke in this manere / amonge folke as I now do," he thinks,

. . . none errowr
of suspecte loke may in my face appere,
this countinance, I am sure, and this chere,
If I forthe use is no thinge reprevable. (163–67)

Hoccleve's busy labor "to peinte countinaunce, chere and loke" only under-lines the distance between inner self and outer persona. And yet Hoccleve is not, he claims, trying to obscure the "sothe" of himself; quite the opposite. What he struggles to paint externally is an accurate reflection of his inner state, so that he will look to others the way he knows himself to be. Like the nuns at Syon, he needs to be able to see himself so that he can show his inner state outwardly and accurately, bringing private seeing and public showing into perfect harmony. Hoccleve will enact himself, bringing his interiority before the public through self-consciously assumed gestures and postures, constructing a persona all the more accurate, paradoxically, for its studied artifice.

Hoccleve's real reconstruction of himself will require a different kind of mirror: the mirror of a text. At the end of the complaint, Hoccleve picks up a book in which he finds the complaint of another "hevy man wooful and angwisshous" (316).[9] For three stanzas, Hoccleve submerges himself in the voice of this other "I"; then he performs the voice of that text's consol-ing Reason figure, who explains that "Woo, heviness and tribulacioun / Comen aren to men alle and *profitable*" (351, emphasis mine). He recognizes his own condition and receives his consolation, a consolation that will allow him to break his silence and write his own complaint, for the profit of oth-ers. The anguished Hoccleve "had lost [his] tunges keie"—but now he will overcome his isolation and give others the means to transform themselves as he has been transformed (144). His own "I" will become available for rhetorical performance, recognition, and appropriation.

But Hoccleve's determination to publish his complaint as proof of his sanity (and the Friend, at least, thinks that writing drove Hoccleve mad to begin with) suggests that this piece of writing may be just another version of the "sane faces" Hoccleve practiced in his chamber glass. Just as Hoccleve jumps in front of the mirror, trying to surprise himself in a look of madness, so too he writes about how he is just this minute writing poetry, as if trying to catch himself in the very act. Here too he only calls attention to the impassable gulf between the one "himself" and the other. In his poetry, Hoccleve presents himself presenting his true face to an audience, looking inward and showing himself outward. Yet we should remember the self-conscious care and steady purpose with which the poet manipulates his own image, the literary games he plays trying to catch himself being himself. Hoccleve may style his confessional outbursts as spontaneous ("I braste oute on the morwe and thus bigan") and therapeutic, but even their evocation of devotional convention is witty and literary—and self-promotional, as Hoccleve addresses his confessions to the most powerful patrons he can find.[10] There are, after all, other profits to be gained from tribulation.

The value of Hoccleve's personal revelations to London audiences—and some of the wry cynicism of those revelations—can be linked to specific changes in government administration and patronage, as critics such as Ethan Knapp have suggested.[11] Hoccleve himself emphasizes that the fifteenth-century English court was becoming increasingly bureaucratized, as government functions were transferred from the king's personal retainers to an army of salaried clerks and administrators. Knapp writes,

the widespread social instabilities of late-fourteenth- and early-fifteenth-century England combined with problems in payment specific to the central bureaucracy to create a profound sense of anxiety in Hoccleve and his colleagues. The old structures that had given security to both the identity and the finances of these clerks, namely, their ecclesiastical status and membership in the king's household, were giving way as the administration became increasingly laicized and increasingly distant from the household of the king.[12]

In the *Regiment of Princes*, Hoccleve describes his scribal labors in the Office of the Privy Seal as intensely impersonal and alienating, as well as very unreliably reimbursed. It is bad enough that these clerks must "labour in travaillous stilnesse" (1013), to the detriment of their eyes, backs, and stomachs; what is worse is that they are without "lordshcepe," without *familia*, without anyone to look after their precarious welfare. They are "Nobody's men"—for as Hoccleve wryly explains, Nobody is their only benefactor: "He hem avanceth; he ful hir frende is; / Sauf only hym, they han but fewe frendes" (1490–91).[13] Nobody will protect them from the unscrupulous manipulators of an impersonal system. The Old Man can remember a time when an appeal to one's lord provided recourse, but Hoccleve denies that he lives in that past world. "The world is naght swich now, my fadir deere," he laments, "As ye han seene; farwel, frendely maneere!" (1796–97). These days, he explains, a lord has so much to attend to, and so little personal connection to his petitioners, "that my mateere / Out of his mynde slippeth away soone" (1794–95).

But where personal relation has been replaced by other forms of economic organization, nostalgia for that relation makes its literary semblance all the more valuable. Larry Scanlon observes that the begging poem was a late development in Europe, the product of a court "sufficiently bureaucratized that petitions for small sum of money have become routine, but still sufficiently invested in the personal to want to see the granting of such petitions as the whimsical response to a *jeu d'esprit*."[14] In such an economy, Hoccleve's literary self-exposures not only re-create the semblance of personal connection but produce "remembraunce," impressing Hoccleve and his "mateere" into the memory of a lord who may not know him very well, but who may be a crucial source of his small income. As Hoccleve writes in "La Male Regle," a man who "thurgh arghnesse [reluctance] his owne self forgetith, / No wondir thogh an othir him forgete" (57–58). The self-remembrance of Augustine and Abelard is twisted from a penitential into a self-promotional aesthetic. The familiar admonition to "Forget not thyself" becomes something more like "look out for number one"—because if you don't, only Nobody will. The Old Man notes that a beggar knows how to show passers-by his shameful diseases, and thus profit by them: "ffor, and he kepe hym cloos, & holde his pees, / And noght out schewe how seek he inward is, / He may al day so sytten helpelees" (253–55). A hidden malady is an unprofitable malady, and Hoccleve admits that shame is an emotion he cannot afford: "As the shameless cravour wole it gooth. . . . But poore shamefast man ofte is wrooth." In his confessional works, Hoccleve reveals himself to his audience through the fractured paradigms of devotional self-knowledge; what he offers, he suggests, is a clear and instructive view of his otherwise hard-to-know heart, in all its shame and misery. What he asks in return is to be remembered—to introduce his imprint into the patron's own heart, and from there into his purse. His singularity and failure become valuable commodities for an audience interested in the cultivation and reformation of the inner life, trained to identify abjection with self-knowledge, and pleased to be granted the intimacy of personal access to the supplicant's heart, here created as a clever literary effect.

Hoccleve's Virgin and the Politics of Complaint

Hoccleve was not just interested in the representation of private selves and their hidden maladies, however. He was also deeply concerned with—and implicated in—the public, political uses of such representation. And here I would like to turn again to a devotional poem: this time Hoccleve's longest and perhaps most popular, "The Complaint of the Virgin." Like the more famous "Hoccleve's Complaint," this work provides a fascinating exploration of the troubled relationship between the private "I" and the public gaze, between personal suffering and its representation in the public sphere. Conventional as it is, the poem demonstrates how those very conventions could provide Hoccleve with an important arena for the negotiations of identity that continue to interest us in his poetry.

Hoccleve's source for "The Complaint of the Virgin" was a section of Guillaume Deguilleville's *Le Pèlerinage de l'Ame*, a rather thin allegory in which the Green Tree (Mary) laments the loss of her Apple (Jesus).[15] Hoccleve offers a reasonably faithful translation of the episode, eliminating the allegorical level, cutting off the end of the lament, and expanding the remaining material slightly to make it fit his rhyme royal stanzas. At 245 lines, it is by far his longest devotional poem. It may also have been his most popular. It seems to have been widely available, occurring as it does in all ten complete manuscripts of the Middle English translation of the *Pèlerinage*, as well as Huntington MS 111.[16]

According to a note at the end of the poem in the Huntington manuscript, Hoccleve undertook the translation at the request of Joan Fitzalan, Countess of Hereford (1347–1419).[17] Joan was a pious widow, probably in her fifties or sixties at the time of the translation, which must have been completed by 1413. She was also very well connected. She was Bishop Arundel's sister, and mother of Henry IV's first wife, Mary; she was thus Henry V's grandmother. Her first daughter married the Duke of Gloucester (and left a "notable" book collection).[18] The presence of a female patron may be significant, for although the Virgin was a favorite subject of Hoccleve's devotional verse, this is the only poem in which she appears as the speaking subject, rather than as the object of the sinful poet's pleas for mercy and remembrance.[19] And Joan was in a position to know something about the sacrificial demands of power, and the public uses of mourning and complaint.

"The Complaint of the Virgin" belongs to a tradition of *planctus Mariae* popularized by St. Bernard and fairly common in Middle English lyric, but with roots in Byzantine Marian laments of the sixth century and earlier.[20] Margaret Alexiou has suggested that the genre originates in the Greek ritual laments of antiquity[21]—and indeed, it is difficult not to hear in Hoccleve's poem an echo of Chaucer's interest in the elegiac, Ovidian female subject. Chaucer had been fascinated by the elegiac female voice. *The Book of the Duchess, The House of Fame, Anelida and Arcite, The Legend of Good Women, The Physician's Tale*—all take up the question of female complaint. Again and again, Chaucer had experimented with questions of betrayal, speech, death, and poetry through women such as Alcyone, Hypsiple, Dido, and Virginia: women whose deaths become central to masculine representations, but whose own laments are often severely curtailed. As Jennifer Summit puts it, "the Chaucerian woman writer is repeatedly conceived as a figure of loss, whether in terms of literal loss, as an elegiac or suicidal figure, or of textual loss, as one whose writing is impaired by illegibility, misapprehension, or disappearance."[22] Hoccleve's interest in Marian lament seems to have been influenced at least in part by this Chaucerian poetic.

But if Hoccleve's "Complaint of the Virgin" takes up the elegiac female voice in a particularly Chaucerian way, it also uses the Christian devotional context to turn that voice toward more typically Hocclevean concerns. For where Chaucer was fascinated by classical poets and stories, Hoccleve was interested primarily in his own social and political world. The complaining Virgin Mary allows Hoccleve to play with issues of speech, power, and sacrifice—with the translation of private emotion into public meaning and value—in a more local and contemporary idiom, reflecting a world in which both religion and poetry were becoming increasingly politicized.

Thus where Chaucer had used the figure of Dido to explore the dependence of male empire on female sacrifice, Hoccleve turns to the inconsolable Virgin Mary, lamenting the loss of her only son in the cause of mankind's salvation. Like Dido, the Virgin figures the private relationships that must be sacrificed for the sake of public duty, the personal history that must be written over by masculine narratives of destiny. Aeneas abandons Dido for the Roman empire, while Christ forsakes his mother to found a Christian one. Both women speak from fissures in the narratives of triumph and unity, and from the verge of death. "The wownde of deeth ne may I nat asterte," Mary laments (53); "Thynke nat, sone, in me that any breeth / Endure may, that feele al this grevance; / My martirdom me hath at the outrance" (80–82).

Like Dido or any of Chaucer's "good women," the Virgin represents her immanent death as the result of male abandonment. She has been betrayed by a fierce, cruel father God and a fickle Holy Ghost; by the smooth-talking Gabriel, who gave her no "warnyng / Of that grace that veyn is and faylyng" (32–33); and especially by her beloved Christ, who once belonged wholly to her and now gives himself to another purpose. Late medieval *planctus Mariae* tend to present Mary as hysterically inconsolable, and this one is no exception. The Virgin refuses to accept Christ's saving mission; instead, she complains bitterly of the torments in which he has left her, seemingly by his own choice. "Mighte nat, sone the Redempcioun / Of man han bee withoute effusioun / Of thy blood?" she asks, answering with a defiant "yis, if it had been thy lust. / But what thow wilt be doon souffre me must!" (116–19). In her eyes, the desertion is unnecessary, her suffering arbitrary. "[T]how mak-ist departynge / Twixt thee & me for ay withoute endynge," she laments, as Christ bequeaths her to his disciple John (174–75); "Thow my ioie appallist" (178). Worst of all, her "special" beloved now refuses even to call her by name, referring to her instead with the cold (and biblical) "woman" (176). Refusing to be thus impersonally passed on, she insists on the swiftness of her impending death. All that is missing is a funeral pyre.

Hoccleve dramatizes this conflict between the personal and the public, between love and necessary sacrifice, in part through the spectacle of Christ's body and the possessive gazes of the Virgin and the people upon it.[23] Mary's unwavering look expresses her exclusive loyalty: "oonly on thee / My look is set," she swears (72–73). The exposure of Christ's naked body to the public gaze, on the other hand, signifies the end of her private access, and she laments that she must see her son "shamely naked" (84) in the "open sight / Of the folk heere unkevered" (136–37). Not the violent making— which is the concern of the *Pèlerinage*—but the public *showing* of the wounds obsesses and destroys her:

And this me sleeth, that in the open day
Thyn hertes wownde shewith him so wyde
That alle folk see and behold it may,
So largeliche opned is thy syde.
O! wo is me, syn I nat may it hyde! (85–89)

She no longer wishes to close the wound, as in Deguilleville's text, but to *hide* it, a word she uses repeatedly. This desire to hide the wounds reverses a familiar devotional trope: the moment when Christ appeals to the reader or viewer to behold his wounds, and particularly his heart-piercing side wound. "Lift up thin eye and thou maist see / My woundes wide, blody, all bare," Christ enjoins the reader in one late fourteenth-century lyric. And in another: "Bihold my side, / My woundes sprede so wide; / Restless I red: / Lok upon me!"[24] The spectator who does so gains access to Christ's heart; in Julian's vision, that wound is large enough for all mankind. The intruding, voyeuristic "folk" of Hoccleve's poem, then, are not Jews and Romans so much as they are the contemporary Christian community, viewers of countless images of the Passion.[25] Mary resents desperately the use of her son's body as an image of devotional contemplation. Her singular understanding of a personal body is deployed against the Christian public and its need to manufacture emotional experience for spiritual benefit. And so she exhorts the sun to withdraw the bright beams that illuminate Christ's body, making it available to the "open sighte" of the people. Hide him, she pleads, "For shame hyde my sones nakidnesse!" (144). The eroticized wounds must remain hidden, covered, private; the naked body, open to the Virgin's devoted and singular gaze alone.

Not only Christ's body but also his name becomes visible and available for public consumption through Pilate's inscription above the cross:

And, lest that somme folk par aventure
No knowleche hadde of thy persone aright,
Thy name, Pilat hath put in scripture,
That knowe mighte it every creature,
For thy penance sholde nat been hid. (93–97)

Pilate's mocking proclamation that "this is Jesus, king of the Jews" inadvertently reveals his true identity (Matt. 27:37). But the satiric title does not concern the Virgin. Instead, her sorrow springs from the exposure of the personal name: the name that, like the wounds, would become a focal point of Christian worship, the object of one of late medieval England's most popular devotions. As Duffy has observed, the cult of the Holy Name was primarily an aristocratic innovation, "seized on by elites in every community as a convenient expression, and perhaps an instrument, of their social dominance" (115). By introducing Jesus' name into written "scripture," Pilate replaces Mary's personal knowledge of Christ with a public identity—one that, in addition to re-creating her emotional connection for popular use, serves the elites who control the representations of orthodoxy.[26]

Of course Mary is Christ's bride as well as his mother, and her fierce insistence that Christ is "al hoolly myn," and "myn . . . nat thyn" is infused with an implicitly sexual jealousy (109, 155). She recollects the tender intimacies of former days, when Jesus lay in her arms, receiving "many a kus of me" as he sucked at her breast (72–77). Those shared caresses, that eroticized past, form the basis of the "special" (211) claim she now pits against the generalized, unspecial *caritas* of salvation.

If the Virgin stands for a while against the claims of the public realm, however, she is eventually absorbed into it, her speech and memory appropriated for its use. As the poem progresses and Mary loses her "special" love, her subjectivity begins to dissolve, and she becomes so estranged from and emptied of herself that she can finally adopt a public voice and assume her designated role in salvation history.

Hoccleve dramatizes this loss of subjectivity through various distortions and dislocations of her name, "Maria." These begin with Christ's devastating refusal to use that name. As he becomes "Jesus, king of the Jews," she becomes merely "woman"; he becomes known to every creature, while she becomes "straunge . . . and unknowe" to the one person who mattered (177). But Mary's name is not simply refused. Christ's rejection radically alters it, deforming the name by removing part of its significance, embedded in the letter "*i*." "Of sorwe talke may I nat ynow," mourns the Virgin, "Syn fro my name 'I' doon away is now" (181–82). Her assertion of a lost "I" is repeated twice more in the following stanza, as she explains the significance of her name's distortion:

Wel may men clepe and calle me "Mara"!
From hennes forward, so may men me call.
How sholde I lenger clept be "Maria,"
Syn 'I', which is Ihesus, is fro me fall
This day al my swetnesse is in-to gall
Torned, syn that 'I', which was the beautee
Of my name this day bynome is me. (183–89)

The missing "I" that Hoccleve reiterates so carefully here is part of a web of clever word play in the French text. There, as here, the letter "I" represents "Ihesus," and when he is taken away, so too is that crucial letter: "Puis que de moi t'es transportes/ Ainsi ostant i de mon nom" (6552–53). Without the "I," Maria becomes "Mara," or bitterness, a metamorphosis Hoccleve translates faithfully. Guillaume continues this play further on, changing *Marie* to *marrie*, and *mere* to *amer*, while playing too with *mer*: "Et n'est femme de mer a mer / Que miex de moi on doie amer" ("and there is no woman from sea to sea / who should be better loved than I," 6595–96). Hoccleve gamely follows the "Marie-marred" transition, but cannot hope to reproduce the elaborate six-line riff on *mere-amere-amer-mer* (mother-bitterness-love-sea) and so abandons it altogether, substituting a poignant description of Mary as a lost ship, driving "steerelees" and "confortles" among the waves (223–24).

What Hoccleve gains in the English, of course, is "I" as the first-person pronoun, the marker of the speaking subject who was named Maria and constituted through her special relation to Ihesus. The Virgin has indeed lost her "I," and this, rather than the play of signification, becomes the more direct focus of the poem's concern with naming. The Virgin's voice undergoes a gradual change, as she begins to address herself in the second person—"O poore modir, what shalt thow now seye? / Poore Marie, thy wit is aweye!" (216–17). The French text does not refer to Mary's lost wits, but madness is a favorite theme of Hoccleve's. (We might also hear the echo of Chaucerian complaint, Anelida's "my wit is al aweye.") His own mental infirmity, as Hoccleve writes later in his "Complaint," "me owt of my selfe cast and threw" (42). And this distancing creates a propensity for speaking to oneself, as we see in the "Male Regle," where Hoccleve thinks with horror, "Ey, what is me that to my self, thus longe / Clappid have I; I trowe that I rave" (393–94). In the Virgin's complaint, the assertion of lost wits comes just as Mary begins to speak to herself this way, as an other, a "thou." "Marie?" she asks herself, "nay but 'marred' I thee call / So may I wel for thow art wel I woot" (218–19). Addressing herself as "thow, woful womman," the Virgin renames and un-names herself just as Jesus did: "of modir haast thow eek lost the style" (225). In the French text, again, this was part of an elaborate word play on *mere-amer*, but here Hoccleve simply refers it back to Mary's initial loss of identity: "no more maist thow clept be by thy name!" (226). She has finally become the emptied-out "womman" of Christ's cruel speech, and her voice too becomes emptied of its personal grief. In the dramatic turn of the poem's concluding stanzas, the Virgin does not speak of herself at all. Her voice becomes exhortative and exemplary in the service of the public spectacle of the Passion. Like the complaining heroine of Chaucerian poetry, realizing that she is losing her private identity to public history and moralization, the Virgin takes her place at last in the dominant discourse of futurity. (We might also recall the disappearance of Lydgate's "I" in the concluding stanzas of the *Testament*, as he abandons his childhood memories and fixes his gaze instead on heaven.)

And so in the poem's final stanzas, the Virgin turns to address the same intruding onlookers from whose penetrating eyes she had previously desired to shield her son. Where once she had wished to clothe him in darkness, she now exhorts them to gaze openly, actively directing and focusing their look: "His blody stremes, see now & behold!" (232). She offers up both her own and Christ's torn outer "clothing," or flesh, for public inspection and the production of public meaning (242–43). At last she performs her ordained role, mediating between sinful humanity and crucified Christ:

O sones of Adam, al to long whyle
Yee tarien hens; hieth hidir for shame!
See how my sone for your gilt & blame,
Hangith heer al bybled up on the crois!
Bymeneth him in herte & cheere & vois! (227–31)

Calling men to the spectacle of the crucifixion, she urges the meditative gaze and its proper effect: "Now for his wo, your hertes oghten colde. / Shewith your love and your dileccioun; / For your gilt makith he correccioun" (234–36). The necessity of Christ's sacrifice comes to the fore, and Mary transfers her relationship with Christ to all who look on him. Christ "hath his blood despent in greet foysoun," she concludes, "And al it was for your Redempcioun" (244–45). What was once wholly hers and wholly of her is now spent for them—just as the Virgin's private history and power have, in the process of the complaint, been spent. It was all for them all along, anyway. Her relationship becomes theirs; her love enables theirs; her erotic loss becomes the grounds of their productive and salvific guilt. The exposure and destruction of her private self not only gives power and authority to her new, public voice, but also makes possible the audience's emotional catharsis and redemption. "Your Redempcioun" is in fact the final phrase of the poem, as Hoccleve abruptly cuts off his translation. ("*Cest tout*" appears at the end of the poem in the Egerton manuscript, as if to ward off future misunderstandings about its state of completion.)

Fradenburg writes that "Elegies construct power; they threaten us with retribution, with deprivation and isolation."[27] Hoccleve's "Complaint of the Virgin" gives powerful voice to just such a threat. The Virgin's private, erotic joys result in an overwhelming, self-destructive anguish. Meanwhile, her tormented complaint is destined to serve the very thing she protests. Her subjectivity becomes publicly available and is thus effectively erased; what she offers her viewers, as they step into her place, is but the literary simulacrum of now-lost private relation. In Fradenburg's words, "traditional systems valorize unity, identity, continuity; division and difference must be triumphed over in order to assert the eternity of undifferentiated community. Death is proclaimed as a new beginning, as regenerative. And women, perhaps because of their association with biological birth, are with sobering frequency made to stand, in mortuary rituals, for division, death, and sorrow" (185). For the sake of this "eternity of undifferentiated community," singular subjectivity is projected onto the Virgin, where it can be nostalgically, even pleasurably articulated, in the very process of its loss and reincorporation into the structure of Christian response. For of course the Virgin's anguish is as powerful and fascinating as it is threatening. It carries the poem in a way that her calm resignation, though doctrinally more correct, could not. Her sorrow for the crucified Christ provides both a model and a warning for all good Christians, who are so often enjoined to stand with her beside the cross, to see Christ through her eyes, to take her place—and yet to be somehow less than she, to mimic but not to topple over into excess. (Recall the *Tretys of Love*: "his blessid moder dide him thenne more of sorow than of comforte.")[28]

Thomas Bestul has argued that the increasingly violent emotionalism of early Marian laments may have been linked to growing female devotion to Christ, a devotion church authorities often considered excessive—compelling, but in need of restraint.[29] Since Hoccleve's "Complaint of the Virgin" was "englisht" for Joan Fitzalan, we might well see it as directed at the excesses of female affectivity (or heterodoxy, or other forms of protest). But in fifteenth-century England, *all* Christians were encouraged to see Mary's spiritual crucifixion, her inward *imitatio*, as a model for their daily imitations of Christ. In the Virgin's desolation, readers could discipline their own complaining subjectivities—learning to take her place but in a much more limited, distanced way, vicariously thrilling to her sacrifice, grounding their more contained, aestheticized devotional response on her powerful and transgressive emotion, her passionately dissenting voice.

What it might mean to invoke a Chaucerian rhetoric of feminine complaint in a poem about the Virgin Mary, in the early years of the fifteenth century? In recalling the bitter, suicidal anguish of a Dido, Hoccleve's Virgin transforms a familiar devotional scene—the crucifixion—into a meditation on the requirements of power, and on the futility of resistance to narratives of political triumph. Aeneas and his Rome are replaced by Christ and his powerful church—a church that was, in fact, being marshaled in support of the monarchy, as Henry IV forged a closer alliance between civil and ecclesiastical authority, strengthening his fractured state through the promotion of religious unity and the persecution of heresy as treason. The resulting emphasis on the proper forms of piety and obedience has been much discussed, as has the cultivation of communal and national identity based on material displays of devotion, prosperity, and conformity. Hoccleve's Virgin seems to lament what is lost, as her fiercely private vision of Christ is replaced by the sterile, acquisitive gaze of "all the folk," by devotional cults whose showy rituals stand in for her sorrow, whose claims to devotional legitimacy, social precedence, and national identity are staked on the display of her emptied-out self.

Poetry, like religion, played its part in the "redempcioun" of the English monarchy. So too the interiority that a complaining Hoccleve repeatedly exposes to his readers—while imagined as extreme, divisive, and alienating, and eventually abandoned for the voice of public counsel—might well function as a locus of discontent vicariously experienced and productively recuperated. We can see this with particular clarity in the *Regement of Princes*, Hoccleve's great autobiographical-political poem. Here the introspective, confessional Hoccleve initially occupies and pushes to its extreme limits a potentially idealized space—the space of rational thought, of self-conscious interiority—in order to evacuate it of ideal value, thereby creating the grounds for a public discourse more attuned to contemporary political and economic realities. Like the complaining Virgin, Hoccleve habitually presents himself as alienated from power and yet unable to keep himself from serving it.[30]

Written around 1412 and addressed to the Prince of Wales, soon to be Henry V, the *Regement* consists of two parts: the "Prologue," which actually comprises about forty percent of the poem, and the *Regement* proper, a *speculum principis* on the art of effective governing, translated mostly from the *Secreta Secretorum*. As in the *Series*, Hoccleve begins in his private life, with a recital of personal woes and worries, and moves from there into the role of translator to the political elite. And as in the *Series*, his initial, woeful litany is labeled "complaint": "Compleyne unto his excellent noblesse," advises the Old Man, his confessor-figure, "As I have herd the un-to me compleyne" (1849–50).

The *Regement* is notable for the extent to which it tropes interiority as sickness and sin.[31] The horror of mental isolation is even more vivid here than in "Hoccleve's Complaint," where Hoccleve claims to be recovering from an actual mental illness. In the *Regement*, Hoccleve presents himself as not only "inly pensif" but "ful mad" (85, 757), plagued by angry waking dreams and driven to seek himself with such desperate absorption that he knows nothing of his surroundings, or even of the actions of his external self: "no thing wyste I / What that I to yow spak, or what I thoghte, / But here & there I my selven soghte" (763). Like many an aspiring contemplative reader, his "moste desire is to be solitarie" (86), but even in the presence of others he is capable of complete disengagement. Men speak to him, but his "hevy thoghtes" so preoccupy him and his wits are so far gone that he does not hear or understand (101–5). The Old Man rouses him out of himself, and is asked to please go away. In Saint Cecilia this disengagement would be ideal; in Hoccleve it is a kind of insanity. The detachment from the world that so many texts of the period present as an ideal here shades into solipsism, imprisoning Hoccleve in his own head. Deploying common metaphors of religious inwardness, he digs the deepest of all sicknesses; he wades heart-deep in his own woe; he is a vessel of torment (83, 118, 81). For Augustine, thought was the sign of a rational mind, the ineradicable image of God. For Hoccleve, it becomes a "wastyng seed," a "fretynge adversarie," sucking his very heart's blood (201, 88–90). As the Old Man says, Thought commits outrageous violence against the self, and "besy thoght," especially, must be avoided at all costs:

In whom that he his mortel venym schedeth,
But if a vomyt after folwe blyve,
At the port of despeir he may arryve.

Sone, swych thoghte lurkynge the[e] with-ynne,
that huntith after thi confusioun,
Hy tyme it is to voyde & late hym twynne,
And walke at large out of thi prisoun. (270–77)

The metaphor is mixed, but the general idea is the same: with poison and prisoners alike, outing is healing. The thoughtful man must *show* "how seek he inward is," must "telle oute al [his] herte"—but even the promise of confessional relief is endangered by the excesses of his introspection. For if he becomes overwhelmed by guilt, despair may render him unable to confess, unable to break out of his mental isolation. "What profyt is for to be pensyf?" asks the Old Man, and the tormented Hoccleve has no answer (231).

Of course, Hoccleve initially presents his solitary thoughtiness, his poisonous flirtations with despair, not as the cause of his social alienation, but as the result: the result, that is, of the instability of fickle Fortune (a traditional Boethian cause for complaint). But the problem of "thought" grows and reverberates throughout both segments of the *Regement* to become—if it was not so all along—the heart of the problem itself. Fortune seems more and more like a convenient smokescreen, a refusal to specify who is kicking whom—as in the beginning of the poem, where Hoccleve attributes King Richard's fall, quite innocently, to the "stroke" of that unstable goddess.

For if thought endangers individual sanity, it also threatens the monarch and his attempts to re-create national stability and harmony in the chaotic years after Richard's deposition and murder. What happens if these "tribulations" forces people to inhabit the houses of their own hearts? Warning Henry to cultivate love rather than fear, Hoccleve points to the dangers of a populace that obeys outwardly but not inwardly, "And unto god they compleyne her grevaunce" (*Regement*, 4823). In a world where private prayer and complaint have become the norm, he suggests, no state can hold itself together. The cultivation of private relationships between men and God only alienates the king from the knowledge of his subjects that would enable him to rule them. The anger of the people is one thing, Hoccleve writes, but when that anger is kept locked in the mind and heart, the danger grows urgent: "who is with grevous thoughtes twight, May with himself nor othir folk a-right / Have no pees; a man mot nedys smert / Whan irous thoughtes occupye his hert" (5058–5061). Feigned peace, so much worse than public discord, is now widespread in England:

Many an hony worde and many a kus
Ther is; but wayte on the conclusioun,
And pryve galle all turnyth up-so-doun;
Ther leveth naght of pees, but contenance,
ffor al the peyntyd chere and daliance. (5085–89)

The last line looks forward to Hoccleve's attempts, in the "Complaint," to paint what he thinks is an accurate "chere" for the crowds of Westminster. Here it is clear how dangerous such painting might become. For Hoccleve's thoughty malady does not belong to him alone. Rather, his poisonous interiority is symptomatic of deeper fissures in the body politic—or rather, in its mind and will, which now threaten to fragment into a series of private enclosures, becoming frustratingly inaccessible to public regulation.

The Lollard John Badby, burned at Smithfield in 1410, embodies precisely this kind of interiority run amok. Badby's reckless thought leads him into heresy, and his mental isolation prevents the confession and renunciation of error that Prince Henry so generously offers. Badby rejects the offer, "by any outward tokyn resonable," and keeps his soul secret from the prince and the community: "If he inward hadde any repentaunce, / That wote he, that of no thing hath doutaunce" (320–22). The nature of his inner state remains a problem for public meaning even after his death, as learned divines debate where his soul has gone—a conversation from which the Old Man tactfully excuses himself. Badby has become one of those people who complain only to God. Unlike the lamenting Virgin, he refuses to give up his private soul to public catharsis and the production of undifferentiated community. And as various critics have pointed out, Badby looks suspiciously like the alter-ego, or dangerous double, of the thoughty, tormented, complaining Hoccleve.[32] Hoccleve too must be cajoled to complain to Prince Henry, to release his poison and walk "at large" out of his (mental) prison.

As we saw in Chapter 1, public displays of "inwardness" were a familiar strategy in early fifteenth-century political life. Vernacular liturgical guides brought mouths and hearts into meaningful harmony, realigning inner desire with outward sign and turning private piety into ritual participation. Henry V used the vernacular to declare the "secrets of his will" to the people, expecting them to do the same. In the *Regiment*, Hoccleve instructs the future king to unify inside and outside, clothing his heart inward with the same honorable and precious garments that array his exterior (3634–37). Virtues must displace any "Inward fickleness" disguised by the appearance of "trouth outward" (2224–25).[33] The king must set the example. It is in the context of fifteenth-century anxieties over all kinds of secrecy, "doubleness," and interiority that we must place the solitary ramblings of the brain-turned clerk of the Privy Seal.[34]

This most inward of poets cannot be accused of doubleness, precisely because he has already displayed his own inner life to such an intimate degree that we can hardly suspect him of harboring anything deeper. We assume that Hoccleve is telling the unvarnished truth—so present does he seem, so guileless in his rambling anguish. The Virgin's Complaint, as we have seen, serves both to evacuate the private and to transfer its undeniable power to the public realm. The emptying out of the private self renders the poem emotionally compelling, while the magnitude of the Virgin's sacrifice becomes the grounds of her public voice and power. In the "complaint" that is the *Regement*'s prologue, we can see a similar dynamic of exposure and transfer. Here, Hoccleve will confess and complain not only for the voyeuristic pleasure of his audience, but as the price of a public voice, cast as the remedy for private woes. Rather than leading him into Lollardy, Hoccleve's busy thought will serve as the occasion for public healing, reaffirming stable community and grounding his claim to participate in the redemptive narrative of Henry's accession to the throne of England. Hoccleve creates his elaborate spectacle of singular inwardness in order to erase it.

Or to make a show of erasing it. For Hoccleve's poetry assumes an ineradicable split between inside and out. The alienation of the self from its social identity is a recurring problem, which can only be remedied, in stopgap fashion, through compelling the inner to confess itself over and over again, offering itself to public power without ever being able to fully cement the transaction. The intractability and alluring unknowability of the private self—the persistence of the dark image of sin—requires constant introspection, and serves as the occasion for repeated speech acts, an incessant "voiding," "vomiting," and "telling out" of the heart that is as lucrative for its teller as it is compelling and reassuring for its viewers. Like Mary, whose lament *creates* each devotional subject's desire for Christ, even as her loss threatens and disciplines that desire, Hoccleve's complaints produce interiority as fascinating, unavoidable, and destructive, a space his audience is called on both to occupy and to incessantly void. Renewal and regeneration are promised for the sacrifice, as public discourse is infused with the tremendous—if unstable—emotional power of the inner life. Hoccleve's subjectivity is not simply the deplored opposites of Lancastrian singularity, but its necessary other and the object of its desire.

Thus as much as Badby is the alter-ego of Hoccleve, we must also recognize the extent to which Hoccleve's audience is implicated in, and threatened by, the complaining "I" of his poems. His excesses, like the Virgin's, may turn out to be their own. And here I would like to examine one final poem: the short "Balade to my gracious Lord of York," probably composed between 1411 and 1415 and intended as a dedicatory preface to a presentation copy of the *Regement of Princes*. It serves as a kind of confessional-preface-to-the-confessional-preface, neatly crystallizing and miniaturizing Hoccleve's aesthetics of literary self-revelation and display, and suggesting the kinds of pleasure—and discipline—he expects his patrons to derive from it.

The dedication takes the form of an author's address to and apology for his book. Its opening "Go, little pamfilet" echoes Chaucer's "Go, litel bok, go, litel myn tragedie." But where Chaucer might send his little book to be "kis the steppes where as thow seest pace / Virgile, Ovide, Omer, Lucan, and Stace,"[35] this book prostrates itself before the mighty Duke of York—who is, after all, more likely than Virgil or Ovid to reimburse his petitioners' flattering subjection. (Once again, Hoccleve diverts Chaucerian forms from a classical into a contemporary context, with a satirical edge.) But Hoccleve does not want the Duchess to see his book, for, as he tells it, it is neither beautiful nor eloquent enough to show itself to her clear eyes. Hoccleve cannot display his inadequate "chere" before this "mirour of wommanly excellence" (24)—and yet, he admits after a small pause, he has nothing else to recommend himself to her. The book must be shown, so that Hoccleve may be kept "out of drede"—as he rather delicately puts the matter (34).

The following stanza traces a similar game of hide and seek with Master Picard (perhaps the prince's tutor). "I warne thee," Hoccleve admonishes his book, "that it shal be ful hard / For thee & me to halte on any syde, / But he espie us" (41–43). But here again, he brushes off his first fears: "yit no force, abyde! / Let him looke on," he says, for "his herte is to me ward / So freendly that our shame wole he hyde" (43–45). Hoccleve goes on to show Picard the shame of his "foul book" on the spot, confessing his writing's folly and disorder, and praying Picard to correct it if he will—just as, in the *Regement*, he will submit to the "correccioun" of the fatherly Old Man (756).

The "foleye" of Hoccleve's text is not all he is exhibiting to the clear eyes of his patrons; the ultimate object in this game, of course, is Hoccleve himself. "Be thow an owter of my nycetee" he instructs his little book—*nycetee* meaning foolishness, simplicity, and/or sin—"For my good lordes lust, and game, & play" (17–18).[36] As the *OED* observes, Hoccleve elsewhere uses the word "outeris" to refer to those who circulate false coin, and I think the link is revealing—for what is Hoccleve "coining" and circulating in the *Regement* but himself?[37] (Remember the metaphor of the inner image as a lost or stamped penny.) Here he demonstrates in graceful miniature the kind of confessional "outing" that he performs to such pleasurable, and lucrative, effect. Still instructing his little book, he writes:

. . . un-to my lord seye also,
that pryde is un-to me so greet a fo,
that the spectacle, forbedith he me,
And hath y-doon of tyme yore ago;
And for my sighte blyve hastith me fro,

And lakkith that that sholde his comfort be,
No wonder thogh thow have no beautee. (55–61)

No doubt Hoccleve's fifteenth-century audience found this off-handed moment of self-revelation as charmingly intimate as have most nineteenth- and
twentieth-century readers. Poignantly acknowledging the self-destructive
vanity of his old age, Hoccleve here executes the maneuver so typical of
poems such as "La Male Regle," "Hoccleve's Complaint," and the *Regement
of Princes*: a standard confession of pride made irresistible by the addition of
trivial, personal detail and its creation of what feels like an authentic authorial presence within the poem. "Out up-on pryde, causer of my wo!" ex-
claims the weak-eyed and movingly penitent old poet Thomas Hoccleve,
and again I would suggest that "out" signifies display as much as purgation
(62). (And *production* as well, if we again hear the echoes of counterfeiting.)
Hoccleve may not be able to see very well, but his strong-eyed audience
glimpses him clearly, as he offers both himself and his book, after an initial
pose of reticence, to the voyeuristic gaze of power. The "spectacle" that pride
forbids is not only a pair of glasses. It is the poem-as-glass, making a show
out of Hoccleve's private follies while subtly assuring his readers that he
hasn't the power—optical or otherwise—to look back. "My sighte is hurt,"
he laments, admitting the damage he has done himself in refusing to admit,
and thus correct, his weakness (63).

And to what end? Throughout the poem, Hoccleve hints at his need for
the "freendly manere," the "remembraunce," the financial assistance, that
have become so important in his impersonal world. He asserts that the duke
had before shown him "grace & favour." He hints that he needs to be kept
"out of drede." And he concludes the poem with a final, abject profession of
loyalty and service to his superiors, studded with reminders of the recom-
pense he expects for his outing of his heart:

And graunte hem ioie & hy prosperitee,
Nat to endure oonly two yeer or three,
But a .Ml.! and if any plesance
Happe mighte, on my poore souffissance,
To his prowesse & hir benignitee,
My lyves ioie it were, and sustenance! (67–72)

The reference to his readers' lasting "prosperitee" is pointed enough. Hoccleve's assertion that he would do his prospective patrons "any plesance"

merely emphasizes that, in his "poore soufisssance," he has already offered them the only currency he has, and expects some form of more material "sustenance" in return.

At the same time, the confessional paradigm suggests a certain exemplarity in Hoccleve's situation. I have suggested that part of the power of the Virgin's Complaint comes from its ability to voice excesses that the public spectator must identify *with*, as well as against. The Virgin is not merely pitiable; she occupies a privileged, even idealized position in relation to the reader, as indeed she must in order to perform her disciplinary function, to adequately "threaten us," to ground effectively a public regeneration and renewal. The Virgin stands for every Christian and, once emptied of her transgressive subjectivity, becomes a conduit for devotional imitation. So too, Hoccleve's weak eyesight not only highlights, but threatens the powerful gazes of his patrons. Their clear eyes may be ruined like his; their "hy prosperitee" may become his "poore souffissance," though he pointedly prays to the Virgin to "graunte hem ioie & hy prosperitee, / Nat to endure *oonly two yeer or three*" (67–68, emphasis mine). In the unstable world of Lancastrian politics, they too may be forgotten, may wake to find "Nobody" their benefactor and defender. They may become Richard, that figure of warning who hovers around the *Regement*'s opening stanzas. The Ballad to York can easily be taken as a plea for money. That reading helps to suggest the real power of Hoccleve's mesmerizing performances of subjectivity, and the pleasures at stake in them. But we might also see this little preface as a guide to subjection, as Hoccleve enacts an exemplary performance of whole-hearted submission—"with hertes humblesse," "Hertily," "with herte enteer," and "With al myn herte"—to the household of his "Prince" of York. If his patrons wish to ensure the sovereign of their whole-hearted submission, perhaps they too should enact a confessional outing of those hearts, lest they become mirrors of, rather than for, that old clerk of the Privy Seal, too proud to admit his age, too vain to accept the optical correction that would have protected his sight and his literary production. As Pearsall notes, many prospective allies of Prince Henry seem to have possessed very expensive presentation copies of the *Regement*, surely paid for by someone other than the impoverished Hoccleve.[38] The *speculum principis* that Thomas Hoccleve offers to his patrons functions as a mirror in more ways than one.

I began this chapter by asking how the apparently marginal and singular Thomas Hoccleve might share a voice and a self with the powerful residents of London, his superiors and patrons. From the abject devotional "I" to the bitter Virgin's lost "I" to Thomas Hoccleve's confessional, complaining "I," the rhetorical selves of Hoccleve's poetry are at once reflexive and reflective, personal and exemplary. Hoccleve not only follows the devotional injunction to see himself, building his profitable poetry out of the anxieties and paradoxes of the private, inward self in early fifteenth-century political and devotional culture. Hoccleve also sees and shows himself in a way that instructs other readers. In doing so, he adds to the ways in which English men and women might understand the nature and profits of tribulation, the boundaries between private and public, the uses of autobiographical speech, and the relationships between books, mirrors, and selves. He complicates further the vernacular paradigms of busy self-beholding that gave late medieval English readers so many ways to see and know themselves.

Afterward

In 1530, a little more than a century after Syon's spiritual directors had first wrestled with the question of how to have a community of private readers who would valorize internal devotion and individual spiritual progress, but remain tied to the liturgical and the communal—who would labor to see themselves, but also to reflect someone else—the *Myroure of Oure Ladye* was printed by Richard Fawkes. Fawkes promoted it as "very necessary for all relygyous persones and other good devoute persons."[1] That year also saw Bridgettine Richard Whytford's translation of Thomas à Kempis's *Imitatio Christi*, and the publication of two practical and immensely popular works for laymen: Whytford's *A Werke for Housholders* and the *Pomander of Prayer*, written by a Sheen Carthusian and introduced by a Syon monk.[2] It seems to have been a high point in Syon's outreach, as the "spiritual power-house of England"[3] redoubled its efforts to model devout, literate behavior for a world now saturated with controversy and printed debate. As the storm gathered, Syon remained one of England's preeminent religious houses. Its revenues were vast, its reputation for holiness was unimpeachable, and the men's library drew scholars such as More, Erasmus, and Colet.[4] England's most readerly and inward convent was also its most devout, its most admired, and its most staunchly orthodox.

It was one of the few houses whose approval for the Act of Supremacy Henry VIII felt he had to have—and one of the few to withhold it, until the weight of threats, intimidation, executions, and official harassment finally brought its opposition to an end in 1535. One of Cromwell's agents wrote, "If it were not for the opinion whiche men had and som yet have, in their apparent holinese, which is and was for the most part, covert hipocrysy, it made no great mater what became of thaim."[5] His comment testifies to the continuing power of the language of show and substance, of doubleness and secrecy. When the king's agents visited the chapterhouse to secure the nuns' consent for Henry's title, they advised any dissenters to rise and walk out, on "peril of their souls." None of the sisters is recorded to have walked. But "one Agnes Smith, a sturdy dame and a wylful" took it upon herself to "[labour] diverse of her susters that we should not have their convent seal."[6] Sturdy, willful Agnes Smith: her brief but vivid appearance in the record invites us to ponder again the unanswerable questions of what all these negotiations of inwardness and specularity might mean for real people, whether the inward care of the heart might result in, for example, a self less vocal or empowered; more self-involved, individualistic, or autobiographical; more autonomous or less so; more modern or less so.

Thomas More, for his part, could not say. Speculating vainly about why so many of his countrymen had accepted Henry's Oath of Succession without a struggle, he wrote from the Tower in 1534: "Some may doe for favour, and some may doe for feare . . . and some might hap to frame himself a conscience and thinke that while he did it for feare God wolde forgive it. And some may peradventure think that they will repent, and be shryven thereof . . . and some may peradventure be of that minde, that if they say one thing and thinke the while the contrary, God more regardeth their harte than their tonge."[7] More postulates some inner reasons and some outer ones. His speculations as to the hearts of his countrymen include some who hope God will forgive them for the sake of their good intentions, some who hope God will privilege the secret thoughts of their hearts, and some who just hope to confess and receive pardon later. In his account, the separation of heart from mouth is not a cause; it does serve as one potential excuse. We cannot know which excuses occurred most often to the sisters at Syon, or how they thought about them afterward. We know that they reconstituted their community abroad and that their order survives to this day.

During the long, recursive religious upheavals of the sixteenth century, English readers would grow numerous beyond anything medieval devotional writers could have expected. And these readers would have ample cause to keep their devotional lives locked in the secret chambers of their hearts, and to ponder the profits of tribulation and the persecutions of the world, whose affiliations could hardly be predicted from one year to the next. Both Protestant and Recusant readers would have cause to imagine their "true" selves as distinct from their social ones, while continuing to imagine those true selves as feminized, marginalized, abject, longing. These were the "inner resources" with which they faced a vertiginously changing world. As Susan Foster writes, "private devotion was hard to police. . . . Throughout the 1530s, the imagery of private devotion still permeated court and country alike."[8] As the pendulum swung, both Protestant and Recusant devotional culture became still more Augustinian; the influence of the *Devotio Moderna*, especially the *Imitatione Christi*, grew. And the problem of public and private worship, of defining the nature and limits of outward and inward devotion, became more urgent and dangerous than ever before— even as the concept of interiority, portable and adaptable as usual, allowed at least this strain of English devotion to survive and thrive in yet another set of altered circumstances.

It also continued to feed English literary traditions both sacred and secular, in prose and verse. A century after Hoccleve wrote his *Series*, another bitter, self-absorbed poet would lament his exclusion from a Henrician court. "I cannot with my words complain and moan," Thomas Wyatt writes to his friend John Poins in 1536; "Nor suffer naught, nor smart without complaint." Describing a corrupt, heartless world full of feigning and flattery, Wyatt laments that Londoners judge "Without regard what doth inward resort." Wyatt's poem is a classical imitation—but like Hoccleve before him, Wyatt excelled at infusing borrowed conventions and translations with a sense of contemporary immediacy and personal revelation. Like Hoccleve, he combined confession and complaint, public and private despair, to create a witty, cynical, autobiographical persona betrayed by the social world, burdened and isolated by his own self-consciousness and self-loathing, and driven repeatedly to "tell out" the bitter contents of his swelling heart. (He sounds much more like Hoccleve, I think, than like Petrarch.) The sonnet tradition that Wyatt initiated would add another strand, another complication, to the discourses of inwardness and self-reflection already proliferating in English culture.

We might trace the devotional strand of this vibrant tradition through English verse from Donne and Herbert all the way to Hopkins: "Selfyeast of spirit a dull dough sours. I see / The lost are like this, and their scourge to be / As I am mine, their sweating selves; but worse" (Sonnet 67). But we might also look to the many developing prose forms for representing the inner life, especially the meditative and autobiographical works of writers like Browne and Bunyan. Recusants, Anglicans, Puritans—in one way or another, all inherited and transformed the preoccupations of late medieval English devotional reading, the diverse forms of self-consciousness cloaked under bland terms such as "inwardness," "contemplation," and "meditation on the Passion." Though these preoccupations eventually issued in different religious traditions, different forms of reading, different kinds of spiritual exercises, what remained constant was the exhortation to see oneself, and to be busy about it. Or as Thomas à Kempis put it, in that first English translation, "Wake upon thiself, styre thiself, amonisshe thiself; and hou ever it be of othir, foryete not thiself."

Notes

The following abbreviations are used in the notes.

BL   British Library
EETS   Early English Text Society: o.s. (Original Series), e.s. (Extra Series)
JMEMS   *Journal of Medieval and Early Modern Studies*
OED   *Oxford English Dictionary*
PMLA   *Publications of the Modern Language Association of America*
STC   Short Title Catalogue

Introduction

Note to epigraph: Langland, *The Vision of Piers Plowman*, passus 12 ll. 17–18.

1. *Speculum Devotorum*, ed. Hogg, 2.

2. *Orologium Sapientiae*, ed. Horstman, 326.

3. Although it has recently become a subject of greater interest, the predominance of devotional texts in vernacular collections has been widely accepted since Deanseley's 1920 "Vernacular Books in England." Among many other important studies of ownership and circulation, see Harris, "Patrons, Buyers, and Owners"; Hutchison, "Devotional Reading"; Friedman, *Northern English Books, Owners, and Makers*; Bell, "Medieval Women Book Owners"; Meale, "Laywomen and Their Books"; Bell, *What Nuns Read*; and Ker, *Medieval Libraries of Great Britain*. For ownership records of many important texts, usefully summarized, see Innes-Parker, "The Legacy of *Ancrene Wisse*."

4. *Contemplations of the Dread and Love of God*, ed. Connolly, 5. For the spread of contemplative texts to the laity, see, for example, Gillespie, "Vernacular Books of Religion"; Sargent, "Russbroek in England" and "Bonaventura English"; Keiser, " 'Noght how lang man lifs' "; Hussey, "The Audience for the Middle English Mystics"; Hutchison, "Devotional Reading"; Erler, "Exchange of Books"; Thrupp, *Merchant Class*, esp. 174–90; and Tanner, *The Church in Late Medieval Norwich*.

5. See Guigo II, *The Ladder of Monks*, and "A Ladder of Foure Ronges by the which Men Mowe Wele Clyme to Heven: A Middle English Translation of *Scala Claustralium*," appendix B in *Deonise hid Divinite*, ed. Hodgson. Windeatt prints just the English translator's additions in *English Mystics of the Middle Ages*, 248–252.

6. See Francis's introduction to *The Book of Vices and Virtues*.

7. *The Growth of English Education*, 94–96. See also Deanseley, "Vernacular Books" 355.

8. See, for example, the work of Walter Ong, particularly *Orality and Literacy*; much of the work of Brian Stock, particularly *The Implications of Literacy* and *After Augustine*; Carruthers, *The Book of Memory*; and Jager, *The Book of the Heart*.

9. See Patterson, "On the Margin," and the introduction to *Chaucer and the Subject of History*. See also Aers, "A Whisper in the Ear of Early Modernists"; and Travis, who discusses the "status, being, and meaning of 'I'" in *The Book of the Duchess* in "White."

10. *The Poetry of Petrarch*, trans. David Young, 4. The Italian reads, "Era il giorno ch' al sol si scoloraro / per la pietá del suo fattore i rai / quando i' fui preso, et non me ne guardai, / ché i be' vostr' occhi, Donna, mi legaro. / Tempo non mi parea da far riparo / contr' a' colpi d'Amor; peró m'andai / secur, senza sospetto, onde i miei guai / nel commune dolor s'incominciaro." Petrarch, *The Canzoniere*, 4. Simpson discusses the "distorted . . . account of Petrarch's influence" on English poetry in "Breaking the Vacuum."

11. Taylor, "Into His Secret Chamber," 48.

12. Partner, "The Hidden Self," 42.

13. *Pype or Tonne of the Lyfe of Perfection*, vol. 4, pt. 3, 451. Cited in Ellis, "Spirituality of Syon Abbey."

14. See, for example, Hamburger, *The Visual and the Visionary* and *Nuns as Artists*; and Newman, "What Did It Mean to Say 'I Saw'?" See also Dimmick et al., *Images, Idolatry, and Iconoclasm*.

15. On education and literacy see, for example, Bennett, "Education and Advancement"; "quiet revolution" is his phrase (94). See also Alexander, *The Growth of English Education*; Coleman, *Medieval Readers and Writers*; Moran, *The Growth of English Schooling*; and Parkes, "The Literacy of the Laity." For changes in book production, see especially the essays in Griffiths and Pearsall, *Book Production and Publishing*; and Friedman, *Northern English Books*.

16. Keiser, "'To Knawe God Almyghtyn,'" 120. Keiser finds Thornton's tastes indicative of broader patterns. See also Thompson, *Robert Thornton*.

17. Friedman, *Northern English Books*, 16. For Stapleton, see Bazire and College's introduction to *The Chastising of God's Children*.

18. Tanner, *The Church in Late Medieval Norwich*, 112.

19. Pantin, *The English Church in the Fourteenth Century*, 189.

20. Sargent, "Walter Hilton's *Scale of Perfection*," esp. 205 ff. See also Scase, "Reginald Pecock."

21. On the demand for and production of early printed devotional works, see, for example, Deansely, "Vernacular Books"; Keiser, "The Mystics and the Early English Printers"; Hughes, *Pastors and Visionaries*, e.g., 357; and Alexander, *The Growth of English Education*, 94–96.

22. Saenger, "Silent Reading." See also his "Books of Hours and the Reading Habits of the Later Middle Ages."

23. "One of the most marked features of late medieval domestic architecture was the growing desire for privacy," Pantin asserts ("Instructions for a Devout and Liter-

ate Layman," 406). Of course medieval prayer closets were nowhere near as elaborate as their seventeenth-century descendants. On the partitioning of monastic space, see Gilchrist, *Gender and Material Culture*, 122. On the creation of private space more generally, see Barthélemy and Contamine, "The Use of Private Space" in *A History of Private Life II*. For a good discussion of private reading and reading practices, see Taylor, "Into His Secret Chamber."

24. *Sir Gawain and the Green Knight*, ed. Cawley and Anderson, l. 934.

25. For Cicely, see especially Armstrong, "The Piety of Cicely, Duchess of York." For Margaret Beaufort, see, for example, Bell, "Medieval Women Book Owners"; Hutchison, "Devotional Reading"; Krug, *Reading Families*, ch. 2, and *The English Works of John Fisher*, ed. Mayor, 1:294–95.

26. Pantin, "Instructions," 399. The work is written in Latin; the English translation is Pantin's.

27. *The Book of Margery Kempe*, ed. Meech and Allen, 143.

28. Coleman, *Public Reading and the Reading Public*. For a study emphasizing the communal nature of many late medieval women's literate experience, see Krug's *Reading Families*.

29. Camille observes, for example: "This is where our modern categories of public and private break down, since so many openly displayed images in churches became the focus of intensely individual devotions and private mysticism." *Gothic Art: Glorious Visions*, 128–29.

30. *Ennobling Love*, 192.

31. *The Earliest English Translation of the De Imitatione Christi*, 23. Biggs's new edition of the text, collated from the four extant manuscripts, has "hit behoveth him to declyne fro the prees" (25).

32. Love, *The Mirror of the Blessed Life of Jesus Christ*, ed. Sargent, 73.

33. *Orologium Sapientiae*, 353.

34. Ed. Vaissier, 154, 29.

35. Ed. Francis, 140.

36. In Horstman, ed., *Yorkshire Writers*, 441–42.

37. Ed. Sargent, 12.

38. Stock, *After Augustine*; see ch. 7, "*Lectio Spiritualis*."

39. Ibid., 105.

40. De Hamel, *Syon Abbey*, 103.

41. *The Orcherd of Syon*, ed. Hodgson and Liegy, 1.

42. I.3177. All citations are to *The Riverside Chaucer*, ed. Benson.

43. See Pearsall, ed., *Studies in the Vernon Manuscript*.

44. *The Myrour of Recluses*, ed. Harley, 618, 631. For the classic discussion of such manuscript apparatuses, see Parkes, "Concepts of *Ordinatio* and *Compilatio*."

45. Hughes, *Pastors and Visionaries*, 355.

46. Warren, *Anchorites and Their Patrons*. On the importance of solitaries to northern religious movements, see Hughes, *Pastors and Visionaries*.

47. Allen, introduction to *The English Writings of Richard Rolle*, x. All subsequent references are to this edition.

48. See Allen's introduction, and Watson, *Richard Rolle and the Invention of Author-*

ity. Besides the more than 400 English manuscripts, there are also more than 70 Continental manuscripts and ten printed editions of his works.

49. *Contemplations of the Dread and Love of God*, xvii. For the confusion surrounding Rolle's works, see also Horstman's introduction to *Yorkshire Writers*. In *Northern English Books*, Friedman observes that "books containing pictures of contemplative hermits of the Desert Fathers type, sometimes labeled Richard Rolle, or 'St. Paul the first hermit' . . . were important models of devotional practice and popular piety" (148). Hamburger notes that three manuscripts of *The Desert of Religion* link the veneration of Rolle to the Desert Fathers; see "The Use of Images in the Pastoral Care of Nuns." For Carthusian interest in Rolle and the Desert Fathers, see Brantley's forthcoming study, *Reading in the Wilderness*.

50. See Warren, *Anchorites and Their Patrons*, ch. 4 and appendix 2; and Watson, "*Ancrene Wisse*, Religious Reform and the Late Middle Ages," in *A Companion to "Ancrene Wisse."*

51. *Sancti Anselmi opera omnia*, 5:360, cited in Warren, *Anchorites and their Patrons*, 105.

52. On the English Carthusians, see Thompson, *The Carthusian Order in England*; and Knowles, *The Religious Orders in England*, 1:129–38. For Carthusian involvement in the production and circulation of devotional texts, see Gillespie, " 'Cura pastoralis in deserto' "; Keiser, " 'Noght How Lang Man Lifs' "; Lovatt, "The Imitation of Christ"; and Sargent, "Transmission by the English Carthusians" and "Walter Hilton's *Scale of Perfection*."

53. Warren, *Anchorites and Their Patrons*, 282. This is again in contrast to the situation on the Continent, where solitaries did not have a strong presence in urban areas. Hughes observes that confessing to a hermit was a much more private affair than confessing to a priest; see *Pastors and Visionaries*, 121.

54. See *The Church in Late Medieval Norwich*, 57, 64 ff.

55. "alle the bokes that I have," 137. See also Bartlett, *Male Authors, Female Readers*, esp. ch. 1; Bell, "Medieval Women Book Owners"; Boffey, "Women Authors and Women's Literacy"; and Riddy, " 'Women Talking About the Things of God.' "

56. Erler, "Exchange of Books," 361; see also Taylor, "Reading and Privacy," 52–61. For the similarities between laywomen's reading and the reading at the Abbey of Syon, see Krug, *Reading Families*.

57. *The Book of Margery Kempe*, 144.

58. Hamburger, "The Use of Images," 45; Gillespie, " 'Lukynge in haly bukes,' " 4; Bell, *What Nuns Read*, 76.

59. For nuns' relationships with their patrons, see Gilchrist, *Gender and Material Culture*, 50–62. On conventual education see, for example, Bell, *What Nuns Read*, 59, and Alexander, *The Growth of English Education*, 57.

60. Cited in Gillespie, "Vernacular Books of Religion," 321. The translator of *De Exterioris et Interioris Hominis Compositione* writes similarly, "though yt so be that thys books . . . towche principally the religious persons, never the later every seculer man or womman . . . may fynde here in sufficient instruction" (Gillespie, " 'Lukynge in haly bukes,' " 17).

61. *Contemplations of the Dread and Love of God*, xvi.

62. *Orologium Sapientiae*, 325. There are thirteen extant manuscripts of the *Seven Poyntes*, five of them complete. Two more manuscripts contain excerpts, and one has an altered version. Independent translations of Suso's *Horologium* include part of the end of Love's *Mirror*, Hoccleve's "Learn to Die," a bit of the *Chastising of God's Children*, the monastic play *Wisdom*, a separate translation of II.2 extant in two manuscripts, and another distinct version extant in one. See Sargent, *James Grenehalgh*, 1:216–19; his footnotes provide a more complete bibliography. See also Lovatt, "Henry Suso."

63. For Margaret Beaufort's interest in Hilton, see Sargent, "Transmission by the English Carthusians." For early prints of the *Scale*, see Sargent, "Walter Hilton's *Scale of Perfection*," 206–7.

64. 114. All citations for the *Epistle on the Mixed Life* are from Windeatt, ed., *English Mystics of the Middle Ages*, 108–30. Hughes provides further discussion of the mixed life in *Pastors and Visionaries*, esp. 215 ff. and 251 ff.

65. See Sargent's introduction to the *Mirror*, xxiv. Sargent also points out that book one of the *Scale of Perfection* typically circulated with Love's *Mirror*, even in early printed editions.

66. Horstman, ed., *Yorkshire Writers*, 1:321. The *Book of Vices and Virtues* similarly observes that Knowledge "is the priour in the cloistre of the hert" (149).

67. Davis #72, but cited and modernized in Castor, *Blood and Roses*, 179.

68. Connolly, 40.

69. That this could serve as a basis for institutional critique is illustrated by the fourteenth-century *Book to a Mother*, in which the priest-author tells his mother to stick to the "cloister of Christ" rather than the cloisters of England, for this inner cloister charges nothing and is free of monastic abuses. See *Book to a Mother*, ed. McCarthy, 122. Watson's "Methods and Objectives of Anchoritic Devotion" is an important treatment of the subject.

70. Ashley, "Historicizing Margery," 374.

71. Coletti, "*Paupertas est donum Dei*," 375.

72. Horrox, introduction to *Fifteenth Century Attitudes*, 2. See also Bennett, "Education and Advancement" and "Careerism in Late Medieval England"; and DuBoulay, *An Age of Ambition*.

73. For courtesy manuals, see, for example, Mertes, "Aristocracy." Mustanoja observes that while French courtesy manuals were written exclusively for aristocrats, in England they were addressed to various levels of society (*How the Good Wife Taught Her Daughter*, ed. Mustanoja). For fifteenth-century conduct books directed at middle-class youth, see Hanawalt, "'The Childe of Bristow.'" For urban guilds, see McRee, "Religious Gilds and Regulation of Behavior"; and Thrupp, *Merchant Class*.

74. Malory, *Le Morte Darthur*, ed. Shepherd, 817.

75. Spenser, *The Faerie Queene*, ed. Roche and O'Donnell, 15.

76. *Canterbury Tales*, I.374–78; 449–52.

77. Richmond, "Religion," 196. See also his "The English Gentry and Religion."

78. Charles Eliot Norton Lectures, 97–98.

79. For the Constitutions, see especially Watson, "Censorship and Cultural Change." Aers and Staley in *Powers of the Holy* also comment on the paucity of

fifteenth-century writing. Watson and others argue not that spiritual writing was actively discouraged, but that writers exercised caution in response to a generally hostile political climate—for as Hudson observes, the "formidable" powers of the bishops "were used only sporadically" (*Premature Reformation*, 444). For a different view of the Constitutions see Somerset, "Professionalizing Translation." For Watson's recent reassessment of his own argument, see "Cultural Changes." For fifteenth-century writers' claims of inadequacy, see, for example, Lawton, "Dullness and the Fifteenth Century," and Lerer, *Chaucer and His Readers*.

80. Watson, "Middle English Mystics," 562.

81. Ibid., 561–62.

82. Hussey makes precisely this point in "Walter Hilton," in his discussion of the fifteenth-century popularity of the *Ancrene Wisse* and the works of Rolle, Hilton, and pseudo-Bonaventura. See also Sargent, "Bonaventura English," 176.

83. Horrall, "*Cursor Mundi* and Its Background." See also Thompson's discussion in *Robert Thornton*, 49.

84. Bestul, "Devotional Writing in England," 18. Bestul documents the rich tradition of Latin contemplative writing that gave rise to many of the texts in this study.

85. See Bazire and College's introduction to the text for manuscripts and circulation.

86. Sargent, "Ruusbroek in England."

87. *Reform and Cultural Revolution*, 64. Patterson argues for the importance of studying the appropriations of earlier by later texts in *Negotiating the Past*.

88. See Cooper, "Romance after 1400," in *The Cambridge History of Medieval English Literature*, 690–719, and Pearsall, "The English Romance."

89. Guillerm, "L'intertextualité démontée," 60.

90. *Sacrifice Your Love*, 50–51.

91. Heffernan, "Orthodoxies' Redux," 79. See also Turville-Petre, "Vernon and Clopton Manuscripts." Sargent is among those who discuss the dissemination of vernacular devotion as a conservative phenomenon; see "Ruusbroec in England" and "Bonaventura English."

92. Hughes, *Pastors and Visionaries*, 247.

93. See, for example, Brady, "Lollard Interpolations and Omissions."

94. *Premature Reformation*, 417–18.

95. See Barnum, *Dives and Pauper*, 1:xi.

96. See, for example, Swanson, "Passion and Practice"; and Rhodes, "The Body of Christ."

Chapter 1. A Very Inward Man

Note to epigraph: *Holy Bible*, Douay-Rheims Version.

1. Hodgson, ed., *The Cloud of Unknowing*, 96. "Inward" is not the only spiritual direction the *Cloud* author worries about; as Watson has observed, he is capable of "devoting entire chapters to the meaning of the word 'up'" ("The Middle English Mystics," 552).

2. Quoted by Horsfield in *"The Pomander of Prayer,"* 210.

3. *English Writings of Richard Rolle*, ed. Allen, 117.

4. Ed. Bestul, 32–33 (I.iii).

5. *Pype or Tonne of the Lyfe of Perfection*, ed. Hogg, 451. Cited in Ellis, "Spirituality of Syon Abbey."

6. *The Myroure of Oure Ladye*, ed. Blunt, 69.

7. *De Imitatione Christi*, ed. Ingram, 41.

8. *The Book of Gostlye Grace*, ed. Halligan, 184.

9. *The Doctrine of the Hert*, ed. Candon, 1.

10. "A tretise of miracleis pleyinge," in *English Wycliffite Writings*, ed. Hudson, 102. Searching for a more inclusive and accurate label for the field than "Middle English mystical writing," Watson has suggested calling it instead "the Middle English literature of interiority" ("The Middle English Mystics," 544, 551).

11. "The Repressor of Over Much Blaming of the Clergy," in *The Idea of the Vernacular*, ed. Wogan-Browne et al., 97–105; 102.

12. *The Testament of Love*, 5–6; excerpted in *The Idea of the Vernacular*, 28–34.

13. See especially Despres, *Ghostly Sights*.

14. See Stock, *After Augustine*, ch. 4 in particular.

15. The passage does not seem entirely definitive, but see Bestul's edition, 236. For the notation, see Sargent, *James Grenehalgh*, 1:88.

16. *OED Online*, s.v. "inward," December 2, 2004. Four pages in the *Middle English Dictionary* are devoted to various permutations of the word, a very large number of which are documented using quotations from Lydgate, Bishop Pecock, or the English *Imitatio Christi*. Cited definitions include "the inner spiritual nature or affections; the inner resources of (one's) reason" (n. 4), "of faculties, actions, experiences, etc: located or operating within the inner nature of man or God; spiritual, mental, contemplative" (adj. 2a), "of feeling, emotions, effort, etc.: sincere, genuine, earnest, heartfelt; also fervent, intense" (adj. 2b), "spiritually minded" (adj. 2c), and "secret, hidden, undisclosed" (adj. 3) (ed. Kuhn and Reidy, I.I 258–61).

17. Jager, *The Book of the Heart*, xx.

18. Summit describes the standard narrative: "the beginning of early modernity . . . signals the rejection of the Roman church in England, the construction of a new religion of inwardness in its place, and the emergence of a new sense of distance from the historical past" (*Lost Property*, 109). For a good example, see Lake, "Religious Identities in Shakespeare's England." Lake cites Duffy's picture of late medieval England as "a world in which there was no real divide between individual religious affect or interiority and outward communal practice" (72).

19. Targoff, *Common Prayer*, 2.

20. Bacon, *Works*, vol. 1, ed. Spedding, 178; cited in Targoff, 2. Targoff notes that Claudius's famous lament has also been taken as emblematic of the new inner/outer gap: "My prayers fly up, my thoughts remain below; / Words without thoughts never to heaven go." But Claudius's lament echoes contested but very common observations in late medieval devotional texts about the uselessness of prayers, confessions, and penance that are less than heartfelt. Hilton, for example: "a bodily turnynge to God without the herte folwynge is but a figure or a likenes of vertues and no soothfast-

nesse" (*Scale* I.i, ed. Bestul, 31). Dozens of medieval texts could be cited for either position.

21. Targoff, 6, 18.

22. *After Augustine*, 69.

23. See Watson, *Richard Rolle and the Invention of Authority*.

24. Some contemporary critics charged that Rolle made men "judges of themselves." The charge was apparently leveled by a Carthusian and reported by the hermit Thomas Basset in his defense of Rolle, circa 1400 (Allen, lvii). For Hilton's reservations about Rolle, and for Bassett's *Defensorium*, see Sargent, "Contemporary Criticism of Richard Rolle."

25. *Form of Living*, in Allen, 110.

26. *Ego Dormio*, in Allen, 66.

27. *Form of Living*, in Allen, 110, 111.

28. For a discussion, see Allen, xlvi.

29. "The Middle English Mystics," 549–50. Watson describes Rolle's work as "an extension, not a denial, of the pastoral project" (548), but adds, "It can be no accident that, despite Wynkyn de Worde's fondness for Rolle's name on his title pages, none of his genuine English works was printed before modern times" (550).

30. *Invention of Authority*, 215.

31. *Form of Living*, in Allen, 104.

32. "A Song of the Love of Jesus," in Allen, 45.

33. "Gastly Gladnesse," in Allen, 52.

34. Allen, lxiii. For more on courtly interiority, see, for example, Fradenburg, *Sacrifice Your Love*. Fradenburg writes that *fin amour* "policed and enhanced the identities of those who could use it well," those who were "set apart by the delicate complications of their knowledge and practice of 'sentement' " (120).

35. Jaeger, *Ennobling Love*, 5.

36. Cited by Hogg in "Adam the Carthusian's *De Quadripartito Exercitio Cellae*," 79.

37. The connection between theological and linguistic concerns in this period is a theme of much of Watson's work. See particularly "Conceptions of the Word" and "Censorship and Cultural Change."

38. "The Soul Selects her own Society," in *The Collected Poems*, 9–10.

39. *The Letters of Abelard and Heloise*, trans. Radice, 75.

40. *Gender and Material Culture*, 5. Warren describes the Benedictine profession ceremony as a kind of spiritual wedding; see *Spiritual Economies*, ch. 1.

41. *Nuns as Artists*, 159.

42. Hamburger, *Nuns as Artists*, 157, 138.

43. *The Goodman of Paris (le ménagier de paris)*, trans. Power, 107.

44. *The Doctrine of the Heart*, ed. Candon, 14.

45. Aelred's *De Institutione Inclusarum* provides another, earlier English example. For further discussion, see Price, " 'Inner and Outer.' " For a discussion of the ways in which the text engages with twelfth-century intellectual currents, see Georgianna, *The Solitary Self*.

46. Cited in Hogg, "Adam the Carthusian's *De Quadripartito Exercitio Cellae*," 75.

47. See Edwards, "Early Readers of *Ancrene Wisse*"; Innes-Parker, "The Legacy of

Ancrene Wisse"; Watson, "*Ancrene Wisse*, Religious Reform and the Late Middle Ages"; and Robertson, " 'This Living Hand.' "

48. Lovatt, "Henry Suso."

49. *Yorkshire Writers*, ed. Horstman, 1:324. See Whitehead, "Making a Cloister of the Soul." The author of *Book to a Mother* advises that "yif thou kepe wel this cloister and holde the therinne to thi lives ende, Crist, that is Abbot and Priour of this cloister, wol ever be therinne with the where-evere thou be" (122). *The Book of Vices and Virtues* pictures the heart as a cloister, a private ravishing couch, a restful chamber of clean conscience, and a city whose gates are the five senses.

50. The *Mirror* survives in close to sixty manuscripts; it went through nine print editions between 1484 and 1530. See Sargent, ed., lxiii–lxxxiv.

51. *Mirror*, 181, in a passage original to Love's version; see Sargent, ed., xli.

52. *Book to a Mother*, 13, emphasis mine. The same passage is quoted from *Pore Caitiff* by Brady, in "Lollard Interpolations and Omissions," 201.

53. See Sargent, ed., xlvi. For the critique of Love, see, for example, Watson, "The Middle English Mystics" (562), "Conceptions of the Word," and "Models and Images of the Reading Process," where he writes that the book's meditative practice "is explicitly aimed at preempting detailed and intellectually demanding study, and even at inviting readers to internalize a view of themselves as inherently incapable of such study" (216). In the same volume, Wogan-Browne writes that Love makes Cecilia "into a figure for a privatized and silent devotion whose mode is affective and repetitive, not progressive" (255 n. 23). Staley sees Love's text as an effort to contain the threat of vernacular devotion (*Margery Kempe's Dissenting Fictions*, 145). Beckwith calls Love's image of Christ "a means of social and linguistic condescension," an image that refuses any "licensing porosity of categories" (*Christ's Body*, 65). For more positive assessments, see Gibson, *The Theater of Devotion*, and Simpson, *Reform and Cultural Revolution*, 434 ff.

54. Sponsler's assessment of English books of hours offers an example of this line of critique. Focusing on the model of private reading promoted by these books' tiny owner portraits, Sponsler finds a "safely enclosed subject" in a "sumptuous consumerist space." These pseudo-monastic books, she argues, teach their patrons to look inward in order "to avoid direct confrontation with disturbing events." Subjects thus created are "[p]rohibited even from looking outside . . . absolutely cut off . . . enclosed, controlled, passive, inert, and contained . . . like the foodstuffs, utensils, and household objects surrounding them" (*Drama and Resistance*, 112, 118, 120). In a similar vein, Swanson argues that "interiorised" and "essentially self-centred" Passion meditations "undermined the *caritas* which underpinned the concern with social responsibility in the medieval religious framework" ("Passion and Practice," 14, 11–12). Much of Richmond's work on the religion of the gentry makes the same argument.

55. Cited in Little, "Chaucer's Parson and the Specter of Wycliffism," 234.

56. Hudson, *The Premature Reformation*.

57. Little, "Chaucer's Parson," 234.

58. This is typical of "orthodox" texts. As Brady observes, sacramental confession is "hardly mentioned" in orthodox versions of the *Pore Caitif*; only a few minor substitutions were necessary for the creation of Lollard versions ("Lollard Interpolations,"

191). In a similar vein, Ghosh points out that although Love's biblical hermeneutics are anti-Lollard, most of the manuscripts of the *Mirror* are carefully annotated to distinguish biblical from non-biblical material and to identify cited authorities—a presentation in keeping with Lollard practice. See "Manuscripts of Nicholas Love's *The Mirror of the Blessed Life of Jesus Christ*."

59. Hamburger, *Nuns as Artists*, 152.

60. Cited by du Boulay, *The England of Piers Plowman*, 71. Beckwith calls this "a common analogy in Lollard writings" (*Christ's Body*, 159 n. 61).

61. *Orologium Sapientiae*, 377.

62. *The Myroure of Oure Ladye*, ed. Blunt, 331. For discussion, see Rhodes, "The Body of Christ," 398. Similarly, Lollard insistence that only inward contrition made penitence acceptable was echoed by a broad spectrum of orthodox writers, including Hilton (see n. 21 above).

63. Strohm, describing orthodox reactions to Lollardy in "Counterfeiters, Lollards, and Lancastrian Unease," 43.

64. Cited in Hudson, *Premature Reformation*, 149.

65. See Brady, "Lollard Interpolations and Omissions," 197.

66. See, for example, Aers, *Powers of the Holy*, ch. 1.

67. He writes, "the persecutive machinery put in place in the early fifteenth century itself effectively produces this peculiarly 'modern' subjectivity, so that the act of being an individual, being true to one's inner self or truth, requires a collision with the demands of the world and the community" (279). See "Anne Askewe, John Bale, and Protestant History."

68. "Epistle on the Mixed Life," in *English Mystics of the Middle Ages*, ed. Windeatt, 108–30; 112.

69. *The Imitation of Christ*, ed. Biggs, 24.

70. *Caxton's Own Prose*, ed. Blake, 58. The complaint appears in the prologue to *Blanchardin and Eglantine* (circa 1489), and is addressed to Margaret Beaufort, herself the translator of book four of *De Imitatione Christi*.

71. Hughes, *Pastors and Visionaries*, 296.

72. In " 'Of Three Workings in Man's Soul,' " the Virgin is so involved in her inner devotion that all her blood goes to her heart, leaving her body a pale, ghostly white, barely alive at all. She reads "without showing of voice" and with her eyes closed. See Stephen Hayes, " 'Of Three Workings in Man's Soul.' "

73. *Orologium Sapientiae*, 354.

74. The *Ymage of Love* (STC 21471) was translated by John Gough from a work by John Ryckes. Krug argues that although the text was not necessarily heretical, its implicit leanings might have raised eyebrows among "influential lay believers." See *Reading Families*, 205. On the complexity of medieval attitudes toward images, see *Images, Idolatry, and Iconoclasm*, ed. Dimmick et al.

75. The treatise appears as Appendix II in *The Book of Margery Kempe*, ed. Meech and Allen. The full contents of Pepwell's edition are modernized and revised in *The Cell of Self-Knowledge*, ed. Gardner.

76. "Margery Kempe and Wynkyn de Worde," 35.

77. Lochrie, *Margery Kempe and the Translations of the Flesh*, 221, 224. Anthony

Goodman writes that Pepwell "transposed Margery to where the secular world always wants to put spiritual dissidents—out of it" ("The Piety of John Brunham's Daughter," 357–58).

78. "Chaucer's Pardoner on the Couch," 669.

79. Summit has argued that the Pepwell text, which opens with an indulgenced "Image of Pity," is a careful response to Luther's attack on indulgences (*Lost Property*, 134). She suggests that the practice of indulgences is both a central concern of the text (a serious misreading, in my view), and the key context for the its reception. However, she also points out that post-Reformation readers of the one surviving copy have simply crossed out the opening indulgence, failing to alter the text itself in any way. Summit interprets this as a large-scale reframing of the meaning of devotional reading; though the text is materially unaltered, its "traditional" significance as a devotional object has been stripped away: "the marks that score through Pepwell's indulgence come out of an effort . . . to reshape the medieval cultural heritage of the indulgenced prayer and thereby to redefine the uses of its texts for a new, reformed book culture" (136). I contend that although Pepwell's edition might seek to create its *own* reception as an indulgenced devotional object in response to Lutheran politics, the reframing provides cover for suddenly dangerous doctrine, rather than indicating a long-standing "cultural heritage" of reading that must be stripped away. Wynkyn de Worde's earlier edition, after all, does not include an indulgence.

80. *The Book of Vices and Virtues*, 233.

81. Bibliothèque Nationale, Paris; in Camille, *Gothic Art: Glorious Visions*, 109.

82. For later interpretations of mass according to events in the life and Passion of Jesus, including Gherit van der Goude's important "Interpretacyon and sygnyfycacyon of the Masse" (1532), see Rhodes, "The Body of Christ," esp. 394–95. See also *Tracts on the Mass*, ed. Legg; and Marshall, *The Catholic Priesthood and the English Reformation*.

83. The work survives at least partially in 13 manuscripts and a printed edition. See *The Minor Poems*, 87–115. Line numbers are cited parenthetically above. For ownership, see Boffey, "Lydgate's Lyrics and Women Readers."

84. Gibson, *Theater of Devotion*, 96.

85. 489, 493. Lydgate's list of the rewards of hearing mass also includes temporary freedom from aging, improved digestion, safety at sea, and successful pregnancy—just in case the prospect of inner understanding is not enough to get every reader to the church on time.

86. See Catto, "Religious Change Under Henry V."

87. See especially Patterson, "Making Identities in Fifteenth-Century England"; Strohm, *England's Empty Throne*, esp. ch. 3, "Plots"; and Watson, " 'Yf wommen be double naturelly.' "

88. Cited by Patterson in "Making Identities," 82. See also Fisher, "A Language Policy for Lancastrian England."

89. Cited in Gillespie, "Vernacular Books of Religion," 318. In the *Convivio*, Dante claims that "one's own vernacular . . . is not simply near but supremely near to everyone" (trans. Lansing, 29 [I.12]).

90. Lollards also cast things they were opposed to in terms of privacy, namely private confession: in the tract *Nota de confessione*, priests and women turn their faces together and speak of lustful thoughts and deeds, which harm them both. Good confession is either to God alone, or openly—not "priuely & rownyngly, as men confessen nowe-adaies." Cited in Little, "Chaucer's Parson," 234.

91. *The Myroure of Oure Ladye*, 4.

92. Duffy, *The Stripping of the Altars*, 39.

93. Ibid., n. p. 120; 19.

94. Ibid., 39.

95. I am hesitant to join the chorus of attacks on Duffy's work, which I deeply admire. The criticism, much of which has been unnervingly polemical, goes too far in my view toward reinstating the heroic Protestant version of the English Reformation that Duffy's work so effectively challenges.

96. Critiques range from Dix's lament that "The old corporate worship of the eucharist is declining into a mere focus for the subjective devotion of each separate worshipper in the isolation of his own mind" (*The Shape of the Liturgy*, 599–600) to Sponsler's characterization of inward-looking devotional subjects as presenting little challenge to the forces of social control (*Drama and Resistance*, described in n. 54 above). Richmond regrets the lack of passion, emotion, "extremes of behavior" and "sensational . . . enthusiasm" in the fifteenth-century English church, writing that "the spirit had gone out of religion in England" ("Religion," 195, 191). Despres compares the public, theatrical, evangelical, prophetic, charitable qualities of Italian sanctity to the enclosed, meditative, private, non-visionary, self-contained, regulatory qualities of fifteenth-century English piety in "Ecstatic Reading and Missionary Mysticism." Lovatt describes an English mentality that favored the sober, moralistic, practical, and prosaic over the elevated and flamboyant ("Henry Suso"). Inwardness has been identified, with obvious disapproval, as a "bourgeois conviction" in much scholarship—see, for example, Lindenbaum, "London Texts and Literate Practice," in *Cambridge History*, ed. Wallace, 284–309; 308.

97. See *The King's Book*, ed. Lacey.

98. Walter Hilton responds to just this problem in the *Scale of Perfection*. His answer is approximately George Herbert's (e.g., "The Flower"): this fragmented, scattered emptiness keeps the believer from trusting too much in her own powers of self-discipline, and so falling victim to the sin of pride.

99. Cited in Targoff, *Common Prayer*, 53; the sermon can also be found in *The Sermons of John Donne*, ed. Potter and Simpson, 5:13.

100. 117 copies of the *Pricke* survive.

101. *The Pricke of Conscience*, ed. Morris. Subsequent references are cited parenthetically.

102. In Horstman, *Yorkshire Writers*, 2:439. The treatise is loosely adapted from the *Speculum Peccatoris*; it is attributed in various manuscripts to St. Augustine, St. Bernard, and Rolle. For more of the same, see the "Speculum S. Edmundi," 219, in the same volume.

103. See especially Leicester's discussion in *The Disenchanted Self*; Dinshaw, "Eu-

nuch Hermeneutics," in *Chaucer's Sexual Poetics*; and Patterson, "Chaucer's Pardoner on the Couch."

104. Ed. Ingram, 45.

105. *Confessions* 10.8 and 10.17. I am using Pine-Coffin's translation; subsequent citations are included parenthetically in the text.

106. *Confessions* 10.17 (223–24). I have found Cary's discussion of Augustinian memory very useful: *Augustine's Invention of the Inner Self*, esp. ch. 10, "The Origin of Inner Space."

107. Hughes, *Pastors and Visionaries*, 95, 184, 275–77.

108. Ibid., 275.

109. I Corinthians 13:12. Paul, like Augustine after him, was heavily indebted to the Platonists for his mirror analogies. See Goldberg, *The Mirror and Man*, ch. 7.

110. *Augustine: Later Works*, ed. and trans. Burnaby, 141. Subsequent references are noted parenthetically. The best new edition is *On the Trinity: Books 5–11*, ed. Matthews, trans. McKenna.

111. Taylor, *Sources of the Self*.

112. *Augustine the Reader*, 111.

113. See, for example, Benton, "Consciousness of Self," 264.

114. Bestul, "Devotional Writing in England," 22. See also Goldin, *The Mirror of Narcissus*, 209. Kieckhefer's *Unquiet Souls* provides a wonderful account of how the new Augustinianism was transforming expectations of holiness across Europe.

115. Hughes, *Pastors and Visionaries*, 277.

116. For example, *Benjamin Minor*: "i rede that a man sek [first] besile forto knaw hym-self, the wilk is made to the ymage of gode os in saule. & witt tho wele that he that desirs forto se gode, hym behose clens his saule, the wilk is os a myroure in the wilk all yngis are clerle sen wen it is clene" (*Yorkshire Writers*, 1:171).

117. Henry's book strongly recalls the *Ancrene Wisse*, both in the vividness of its metaphors and in the way Henry imagines his inner self as an enclosed space vulnerable to penetration from the outside. For the increasing popularity of "heart-centered" piety more generally, see Jager, *Book of the Heart*, ch. 6; for the heart as a text to be read and understood as the record of a private, unique individual, see ch. 3.

118. Books I and II are quite different works, though both concentrate on the soul's reformation in the image of God. Book I often circulated independently of Book II; there are eighteen surviving manuscripts with I alone, twenty-three with I and II, and one with II alone. Only half the surviving manuscripts have the title *The Scale of Perfection*; BL MS Harley 2397 calls it *The Reformyng of Mannys Soule*. See Bestul, *Scale of Perfection*, 6; see also the introduction by Clark and Dorward to their modern translation of the *Scale*, and Hussey, "Editing *The Scale of Perfection*." For further discussion of the image in Hilton, see Clark, "Image and Likeness in Walter Hilton," and Watson, "Idols and Images in Walter Hilton."

119. Thomas Fishlake produced a Latin translation of both books, and the work was printed several times by Wynkyn de Worde beginning in 1494. MS Lambeth Palace 472, on which Bestul's edition is based, was made for John Killum, a London grocer who died in 1416, as a "common profit book" to be passed from one reader to another (see Bestul's discussion, 7–11). The Lambeth manuscript, like many others circulating

in the London area, is based on a slightly expanded version of the *Scale*, with some additions that have been described as "Christo-centric." Wynkyn de Worde's editions were probably based on this version as well. See Sargent, "Walter Hilton's *Scale of Perfection*."

120. Bestul, ed., *Scale of Perfection*. Subsequent references are cited parenthetically above.

121. *The Seven Poyntes* has similar troubles, asking readers to close the doors of their hearts "fro the formes of outewarde thinges and ymagynayouns of erthly things," while depending on a plethora of vivid earthly and social metaphors—architectural, chivalric, romantic—for its own instructional program (354).

122. See Watson, "The Trinitarian Hermeneutic."

123. *A Book of Showings*, ed. Colledge and Walsh, 1:236 (ch. 11). Subsequent references are to the Long Text in vol. 2 unless otherwise indicated, and are cited by chapter and line. See 235n.1.

124. Technically, the word's first appearance is in chapter 13, where Christ's scorn of the devil causes Julian to laugh. She does not see Christ laugh, but nevertheless Julian understands an inner expression of scorn: "And ther I sawe hym scorne [the devil's] malis, is was be holdyng to my understandyng in to oure lorde, that is to say an inward shewyng of sothfastnesse without changngyng of chere" (13.31–35). This sentence does not appear in the Short Text, and it seems to refer forward in the Showings to the two "cheers" with which the Lord beholds his Servant (ch. 51). There are a handful of other instances in the work; see 27.20, 30.6, 41.56–60, 79.17, and 80.5.

Chapter 2. Seeing a Difference

Note to epigraph: For authorship and identity in *Piers Plowman*, see especially Middleton, "William Langland's 'Kynde Name.'" See also Kruger, "Mirrors and the Trajectory of Vision in *Piers Plowman*."

1. Newman provides a useful survey and typology of the confusion in "What Did It Mean to Say 'I Saw'?"

2. See Stock, *Augustine the Reader*, esp. 241–44.

3. Ong, *Orality and Literacy*, 105.

4. Stock, *Augustine the Reader*, 89.

5. *Ennarratio in Psalmum CIII*. Cited in Goldin, *The Mirror of Narcissus*, 4.

6. From the preface to *Moralia in Job*, IIi and I.xxxiii, ed. Adriaen. The translation is Carruthers's; see *The Craft of Thought*, 159.

7. *Confessions*, 160, 164 (8.2, 8.5).

8. *Confessions*, 168 (8.6).

9. *Confessions*, 169 (8.7).

10. "Not in reveling and drunkenness, not in lust and wantonness, not in quarrels and rivalries. Rather, arm yourselves with the Lord Jesus Christ; spend no more thought on nature and nature's appetites" (Rom. 13:13–14).

11. For a discussion of the Augustinian heart, see Jager, *The Book of the Heart*, ch. 2.

12. Grabes, *The Mutable Glass*, 29. Grabes also notes that in the fifteenth century,

England was eclipsed by southern Germany and the Netherlands in the production of mirror-titled texts. Dutch interest in mirrors is most famously on display in Jan van Eyck's *Arnolfini Marriage* of 1434, where the painter is reflected in a looking glass framed by scenes from the life of Christ.

13. Ibid., 71. Though Grabes's study is the most comprehensive, see also Goldin, *The Mirror of Narcissus*; Goldberg, *The Mirror and Man*; Knoespel, *Narcissus and the Invention of Personal History*; Nolan, *Now Through a Glass Darkly*; Torti, *The Glass of Form*; and Wimsatt, *Allegory and Mirror*. For mirrors as symbols of spiritual development, see Bradley, "The Speculum Image"; and Beckwith, "A Very Material Mysticism."

14. See, for example, Goldberg, *The Mirror and Man*. Goldberg observes that European demand for Venetian mirrors increased in the early fourteenth and again in the first half of the fifteenth centuries (138). Clear crystal mirrors were not invented until 1507 (Grabes, 4).

15. Kruger notes that the Langlandian mirrors "appear in that section of [the text] which is most concentratedly introspective and most intensely concerned with problems of epistemology" ("Mirrors and the Trajectory of Vision," 75).

16. *The Myrour of Recluses*, ed. Harley, xxiii.

17. Sargent, 27.

18. *Book to a Mother*, ed. McCarthy, 38, 31.

19. Meier-Ewert, "A Middle English Version of the Fifteen Oes" (see Oes 5 and 7); *The Prickynge of Love*, ed. Kane, 184.

20. *The Orcherd of Syon*, ed. Hodgson and Liegy, 419–20.

21. Grabes, 75.

22. Belting, *Likeness and Presence*, 422. I am grateful to Jessica Brantley for drawing it to my attention.

23. In *Nuns as Artists*, Hamburger quotes a German homily comparing the image of Christ on the soul to the image on a shield (2). Here the image of Christ replaces, rather than supplementing or serving as the flip side of, the heraldic insignia as symbolic of the self.

24. Goldin, 3, 146 n. 36.

25. For the history and spirituality of Syon, see de Hamel, *Syon Abbey*; Knowles, *The Religious Orders in England*, vol. 3, ch. 18.; Aungier, *The History and Antiquities of Syon*; Beckett, "St. Bridget, Henry V and Syon Abbey"; Ellis, *Viderunt eam filie Syon*; and Ellis, "Spirituality of Syon Abbey." See also Blunt's introduction to the *Myroure of Oure Ladye*.

26. De Hamel, 53.

27. "Vast sums were spent on building," de Hamel observes, "and if it had survived, Syon Abbey might have rivaled the chapels of Eton or Windsor or King's College as a monument of the high gothic" (62).

28. Ed. Blunt, xxxix.

29. For Syon's books and influence on devotional culture, see, for example, de Hamel, *Syon Abbey*; Gillespie and Doyle, *Syon Abbey*; Bateson, *Catalogue of the Library of Syon* (for the brothers' library); Hogg, "The Contribution of the Brigittine Order"; Rhodes, "Syon Abbey and its Religious Publications"; Hutchison, "Devo-

tional Reading"; Hutchison, "What Nuns Read"; Krug, *Reading Families*, ch. 4; Sargent, *James Grenehalgh*; Powell, "Syon, Caxton, and the Festial"; Keiser, "Patronage and Piety"; Keiser, "The Mystics and the Early English Printers"; and Rhodes, "The Body of Christ."

30. Gillespie, *Syon Abbey*, xxxiii. Duffy discusses Syon's "extensive lay clientele" in *The Stripping of the Altars*, 86.

31. De Hamel, 58, 82.

32. The only book known to have belonged to the Yorkist Queen Elizabeth Woodville was associated with Syon. See Sutton and Visser-Fuchs, "The Cult of Angels."

33. Gibson, *The Theater of Devotion*, e.g., 20, 97–98.

34. Krug, *Reading Families*, 191. In "The Body of Christ," Rhodes points to a manuscript full of Syon-related Passion materials copied for Dame Anna Bulkley, who was perhaps related to Syon sisters Alice Bulkeley (d. 1495) and Joan Bulkeley (d. 1532) (398 and n. 71).

35. For the catalog, see Bateson, *Catalogue*, and Gillespie, *Syon Abbey*. De Hamel writes, "By the time of the catalogue, Syon Abbey could boast a collection of nearly one and a half thousand books which would be the envy of any library of renaissance scholarship" (79).

36. Bell finds some evidence of Latin learning at Syon and a few other houses; see *What Nuns Read*, 61. A typical response to the problem can be seen in the prologue to the English register of Godstow Abbey (ca. 1460); see Goldberg, *Women in England*, 266.

37. Henry VIII would answer just this question with a decree that "the unlearned people should use to make their prayers in their mother tongue, which they best understand, whereby they may be the more moved and stirred unto devotion, and the more earnestly mind the thing that they pray for" (*The King's Book*, 123). Some Protestants, however, objected to voiced prayer even in the vernacular, believing that it "sustain[ed] an undesirable gap between the individual's outward performance and inward state of mind" (Targoff, *Common Prayer*, 39).

38. Ed. Vaissier, 27.

39. *The Chastising of God's Children*, ed. Bazire and Colledge, 221. The text was owned by and perhaps written for the convent at Barking, with which Syon originally had strong affiliations.

40. *The Myroure of Oure Ladye*, ed. Blunt, 71. Subsequent references appear parenthetically in the text. Other studies include Hutchison, "*The Myroure of Oure Ladye*"; and Grise, "Female Religious Readers and Textual Reception."

41. See Saenger, "Books of Hours and the Reading Habits of the Later Middle Ages."

42. The quality of the sisters' spiritual directors was apparently very high as well; see Knowles, *The Religious Orders*, 3:212–13.

43. Ed. Bestul, 183.

44. For a discussion of the Rule, see Ellis, *Viderunt Eam*; for the legislation of private devotion, see p. 111.

45. See, for example, Hutchison, "Devotional Reading," 215.

46. Hogg, ed., *The Rewyll of Seynt Savioure*, 4:72. See Hutchison, "Devotional Reading," 217.

47. For the Chambress's account, see Blunt, xxvii. For manuscript indexing, see de Hamel, 103.

48. The *Myroure* refers to English Bibles that the nuns might have "license thereunto." Dame Anne Danvers, widow of Sir William Danvers, donated an English Bible in 1517; it is now Manchester Rylands Eng. 81, which preserves no sign of a license. See Hudson, *The Premature Reformation*, 23 and 233 n. 4; depending on Ker, *Medieval Libraries of Great Britain*; see also de Hamel, 82.

49. Rhodes, "Syon Abbey," 16. *De Exterioris* (also known as *Formula Noviciarum*) was translated by Thomas Prestius of Syon.

50. See Bell, *What Nuns Read*, 43, and de Hamel's list of surviving manuscripts.

51. De Hamel, 81. The manuscript is inscribed with the names of two Syon nuns; the scribe's signature is dated 1459.

52. De Hamel, 97. The work was printed in Lyons in 1483.

53. Richard Whytford, *Pype or Tonne of the Lyfe of Perfection*, ed. Hogg, vol. 4, pt. 3, p. 335. Gilchrist observes that convents sought to "[numb] any private experience of self through the construction of collective identity" (*Gender and Material Culture*, 20).

54. Krug also discusses the obsessive visuality of the text; see *Reading Families*, 168 ff.

55. See, for example, Augustine, "De Trintate," in *Later Works*, ed. and trans. Burnaby, 143; see also Hamburger, "The Visual and the Visionary," 180.

56. "The Visual and the Visionary," 180. Rolle, for example, devalued the textual aspects of seeing, holding that only the lower part of contemplation was involved in meditating on holy writing, whereas the higher part was a beholding of the things of heaven. James Simpson takes a dim view of the trend: "throughout the period . . . the visual is characterized as the realm of the unlearned because it is restricted to the corporal and fleshly. The visual is deployed in official religious practice to provoke powerful feelings of devotional piety and penitential regret, but precisely as such it precludes abstract thinking" (*Reform and Cultural Revolution*, 442).

57. See Despres, *Ghostly Sights*, e.g. 8.

58. Newman writes, "[t]he penchant for cultivating visionary experience . . . eventuated finally in a kind of category mistake, a pervasive intellectual confusion, that compounded late medieval churchmen's anxiety about uncontrolled visionaries" ("What Did It Mean to Say 'I Saw'?" 5).

59. Saenger, "Books of Hours," 147.

60. Newman, "What Did It Mean to Say 'I Saw'?" 25.

61. Gillespie, *Syon Abbey*, 753. References to Mechtild can be found in at least fourteen other English devotional works. There are four extant English manuscripts of an abridged version of the Latin *Liber Spiritualis Gratiae*; the English translation survives in two—one of which, BL Egerton 2006, belonged to Richard III and his wife Anne—and seems to have been popular with women in particular. See Halligan's introduction to *The Booke of Gostlye Grace*. For BL Egerton 2006, see Sargent, *James Grenehalgh*, 34. See also Voaden, "The Company She Keeps."

62. *The Orcherd of Syon*, ed. Hodgson and Liegy, 47.

63. Emphasis mine. Cited in Keiser, " 'To Knawe God Almiyghtyn,' " 113–14. The sermon was included in Thornton's fifteenth-century devotional collection, but also forms a part of John Gaytryge's *Lay Folks' Catechism*, produced in 1357.

64. Richard Whytford would echo this injunction in the early sixteenth century: "bende thy mynd willingly and esysely to readinge . . . seeke not for curiosity, nor for superfluous intelligence and science: nor yet for ornamente and eloquence of words" (de Hamel, 178, n. 71). The admonition apparently had little force on the other side of the Bridgettine wall, where Richard Pace was becoming expert in Hebrew and Chaldaic, and where the brothers were amassing their library of renaissance scholarship (de Hamel, 99).

65. Sargent documents the close association of Syon, Sheen, and the London Charterhouse with the *Scale* in "Walter Hilton's *Scale of Perfection*."

66. Sargent, *James Grenehalgh*, 1:35. The book is Bell A.19, de Hamel item 11, now Glassgow Hunterian MS.T.6.18.

67. De Hamel item 126. Clemence was re-enclosed during Mary's reign, in 1557.

68. Sargent, *James Grenehalgh*, 1:172; see also Krug's discussion on 196. Grenehalgh was a Carthusian monk, born ca. 1465–70, professed at Sheen before 1499 and removed to Coventry by 1508, apparently for disciplinary reasons (Sargent, 103). His annotations appear in twelve extant manuscripts and two printed books (213).

69. See Goldberg, *The Mirror and Man*, 150.

70. Gibson, *Theater of Devotion*, 176.

71. *Reading Families*, 172. Although my reading of *The Myroure* differs somewhat from Krug's, I admire and have benefited from her careful and insightful work.

72. Krug, *Reading Families*, 183–84.

73. Bodleian MS.Rawl.C.941, item 14 in de Hamel's list of surviving manuscripts (p. 198); see Blunt, viii. There are also seven known copies of the 1530 print edition.

74. *PL* 175, 976A; quoted in Hamburger, *Nuns as Artists*, 129.

75. *The Cloud of Unknowing*, ed. Hodgson, 32. Subsequent references are cited parenthetically.

76. Trans. Babinsky, 153 (ch. 78).

77. Here I am quoting from the "Book of Privy Counseling," in Hodgson, *The Cloud of Unknowing*, 157.

78. The *Cloud*-author recommends picking one single word of one short syllable and using it to drive out all other language.

79. See Haren, "Social Ideas in the Pastoral Literature of Fourteenth-Century England," 46–47.

80. There are seventeen extant versions of the *Cloud* and ten of *The Book of Privy Counseling* (Hodgson, ix). None of them are bundled into large, diverse collections of vernacular texts; all seem to be "specialist" manuscripts.

81. *The Middle English Mystics*, trans. Standring, 60.

82. Watson makes a similar argument about Hilton's relation to the *Cloud*-author, observing that Hilton "rejected the *Cloud*-author's wholesale refusal of the visual, concluding the *Scale* with accounts of the purified soul's exploration of truth, in which the soul's intuitive knowledge of all it sees is still a version, however distant, of the seeing associated with images" ("Idols and Images in Walter Hilton," 110). While

not naming the *Cloud* explicitly, Hilton describes erring contemplatives in terms that strongly recall it, even troping their arrogance as two clouds. Such people "are not bisy for to entren into hemself" to examine the wickedness of their hearts, but "astite as thei han forsaken the werld as it were outward in liknes," they believe that they love God perfectly (2:26). (This neatly reverses the *Cloud*-author's criticism of simple people trying to be inward.)

83. 131–32. These passages are translated from Ruysbroek's *Spiritual Espousals*, a text that is interested in the possibility of mystical union. In Ruysbroek's text, these criticisms are directed against the heresy of the Free Spirit. Bazire and Colledge assume that since this is what the passages refer to in the original, this is what they refer to in the translation as well. But the *Chastising* is not a faithful translation of Ruysbroek; rather, it is a carefully sewn patchwork of excerpts from Ruysbroek and many other writers, along with one chapter that seems to be original—all together forming a work of remarkable thematic unity. The largest borrowing is from only one of the three parts of Ruysbroek's work: the middle part, the "Life of Yearning for God." England had no problem with the heresy of the Free Spirit, and it makes no sense that in a text so carefully constructed, the author would waste space criticizing a heresy that his readers were unlikely to encounter. The language he uses is similar enough to the *Cloud*'s that I think we can guess which false contemplatives he really had in mind.

84. Bazire and College, 147. For a discussion of the visual tradition associated with the verse, see Hamburger, *Nuns as Artists*, 81–92.

85. Compare the popular *Remedy Against the Troubles of Temptations*, translated from William Flete's Latin: "Ryght so yf a man be in perfyte rest and quyetnes of herte / it is no maystry for hym to serve god: But it is a maystry to hym that is in travalyle and out of quyetnes of herte to serve hym" (Horstmann, *Yorkshire Writers*, 2:115). Virtues are more profitable if they are acquired with more difficulty.

86. Gibson, *Theater of Devotion*, 7.

Chapter 3. Private Passions

Note to epigraphs: *The Imitation of Christ*, ed. Biggs, 57–58 (2.12). Three separate English translations of Books I–III were made in the fifteenth and early sixteenth centuries. For Lady Margaret Beaufort's translation of book IV, see the earlier EETS edition, ed. Ingram. Yates, *The Art of Memory*, 16.

1. For the text, see *The Minor Poems I*, ed. MacCracken, 329–62. The poem survives in fourteen manuscripts and an early print edition, as well as some painted verses in the Clopton chantry at Long Melford. Line numbers are cited parenthetically.

2. The association of the crucified Christ with meditation on "the past" goes back to Aelred's *De Institutione Inclusarum*, which advises a three-stage meditation on past (the Passion), present (one's own spiritual state), and future (judgment).

3. Lydgate describes the floral chaplet earlier, in the description of his childhood springtime, but the iconographic detail is significant enough to linger in the mind, particularly in light of the rhetoric of Voragine's *Golden Legend*, which Lydgate un-

doubtedly knew: "Thou art a man and hast a chaplet of flowers, and I am God and have a chaplet of thorns. Thou hast gloves on thy hands, and I have nails fixed in my hands" (quoted from the fifteenth-century English translation in Bennett, *Poetry of the Passion* 46–47).

4. The *OED* lists this poem as the first example of a semantic shift for the word "talent," from the older sense of "inclination or disposition" ("'mind,' 'will,' wish, desire, appetite") to a newer sense of "mental endowment or natural ability" ("power or ability of mind or body viewed as something divinely entrusted to a person for use and improvement"). Of course when Lydgate resolves "taccount for my talent," he has in mind the unit of money in the Biblical parable of the talents (Matt. 25.14–30)—like Milton, lamenting "that one talent which is death to hide." Milton means "talent" in the modern sense, of course, his "*one* talent" being poetry. It is interesting to see Lydgate—who is also concerned with his poetic making here, if much less openly than Milton—moving in that direction, trying to imagine how the ability he has been granted should be accounted for, and whether it even matters.

5. For Lydgate's biography, and a somewhat different reading of the *Testament*, see Pearsall, *John Lydgate*. Pearsall writes, "every mask [Lydgate] puts on is a well-worn medieval one, and it is well to recognise these masks for what they are, otherwise we may find ourselves interpreting poems like the *Testament* as personal documents" (5).

6. The association of monastic regrets with Lot's wife appears to be traditional. Compare Heloise's account: "When you hurried towards God I followed you, indeed, I went first to take the veil—perhaps you were thinking how Lot's wife turned back when you made me put on the religious habit and take my vows before you gave yourself to God" (trans. Radice, 117).

7. Various critics have noted Lydgate's valorization of coherent selfhood. See, for example, Pearsall, *John Lydgate*; Watson, "'Yf Wommen Be Double Naturelly'"; and Patterson, "Making Identities in Fifteenth-Century England."

8. See Gibson, *The Theater of Devotion*, 86–90, for images and discussion.

9. Duffy puts it this way: "the Bernardine tradition of affective meditation on the Passion, enriched and extended by the Franciscans, had become without any rival the central devotional activity of all seriously minded Christians" (*Stripping of the Altars*, 234–35). This "central devotional activity" could of course be accomplished without texts. This is not the place to consider the proliferation of images and windows, Jesus masses and Jesus brotherhoods, dramatic re-enactments, devotions to the Holy Name, and cults of the Wounds that sprung up across late medieval England. See, for example, *Stripping*, 115, 245 ff.; Rubin, *Corpus Christi*; and the essays in MacDonald et al., *The Broken Body*. On the Passion in the visual arts, see especially Marrow, *Passion Iconography*; and van Os, *The Art of Devotion*.

10. Shuger speculates that "before the Enlightenment the dominant models of subjectivity in the Christian West originate as Passion narratives" (*The Renaissance Bible*, 8). Much recent scholarship has elaborated the truth of this proposition for the late Middle Ages. Bynum and Beckwith have traced the symbolism of Christ's body in relation to gender and social identity (see Bynum, *Jesus as Mother* and *Holy Feast and Holy Fast*; and Beckwith, *Christ's Body* and "A Very Material Mysticism"). Feminist critics such as Robertson (*Early English Devotional Prose*) and Bartlett (*Male Authors,*

Female Readers) have investigated its meaning for the sexual identities of religious women. Aers and Staley's *Powers of the Holy* is an important intervention in the conversation about whether the image of Christ's bleeding body could really "empower" those who used it. Newman, however, dismisses the "subversion question" as an inadequate way of thinking about medieval people and their relation to Christianity (*From Virile Woman to Woman-Christ*). Watson addresses the issue—sensitively as usual—in "Conceptions of the Word."

11. Gillespie, "Strange Images of Death." Both this work and Gillespie's "'Lukynge in haly bukes'" are important to the following discussion.

12. See Bestul, *Texts of the Passion*.

13. Love calls meditation on Christ's humanity the most "needful and edifying" exercise for simple souls (ed. Sargent, 78). We have seen that the *Cloud*-author assigns it to the middle stages of the spiritual life, where the devout are "within themselves and even with themselves." These writers echo a school of thought influential since Bernard that considered the humanity and flesh of Christ a more suitable meditative subject for beginning contemplatives than his divinity. Of course not everyone accepted the idea that such exercises were a lesser form of devotion. For further discussion, see, for example, Gillespie, "Strange Images," and Watson, "Conceptions of the Word," esp. 91 ff.

14. The first was the *Meditations on the Supper and Passion of Our Lord*, attributed to Robert Mannyng of Brunne; it survives in nine manuscripts. Others include *The Privity of the Passion*, which survives in four manuscripts and seems to have circulated widely. For other works, see Sargent's introduction to Love's *Mirror*, esp. xix–xx, and Salter, *Nicholas Love's "Myrrour of the Blessed Lyf of Jesu Christ."* See also Sargent's "Bonaventura English." For a useful introduction to the texts, see Despres, *Ghostly Sights*, ch. 1. On Middle English lives of Christ more generally, see Johnson, "Prologue and Practice" and Salter, "*Myrrour.*"

15. Pantin, *The English Church*, 222.

16. Pezzini, "'The meditacion of oure lordis passyon.'"

17. For a prose version, see Meier-Ewert, "A Middle English Version of the 'Fifteen Oes.'" All the printed books of hours contain the *Oes* (Duffy, 238). The text is the subject of excellent discussions in Duffy (218 ff. and 249 ff.), in White, *The Tudor Books of Private Devotion*, ch. 13, and in Summit, *Lost Property*, ch. 3.

18. For excerpts from both works, see Barratt, *Women's Writing in Middle English*. For Barratt's discussion, see "*Stabant matres dolorosae.*"

19. Bennett discusses Henryson's "Bludy Serk" and Dunbar's "Table of Confession" in *Poetry of the Passion*, 120 ff. See also MacDonald, "Passion Devotion in late medieval Scotland."

20. The English translation of Ludolphus's text was from Guillaume le Ménard's French translation, frequently printed after 1470; see MacDonald, "Passion Devotion in Late Medieval Scotland," 128. On Jordanus, see Rhodes, "Prayers of the Passion." Several manuscripts of the *Meditations* are associated with Syon nuns, and one abbreviated version exists in Scots (Rhodes, 31). John Fewterer was confessor general at Syon; his *Myrrour* is STC 14553. See Rhodes, "Syon Abbey and its Religious Publications," 16. Rhodes notes that the *Myrrour* seeks to imprint each episode on the

reader's heart " 'as yf he had only suffred them for us. And so . . . all the prayers be fourmed and made in the singular nombre, to the intent that we may applye them to our selfe" (STC 14553, fo. 57). See also Salter, "Ludophus of Saxony." For discussion of Kennedy's poem, see Bennett, *Poetry of the Passion*, 128.

21. See Gray, "Books of Comfort."

22. Horrall, "*Cursor Mundi* and Its Background," 106. See also Brown, "The Cursor Mundi and the Southern Passion."

23. *The Minor Poems*, ed. MacCracken, xxix and 329.

24. Bodleian 3938 and BM Add. 22283. Westra observed that the text "ranked with the most popular devotional works of the fourteenth century" (xxxi). All references are to Westra, ed., *A Talkynge of the Love of God*; I have modernized the punctuation. The work is also included in Horstman's *Yorkshire Writers*, 2:345–66.

25. Westra details these changes in the introduction, xxx–xxxi.

26. Westra, xxxi. For debate over the audience for these manuscripts, see especially *Studies in the Vernon Manuscript*, ed. Pearsall.

27. This is Bartlett's argument in *Male Authors, Female Readers. The Idea of the Vernacular* also identifies it as a work for nuns, both in the headnote to excerpt 3.1 and in Watson's essay on "The Politics of Middle English Writing" (222, 339). On the cultivation of desire in female religious, see also Robertson, *Early English Devotional Prose*. The most interesting work on the subject is Sarah McNamer's forthcoming study on the history of compassion; I am grateful to have had the opportunity to see that work in progress.

28. *Ureisun*, 5. All references are to *The Wohunge of Ure Lauerd*, ed. Thompson.

29. The idea of Christ's crucified arms outstretched in a loving embrace is common; it appears in the sermon tradition, for example, and in many of the *ars moriendi*, including "The Book of the Craft of Dying" (in Horstman, *Yorkshire Writers* 2:410).

30. See Bynum, *Jesus as Mother* (161 ff.) for men using the trope of the female soul to explore sexual union with God. See also *Fragmentation and Redemption*, esp. 153. Anselm's meditation on Christ at the age of thirteen lingers on his sensual beauty, as does the *Letter of Lentulus*. For an argument that stresses the homoerotic, rather than feminized, aspect of male devotional desire (in seventeenth-century poetry), see Rambuss's *Closet Devotions*.

31. "Prayer to John the Baptist," in *The Prayers and Meditations of St. Anselm*, trans. Ward, 134.

32. *The Prayers and Meditations*, 9–10.

33. Carruthers, *The Craft of Thought*, 105. For in-depth discussion of Anselm's prayers, see, for example, Fulton, *From Judgment to Passion*, ch. 3.

34. "Meditations at Lagunitas," ll. 24–25, in *Praise*.

35. 60. The image of the greyhound as a symbol of desire can be found in other religious texts; cf. *The Cloud of Unknowing*: "lache not over hastely, as it were a gredy grehounde," or Sister Elsbeth Hainburg of Villingen: "The greyhound renneth . . . for gret desyr. . . . The holy man renneth as greyhoundes for thei have evere here eighen to hevene, for there thei seen the praie that thei honten and chaseth after" (cited in Riehle, *The Middle English Mystics*, 71 n. 41).

36. Cited in Horsfield, "*The Pomander of Prayer*," 211.

37. *The Book of Vices and Virtues*, ed. Francis, 140.

38. Bartlett makes essentially this argument in *Male Authors, Female Readers*, although she connects the text's erotic rhetoric to medical discourses about female sexuality, assuming that male writers were trying to arouse religious women's naturally cold, dry, slow bodies to erotic excitement for Christ. Carruthers's investigation of medieval theories of memory in *The Book of Memory* provides an important counterbalance to the gender specificity and body-centeredness of this argument, showing that the mind was regarded as unfortunately inclined to torpor in both sexes. I share Bartlett's sense, however, of the surprising nature of what such texts had to offer real women with real bodies.

39. *The Tretys of Love*, ed. Fisher. For further discussion see Innes-Parker, "The Legacy of *Ancrene Wisse*."

40. Wakelin has observed that the Passion is generally less erotic and emotional in sermons than in texts meant for private meditation. See "English Mysticism and the English Homiletic Tradition," 49.

41. *The Renaissance Bible*, 191. But Rambuss cautions us about describing all male erotic desire for Jesus as "feminine" in *Closet Devotions*.

42. Gibson, *The Theater of Devotion*, 98.

43. *Troilus and Criseyde*, I.297–98.

44. See Miles, *Image as Insight*, 45, and Lindberg, *Theories of Vision from Al-Kindi to Kepler*.

45. Miles, *Image as Insight*, 97, and Lindberg, *Theories of Vision*, chs. 5–6. Boethius refers to the theory as outdated in the *Consolation of Philosophy* V, poem 4.

46. Miles, "Vision: the Eye of the Body and the Eye of the Mind." The relevant discussions can be found in Book 11 of *De Trinitate*. Wolfgang Riehle notes that Origen first developed the doctrine of the spiritual senses; see *The Middle English Mystics*, 104.

47. *A Book of Showings*, 1.268 (short text, ch. 22). This is an insight familiar to modern film theory; as Pribram writes, "subjectivity is produced and affirmed, and ideology disseminated, through spectatorial identification" (*Female Spectators*, 4).

48. *The Treatise of Perfection of the Sons of God*, excerpted in *English Mystics of the Middle Ages*, ed. Windeatt, 263.

49. There is a large body of work on this subject, but see especially the work of Hamburger, for example, *Nuns as Artists* and *The Visual and the Visionary*. See also Erikson, *The Medieval Vision*.

50. *On the Trinity*, ed. Matthews, trans. McKenna, 66 (book 11).

51. Ibid., 69.

52. Trans. Radice, 68.

53. Quoting Hugh, Bonaventure writes that "the power of love transforms the lover into the beloved's likeness" (*Opera Omnia* IX, 695, cited in Camille, "Mimetic Identification," 206).

54. The treatise can be found in Clark, *The Cloud of Unknowing*, 3:67–69.

55. *The Orcherd of Syon*, ed. Hodgson and Liegey, 114.

56. Ed. Hogg, IV.451. Cited in Ellis, "Spirituality of Syon Abbey."

57. Yates, *The Art of Memory*, 4, 9; see Carruthers, *The Book of Memory*, 130–38.

58. Cary, *Augustine's Invention of the Inner Self*, 127 ff.

59. Carruthers, *The Craft of Thought*, 99. She writes, "the notion that memories are produced and recalled affectively, that memory itself is an 'affection' of the body, was basic" (99). For a provocative study of the links between torture and medieval theories of truth production, see Enders, *The Medieval Theater of Cruelty*.

60. Carruthers, *Craft of Thought*, 103.

61. Lydgate, *Minor Poems I*, 250. See also "Cristes Passioun," "A Saying of the Nightengale," "The Fifteen Oes," "On the Image of Pity," in the same volume.

62. *The Book of Margery Kempe*, 143. The list of works also appears on 39.

63. Ibid., 154. Cf. *Prickynge of Love*, ed. Kane, 20. Subsequent references are cited parenthetically above. I have modernized the punctuation.

64. For Kempe's relation to the Passion, see Beckwith, "A Very Material Mysticism," and Manter's recent response, "The Savior of Her Desire." For the other side again, see Barratt, "*Stabant matres.*" All three critics concur that the authors of Passion meditations intend to oppress women, whether or not they succeed in Margery's case.

65. Fleming, *Franciscan Literature*, 214. Sargent describes the work in *Nicholas Love's Mirror*, xiii–xiv.

66. Kirchberger (editor of *The Goad of Love*) was confident of Hilton's authorship; Kane is skeptical, noting among other problems that Margery Kempe—she would have liked being cited as an authority, I think—seems not to have connected the work to Hilton. Watson accepts the attribution (see "Middle English Mystics"), as does Hughes (*Pastors and Visionaries*). Lagorio and Sargent consider it probable ("English Mystical Writings"). My gut feeling is that Hilton is not the translator. Given the number of treatises wrongly attributed to Rolle, it is not surprising that some popular works should also be attributed to Hilton; *The Privity of the Passion*, a translation of pseudo-Bonaventure roughly contemporary with the *Stimulus* and appearing alongside it in one surviving manuscript, was also attributed to him, as was *The Chastising of God's Children* (Keiser, "Middle English Passion Narratives," 85; Lagorio and Sargent, 3080–81). For further discussion of the authorship question, see Sargent, "Bonaventura English," 161.

67. Judging by the divergences in the manuscript tradition, many more must have been lost. Only eleven of the manuscripts are complete or originally complete; there are four sets of extracts and one fragment. See Kane, *Prickynge*, xiv, and Kirchberger, *Goad*, 13, for the manuscripts.

68. *The Tree and xii Frutes*, ed. Vaissier, 32. We have particularly good records of female readership, from bourgeois widows to waiting-gentlewomen to countesses to Dominican nuns. See Kane, ed., vi; Erler, "Exchange of Books," 361–62; and Tanner, *The Church in Late Medieval Norwich*, 112.

69. My discussion here is indebted to Kirchberger's introduction. For the Latin text, see Jacobus Mediolanensis (James of Milan), *Stimulus Amoris*, Quaracchi editors. For the later version, see *S. Bonaventura Opera Omnia*, v. 12, ed. Peltier.

70. The translator's practice here parallels the practice and effect of English translations of Latin lyrics as described by Woolf in *The English Religious Lyric*. Woolf argues that where the Latin lyrics are witty, the English are loving; the rough and

humble qualities of the English language coincide with their translators' desires to describe personal and private relationships rather than expressing ingenious ideas in formal and ornate style. In a similar vein, Ong observes that "There is no way simply to 'translate' a language such as learned Latin into languages like the vernaculars," in part because Latin was so "consciously metaphorical," whereas the vernaculars were less so (*Orality and Literacy*, 114).

71. Quaracchi 118/ Peltier 666, Kane, 84.

72. See, for example, Kane, 3 (Quaracchi 67, Peltier 633), 24 (Q 77–78, P 638), 32 (P 640), 91 (Q 44, P 667), 93 (Q 46, P 668), 101 (Q 113, P 670).

73. For the metaphors, see, for example, 24, 81, 98, 49. On degree-appropriate devotion, see, for example, Kane, 50 (compare P 647); 112 (compare Q 125, P 673), and 125, where "conjoin yourself to him alone" becomes "suffer thy body be occupied in god's service as falls to your state" (Q 20, P 677).

74. Kane, 22 (Q 13, P 638). C.f. 8 (Q 71, P 634), 19 (P 637), 62–63 (P 651).

75. When the soul is mentioned, the pronouns shift. For example: "And ryght so wenne *a man* is besi in al that <u>he</u> may to conforme <u>him</u> to that pite. That crist shewid in his passioun. sothely <u>he</u> plesith mykel criste. soche *a soule* criste loveth tendirli for <u>hit</u> is like hym. <u>she</u> felleth als he dothe. <u>sheo</u> hatith synne in <u>hir-self</u> and in all odir as crist doth in us. <u>sheo</u> hath pite & compassioun of othere" (50, emphasis mine). Cf. 39, 41.

76. Crawford and Chaffin present research suggesting a link between gendered pronouns and textual comprehension in "The Reader's Construction of Meaning." Women were more likely to remember texts using gender-neutral language. Medieval writers seem to have grasped this idea readily; in translations intended especially for female readers, the universal "man" is often changed to "men and women" or "devout religious folk" or some similar tag, suggesting a clear sense of the importance of gender in the process of memory and devotional identification.

77. Chapters 31 and 16, respectively. There is no equivalent to chapter 16 in James of Milan's treatise; the material is based on the enlarged edition of the *Stimulus* (Peltier), but has been expanded a great deal.

78. The Franciscan life generally struggles with this "double movement," as Fleming calls it; see *Franciscan Literature*, 8–9). The pseudo-Bonaventuran *Meditationes*, in a revision of traditional hierarchies, makes contemplation an intermediate step between the two phases of the active life.

79. On the cult of the Wounds, see Duffy, *Stripping of the Altars*, 245. For the mystical theme of wound as vulva, see Riehle, *Middle English Mystics*, 46. For the same theme in preaching, see Ross, *Middle English Sermons*, 216–18. For lyric, see Gray, *Themes and Images*. For a discussion of the wound in relation to *arma christi* and *mapa mundi*, see Areford, "The Passion Measured."

80. For entering the wound as returning to the womb, see Bynum, *Jesus as Mother*, 120–22. Lewis observes that depictions of the wound sometimes served as talismans against death in childbirth; they were included in birth girdles and accompanied by indulgences for women in labor ("The Wound in Christ's Side," 217). For her discussion of *Stimulus Amoris*, see 214–16. Lewis argues that medieval men and women did consider the physical messiness of birth in connection to Christ's own birth and his

womb-wound; Aude Fauré, for example, could not stop herself from thinking about the "filthiness of the placenta" in connection to the Eucharist (216). Fulton argues that earlier medieval defensiveness about Mary's womb was connected to Jewish revulsion at the idea that God would allow himself to be confined for nine months in the slime of a woman's womb (*Judgment to Passion*, 282 ff.). The gender fluidity of Christ's body, epitomized by the wound as vulva and womb, has provided queer theorists with a way of thinking about the possibility of more fluid sexual identities in the Middle Ages. Lochrie, for example, argues that the mystical maternal body of Christ "opens a mesh of possibilities" for the queering of categories ("Mystical Acts, Queer Tendencies," 188). "In the *Stimulus Amoris* and elsewhere," she argues, "gender and sexuality are transitive rather than binary and monolithic" (189–90). See also Salih, "Queering Sponsalia Christi."

81. Watson argues that this passage valorizes Christ's flesh and makes his divinity accessible to the vernacular reader; see "Conceptions of the Word," 109 ff.

82. "Strange Images of Death," 127–28. Gillespie's important article describes some late medieval Passions as enacting a shift from clerical, Biblical literacy to a devotional literacy based on "reading" Christ's body, a body that is "simultaneously an image and a text" (111).

83. Ibid., 122, 129.

84. *Christ's Body*, 59.

85. *The Orcherd of Syon*, 114.

86. In *Nuns as Artists*, Hamburger explores the iconography of the heart in relation to the wounding look of love. The look, he writes, has its roots in both the piercing of Christ's side by Longinus and the *Song of Songs*: "Thou hast wounded my heart, my sister, my spouse, thou hast wounded my heart with one of thy eyes" (4:9).

87. For the text's concern with imprinting, see, for example, Kane 6, 71, 107, 112, 132, 165.

88. See, for example, Kane 4, 5, 12, 26–28, 39–40, and 58; most of ch. 7 (which is about being conformed through imitation); 71, 75, 91, and 99; chs. 20 and 21; 175, 184, and 187.

89. Kane 100/ Quaracchi 111 (Peltier 669), Kane 134/ Quaracchi 40 (Peltier 680).

90. Kane 98/ Quaracchi 108 (Peltier 669).

91. The translator adds phrases such as: "in beholding of his Passion" (14); "with my inner eye" (22); "set Christ in sight of thy soul" (26); "thou might see in this Passion" (30); "the fouler his death was, the fairer ought it to be in our sight"(30); "in Christ is his eye set" (43); "of this sight a man is ashamed" (44); "He hath no other sight" (45); "And though he cannot see him bodily, he is glad and thanks him that he may see him ghostly" (97); "make Jesus Christ always present before the sight of thy soul" (125); and "always having him in their sight whatsoever they do" (130).

92. For a parallel dynamic in fifteenth-century painted images of the Man of Sorrows, see Camille, "Mimetic Identification," 190.

93. Quaracchi 32–33: "quomodo dignatur tam rem foetidam coram suis oculis praesentare et te ad momentum patitur in sua praesentia commorari?"

94. Kane 110. Quaracchi, 123: "Servus Dei nunquam deberet nec aliud nec aliter cogitare, loqui et operari, quam si Deum facie ad faciem videret."

95. Kane 111. In his reading of medieval martyr narratives, Mills argues (via Žižek) that being seen by the Other is part of the masochist's desire: "the desiring subject wishes to be the object of the Other's gaze." See "A Man is Being Beaten," 137.

96. Kane 87. See also 53, where the translator adds, "Because no man may flee from the face of God. Whatever sin you do or think, be it never so privy, you do it even before his face."

97. See, for example, Kane 3, 20, 30, 35, 39, 80, 123, 124.

98. *Puro corde*: see Peltier 637/ Kane 20. *Cor altum*: see Peltier, 641/ Kane, 33.

99. Peltier 641/ Kane 34.

100. On Margery's relation to the Franciscan meditative tradition, see Despres, *Ghostly Sights*, ch. 2; Gibson, *Theater of Devotion*, ch. 3; and Beckwith, *Christ's Body*, ch. 4. Beckwith also focuses on the tension between interiorized and exteriorized devotion in Margery's practice.

101. Kane 45/ Peltier 645.

102. Other late medieval devotional texts exhibit a similar tendency to allegorize the *imitatio Christi* and the comtemplative life in remarkably flexible and open ways. Barratt observes that the fifteenth-century *Faits and the Passion of Our Lord Jesu Christ* "is even rendered whimsical by the unlikely allegorical parallels to Christ's suffering that [the author] finds in her own restricted life" ("Stabant Matres," 60). The 1530 *Pomander of Prayer* explains that alms-giving is the same as despising the world (cited in White, *Tudor Books*, 154).

103. *The English Works of John Fisher*, ed. Mayor, 390–91.

Chapter 4. Profitable Sights

1. 3.25–8. Unless otherwise indicated, all citations are from the Long Text in Colledge and Walsh's edition. I refer to the text by chapter and lines (though the lines will be exact only in Colledge and Walsh) to make it easier for readers using other editions, particularly Watson and Jenkins's *The Writings of Julian of Norwich*.

2. *The Dialogue*, trans. Noffke, 25.

3. For the *Showings* as a kind of spiritual autobiography, see, for example, Windeatt, "The Art of Mystical Loving"; Abbot, *Julian of Norwich*; and Baker, *Julian of Norwich's* "*Showings*," esp. ch. 5, "Reconceiving the *Imago Dei*." Baker details Julian's revisions of the Augustinian system, emphasizing her "original theory of an androgynous God who creates the soul in an asexual image" (113).

4. For Julian's balancing of opposites and subversion of contemporary hierarchies, see in particular Staley, "Julian of Norwich and the Late Fourteenth-Century Crisis of Authority," in *Powers of the Holy*. See also Watson's brilliant work on Julian, including " 'Yf wommen be double naturelly' " and "The Trinitarian Hermeneutic."

5. Watson, " 'Yf wommen,' " 24 n. 42; and Aers, "The Humanity of Christ: Reflections on Julian of Norwich's *Revelation of Love*," in *Powers of the Holy*, 82.

6. See, for example, Ward, "Julian the Solitary."

7. "The Composition of Julian of Norwich's *Revelation of Love*." For a detailed ac-

count of Julian's revisions emphasizing the complex, interconnected structuring of her argument, see Baker, *Julian of Norwich's "Showings."*

8. For an argument against Watson's redating, see Aers and Staley, 79 n. 4, and 126.

9. Watson has observed the "polyphonic complexity" of Julian's uses of visual language, the way she deploys Augustinian categories of bodily, imaginative, and intellectual vision only to overwhelm them and render them essentially irrelevant through her shifting descriptions of the modes of revelation. See "The Trinitarian Hermeneutic," 66.

10. In the Short Text, the hazelnut comes first.

11. Hayes, " 'Of Three Workings in Man's Soul.' " The text is derived from Richard of St. Victor's *Benjamin Major* and is extant in four English manuscripts. See also Love's *Mirror*, ch. 3, which emphasizes that Mary is reading in her "pryve chaumbur," or another translation of the *Meditationes Vitae Christi* called "De Sancta Maria," or "The Rule of the Life of Our Lady," found in Horstman, *Yorkshire Writers*, vol. 1.

12. See Watson and Jenkins's gloss in *The Writings of Julian of Norwich*, 142.

13. We might compare some Continental female mystics' embrace of abjection as a means of imitating Christ in his Passion: kissing lepers, swallowing scabs, punishing their own flesh, and so forth. Unlike Julian, these women do not try to suggest that the flesh in its most loathsome aspects is anything but repellent; that is what gives it its power to propel them toward transcendence. See Lochrie, "The Language of Transgression."

14. For the death-bed struggle, see Duffy, *Stripping of the Altars*, 315 ff.

15. A similar moment occurs in the fifth showing, where Julian sees that the fiend is overcome and laughs. "[A]nd that made them to lagh that were abowte me," she writes, "and ther lawchyng was a liking to me. I thought that I wolde that alle my evyn crysten had seen as I saw. Then should all they a lawchyd with me" (13.25–28).

16. For an excellent discussion of how Julian's revisions to the Short Text work toward universality, see Watson, "The Middle English Mystics," 558.

17. *Prickynge of Love*, 96; cf. *Stimulus Amoris* (Quaracchi), 106–7.

18. Aers and Staley, 175.

19. See, for example, Bradley, "Patristic Background"; Heimmel, *"God is Our Mother"*; and McNamer, "The Exploratory Image."

20. Other critics have seen this as an indication that Julian is rejecting "feminine" spirituality (e.g., Watson, " 'Yf wommen,' " and Aers, "The Humanity of Christ"), but the bride-of-Christ figure was associated with male as well as female religious.

21. *Anchoritic Spirituality*, trans. Savage and Watson, 132.

22. Fulton, *From Judgment to Passion.*

23. Innes-Parker notes that the absent mother-God also appears in William of Flete's *De Remediis*, *The Pore Caitiff*, and *The Doctrine of the Heart*, and that it made its way from the *Chastising* into *Disce Mori* and *Ignorancia Sacerdotum*. See "Subversion and Conformity."

24. For the passage in an English translation (one of at least three), see *Yorkshire Writers*, 2:118–19.

25. Watson, *Anchoritic Spirituality*, 47.

26. Coiner, "The 'Homely' and the Heimliche," 318.

27. On the theme of doubleness, see Coiner, "The 'Homely' and the Heimliche," and Watson, " 'Yf wommen.' "

28. For extended discussions of the *planctus Mariae*, see McNamer, "The Virgin and the Voice of Protest," and Keiser, "The Middle English *Planctus Mariae*."

29. Watson discusses this episode as a "love-test" in "Remaking 'Womman,'" 4–5.

30. Lynn Staley makes much of Julian's failure to see the Virgin bodily, arguing that it is part of Julian's overall rejection of affective expectations. See "Crisis of Authority" in Aers and Staley, *Powers of the Holy*.

31. "The Trinitarian Hermeneutic," 64–65.

Chapter 5. Hoccleve's Glasses

1. *Hoccleve's Works: The Minor Poems*, xxxviii. Subsequent references are cited parenthetically above. Furnivall goes on to add, with greater sympathy, that "all of those who've made fools of themselves, more or less, in their youth, will feel for the poor old versifier." For a more scathing judgment of Hoccleve's personal failures, see Richardson, "Hoccleve in his Social Context."

2. Burrow, "Hoccleve's *Series*," 268. Ellis calls him "a figure who can speak very directly to our own uncertain and privatized age," in "'*My Compleinte' and Other Poems*," 41. On the autobiographical elements in Hoccleve's poetry, see, for example, Burrow, "Autobiographical Poetry"; Knapp, "Bureaucratic Identity" and *The Bureaucratic Muse*; Mitchell, "The Autobiographical Element"; Pearsall, "Hoccleve's *Regement of Princes*"; Spearing, "Hoccleve's Misrule"; and Thornley, "Middle English Penitential Lyric."

3. See, respectively, Burrow ("Hoccleve and the Middle French Poets"), Spearing ("Hoccleve's Misrule"), and Knapp ("Bureaucratic Identity" and *Bureaucratic Muse*). The reluctance of most critics to foreground religious models may stem in part from the frequent assumption that if Hoccleve's self-revelations are penitential, they are merely conventional and not really autobiographical. In 1982, Burrow attacked this assumption; if Hoccleve's poetry is penitential, he argues, it is because that is how men and women of the time thought about and expressed themselves ("Autobiographical Poetry"). Modern audiences would never assume that because an autobiography draws on popular psychology, it is merely conventional and not really about the author "herself." Autobiography is the most conventional of genres.

4. It is sometimes assumed that Hoccleve's devotional verse belongs to the earliest phase of his career, before his 1402 "Letter of Cupid." But none of these poems can be dated with much certainty, and there seems to be no real reason for assuming such a reverse-conversion narrative. Most of the devotional poems can be found in *The Minor Poems*; there are fourteen additional devotional poems, from a prose version of Deguilleville's *Pélerinage de l'ame* (ms. Egerton 615, produced in 1413) that may also be Hoccleve's; they form an appendix to *The Regement of Princes*, ed. Furnivall.

5. "Invocacio ad Patrem," 100–101, in *The Minor Poems*.

6. "Invocacio ad Patrem," 129–30, in *The Minor Poems*.

7. All from *The Minor Poems*.

8. Line 70. For the *Series*, see *Minor Poems*; I also like Ellis's *"My Compleinte" and Other Poems*.

9. Isidore of Seville's *Synonyma*, not named in the text itself, but identified by Rigg in 1970 ("Hoccleve's Complaint and Isidore of Seville"). Hoccleve was evidently working with a drastically shortened epitome of the text (Burrow, "Isidore of Seville Again"). The *Synonyma* presents a traditional explanation of tribulation: that it is God's punishment for sin.

10. The tales and treatises that make up the remainder of the *Series* are addressed to Duke Humphrey, Henry V's younger brother and, at the time of the *Series'* writing (1421–22), his regent in England.

11. See Knapp, "Bureaucratic Identity" and "Eulogies and Usurpations."

12. Knapp, "Bureaucratic Identity," 360.

13. The parodic hagiographic tradition of "Saint Nobody" may inform Hoccleve's complaints here. See Bayless, *Parody in the Middle Ages*, 57–86, and appendices 2–5 (259–310) for texts and translations. For further exploration of bureaucratic anonymity in Hoccleve's poetry, see Simpson, "Nobody's Man."

14. "The King's Two Voices," 230. Burrow also highlights the entertainment value of personal detail ("Autobiographical Poetry" 411). See also Hasler, "Hoccleve's Unregimented Body," and for another discussion of late medieval patronage, Fradenburg, "The Manciple's Servant Tongue."

15. Guillaume de Deguilleville, *Le Pélerinage de l'Ame*, ed. Stürzinger, ll. 6552–53.

16. Burrow, *Thomas Hoccleve*, 24.

17. Doyle speculated that Joan might have been the "Joan Boun" (Bohun) whose name appears in a tiny hand in the middle of the Simeon manuscript. She had married Humphrey de Bohun, Earl of Hereford, Essex, and Northampton, but had been widowed in 1372. She had taken a vow of fasting sometime before 1414, when she was allowed to modify it on account of infirmity (*The Vernon Manuscript*, 15–16).

18. Doyle, *The Vernon Manuscript*, 15.

19. For the potential impact of a gendered "horizon of expectation," see, for example, Gill, "Women and Religious Literature"; and Riddy, "'Women Talking About the Things of God.'"

20. Keiser, "The Middle English *Planctus Mariae*," 169. See also Bestul, *Texts of the Passion*, ch. 4.

21. *The Ritual Lament in Greek Tradition*, cited in Keiser, "The Middle English *Planctus Mariae*."

22. *Lost Property*, 28. On Chaucerian complaint, see, for example, Davenport, *Chaucer: Complaint and Narrative*; and Patterson, "Writing Amorous Wrongs."

23. For a description of this theme, see Stanbury, "The Virgin's Gaze."

24. Lyrics 583 and 2150 in Brown and Robbins's Index of Middle English verse.

25. Knapp also sees the Virgin's Complaint as anxious about fifteenth-century devotional practice, though he is more interested in Hoccleve's ambivalent stance toward Lollard iconoclasm. Knapp reads the poem as establishing a devotional image, which is also how I want to think about the Virgin's reaction. See *The Bureaucratic Muse*, ch. 5.

26. Mary's description of the naming as public "penance" again recalls Chaucerian female complaint, in which the speaker is often obsessed with the publication of her name, which becomes central to her exemplary function.

27. "Voice Memorial," 184.

28. *The Tretys of Love*, ed. Fisher, 63. In "The Virgin and the Voice of Protest." McNamer reads fifteenth-century Marian laments as protests against contemporary violence. See also her forthcoming *Reading the Literature of Compassion*.

29. Bestul, *Texts of the Passion*.

30. It is interesting to compare Hoccleve's autobiographical stance to that of Christine de Pisan, whose work Hoccleve knew and imitated. She too stakes her claim to participation in the redemption of the (French) monarchy on a personal history of loss, defeat, and transformation. Hoccleve's interest in the politics of gender can be traced throughout his career, from the 1402 "Letter of Cupid" to the moral stories about women in the *Series* of 1421–22. For Hoccleve's gender politics, see especially Nissé, " 'Oure Fadres Olde.' "

31. For a simliar argument see Nissé, " 'Oure Fadres Olde,' " esp. 281. Nissé links excessive interiority to both Lollardy and femininity.

32. Tolmie, in "The *Prive Scilence* of Thomas Hoccleve," makes a good case for the importance of Badby as a kind of "monstrous double" for Hoccleve, "the most potentially disorderly and reversing aspect of the kind of silent, suffering, unrevealing will that is also exhibited by the repressed figures of the clerks laboring in the Privy Seal office" (299). See also Nissé.

33. The disjunction between inner and outer is a recurrent feature in Hoccleve's poetry. In the 1402 "Letter of Cupid," he makes interiority central to the difference between men and women and the focus of Cupid's complaint: "Ful herd yt is to know a manys hert," Cupid laments, "for outwarde may no man the trouthe deme" (36–37). Whereas male subjectivity separates inner truth from outer display, and fair speech from false thought, women have no such hidden interiority: "what they be Inward sheweth outwarde sygne" (343).

34. On early fifteenth-century political rhetoric about "doubleness," see Patterson, "Making Identities"; Strohm, *England's Empty Throne*; and Watson, " 'Yf Wommen Be Double.' "

35. *Troilus and Criseyde*, 5.1790–91.

36. The word "nycetee" is somewhat ambiguous, signifying variously simplicity, stupidity, foolishness, lust, reticence, and shyness; Hoccleve uses it elsewhere as a synonym for sin. All are likely in play here. On Hoccleve's penchant for dark puns, see Tolmie, "The *Prive Scilence* of Thomas Hoccleve."

37. The *OED* defines an "outer" as "one who or that which puts out, utters, or gives vent to," or "one who utters or circulates false coin," listing this instance and Hoccleve's earlier *Dialog*, where Hoccleve writes, "Vengaunce on yow, ye false moneyours, and on yowre outeris" (175). In "Counterfeiters, Lollards, and Lancastrian Unease," Paul Strohm links Hoccleve's interest in counterfeiting to his concerns about Lancastrian legitimacy and the Lollard threat.

38. "Hoccleve's *Regement of Princes*," 393–94.

Afterward

1. The surviving manuscript copy ended up in the sixteenth-century hands of one William Cudde (Blunt, viii; de Hamel item 14). There is no record of how necessary or useful he found it.

2. White, *Tudor Books*, 153, 157.

3. De Hamel, 48.

4. De Hamel, 48.

5. Cited in Hogg, *Richard Whytford*, 1.1, p. 44. Knowles discusses the "long and tortuous process of persuasion, oppression, and intimidation" in *Religious Orders*, 3:216.

6. Knowles, *Religious Orders*, 3:219.

7. Ibid., 3:179 n. 5; citing the correspondence of Sir Thomas More.

8. Foster, "Private Devotion," in *Gothic: Art for England*, 335.

Works Cited

Primary Texts

Abelard, Peter. *The Letters of Abelard and Heloise.* Trans. Betty Radice. New York: Penguin, 1974.

Aelred of Rievaulx. *De Institutione Inclusarum: Two English Versions.* Ed. John Ayto and Alexandra Barratt. EETS 287. Oxford: Oxford University Press, 1984.

Andreas Capellanus. *The Art of Courtly Love.* Trans. John Jay Parry. New York: Norton, 1941, 1969.

Anselm of Canterbury. *The Prayers and Meditations of St. Anselm.* Trans. Benedicta Ward. Foreword by R. W. Southern. New York: Penguin, 1973.

Augustine. *Confessions.* Trans. R. S. Pine-Coffin. New York: Penguin Classics, 1961.

———. *Later Works.* Ed. and trans. John Burnaby. Philadelphia: Westminster Press, 1955.

———. *On the Trinity: Books 5–11.* Ed. Gareth Matthews. Trans. Stephen McKenna. Cambridge: Cambridge University Press, 2002.

Barratt, Alexandra, ed. *Women's Writing in Middle English.* New York: Longman, 1992.

The Holy Bible: *Douay-Rheims Version.* Rev. Richard Challoner. Rockford, Ill.: Tan Publishing, 1989.

Bonaventure [pseud.]. "Stimulus Amoris." *S. Bonaventura Opera Omnia,* v. 12, 631–703. Ed. A. C. Peltier. Paris, 1868. See also James of Milan.

Book to a Mother: An Edition with Commentary. Ed. Adrian James McCarthy. Salzburg Studies in English Literature; Elizabethan and Renaissance Studies 92. Salzburg: Institut für Anglistik und Amerikanistik, Universität Salzburg, 1981.

The Book of Vices and Virtues. Ed. W. Nelson Francis. EETS 217. London: Oxford University Press, 1942.

Borges, Jose Luis. *This Craft of Verse: The Charles Eliot Norton Lectures, 1967–68.* Ed. Calin-Andrei Mihailescu. Cambridge: Harvard University Press, 2000.

Catherine of Siena. *The Dialogue.* Trans. Suzanne Noffke. New York: Paulist Press, 1980.

Caxton, William. *Caxton's Own Prose.* Ed. N. F. Blake. London: Andre Deutsch, 1973.

The Cell of Self-Knowledge: Seven Early English Mystical Treatises Printed by Henry Pepwell in 1521. Ed. and introduced by Edmund Gardner. New York: Cooper Square Publishers, 1966.

The Chastising of God's Children. Ed. Joyce Bazire and Eric Colledge. Oxford: Basil Blackwell, 1957.

Chaucer, Geoffrey. *The Riverside Chaucer.* Ed. Larry Benson. 3rd ed. Boston: Houghton Mifflin, 1987.

The Cloud of Unknowing and The Book of Privy Counselling. Ed. Phyllis Hodgson. EETS 218. London: Oxford University Press, 1944; repr. 1973.

Contemplations of the Dread and Love of God. Ed. Margaret Connolly. EETS 303. New York: Oxford University Press, 1993.

Dante Alighieri. *Il Convivio (The Banquet).* Trans. Richard H. Lansing. New York: Garland, 1990.

Davis, Norman, ed. *Paston Letters and Papers of the Fifteenth Century.* 2 vols. Oxford: Oxford University Press, 1971–76, repr. 2004.

Deonise hid Divinite. Ed. Phyllis Hodgson. EETS 231. London: Oxford University Press, 1955.

Dickinson, Emily. *The Collected Poems of Emily Dickinson.* New York: Barnes & Noble Books, 1993.

Dives and Pauper. Ed. Priscilla Heath Barnum. 2 vols. EETS 275, 280, 323. Oxford: Oxford University Press, 1976, 1980, 2004.

The Doctrine of the Hert. Ed. Sister Mary Patrick Candon. Ph.D. diss., Fordham University, 1963.

Donne, John. *The Sermons of John Donne.* Ed. George R. Potter and Evelyn M. Simpson. 10 vols. Berkeley: University of California Press, 1953–62.

———. *The Complete Poetry and Selected Prose of John Donne.* Ed. Charles M. Coffin. New York: Modern Library, 1994.

Fisher, John. *The English Works of John Fisher.* Ed. John E. B. Mayor. EETS e.s. 27. 2 vols. London, 1876.

The Good Wife Taught Her Daughter, The Good Wyfe Wold a Pylgremage, and The Thewis of Gud Women. Ed. Tauno Mustanoja. Helsinki: Suomalaisen Kirjallisuuden Scuran, 1948.

The Goodman of Paris (le ménagier de paris): A Treatise on Moral and Domestic Economy by a Citizen of Paris (c. 1393). Trans. Eileen Power. New York: Harcourt, Brace, 1928.

Gregory. *Moralia in Job.* Ed. M. Adriaen. 3 vols. Corpus Christianorum, Series Latina 143–143B. Turnhout: Brepols, 1979–85.

Guigo II. *The Ladder of Monks and Twelve Meditations.* Ed. and trans. Edmund Colledge and James Walsh. New York: Image Books, 1978.

Guillaume de Deguilleville. *Le Pélerinage de l'Ame.* Ed. J. J. Stürzinger. London, 1895.

Hass, Robert. *Praise.* New York: Ecco Press, 1979.

Henry VIII. *The King's Book.* Ed. T. A. Lacey. London: Society for Promoting Christian Knowledge, 1932.

Henry of Lancaster. *Le Livre de Seyntz Medicines.* Ed. E. J. Arnould. Oxford: Basil Blackwell, 1940.

Hilton, Walter. *The Goad of Love: An Unpublished Translation of the Stimulus Amoris Formerly Attributed to St. Bonaventura.* Ed. Clare Kirchberger. London: Faber and Faber, 1952.

———. *The Scale of Perfection.* Ed. Thomas Bestul. Kalamazoo: Medieval Institute Publications, 2000.

————. *The Scale of Perfection.* Ed. and trans. John Clark and Rosemary Dorward. New York: Paulist Press, 1991.

Hoccleve, Thomas. *Hoccleve's Works: The Minor Poems.* Ed. Frederick J. Furnivall and I. Gollancz. EETS e.s. 61, 73. New York: Oxford University Press, 1892 and 1925. Rev. repr. 1970.

————. *Hoccleve's Works: The Regiment of Princes.* Ed. Frederick J. Furnivall. EETS e.s. 72. London: Kegan Paul, Trench, Trübner, 1897; repr. 1996.

————. *"My Compleinte" and Other Poems.* Ed. Roger Ellis. Exeter: University of Exeter Press, 2001.

Horstman, Carl, ed. *Yorkshire Writers: Richard Rolle of Hampole and His Followers.* 2 vols. New York: Macmillan & Co, 1895.

Hudson, Anne, ed. *English Wycliffite Writings.* Cambridge: Cambridge University Press, 1978.

James of Milan. *Stimulus Amoris.* Bibliotheca Franciscana Ascetica Medii Aevi, v. IV. Quaracchi, 1905. See also Bonaventure [pseud.].

Julian of Norwich. *A Book of Showings to the Anchoress Julian of Norwich.* Ed. Edmund Colledge and James Walsh. 2 vols. Toronto: Pontifical Institute of Medieval Studies, 1978.

————. *The Writings of Julian of Norwich: A Vision Showed to a Devout Woman and A Revelation of Love.* Ed. Nicholas Watson and Jacqueline Jenkins. University Park: Pennsylvania State University Press, 2006.

Kempe, Margery. *The Book of Margery Kempe.* Ed. Sanford Meech and Hope Emily Allen. EETS 212. London, 1940.

Langland, William. *The Vision of Piers Plowman: A Complete Edition of the B-Text.* Ed. A. V. C. Schmidt. Rutland, Vt.: Charles E. Tuttle, 1978.

Legg, J. Wickham, ed. *Tracts on the Mass.* London, 1904.

Love, Nicholas. *The Mirror of the Blessed Life of Jesus Christ.* Ed. Michael Sargent. New York: Garland, 1992.

————. *Nicholas Love's "Myrrour of the Blessed Lyf of Jesu Christ."* Ed. Elizabeth Salter. Analecta Cartusiana 10. Salzburg: Institut für Englische Sprache und Literatur, Universität Salzburg, 1974.

Luria, Maxwell, and Richard Hoffman, eds. *Middle English Lyrics.* New York: Norton, 1974.

Lydgate, John. *The Minor Poems of John Lydgate.* Ed. Henry Noble MacCracken. EETS e.s. 107. London: Kegan Paul, Trench Trübner, 1911 for 1910.

Malory, Thomas. *Le Morte Darthur.* Ed. Stephen H. A. Shepherd. New York: Norton, 2004.

Mechtild of Hackeborn. *The Booke of Gostlye Grace.* Ed. Theresa Halligan. Toronto: Pontifical Institute of Medieval Studies, 1979.

Meditations on the Life and Passion of Christ. Ed. Charlotte D'Evelyn. EETS 158. London: Oxford University Press, 1921.

Meier-Ewert, Charity. "A Middle English Version of the Fifteen Oes." *Modern Philology* 68, no. 4 (1971): 355–61.

The Myroure of Oure Ladye. Ed. John Henry Blunt. EETS e.s. 19. London, 1873; repr. 1898.

The Myrour of Recluses: A Middle English Translation of Speculum Inclusorum. Ed. Marta Powell Harley. London: Associated University Presses, 1995.

The Northern Passion. Ed. Frances A. Foster. 2 vols. EETS 147. London: Kegan Paul, Trench, Trübner, 1913–16.

The Northern Passion (Supplement). Ed. Wilhelm Heuser and Frances A. Foster. EETS 183. London, 1930. Repr. New York: Kraus, 1971.

The Orcherd of Syon. Ed. Phyllis Hodgson and Gabriel Liegy. EETS 258. Oxford: Oxford University Press, 1966.

Orologium Sapientiae, or The Sevene Poyntes of Trewe Wisdame. Ed. Carl Horstmann. *Anglia* 10 (1888): 323–89.

The Passion of Our Lord. Ed. Beatrice Daw Brown. EETS 169. London, 1927.

Petrarch, Francis. *The Canzoniere, or Rerum Vulgarium Fragmenta.* Trans. Mark Musa. Bloomington: Indiana University Press, 1996.

———. *The Poetry of Petrarch.* Trans. David Young. New York: Farrar, Straus and Giroux, 2004.

Porete, Marguerite. *The Mirror of Simple Souls.* Trans. Ellen L. Babinsky. New York: Paulist Press, 1993.

The Pricke of Conscience. Ed. Richard Morris. Berlin, 1863.

The Prickynge of Love. Ed. Harold Kane. Elizabethan and Renaissance Studies 92:10. 2 vols. Salzburg: Institut für Anglistik und Amerikanistik, Universität Salzburg, 1983. See also "Hilton" (*The Goad of Love*).

The Rewyll of Seynt Savioure. Ed. James Hogg, 4 vols. Salzburg: Institut für Englische Sprache und Literatur, Universität Salzburg, 1978.

Rolle, Richard. *The English Writings of Richard Rolle, Hermit of Hampole.* Ed. Hope Emily Allen. Oxford: Clarendon Press, 1931; repr. 1963.

———. *Prose and Verse.* Ed. S. J. Ogilvie-Thomson. EETS 293. London: Oxford University Press, 1988.

Ross, Woodburn, ed. *Middle English Sermons.* EETS 209. London: Oxford University Press, 1940.

Savage, Anne, and Nicholas Watson, ed. and trans. *Anchoritic Spirituality: Ancrene Wisse and Associated Works.* New York: Paulist Press, 1991.

Sir Gawain and the Green Knight, Pearl, Cleanness, Patience. Ed. A. C. Cawley and J. J. Anderson. Rutland, Vt.: Charles E. Tuttle, 1962, 1976.

The Speculum Devotorum of an Anonymous Carthusian of Sheen. Ed. James Hogg. 4 vols. Analecta Cartusiana 11–13. Salzburg: Institut für Englische Sprache und Literatur, Universität Salzburg, 1973.

Spenser, Edmund. *The Faerie Queene.* Ed. Thomas P. Roche, Jr., and C. Patrick O'Donnell, Jr. New York: Penguin, 1987.

Stimulus Amoris. See Bonaventure [pseud.]; James of Milan.

A Talkynge of the Love of God. Ed. Salvina Westra. The Hague: Martinus Nijhoff, 1950.

Thomas à Kempis. *The Earliest English Translations of the First Three Books of the "De Imitatione Christi."* Ed. John K. Ingram. EETS e.s. 63. London, 1893.

———. *The Imitation of Christ: The First English Translation of the "Imitatio Christi."* Ed. B. J. H. Biggs. EETS 309. Oxford: Oxford University Press, 1997.

Tracts on the Mass. Ed. J. Wickham Legg. London, 1904.

The Tree and Twelve Frutes of the Holy Goost. Ed. J. J. Vaissier. Groningen: J. B. Wolters, 1960.

The Tretyse of Love. Ed. John H. Fisher. EETS 223. London: Oxford University Presss, 1951.

The Vernon Manuscript: A Facsimile of Bodleian Library, Oxford, MS. Eng. poet. A.1; with an introduction by Ian Doyle. Cambridge: D. S. Brewer, 1987.

Whytford, Richard. *Pype or Tonne of the Lyfe of Perfection.* Ed. James Hogg. 4 vols. Salzburg: Institut für Anglistik und Amerikanistik, Universität Salzburg, 1979.

Windeatt, Barry, ed. *English Mystics of the Middle Ages.* New York: Cambridge University Press, 1994.

The Wohunge of Ure Lauerd. Ed. W. Meredith Thompson. EETS 241. London: Oxford University Press, 1958.

Reference Works

Jolliffe, P. S. *A Check-List of Middle English Prose Writings of Spiritual Guidance.* Toronto: Pontifical Institute of Medieval Studies, 1974.

The Middle English Dictionary. Ed. Sherman M. Kuhn and John Reidy. Ann Arbor: University of Michigan Press, 1968.

Oxford English Dictionary Online. Oxford: Oxford University Press, 2004. http://dictionary.oed.com/.

Secondary Works

Abbot, Christopher. *Julian of Norwich: Autobiography and Theology.* Cambridge: D. S. Brewer, 1999.

Aers, David. "A Whisper in the Ear of Early Modernists; Or, Reflections on Literary Critics Writing the 'History of the Subject.'" In *Culture and History, 1350–1600: Essays on English Communities, Identities, and Writing.* Detroit: Wayne State University Press, 1992.

Aers, David, and Lynn Staley. *Powers of the Holy: Religion, Politics, and Gender in Late Medieval English Culture.* University Park: Pennsylvania State University Press, 1996.

Alexander, J. J. G., and M. T. Gibson, eds. *Medieval Learning and Literature: Essays Presented to Richard William Hunt.* Oxford: Oxford University Press, 1976.

Alexander, Michael. *The Growth of English Education, 1340–1648: A Social and Cultural History.* University Park: Pennsylvania State University Press, 1996.

Alexiou, Margaret. *The Ritual Lament in Greek Tradition.* Cambridge: Cambridge University Press, 1974.

Areford, David S. "The Passion Measured: A late medieval Diagram of the Body of Christ." In MacDonald et al., *The Broken Body,* 211–38.

Armstrong, C. A. J. "The Piety of Cicely, Duchess of York: A Study in Late Mediaeval Culture." In *For Hilaire Belloc: Essays in Honour of his 72nd Birthday,* ed. Douglas

Woodruff, 73–94. London, 1942. Repr. in *England, France, and Burgundy in the Fifteenth Century*, 135–56. London: Hambledon Press, 1983.

Ashley, Kathleen. "Historicizing Margery: *The Book of Margery Kempe* as Social Text." *JMEMS* 28 (1998): 371–88.

Aungier, G. J. *The History and Antiquities of Syon Monastery.* London, 1840.

Baker, Denise. *Julian of Norwich's "Showings": From Vision to Book.* Princeton: Princeton University Press, 1994.

Barratt, Alexandra. "*Stabant Matres Dolorosae*: Women as Readers and Writers of Passion Prayers, Meditations and Visions." In MacDonald et al., *The Broken Body*, 55–71.

Barthélemy, Dominique, and Philippe Contamine. "The Use of Private Space." In *A History of Private Life II: Revelations of the Medieval World*, ed. Georges Duby, trans. Arthur Goldhammer, 395–505. Cambridge: Belknap Press of Harvard University Press, 1988.

Bartlett, Anne Clark. *Male Authors, Female Readers: Representation and Subjectivity in Middle English Devotional Literature.* Ithaca: Cornell University Press, 1995.

Bateson, Mary. *Catalogue of the Library of Syon Monastery Isleworth.* Cambridge, 1898.

Bayless, Martha. *Parody in the Middle Ages: The Latin Tradition.* Ann Arbor: University of Michigan Press, 1996.

Beckett, Neil. "St. Bridget, Henry V and Syon Abbey." In *Studies in St. Birgitta and the Brigittine Order*, ed. James Hogg, vol. 2 of 2, 125–50. Salzburg: Institut für Anglistik und Amerikanistik, Universität Salzburg, 1993.

Beckwith, Sarah. *Christ's Body: Identity, Culture, and Society in Late Medieval Writings.* New York: Routledge, 1993.

———. "A Very Material Mysticism: The Medieval Mysticism of Margery Kempe." In *Medieval Literature: Criticism, History, Ideology*, ed. David Aers, 34–57. Brighton: Harvester, 1986.

Bell, David. *What Nuns Read: Books and Libraries in Medieval English Nunneries.* Kalamazoo: Cistercian Publications, 1995.

Bell, Susan Groag. "Medieval Women Book Owners: Arbiters of Lay Piety and Ambassadors of Culture." *Signs* 7 (1982): 742–68.

Belting, Hans. *Likeness and Presence: A History of the Image Before the Era of Art.* Trans. Edmund Jephcott. Chicago: University of Chicago Press, 1994.

Bennett, J. A. W. *Poetry of the Passion: Studies in Twelve Centuries of English Verse.* Oxford: Clarendon Press, 1982.

Bennett, Michael. "Careerism in Late Medieval England." In *People, Politics, and Community in the Later Middle Ages*, ed. Joel Rosenthal and Colin Richmond, 19–39. New York: St. Martin's Press, 1987.

———. "Education and Advancement." In Horrox, *Fifteenth-Century Attitudes*, 79–96.

Benton, John F. "Consciousness of Self and Perceptions of Individuality." In *Renaissance and Renewal in the Twelfth Century*, ed. Robert L. Benson and Giles Constable, 263–95. Cambridge: Harvard University Press, 1982.

Bestul, Thomas. "Devotional Writing in England Between Anselm and Richard Rolle." In *Mysticism Medieval and Modern*, ed. Valerie Lagorio, 12–28. Salzburg: Institut für Anglistik und Amerikanistik, Universität Salzburg, 1986.

———. *Texts of the Passion: Latin Devotional Literature and Medieval Society.* Philadelphia: University of Pennsylvania Press, 1996.

Betteridge, Thomas. "Anne Askewe, John Bale, and Protestant History." *JMEMS* 27, no. 2 (1997): 265–84.

Biller, Peter, and A. J. Minnis, eds. *Handling Sin: Confession in the Middle Ages*. Bury St. Edmunds, Suffolk: York Medieval Press in association with Boydell Press, 1998.

Boffey, Julia. "Lydgate's Lyrics and Women Readers." In *Women, the Book and the Worldly: Selected Proceedings of the St Hilda's Conference, 1993*, vol. 2 of 2, ed. Lesely Smith and Jane Taylor, 139–49. Cambridge: D. S. Brewer, 1995.

———. "Women Authors and Women's Literacy in Fourteenth- and Fifteenth-Century England." In Meale, *Women and Literature in Britain*, 159–82.

Bowers, John. *The Crisis of Will in Piers Plowman*. Washington, D.C.: Catholic University of America Press, 1986.

Bradley, Ritamary. "Perception of Self in Julian of Norwich's Showings." *Downside Review* 104 (1986): 227–39.

———. "The Speculum Image in Medieval Mystical Writers." In *The Medieval Mystical Tradition in England: Papers Read at Dartington Hall, July 1984*, ed. Marion Glasscoe, 9–27. Cambridge: D. S. Brewer, 1984.

Brady, Mary Teresa. "Lollard Interpolations and Omissions in Manuscripts of *The Pore Caitiff*." In Sargent, *De Cella in Seculum*, 183–203.

Bradley, Ritamary. "Patristic Background of the Motherhood Similitude in Julian of Norwich." *Christian Scholar's Review* 8 (1978): 101–13.

Brantley, Jessica. *Reading in the Wilderness: Private Devotion and Public Performance in Late Medieval England*. Chicago: University of Chicago Press, forthcoming.

Brown, Carleton. "The Cursor Mundi and the Southern Passion." *Modern Language Notes* 26 (1911): 15–18.

Burrow, John. "Autobiographical Poetry in the Middle Ages: The Case of Thomas Hoccleve." *Read* 4 (1982): 389–412.

———. "Hoccleve's *Complaint* and Isidore of Seville Again." *Speculum* 73 (1998): 424–28.

———. "Hoccleve and the Middle French Poets." In *The Long Fifteenth Century: Essays for Douglas Gray*, ed. Helen Cooper and Sally Mapstone, 35–49. Oxford: Clarendon Press, 1997.

———. "Hoccleve's *Series*: Experience and Books." In *Fifteenth-Century Studies: Recent Essays*, ed. Robert F. Yeager, 259–73. Hamden, Conn.: Archon Books, 1984.

Bynum, Caroline Walker. *Fragmentation and Redemption: Essays on Gender and the Human Body in Medieval Religion*. New York: Zone Books, 1991.

———. *Holy Feast and Holy Fast: The Religious Significance of Food to Medieval Women*. Berkeley: University of California Press, 1987.

———. *Jesus as Mother: Studies in the Spirituality of the High Middle Ages*. Berkeley: University of California Press, 1982.

Camille, Michael. *Gothic Art: Glorious Visions*. New York: Harry N. Abrams, 1996.

———. "Mimetic Identification and Passion Devotion in the Later Middle Ages: A Double-Sided Panel by Meister Francke." In MacDonald et al., *The Broken Body*, 183–210.

Cannon, Christopher. "Monastic Productions." In Wallace, *The Cambridge History of Medieval English Literature*, 316–48.

Carruthers, Mary. *The Book of Memory: A Study of Memory in Medieval Culture.* New York: Cambridge University Press, 1990.

———. *The Craft of Thought: Meditation, Rhetoric, and the Making of Images, 400–1200.* Cambridge: Cambridge University Press, 1998.

Cary, Phillip. *Augustine's Invention of the Inner Self: The Legacy of a Christian Platonist.* Oxford: Oxford University Press, 2000.

Castor, Helen. *Blood and Roses: The Paston Family and the Wars of the Roses.* London: Faber and Faber, 2004.

Catto, Jeremy. "Religious Change Under Henry V." In *Henry V: The Practice of Kingship,* ed. G. L. Harris, 97–115. Oxford: Oxford University Press, 1985.

Clark, John. *The Cloud of Unknowing: An Introduction.* 3 vols. Analecta Cartusiana 119:6, ed. James Hogg. Salzburg: Institut für Anglistik und Amerikanistik, Universität Salzburg, 1995.

———. "Image and Likeness in Walter Hilton." *The Downside Review* 97 (1979): 204–20.

Coiner, Nancy. "The 'Homely' and the Heimliche: The Hidden, Doubled Self in Julian of Norwich's Showings." *Exemplaria* 5 (1998): 305–23.

Coleman, Janet. *Medieval Readers and Writers, 1350–1400.* New York: Columbia University Press, 1981.

Coleman, Joyce. *Public Reading and the Reading Public in Late Medieval England and France.* Cambridge: Cambridge University Press, 1996.

Coletti, Theresa. "*Paupertas est donum Dei*: Hagiography, Lay Religion, and the Economics of Salvation in the Digby *Mary Magdalene.*" *Speculum* 76 (2001): 337–78.

Cooper, Helen. "Romance after 1400." In Wallace, *The Cambridge History of Medieval English Literature,* 690–719.

Copeland, Rita, David Lawton, and Wendy Scase, eds. *New Medieval Literatures V.* Oxford: Oxford University Press, 2002.

Crawford, Mary, and Roger Chaffin. "The Reader's Construction of Meaning: Cognitive Research on Gender and Comprehension." In *Gender and Reading: Essays on Readers, Texts, and Contexts,* ed. Elizabeth Flynn and Patrocinio Schweichart, 3–30. Baltimore: Johns Hopkins University Press, 1986.

Davenport, W. A. *Chaucer: Complaint and Narrative.* Cambridge: D. S. Brewer, 1988.

de Hamel, Christopher. *Syon Abbey: The Library of the Bridgettine Nuns and Their Peregrinations After the Reformation.* Otley: Roxburghe Club, 1991.

Deanseley, Margaret. "Vernacular Books in England in the Fourteenth and Fifteenth Centuries." *Modern Language Review* 25 (1920): 349–58.

Despres, Denise. "Ecstatic Reading and Missionary Mysticism: *The Orcherd of Syon.*" In Voaden, *Prophets Abroad,* 141–60.

———. *Ghostly Sights: Visual Meditation in late medieval Literature.* Norman, Okla.: Pilgrim Books, 1989.

Dickman, Susan. "Julian of Norwich and Margery Kempe: Two Images of Fourteenth-Century Spirituality." In *Spätmittelalterliche Geistliche Literatur in der Nationalsprache,* ed. James Hogg, 2 vols, Analecta Cartusiana 106, 178–94. Salzburg: Institut für Anglistik und Amerikanistik, Universität Salzburg, 1983.

Dimmick, Jeremy, James Simpson, and Nicolette Zeeman, eds. *Images, Idolatry, and Iconoclasm in Late Medieval England: Textuality and the Visual Image.* Oxford: Oxford University Press, 2002.

Dinshaw, Caroline. *Chaucer's Sexual Poetics.* Madison: University of Wisconsin Press, 1989.

Dix, Dom Gregory. *The Shape of the Liturgy.* London: Dacre Press, 1945.

Doane, A. N., and Mark Amsler. "Literacy and Readership." In *Medieval England: An Encyclopedia*, ed. Paul E. Szarmach, M. Teresa Tavormina, and Joel T. Rosenthal, 425–27. New York: Garland, 1998.

du Boulay, F. R. H. *An Age of Ambition: English Society in the Late Middle Ages.* London: Thomas Nelson, 1970.

———. *The England of Piers Plowman: William Langland and His Visions of the Fourteenth Century.* Cambridge: D. S. Brewer, 1991.

Duffy, Eamon. *The Stripping of the Altars: Traditional Religion in England 1400–1580.* New Haven: Yale University Press, 1992.

Dunning, R. W. "The Building of Syon Abbey." *Transactions of the Ancient Monuments Society* NS 25 (1981), 16–26.

Dutton, Anne M. "Passing the Book: Testamentary Transmission of Religious Literature to and by Women in England, 1350–1500." In Smith and Taylor, *Women, the Book and the Godly*, 41–54.

Edwards, A. S. G. "The Middle English Manuscripts and Early Readers of *Ancrene Wisse*." In Wada, *A Companion to "Ancrene Wisse,"* 103–12.

Ellis, Roger. "Further Thoughts on the Spirituality of Syon Abbey." In *Mysticicsm and Spirituality in Medieval England*, ed. William Pollard and Robert Boenig, 9–27. Cambridge: D. S. Brewer, 1984.

———. *Viderunt eam Filie Syon: the Spirituality of the English House of a Medieval Contemplative Order from Its Beginnings to the Present Day.* Analecta Cartusiana 68, vol. 2. Salzburg: Institut für Anglitik und Amerikanistik, Universität Salzburg, 1984.

Enders, Jody. *The Medieval Theater of Cruelty: Rhetoric, Memory, Violence.* Ithaca: Cornell University Press, 1999.

Erikson, Carolly. *The Medieval Vision: Essays in History and Perception.* New York: Oxford University Press, 1976.

Erler, Mary C. "Exchange of Books Between Nuns and Laywomen: Three Surviving Examples." In *New Science out of Old Books: Studies in Manuscripts and Early Printed Books in Honour of A. I. Doyle*, ed. Richard Beadle and A. J. Piper, 360–71. Aldershot, Hants.: Scolar Press, 1995.

Fisher, John H. "A Language Policy for Lancastrian England." *PMLA* 107 (1992): 1168–80.

Fleming, John. *An Introduction to the Franciscan Literature of the Middle Ages.* Chicago: Franciscan Herald Press, 1977.

Foster, Susan. "Private Devotion." In *Gothic: Art for England, 1400–1547*, ed. Richard Marks and Paul Williamson, exhibition catalogue, Victoria and Albert Museum, October 9, 2003–January 18, 2004, 334–36. London: V&A Publications, 2003.

Fradenburg, L. O. Aranye. "The Manciple's Servant Tongue: Politics and Poetry in the *Canterbury Tales*." *English Literary History* 52 (1985): 85–118.

———. *Sacrifice Your Love: Psychoanalysis, Historicism, Chaucer.* Minneapolis: University of Minnesota Press, 2002.

———. "Voice Memorial: Loss and Reparation in Chaucer's Poetry." *Exemplaria* 2 (1990): 170–202.

Friedman, John B. *Northern English Books, Owners, and Makers in the Late Middle Ages.* Syracuse: Syracuse University Press, 1995.

Fulton, Rachel. *From Judgment to Passion: Devotion to Christ and the Virgin Mary, 800–1200.* New York: Columbia University Press, 2002.

Georgianna, Linda. *The Solitary Self: Individuality in the* Ancrene Wisse. Cambridge: Harvard University Press, 1981.

Ghosh, Kantik. "Manuscripts of Nicholas Love's *The Mirror of the Blessed Life of Jesus Christ* and Wycliffite Notions of 'Authority.'" In *Prestige, Authority and Power in Late Medieval Manuscripts and Texts*, ed. Felicity Riddy, 17–34. Woodbridge, Suffolk: York Medieval Press in association with Boydell Press, 2000.

Gibson, Gail McMurray. *The Theater of Devotion: East Anglian Drama and Society in the Late Middle Ages.* Chicago: University of Chicago Press, 1989.

Gilchrist, Roberta. *Gender and Material Culture: The Archaeology of Religious Women.* London: Routledge, 1994.

Gill, Katherine. "Women and Religious Literature in the Vernacular." In *Creative Women in Medieval and Early Modern Italy*, ed. E. Ann Matter and John Coakley, 64–104. Philadelphia: University of Pennsylvania Press, 1994.

Gillespie, Vincent. "Cura pastoralis in deserto." In Sargent, *De cella in seculum*, 161–81.

———. "'Lukynge in Haly Bukes': *Lectio* in Some Late Medieval Spiritual Miscellanies." In *Spätmittelalterliche geistliche Literatur in der Nationalsprache*, ed. James Hogg, 2 vols., Analecta Cartusiana 106, 1–27. Salzburg: Institut für Anglistik und Amerikanistik, Universität Salzburg, 1983.

———. "Strange Images of Death: the Passion in Later Medieval English Devotional Writing." In *Zeit, Tod, und Ewigkeit in der Renaissance Literatur*, ed. James Hogg, Analecta Cartusiana 117:3, 111–59. Salzburg: Institut für Anglistik und Amerikanistik, Universität Salzburg, 1987.

———, and A. I. Doyle, eds. *Syon Abbey, with the Libraries of the Carthusians.* London: British Library in Association with British Academy, 2001.

———. "Vernacular Books of Religion." In Griffiths and Pearsall, *Book Production and Publishing in England*, 317–44.

Goldberg, Benjamin. *The Mirror and Man.* Charlottesville: University of Virginia Press, 1985.

Goldberg, P. J. P. *Women in England, c. 1275–1525: Documentary Sources.* Manchester: Manchester University Press, 1995.

Goldin, Frederick. *The Mirror of Narcissus in the Courtly Love Lyric.* Ithaca: Cornell University Press, 1967.

Goodman, Anthony. "The Piety of John Brunham's Daughter of Lynn." In *Medieval Women: Essays Dedicated and Presented to Professor Rosalind M. T. Hill*, ed. Derek Baker, 347–58. Oxford: Basil Blackwell, 1987.

Grabes, Herbert. *The Mutable Glass: Mirror-Imagery in Titles and Texts of the Middle Ages and English Renaissance.* New York: Cambridge University Press, 1982. Originally published in German, 1973.

Gray, Douglas. "Books of Comfort." In *Medieval English Religious and Ethical Literature: Essays in Honour of G.H. Russell,* ed. Gregory Kratzmann and James Simpson, 209–21. Cambridge: D. S. Brewer, 1986.

———. *Themes and Images in the Medieval Religious Lyric.* London: Routledge and Kegan Paul, 1972.

Greetham, D. C. "Self-Referential Artifacts: Hoccleve's Persona as a Literary Device." *Modern Philology* 86 (1989): 242–51.

Griffiths, Jeremy, and Derek Pearsall, eds. *Book Production and Publishing in Britain, 1375–1475.* Cambridge: Cambridge University Press, 1989.

Grise, C. Annette. " 'In the Blessid Vyneyerd of Oure Holy Saveour': Female Religious Readers and Textual Reception in the *Myroure of Oure Ladye* and the *Orcherd of Syon*." In *The Medieval Mystical Tradition: England, Ireland and Wales, Exeter Symposium VI,* ed. Marion Glasscoe, 193–211. Cambridge: D. S. Brewer, 1999.

Guillerm, Luce. "L'intertextualité démontée: Le discours sur la traduction." *Littératures* 55 (1984): 54–63.

Hamburger, Jeffrey. *Nuns as Artists: The Visual Culture of a Medieval Convent.* Berkeley: University of California Press, 1997.

———. "The Use of Images in the Pastoral Care of Nuns: The Case of Heinrich Suso and the Dominicans." *Art Bulletin* 71 (1989): 20–46.

———. *The Visual and the Visionary: Art and Female Spirituality in Late Medieval Germany.* New York: Zone Books, 1998.

———. "The Visual and the Visionary: The Image in Late Medieval Monastic Devotions." *Viator* 20 (1989): 160–82.

Hanawalt, Barbara. " 'The Childe of Bristow' and the Making of Middle-Class Adolescence." In *Bodies and Disciplines: Intersections of Literature and History in Fifteenth-Century England,* ed. Barbara Hanawalt and David Wallace, 155–78. Minneapolis: University of Minnesota Press, 1996.

Haren, Michael. "Social Ideas in the Pastoral Literature of Fourteenth-Century England." In *Religious Belief and Ecclesiastical Careers in Late Medieval England,* ed. Christopher Harper-Bill, 43–58. Rochester, N.Y.: Boydell Press, 1991.

Harris, Kate. "Patrons, Buyers, and Owners: The Evidence for Ownership and the Role of Book Owners in Book Production and the Book Trade." In Griffiths and Pearsall, *Book Production and Publishing in Britain,* 163–99.

Hasler, Antony. "Hoccleve's Unregimented Body." *Paragraph* 13 (1990): 164–83.

Hayes, Stephen. " 'Of Three Workings in Man's Soul': A Middle English Prose Meditation on the Annunciation." In *Vox Mystica: Essays on Medieval Mysticism in Honor of Valerie M. Lagorio,* ed. Anne Clark Bartlett, 177–200. Cambridge: D. S. Brewer, 1995.

Heffernan, Thomas. "Orthodoxies' Redux: The Northern Homily Cycle in the Vernon Manuscript and its Textual Affiliations." In Pearsall, *Studies in the Vernon Manuscript,* 75–88.

Heimmel, J. P. *"God is Our Mother"*: *Julian of Norwich and the Medieval Image of Christian Feminine Divinity*. Salzburg Studies in English Literature 92:5. Salzburg: Universität Salzburg, 1982.

Hogg, James. "Adam the Carthusian's *De Quadripartito Exercitio Cellae*." In Sargent, *De Cella in Seculum*, 67–79.

———. "The Contribution of the Brigittine Order to Late Medieval English Spirituality." In *Spiritualität Heute und Gestern*. Analecta Cartusiana 35:3, 153–74. Salzburg: Institut für Anglistik und Amerikanistik, Universität Salzburg, 1983.

———, ed. *Richard Whytford's* The Pype or Tonne of the Lyfe of Perfection: *with an Introductory Study of Whytford's Works*. Elizabethan and Renaissance Studies 89. Salzburg: Institut für Anglistik und Amerikanistik, Universität Salzburg, 1979.

Hollbrook, Sue Ellen. "Margery Kempe and Wynkyn de Worde." In *The Medieval Mystical Tradition in England IV*, ed. Marion Glasscoe, 27–46. Cambridge: D. S. Brewer, 1987.

Horrall, Sarah M. "'For the Commun at Understand': *Cursor Mundi* and Its Background." In Sargent, *De Cella in Seculum*, 97–107.

Horrox, Rosemary, ed. *Fifteenth Century Attitudes: Perceptions of Society in Late Medieval England*. New York: Cambridge University Press, 1994.

Horsfield, Rev. Robert A. "*The Pomander of Prayer*: Aspects of Late Medieval English Carthusian Spirituality and Its Lay Audience." In Sargent, *De Cella in Seculum*, 205–13.

Hudson, Anne. *The Premature Reformation: Wycliffite Texts and Lollard History*. Oxford: Clarendon Press, 1988.

Hughes, Jonathan. *Pastors and Visionaries: Religion and Secular Life in Late Medieval Yorkshire*. Wolfeboro, N.H.: Boydell Press, 1988.

Hussey, S. S. "The Audience for the Middle English Mystics." In Sargent, *De Cella in Seculum*, 109–22.

———. "Editing *The Scale of Perfection*: Return to Recension." In *Crux and Controversy in Middle English Textual Criticism*, ed. A. J. Minnis and Charlotte Brewer, 97–107. Cambridge: D. S. Brewer, 1992.

Hutchison, Anne. "Devotional Reading in the Monastery and in the Late Medieval Household." In Sargent, *De Cella in Seculum*, 215–27.

———. "*The Myroure of Oure Ladye*: A Medieval Guide for Contemplatives." In *Studies in St. Birgitta and the Brigittine Order*, 2 vols., Spiritualität Heute und Gestern 19, Analecta Cartusiana 35:10, ed. James Hogg. Salzburg: Institut für Anglistik und Amerikanistik, Universität Salzburg, 1993.

———. "What Nuns Read: Literary Evidence from the English Bridgettine House, Syon Abbey." *Medieval Studies* 57 (1995): 205–22.

Innes-Parker, Catherine. "The Legacy of *Ancrene Wisse*: Translations, Adaptations, Influences and Audience, with Special Attention to Women Readers." In Wada, *A Companion to "Ancrene Wisse*," 145–74.

———. "Subversion and Conformity in Julian's *Revelation*: Authority, Vision, and the Motherhood of God." *Mystics Quarterly* 23, no. 2 (1997): 7–35.

Jaeger, C. Stephen. *Ennobling Love: In Search of a Lost Sensibility*. Philadelphia: University of Pennsylvania Press, 1999.

Jager, Eric. *The Book of the Heart.* Chicago: University of Chicago Press, 2000.

Johnson, Ian. "Prologue and Practice: Middle English Lives of Christ." In *The Medieval Translator: The Theory and Practice of Translation in the Middle Ages*, ed. Roger Ellis, 69–85. Cambridge: D. S. Brewer, 1989.

Keiser, George. "The Middle English *Planctus Mariae* and the Rhetoric of Pathos." In *The Popular Literature of Medieval England*, ed. Thomas J. Heffernan, 167–93. Knoxville: University of Tennessee Press, 1985.

———. "The Mystics and the Early English Printers: The Economics of Devotionalism." In *The Medieval Mystical Tradition in England: Exeter Symposium IV, Papers Read at Dartington Hall, July 1987*, ed. Marion Glasscoe, 9–26. Cambridge: D. S. Brewer, 1987.

———. " 'Noght how lang man lifs; bot how wele': the Laity and the Ladder of Perfection." In Sargent, *De Cella in Seculum*, 145–60.

———. "Patronage and Piety in Fifteenth-Century England: Margaret, Duchess of Clarence, Symon Wynter and Beinecke MS 317." *Yale University Library Gazette* 60 (1985): 32–46.

———. " 'To Knawe God Almyghtyn': Robert Thornton's Devotional Book." In *Spätmittelalterliche Geistliche Literatur in der Nationalsprache*, ed. James Hogg, 2 vols., Analecta Cartusiana 106, 103–29. Salzburg: Institut für Anglistik und Amerikanistik, Universität Salzburg, 1984.

Ker, N. R. *Medieval Libraries of Great Britain: A List of Surviving Books.* 2nd ed. London: Royal Historical Society, 1964.

———. *Medieval Manuscripts in British Libraries.* 3 vols. Oxford: Oxford University Press, 1969.

Kieckhefer, Richard. *Unquiet Souls: Fourteenth-Century Saints and Their Religious Milieu.* Chicago: University of Chicago Press, 1984.

Knapp, Ethan. "Bureaucratic Identity and the Construction of the Self in Hoccleve's *Formulary* and *La male regle*." *Speculum* 74 (1999): 357–76.

———. *The Bureaucratic Muse: Thomas Hoccleve and the Literature of Late Medieval England.* University Park: Penn State University Press, 2001.

———. "Eulogies and Usurpations: Hoccleve and Chaucer Revisited." *Studies in the Age of Chaucer* 21 (1999): 247–73.

Knoespel, Kenneth J. *Narcissus and the Invention of Personal History.* New York: Garland, 1985.

Knowles, David. *The Religious Orders in England.* 3 vols. Cambridge: Cambridge University Press, 1955.

Kratzmann, Gregory, and James Simpson, eds. *Medieval English Religious and Ethical Literature: Studies in Honour of G. H. Russell.* Cambridge: D. S. Brewer, 1986.

Krug, Rebecca. *Reading Families: Women's Literate Practice in Late Medieval England.* Ithaca: Cornell University Press, 2002.

Kruger, Steven. "Mirrors and the Trajectory of Vision in *Piers Plowman*." *Speculum* 66:1 (1991): 74–95.

Lagorio, Valerie, and Michael Sargent. "English Mystical Writings." In *A Manual of the Writings in Middle English*, ed. Albert E. Hartung, vol. 9, 3049–3137. New Haven: Connecticut Academy of Arts and Sciences, 1993.

Lake, Peter. "Religious Identities in Shakespeare's England." In *A Companion to Shakespeare*, ed. David Scott Kastan, 57–84. Oxford: Blackwell, 1999.

Lawton, David. "Dullness and the Fifteenth Century." *English Literary History* 54 (1987): 761–99.

Leclerq, Jean. *The Love of Learning and the Desire for God: A Study of Monastic Culture*. Trans. Catherine Misrahi. New York: Fordham University Press, 1961.

Leicester, H. Marshall. *The Disenchanted Self: Representing the Subject in "The Canterbury Tales."* Berkeley: University of California Press, 1990.

Lerer, Seth. *Chaucer and His Readers: Imagining the Author in late medieval England*. Princeton: Princeton University Press, 1993.

Lewis, Flora. "The Wound in Christ's Side and the Instruments of the Passion: Gendered Experience and Response." In Taylor and Smith, *Women and the Book*, 204–29.

Little, Katherine. "Chaucer's Parson and the Specter of Wycliffism." *Studies in the Age of Chaucer* 23 (2001): 225–53.

Lindberg, David. *Theories of Vision from Al-Kindi to Kepler*. Chicago: University of Chicago Press, 1976.

Lindenbaum, Sheila. "London Texts and Literate Practice." In Wallace, *The Cambridge History of Medieval English Literature*, 284–309.

Lochrie, Karma. *Covert Operations: The Medieval Uses of Secrecy*. Philadelphia: University of Pennsylvania Press, 1999.

———. "The Language of Transgression: Body, Flesh, and Word in Mystical Discourse." In *Speaking Two Languages: Traditional Disciplines and Contemporary Theory in Medieval Studies*, ed. Allen Frantzen, 115–40. Albany: SUNY Press, 1991.

———. *Margery Kempe and the Translations of the Flesh*. Philadelphia: University of Pennsylvania Press, 1991.

———. "Mystical Acts, Queer Tendencies." In *Constructing Medieval Sexuality*, ed. Karma Lochrie, Peggy McCracken, and James Schultz, 180–200. Minneapolis: University of Minnesota Press, 1997.

Lovatt, Roger. "Henry Suso and the Medieval Mystical Tradition in England." In *The Medieval Mystical Tradition in England: Papers Read at Dartington Hall*, ed. Marion Glasscoe, 47–62. Cambridge: D. S. Brewer, 1982.

———. "The Imitation of Christ in Late Medieval England." *Transactions of the Royal Historical Society*, 5th ser. 18 (1968): 97–121.

MacDonald, A. A., H. N. B. Ridderbos, and R. M. Schlusemann, eds. *The Broken Body: Passion Devotion in late medieval Culture*. Grongingen: Egbert Forsten, 1998.

Manter, Lisa. "The Savior of Her Desire: Margery Kempe's Passionate Gaze." *Exemplaria* 13, no. 1 (2001): 39–66.

Marrow, James H. *Passion Iconography in Northern European Art of the Late Middle Ages and Early Renaissance*, vol. 1. Kortrijk: Van Ghennert, 1979.

Marshall, Peter. *The Catholic Priesthood and the English Reformation*. Oxford: Oxford University Press, 1994.

McEntire, Sandra J. *Julian of Norwich: A Book of Essays*. New York: Garland, 1998.

McNamer, Sarah. "The Exploratory Image: God as Mother in Julian of Norwich's *Revelations of Divine Love*." *Mystics Quarterly* 15 (1989): 21–28.

———. *Reading the Literature of Compassion: A Study in the History of Feeling.* Ph.D. diss., UCLA, 1999.

———. "The Virgin and the Voice of Protest." In *Speaking Images: Essays in Honor of V. A. Kolve*, ed. Robert F. Yeager and Charlotte C. Morse, 505–25. Asheville, N.C.: Pegasus Press, 2001.

McRee, Ben. "Religious Gilds and Regulation of Behavior in Late Medieval Towns." In *People, Politics, and Community in the Later Middle Ages*, ed. Joel Rosenthal and Colin Richmond, 108–22. New York: St. Martin's Press, 1988.

McSheffrey, Shannon. "Literacy and the Gender Gap in the Late Middle Ages: Women and Reading in Lollard Communities." In Smith and Taylor, *Women, the Book and the Godly*, 157–70.

Meale, Carol M. "'. . . all the bokes that I have of latyn, englisch, and frensch': Laywomen and Their Books in Late Medieval England." In Meale, *Women and Literature in Britain*, 128–58.

———, ed. *Women and Literature in Britain 1150–1500.* Cambridge: Cambridge University Press, 1993.

Medcalf, Stephen. *The Later Middle Ages.* London: Methuen, 1981.

Meier-Ewert, Charity. "A Middle English Version of the Fifteen Oes." *Modern Philology* 68, no. 4 (1971): 355–61.

Mertes, Kate. "Aristocracy." In Horrox, *Fifteenth-Century Attitudes,* 42–60.

Middleton, Anne. "Narration and the Invention of Experience: Episodic Form in *Piers Plowman.*" In *The Wisdom of Poetry: Essays in Early English Literature in Honor of Morton W. Bloomfield*, ed. Larry D. Benson and Siegfried Wenzel, 91–122. Kalamazoo: Medieval Institute Publications, 1982.

———. "William Langland's 'Kynde Name': Authorial Signature and Social Identity in Late Fourteenth-Century England." In Patterson, *Literary Practice and Social Change in Britain*, 15–82.

Miles, Margaret. *Image as Insight: Visual Understanding in Western Christianity and Secular Culture.* Boston: Beacon Press, 1985.

———. "Vision: The Eye of the Body and the Eye of the Mind in Augustine's *De Trinitate.*" *Journal of Religion* 63 (1983): 125–42.

Miedema, Nine. "Following in the Footsteps of Christ: Pilgrimage and Passion Devotion." In MacDonald et al., *The Broken Body*, 73–92.

Mills, Robert. "A Man is Being Beaten." In Copeland et al., *New Medieval Literatures V*, 115–53.

Mitchell, Jerome. *Thomas Hoccleve: A Study in Early Fifteenth-Century English Prose.* Chicago: University of Illinois Press, 1968.

Moran, Jo Ann Hoeppner. *The Growth of English Schooling: Learning, Literacy, and Laicization in Pre-Reformation York Diocese.* Princeton: Princeton University Press, 1985.

Morris, Colin. *The Discovery of the Individual 1050–1200.* New York: Harper & Row, 1972.

Newman, Barbara. *From Virile Woman to Woman-Christ: Studies in Medieval Religion and Literature.* Philadelphia: University of Pennsylvania Press, 1995.

———. "What Did It Mean to Say 'I Saw'?: The Clash Between Theory and Practice in Medieval Visionary Culture." *Speculum* 80, no. 1 (2005): 1–43.

Nissé, Ruth. "'Oure Fadres Olde and Modres': Gender, Heresy, and Hoccleve's Literary Politics." *Studies in the Age of Chaucer* 21 (1999): 275–99.

Nolan, Edward. *Now Through a Glass Darkly: Specular Images of Being and Knowing from Virgil to Chaucer.* Ann Arbor: University of Michigan Press, 1990.

Ong, Walter. *Orality and Literacy: The Technologizing of the Word.* New York: Routledge, 1982.

Palliser, D. M. "Urban Society." In Horrox, *Fifteenth Century Attitudes*, 132–49.

Pantin, W. A. *The English Church in the Fourteenth Century.* Cambridge: Cambridge University Press, 1955. Reprint: Medieval Academy Reprints for Teaching. Toronto: Medieval Academy in association with University of Toronto Press, 1980.

———. "Instructions for a Devout and Literate Layman." In Alexander and Gibson, *Medieval Learning and Literature*, 398–422.

Parkes, Malcolm. "The Influence of the Concepts of *Ordinatio* and *Compilatio* on the Development of the Book." In Alexander and Gibson, *Medieval Learning and Literature*, 115–41.

———. "The Literacy of the Laity." In *The Mediaeval World*, ed. David Daiches and Anthony K. Thorlby, 555–79. London: Aldus Books, 1973.

Partner, Nancy. "The Hidden Self: Psychoanalysis and the Textual Unconscious." In *Writing Medieval History*, ed. Partner, 42–64. London: Hodder Arnold, 2005.

Patterson, Lee. "Chaucer's Pardoner on the Couch: Psyche and Clio in Medieval Literary Studies." *Speculum* 76 (2001): 638–80.

———. *Chaucer and the Subject of History.* Madison: University of Wisconsin Press, 1991.

———, ed. *Literary Practice and Social Change in Britain, 1380–1530.* Berkeley: University of California Press, 1990.

———. "Making Identities in Fifteenth-Century England: Henry V and John Lydgate." In *New Historical Literary Study: Essays on Reproducing Texts, Representing History*, ed. Jeffrey Cox and Larry Reynolds, 67–107. Princeton: Princeton University Press, 1993.

———. *Negotiating the Past: The Historical Understanding of Medieval Literature.* Madison: University of Wisconsin Press, 1987.

———. "On the Margin: Postmodernism, Ironic History, and Medieval Studies." *Speculum* 65 (1990): 87–108.

———. "Writing Amorous Wrongs: Chaucer and the Order of Complaint." In James Dean and Christian Zacher, eds., *The Idea of Medieval Literature: New Essays on Chaucer and Medieval Culture in Honor of Donald R. Howard*, 55–71. Newark: University of Delaware Press, 1992.

Pearsall, Derek. "The English Romance in the Fifteenth Century." *Essays and Studies* 29 (1976): 56–83.

———. "Hoccleve's *Regement of Princes*: The Poetics of Royal Self-Representation." *Speculum* 69 (1994): 386–410.

———. *John Lydgate.* London: Routledge and Kegan Paul, 1970.

———, ed. *Studies in the Vernon Manuscript.* Cambridge: D. S. Brewer, 1990.

Pezzini, Domenico. "'The meditacion of oure lordis passyon' and other Bridgettine texts in MS Lambeth 432." In *Studies in St. Birgitta and the Bridgettine Order*, vol. 1, ed.

James Hogg, Analecta Cartusiana 35:19, 276–95. Salzburg: Institut für Anglistik und Amerikanistik, Universität Salzburg, 1993.

Powell, Susan. "Syon, Caxton, and the Festial." *Birgittiana* 2 (1996): 187–207.

Pribram, Denise. *Female Spectators: Looking at Film and Television.* New York: Verso, 1988.

Price, Jocelyn. " 'Inner and Outer': Conceptualizing the Body in *Ancrene Wisse* and Aelred's *De Institutione Inclusarum.*" In *Medieval English Religious and Ethical Literature: Studies in Honour of G. H. Russell,* ed. Gregroy Kratzmann and James Simpson, 192–208. Cambridge: D. S. Brewer, 1986.

Rambuss, Richard. *Closet Devotions.* Durham and London: Duke University Press, 1998.

Rhodes, J. T. "The Body of Christ in English Eucharistic Devotion, c. 1500–c. 1620." In *New Science Out of Old Books: Studies in Manuscripts and Early Printed Books in Honour of A. I. Doyle,* ed. Richard Beadle and A. J. Piper, 389–419. Aldershot: Scolar Press, 1995.

———. "Prayers of the Passion: From Jordanus of Quedlinburg to John Fewterer of Syon." *The Durham University Journal* 85 (1993): 27–38.

———. "Syon Abbey and its Religious Publications in the Sixteenth Century." *Journal of Ecclesiastical History* 44 (1993): 11–25.

Richardson, Malcolm. "Hoccleve in his Social Context." *Chaucer Review* 20 (1986): 313–22.

Richmond, Colin. "The English Gentry and Religion, c. 1500." In *Religious Belief and Ecclesiastical Careers in Late Medieval England,* ed. Christopher Harper-Bill, 121–50. Rochester, N.Y.: Boydell Press, 1991.

———. "Religion." In Horrox, *Fifteenth Century Attitudes,* 183–201.

Riddy, Felicity. " 'Women Talking About the Things of God': A late medieval Subculture." In Meale, *Women and Literature in Britain,* 104–27.

Riehle, Wolfgang. *The Middle English Mystics.* Trans. Bernard Standring. Boston: Routledge, 1981; pub. in German, 1977.

Rigg, A. G. "Hoccleve's Complaint and Isidore of Seville." *Speculum* 45 (1970): 564–74.

Ringbom, Sixten. "Devotional Images and Imaginative Devotions: Notes on the Place of Art in Late Medieval Private Piety." *Gazette des Beaux-Arts,* 6th ser. 73 (1969): 159–70.

Robertson, Elizabeth. *Early English Devotional Prose and the Female Audience.* Knoxville: University of Tennessee Press, 1990.

———. " 'This Living Hand': Thirteenth-Century Female Literacy, Materialist Immanence, and the Reader of the *Ancrene Wisse.*" *Speculum* 78 (2003): 1–36.

Rosenthal, Joel. "Aristocratic Cultural Patronage and Book Bequests, 1350–1500." *Bulletin of the John Rylands Library* 64 (1982): 522–48.

Rosenthal, Joel, and Colin Richmond, eds. *People, Politics, and Community in the Later Middle Ages.* New York: St. Martin's Press, 1988.

Rubin, Miri. *Corpus Christi: The Eucharist in Late Medieval Culture.* New York: Cambridge University Press, 1991.

Saenger, Paul. "Books of Hours and the Reading Habits of the Later Middle Ages." *Scrittura e Civilitá* 9 (1985): 239–69. Repr. in *The Culture of Print: Power and the Uses of Print in Early Modern Europe,* ed. Roger Chartier, trans. Lydia G. Cochrane, 141–73. Cambridge: Polity Press, 1989.

———. "Silent Reading: Its Impact on Late Medieval Script and Society." *Viator* 13 (1982): 367–414.

Salih, Sarah. "Queering Sponsalia Christi: Virginity, Gender, and Desire in the Early Middle English Anchoritic Texts." In Copeland et al., *New Medieval Literatures V*, 155–75. New York: Oxford University Press, 2002.

Salter, Elizabeth. "Ludophus of Saxony and his English Translator." *Medium Aevum* 33 (1964): 26–35.

Sargent, Michael. "Bonaventura English: A Survey of the Middle English Prose Translations of Early Franciscan Literature." In *Spätmittelalterliche Geistliche Literatur in der Nationalsprache*, ed. James Hogg, 2 vols., Analecta Cartusiana 106, 145–76. Salzburg: Institut für Anglistik und Amerikanistik, Universität Salzburg, 1984.

———. "Contemporary Criticism of Richard Rolle." In *Kartäusermystik und –mystiker*, ed. James Hogg and Robert Rackowitz, Analecta Cartusiana 55:1, 160–205. Salzburg: Institut für Anglistik und Amerikanistik, Universität Salzburg, 1981.

———, ed. *De Cella in Seculum: Religious and Secular Life and Devotion in Late Medieval England*. Cambridge: D. S. Brewer, 1989.

———. *James Grenehalgh as Textual Critic*. 2 vols. Analecta Cartusiana 85. Salzburg: Institut für Anglistik und Amerikanistik, Universität Salzburg, 1984.

———. "Russbroek in England: *The Chastising of God's Children* and Related Works." In *Historia et Spiritualitas Cartusiensis*, ed. Jan de Grauwe, 303–12. Bruges, 1983.

———. "The Transmission by the English Carthusians of Some Late Medieval Spiritual Writings." *Journal of Ecclesiastical History* 27 (1976): 225–40.

———. "Walter Hilton's *Scale of Perfection*: The London Manuscript Group Reconsidered." *Medium Aevum* 52, no. 2 (1983): 189–215.

Scanlon, Larry. "The King's Two Voices: Narrative and Power in Hoccleve's *Regiment of Princes*." In Patterson, *Literary Practice and Social Change in Britain*, 216–47.

Scase, Wendy, Rita Copeland, and David Lawton, eds. *New Medieval Literatures I*. Oxford: Clarendon Press, 1997.

———. "Reginald Pecock, John Carpenter and John Colop's 'Common-Profit' Books: Aspects of Book Ownership in Fifteenth-Century London." *Medium Aevum* 61 (1992), 261–74.

Shuger, Debora. *The Renaissance Bible: Scholarship, Sacrifice, and Subjectivity*. Berkeley: University of California Press, 1994.

Simpson, James. "Breaking the Vacuum: Ricardian and Henrician Ovidianism." *JMEMS* 29:2 (1999): 325–55.

———. "Nobody's Man: Thomas Hoccleve's *Regiment of Princes*." In *London and Europe in the Later Middle Ages*, ed. Julian Boffey and Pamela King, 149–80. London: Centre for Medieval and Renaissance Studies at Queen Mary and Westfield College, 1995.

———. *The Oxford English Literary History, Volume 2, 1350–1547: Reform and Cultural Revolution*. Oxford: Oxford University Press, 2002.

Smith, Lesley, and Jane Taylor, eds. *Women, the Book and the Godly: Selected Proceedings of the St. Hilda's Conference, 1993*. Woodbridge, Suffolk: D. S. Brewer, 1995.

Somerset, Fiona. "Professionalizing Translation at the Turn of the Fifteenth Century: Ullerston's *Determinacio*, Arundel's *Constitutions*." In Somerset and Watson, *The Vulgar Tongue*, 145–57.

Somerset, Fiona, and Nicholas Watson, eds. *The Vulgar Tongue: Medieval and Postmedieval Vernacularity.* University Park: Pennsylvania State University Press, 2003.

Spearing, A. C. "Hoccleve's Misrule." In *Medieval to Renaissance in English Poetry.* New York: Cambridge University Press, 1985.

Spence, Sarah. *Texts and the Self in the Twelfth Century.* Cambridge: Cambridge University Press, 1996.

Sponsler, Claire. *Drama and Resistance: Bodies, Goods, and Theatricality in Late Medieval England.* Minneapolis: University of Minnesota Press, 1997.

Staley, Lynn. *Margery Kempe's Dissenting Fictions.* University Park: Pennsylvania State University Press, 1994.

Stanbury, Sarah. "The Virgin's Gaze: Spectacle and Transgression in Middle English Lyrics of the Passion." *PMLA* 106 (1991): 1083–93.

Stock, Brian. *After Augustine: The Meditative Reader and the Text.* Philadelphia: University of Pennsylvania Press, 2001.

———. *Augustine the Reader: Meditation, Self-Knowledge, and the Ethics of Interpretation.* Cambridge: Harvard University Press, 1996.

———. *The Implications of Literacy: Written Language and Models of Interpretation in the Eleventh and Twelfth Centuries.* Princeton: Princeton University Press, 1983.

Strohm, Paul. "Counterfeiters, Lollards, and Lancastrian Unease." In Scase et al., *New Medieval Literatures I,* 31–58.

———. *England's Empty Throne: Usurpation and the Language of Legitimation, 1399–1422.* New Haven: Yale University Press, 1998.

Summit, Jennifer. *Lost Property: The Woman Writer and English Literary History, 1380–1589.* Chicago: University of Chicago Press, 2000.

Sutton, Anne F., and Livia Visser-Fuchs. "The Cult of Angels in Late Fifteenth-Century England: An Hours of the Guardian Angel Presented to Queen Elizabeth Woodville." In Taylor and Smith, *Women and the Book,* 230–65.

Swanson, R. N. "Passion and Practice: The Social and Ecclesiastical Implications of Passion Devotion in the Late Middle Ages." In MacDonald et al., *The Broken Body,* 1–30.

Tanner, Norman. *The Church in Late Medieval Norwich, 1370–1532.* Toronto: Pontifical Institute of Medieval Studies, 1984.

Targoff, Ramie. *Common Prayer: The Language of Public Devotion in Early Modern England.* Chicago: University of Chicago Press, 2001.

Tarvers, Josephine Koster. " 'Thys ys my mystrys boke': English Women as Readers and Writers in Late Medieval England." In *The Uses of Manuscripts in Literary Studies: Essays in Memory of Judson Boyce Allen,* ed. Charlotte Cook Morse, Penelope Reed Doob, and Marjorie Curry Woods, 305–27. Studies in Medieval Culture 31. Kalamazoo, MI: Medieval Institute Publications, 1992.

Taylor, Andrew. "Into His Secret Chamber: Reading and Privacy in Late Medieval England." In *The Practice and Representation of Reading in England,* ed. James Raven, Helen Small, and Naomi Tadmor, 41–61. Cambridge: Cambridge University Press, 1996.

Taylor, Charles. *Sources of the Self: The Making of the Modern Identity.* Cambridge: Harvard University Press, 1989.

Taylor, Jane H. M., and Lesley Smith, eds. *Women and the Book: Assessing the Visual Evidence.* London: British Library and University of Toronto Press, 1996.

Thompson, E. Margaret. *The Carthusian Order in England.* London: Macmillan, 1930.

Thompson, John J. *Robert Thornton and the London Thornton Manuscript: British Library MS Additional 31042.* Manuscript Studies II. London: D. S. Brewer, 1987.

Thornley, Eva. "The Middle English Penitential Lyric and Hoccleve's Autobiographical Poetry." *Neuphilologische Mitteilungen* 68 (1967): 295–321.

Thrupp, Sylvia. *The Merchant Class of Medieval London, 1300–1500.* Chicago: University of Chicago Press, 1948.

Tolmie, Sarah. "The *Prive Scilence* of Thomas Hoccleve." *Studies in the Age of Chaucer* 22 (2000): 281–309.

Torti, Anna. *The Glass of Form: Mirroring Structures from Chaucer to Skelton.* Cambridge: D. S. Brewer, 1991.

Trapp, J. B. "An English Late Medieval Cleric and Italian Thought: The Case of John Colet, Dean of St. Paul's (1467–1519)." In *Medieval English Religious and Ethical Literature: Studies in Honour of G. H. Russell,* ed. Gregroy Kratzmann and James Simpson, 233–50. Cambridge: D. S. Brewer, 1986.

Travis, Peter. "White." *Studies in the Age of Chaucer* 22 (2000): 1–66.

Turville-Petre, Thorlac. "The Relationship of the Vernon and Clopton Manuscripts." In Pearsall, *Studies in the Vernon Manuscript,* 29–44.

Van Os, Henk. *The Art of Devotion in the Late Middle Ages in Europe, 1300–1500.* Trans. Michael Hoyle. Princeton: Princeton University Press, 1994.

Voaden, Rosalynn. "The Company She Keeps: Mechtild of Hackeborn in late medieval Devotional Compilations." In Voaden, *Prophets Abroad,* 51–70.

———, ed. *Prophets Abroad: The Reception of Continental Holy Women in late medieval England.* Cambridge: D. S. Brewer, 1996.

Wada, Yoko, ed. *A Companion to "Ancrene Wisse."* Cambridge: D. S. Brewer, 2003.

Wakelin, M. F. "English Mysticism and the Homiletic Tradition." In *The Medieval Mystical Tradition in England: Papers read at the Exeter Symposium, July 1980,* ed. Marion Glasscoe, 39–54. Exeter: University of Exeter Press, 1980.

Wallace, David, ed. *The Cambridge History of Medieval English Literature.* Cambridge: Cambridge University Press, 1999; repr. 2002.

Ward, Sister Benedicta. "Julian the Solitary." In *Julian Reconsidered,* ed. Kenneth Leech and Benedicta Ward, 11–31. Oxford: Fairacres, 1988.

Warren, Anne K. *Anchorites and Their Patrons in Medieval England.* Berkeley: University of California Press, 1985.

Warren, Nancy Bradley. *Spiritual Economies: Female Monasticism in Later Medieval England.* Philadelphia: University of Pennsylvania Press, 2001.

Watson, Nicholas. "*Ancrene Wisse,* Religious Reform and the Late Middle Ages." In Wada, *A Companion to "Ancrene Wisse,"* 197–226.

———. "Censorship and Cultural Change in late medieval England: Vernacular Theology, the Oxford Translation Debate, and Arundel's *Constitutions* of 1409." *Speculum* 70 (1995): 822–64.

———. "The Composition of Julian of Norwich's *Revelation of Love.*" *Speculum* 68 (1993): 637–83.

———. "Conceptions of the Word: The Mother Tongue and the Incarnation of God." In Scase et al., *New Medieval Literatures I*, 85–124.

———. "Cultural Changes." *English Language Notes* 44 (2006): 127–37.

———. " '*Et que est huius ydoi materia? Tuipse*': Idols and Images in Walter Hilton." In Dimmick et al., *Images, Idolatry, and Iconoclasm*, 95–111.

———. "Methods and Objectives of Anchoritic Devotion." In *The Medieval Mystical Tradition in England*, ed. Marion Glasscoe, 132–53. Cambridge: D. S. Brewer, 1987.

———. "The Middle English Mystics." In Wallace, *The Cambridge History of Medieval English Literature*, 539–65.

———. "Models and Images of the Reading Process." In Wogan-Browne et al., *The Idea of the Vernacular*, 211–22.

———. *Richard Rolle and the Invention of Authority*. Cambridge: Cambridge University Press, 1991.

———. "The Trinitarian Hermeneutic in Julian of Norwich's *Revelation of Love*." In *Julian ofNorwich: A Book of Essays*, ed. Sandra J. McEntire, 61–90. New York: Garland, 1998.

———. "Visions of Inclusion: Universal Salvation and Vernacular Theology in Pre-Reformation England." *JMEMS* 27, no. 2 (1997): 145–87.

———. " 'Yf wommen be double naturelly': Remaking 'Woman' in Julian of Norwich's Revelation of Love." *Exemplaria* 8:1 (1996): 1–34.

Webb, Diana M. "Women and Home: the Domestic Setting of Late Medieval Spirituality." In *Women in the Church: Papers read at the 1989 Summer Meeting and the 1990 Winter Meeting of the Ecclesiastical History Society*, ed. W. J. Sheils and Diana Wood, 159–73. Oxford: Oxford University Press, 1990.

White, Helen C. *The Tudor Books of Private Devotion*. Madison: University of Wisconsin Press, 1951.

Whitehead, Christina. "Making a Cloister of the Soul in Medieval Religious Treatises," *Medium Aevum* 67 (1998): 1–29.

Wimsatt, James. *Allegory and Mirror: Tradition and Structure in Middle English Literature*. New York: Pegasus, 1970.

Windeatt, Barry. "The Art of Mystical Loving: Julian of Norwich." In *The Medieval Mystical Tradition in England: Papers read at the Exeter Symposium, July 1980*, ed. Marion Glasscoe, 55–71. Exeter: Exeter University Press, 1980.

———. *English Mystics of the Middle Ages*. Cambridge: Cambridge University Press, 1994.

Wogan-Browne, Jocelyn, Nicholas Watson, Andrew Taylor, and Ruth Evans, eds. *The Idea of the Vernacular: An Anthology of Middle English Literary Theory*. University Park: Pennsylvania State University Press, 1999.

Woolf, Rosemary. *The English Religious Lyric in the Middle Ages*. Oxford: Clarendon Press, 1960.

Yates, Frances. *The Art of Memory*. Chicago: University of Chicago Press, 1966.

Index

Acknowledgments

Though it is very satisfying to see my first book finally finished, it is still more satisfying to reflect on the many wonderful people who helped to make it possible, and who enriched my life while I was writing it. It is a particular pleasure to acknowledge the early and lasting influence of V. A. Kolve, surely one of the most generous, gracious, and wise people in the academy, or anywhere. He introduced me to medieval religious culture, and has shaped my attitudes toward writing, scholarship, and the profession in ways too numerous and significant to count. I continue to look to him as a model of the academic life well lived, and to his works as models of the academic book well written. I am also happy to acknowledge my deep indebtedness to Debora Shuger. I can hardly express the value of her lively interest in this project, or my continuing thankfulness for her keen, wide-ranging, and utterly uncompromising intellect.

Jessica Brantley, Catherine Sanok, and Claire Banchich have heard every idea in this book—and many that did not make it—more times than anyone should reasonably ask of her friends. They have been not only my best and most tireless readers, but also the dearest companions of my intellectual and professional life. They are one of the few reasons I am grateful for email. But because we now live within driving distance, it has been Catherine who has in recent years been most plagued with this manuscript, and who has most persistently interrogated my thinking and pushed me to say what I mean. I also owe Claire a special debt of gratitude for faithfully photocopying the entire Peltier edition of the *Stimulus Amoris* when the University of Arizona library was unable to borrow it for me. Thank you.

Many other friends, mentors, colleagues, and readers have contributed their advice, assistance, and support along the way. Thanks to H. A. Kelly, a treasure-house of knowledge and kindness; to Donka Minkova, my cheerful language guru; to Christopher Cannon, for an insightful early reading; to James Schultz, for comfort and humor; and to Brian Stock, for encouragement about the Augustinian bits. It is a pleasure to recall the generous interest in this project exhibited by my former colleagues at the University of

Arizona, where I gained much from the lively conversation of Alan Bernstein, Albrecht Classen, John Ulrich, and especially Chris Carroll. Roger Dahood and Peter Medine provided helpful references and sage counsel. Carl Berkhout got me started at the British Library. Special thanks to Gregory Jackson for his expertise in American Protestantism, his sharp editorial eye, and his exceptional cheese sandwiches. I wrote many pages in his disciplined company.

It remains to thank the first and last: those whose early guidance and inspiration made me a scholar in the first place—especially Kathy Deinhardt-Hill, Linda Rickard, Lisa Haines Wright, and Clara Claiborne Park, not to mention my puzzled but always supportive parents, Bob and Peggy—and my present colleagues at Oberlin College, who make me think it was a really good idea. Thanks to the Ohio legislature for continuing to fund OhioLink, which puts world-class resources at my small-college fingertips. Thanks to the Interlibrary loan office for stepping into the remaining gaps with unwavering professionalism and speed. (I still remember with wonder the day the Vernon facsimile arrived.) Thanks to Clayton Koppes, Harry Hirsch, and Jeff Witmer, Deans of Arts and Sciences, for the leave that allowed me to finish the book, and for the subvention that will underwrite some of its publication costs. Thanks to the anonymous readers for Penn Press, my good angels of the year, whose advice has improved my writing and saved me at least a little embarrassment. Thanks to the editor of *PMLA* for permission to reprint a version of "Hoccleve, the Virgin, and the Politics of Complaint" in Chapter 5. Thanks to my understanding editor, Jerry Singerman. And finally—first, last, and everywhere in between—I thank Nick Petzak, my patient household saint, who has witnessed the entire, hideous process and loves me anyway. This book is for him.